WHY PEOPLE DRINK

WHY PEOPLE DRINK

Parameters of Alcohol as a Reinforcer

Edited by

W. Miles Cox, Ph.D.

Foreword by

G. ALLAN MARLATT, Ph.D.

GARDNER PRESS

GARDNER PRESS, INC.

New York London Sydney

Gardner Press, Inc.,
19 Union Square West,
New York, NY 10003

Gardner Press Distribution
540 Barnum Avenue
Bridgeport, CT 06608
(203) 366-1900

Foreign orders except Canada,
South America, Australia, and N
Afterhurst Limited
27 Palmeira Mansions
Church Road, Hove,
East Sussex BN3 2FA
England

Orders for Australia and New Zealand to:
Astam Books
27B, Llewellyn Street
Balmain, N.S.W., Australia

Library of Congress Cataloging in Publication

Library of Congress Cataloging-in-Publication Data
Why people drink.

Includes index.
1. Drinking of alcoholic beverages. 2. Alcohol—Physiological aspects. I. Cox, W. Miles II. Title.
HV5035.W355 1988 362.2'92 87-19775
ISBN 0-89876-132-8

Book Design by Raymond Solomon

To the memory of
ROGER W. BLACK,
without whose influence
this book would
never have been written.

CONTRIBUTORS

Marsha E. Bates
Center of Alcohol Studies
Rutgers University, New Brunswick, N.J.

John Brick
Rutgers University, New Brunswick, N.J.

W. Miles Cox
Veterans Administration Medical Center
Indiana University School of Medicine, Indianapolis, Ind.

Donald W. Goodwin
University of Kansas Medical Center, Kansas City, Kans.

Dwight B. Heath
Brown University, Providence, R.I.

Walter A. Hunt
Behavioral Sciences Department
Armed Forces Radiobiology Research Institute, Bethesda, Md.

Valerie Johnson
Center of Alcohol Studies
Rutgers University, New Brunswick, N.J.

Eric Klinger
University of Minnesota

Alan R. Lang
Department of Psychology
Florida State University, Tallahassee, Fla.

James W. Langenbucher
Rutgers University, New Brunswick, N.J.

Elizabeth M. Michalec
Department of Psychology
Florida State University, Tallahassee, Fla.

G. Alan Marlatt
University of Washington, Seattle, Wash.

Peter E. Nathan
Rutgers University, New Brunswick, N.J.

Patricia B. Sutker
Veterans Administration Medical Center
Tulane University School of Medicine, New Orleans, La.

Jeffrey A. West
Veterans Administration Medical Center
Tulane University School of Medicine, New Orleans, La.

Helene Raskin White
Center of Alcohol Studies, Rutgers University, New Brunswick, N.J.

Gail Winger
Department of Pharmacology
University of Michigan, Ann Arbor, Mich.

PREFACE

People use alcohol as a negative reinforcer to alleviate undesirable emotional states such as anger, anxiety, boredom, and depression. They also use it as a positive reinforcer to achieve desirable emotional states such as happiness, elation, and euphoria. It is also often used to enhance the attractiveness of other incentives such as food, sex, and social interactions. The great attraction of alcohol is evidenced by the estimated per capita consumption in the United States—the equivalent of 2.65 gallons of pure alcohol for each person 14 years of age and older (*Alcohol and Health*, 1987, p.1). We pay billions of dollars yearly for alcohol and additional billions in losses due to its misuse (*Alcohol and Health*, 1987, p. 21). In addition, many persons jeopardize their careers, their relationships, their health, and even their lives in order to drink. In short, alcohol is a powerful reinforcer for which some people pay dearly.

During the past decade, the mechanisms by which alcohol functions as a reinforcer have captured the attention of scientists from a variety of disciplines, including biochemistry, physiology, pharmacology, psychopharmacology, psychology, psychiatry, sociology, and anthropology. The primary interest of some scientists has been in establishing appropriate techniques and procedures for studying alcohol's reinforcing effects. From this work, for example, have come successful animal models that are valuable for studying the complex variables involved in human alcohol consumption at a simpler level of analysis.

Notwithstanding the value of animal models, scientists have learned increasingly to recognize the multiple parameters of alcohol's reinforcing effects. Thus they have come to approach the study of alcohol as a reinforcer from an interdisciplinary perspective, thereby resolving much of the engima surrounding the potency of alcohol's reinforcing properties. Some fascinating recent research on the biochemical actions of alcohol and the brain mechanisms involved in these actions have helped to elucidate the reinforcing effects of alcohol from a pharmacological perspective. Yet the work of scientists from other disciplines has shown that these reinforcing effects are far more complex than a molecular analysis of alcohol's pharmacological actions as a mood modifier might imply. For example, psychological, sociological, and anthropological research has indicated that the particular effect that alcohol has is highly dependent upon such variables as the setting or context in which alcohol is consumed and the society and culture in which one lives.

In a similar manner, social psychologists and sociologists have identified social reinforcements derived from the act of consuming alcohol apart from the pharmacological effects experienced. Research in the psychological laboratory, moreover, has found that a person's expectations about the effects of alcohol are in some cases even stronger determinants of actual behavior than are its pharmacological effects. Finally, psychologists and psychiatrists have discovered the important influence of personality factors. Alcohol is especially reinforcing for individuals who exhibit certain constellations of personality characteristics.

The present volume, recognizing the value of the interdisciplinary approach, attempts to integrate knowledge acquired from the various scientific disciplines about the parameters of alcohol as a reinforcer. The book begins with discussions of the various models, processes, and techniques for studying alcohol's reinforcing effects. It proceeds from there with a discussion of the most molecular analysis of these effects and progresses eventually to the most molar analysis. Hence we begin the book by describing the physiological mechanisms involved in the reinforcing effects of alcohol and advance in successive chapters to discussion of psychological, sociological, and anthropological variables. Each chapter presents the relevant issues on a given topic and summarizes the most recent research findings relevant to that topic.

The final, integrative chapter presents a motivational model of alcohol use that depicts all of the variables that are known to affect drinking and shows how these variables are interrelated.

Since this volume utilizes an interdisciplinary approach, the chapters are written by professionals from a variety of disciplines. However, the authors attempt to convey their material in a simple and straightforward manner that can be easily understood not only by professionals from other disciplines but also by nonprofessionals who have an interest in learning more about how and why alcohol functions as a powerful reinforcer.

W. Miles Cox, Ph.D.

REFERENCE

Alcohol and Health, (1987). Washington, DC: U. S. Department of Health and Human Services.

CONTENTS

WHY PEOPLE DRINK

FOREWORD

G. ALLAN MARLATT, Ph.D.

As an undergraduate student majoring in psychology, I took a course entitled "Motivation and Emotion." The professor told us that although the construct of reinforcement was well established as a foundation of learning theory, considerable disagreement existed concerning the role of motivation and affect. Strict behaviorists viewed motivation as an inferred hypothetical construct, a pseudoexplanatory mechanism that should be eschewed in favor of the objective measurement and manipulation of overt consummatory behaviors. We were admonished to avoid making tautological statements implying causality to unobserved underlying motivational states, for example, "The animal drinks because it is thirsty," or "The alcoholic drinks because he craves alcohol." Questions such as "Why did this happen?" were replaced with "What/when/how did this happen?"

One central controversy in motivation and learning theory outlined by my professor involved the debate between those who held that behavior is governed by the direct impact of reinforcement on the target behavior (e.g., Skinner's operant view and the "S-R" school) and those who held that behavior can be influenced by the *expectancy* of reinforcement (e.g., Tolman's expectancy model and the "S-S" school). This controversy characterized the split between behavioral and cognitive camps, fueling the separate development of both schools into radical behaviorism at one extreme and social cognitive theory at the other. Although the material presented in this book stems from research on both sides of this controversy, the editor (and senior author of the final chapter) endorses the view that the motivation for alcohol consumption by humans is rooted in the drinker's *expectations* about the reinforcing effects of alcohol. As stated in the final chapter by Cox and Klinger: "Our model of alcohol use suggests that the many variables demonstrated in this volume to have an impact on people's motivation to drink do so by virtue of the fact that they help to form expectations about the affective changes that will occur if a person drinks." I agree with this conclusion. If motivation is indeed the final, common pathway to alcohol use, it should be possible to gain access to this pathway through the study of alcohol expectancies.

Many variables influence motivation to drink. The material in the following chapters provides an extensive review of these variables, ranging all the way from genetic and biological factors to social and cultural determinants. I am in agreement with Lang and Michalec's statement in Chapter 8 that expectancy is a complex *biopsychosocial* construct:

> Expectancy addresses drinking in terms of an alcohol × person × environment interaction. This permits consideration of the biological actions of alcohol, but anticipates the potential importance of the psychosocial and even physical context in which they occur. Moreover, the expectancy approach makes room for genetic, personality, conditioning and learning, and other influences, without exclusive or exaggerated emphasis on any one such factor.

Expectancy of affective change as a result of drinking, although itself determined by a host of biopsychosocial factors, represents the distillation of a myriad of motivational forces that come into play at the point of choosing to drink or not in any given situation. Expectancy is therefore the most salient proximal factor associated with the motivation to drink (or not to drink) for a particular individual at a specific time and place. In that sense, expectancy truly is a common, final pathway to alcohol use. And unlike other, more uncontrollable factors that may influence drinking (e.g., genetic predisposition), expectancies are modifiable and can be changed. In this sense, all efforts geared toward the prevention and treatment of alcohol dependence represent attempts to change expectancies about drinking.

Biological factors influence expectancies and expectancies influence biological processes. Genetic factors may, for example, increase or decrease the reinforcing effects of alcohol. Evidence reviewed in this book (Chapters 2–5 suggests, for example, that children of alcoholics may manifest increased tolerance to the euphoric effects of alcohol as compared with children of nonalcoholics. Such experience may lead to the expectation in those with a family history of alcoholism that greater consumption of alcohol is required to obtain the desired reinforcing effects. Other biological factors may increase expectancies for the negative effects of drinking. Evidence presented by Hunt in Chapter 3 initiatesa discussion of the role of acetaldehyde (produced in the metabolism of alcohol) as a possible protective factor for alcohol dependence in certain ethnic groups (acetaldehyde appears to mediate the unpleasant "flush response" experienced by some Asians after they have consumed alcohol). Drinkers who experience this unpleasant effect are likely to develop negative outcome expectancies about drinking. Another example, detailed by West and Sutker in Chapter 5, shows that hormonal changes associated with the menstrual cycle may alter the reinforcing effects of alcohol in female drinkers. Again, a biological change is accompanied by a change in alcohol expectancies.

Expectancy and motivational factors may, in turn, influence biological processes. Evidence is growing (see Brick's review in Chapter 7) that expectancy manipulations, as in the balanced placebo design, may trigger biobehavioral reactions that mimic or compensate for alcohol effects, even in the absence of actual alcohol administration. Placebo reactions to drinks disguised as containing alcohol (even though they are alcohol-free) show evidence of powerful expectancy effects, probably mediated through classical conditioning. Motivational factors may affect biological processes as well. Research reviewed in Chapter 7, for example, shows that manipulation of a motivational variable (whether or not subjects were paid) had a significant effect on the development of tolerance to the debilitating effects of alcohol, as measured by performance on a complex motor coordination task. In short, the relation between cognitive expectancies and biological processes is characterized by reciprocal determinism. The mind influences the body, and vice versa. Physical dependency and psychological dependency are two sides of the same coin. Expectancy of changed affect (the "head side" of the coin) is the key to psychological dependency, with clear implications for prevention and intervention. What is the key to physical dependency and what doorways to change does it open?

Although attempts have been made to assess alcohol outcome expectancies (reviewed by Lang and Michalec in Chapter 8), a number of methodological problems remain. Most alcohol expectancy questionnaires developed to date focus on the expected outcomes from alcohol consumption, such as tension reduction or enhanced aggressiveness. What these expectancy measures fail to tell us is the *affective valence* of the outcome for a particular person. As an outcome of drinking, tension reduction may be positive for one individual (alcohol makes him feel relaxed when under pressure) and negative for another (drinking makes her feel tired and introverted). Or the same outcome may be positively valued on one occasion and negatively evaluated on another for the same person (tension reduction may be a desired effect at the cocktail hour but is evaluated as a counterproductive effect at a business luncheon). Expectancy is a fluid or "state" variable that changes over time, both within and between individuals. Despite this fluidity, changes in both expected outcomes and the valence for such outcomes are critical to our understanding of why people drink.

Expectancy effects can be studied in both human and animal subjects. One limitation of animal studies of alcohol dependence is that researchers must go to great lengths to get most animals to drink alcohol in the first place—at least at levels corresponding to human alcohol dependence (see reviews in Chapters 1, 3, and 4). Animals seem to have negative expectancies for alcohol's effects, judged by their natural drinking inclinations (when is the last time you have seen a drunk animal, other than in the lab?). As a result, researchers have to "trick" animals into drinking by various manipulations (ranging from schedule-induced polydipsia to selective inbreeding of extreme genetic strains of rodents who "prefer" alcohol). If human researchers were to follow the same strategy, they would first look for people who did not like to drink (those with negative expectancies), and then attempt to make them drink heavily by whatever means possible in order to develop a human model of animal drinking! Although animal models have contributed in many important ways to our understanding of mechanisms of dependence and abuse (e.g., alcohol's effects on biological and developmental processes, as a means of studying conditioning effects, etc.), there are obvious limitations to this approach to studying human motivation and expectancy for drinking.

Several authors in this volume draw an important distinction between expectancies for the direct and indirect effects of alcohol. In Chapter 8, Lang and Michalec distinguish between what they call *alcohol-response expectancies* (how drinking affects the individual directly) and *response-outcome alcohol expectancies* (beliefs about the indirect effects of drinking, such as the social consequences of being intoxicated). Along similar lines, Cox and Klinger in Chapter 11 draw a distinction between the direct, *chemical effects* of alcohol and the indirect, *instrumental effects*, such as how drinking may enhance or detract from access to other reinforcers (e.g., peer approval). I think this is a particularly important distinction to make in understanding human motivation to drink (it is not clear what the implications are for animal models, since the focus in these studies is almost always on the direct rather than the indirect effects of alcohol). Sometimes the direct and indirect effects are complementary (e.g., a drinker who successfully seeks the sedative effects of alcohol to dull social anxiety in a cocktail party) and sometimes they are antagonistic (e.g., although "liquor is quicker than candy" as a seductive ploy, the direct effects of heavy drinking may impede physical sexual performance). Along these lines, it is important to consider the potentially conflicting interaction of outcome expectancies for both the direct and indirect effects of alcohol. Many drinkers, particularly heavy drinkers, experience a *conflict of expectancies* regarding alcohol's effects. A problem drinker may expect alcohol to provide immediate relief from distress arising from anticipation of delayed negative effects (e.g., disapproval by significant others). Here there is a conflict between the expectancy for immediate gratification (desired direct effects) and the expectancy for negative social reactions (undesired indirect effect). Clinicians who work with problem drinkers will be familiar with this form of conflict or ambivalence in their clients. It gives rise to a variety of practical problems in treatment, including resistance to change, problem denial, and intense motivational conflict.

A related important distinction raised by several authors concerns the difference between the effects of reinforcement as experienced directly by the individual (e.g., both the direct and indirect effects of alcohol for a specific drinker) and the vicarious effects of reinforcement experienced by someone observing another person drink. Research reviewed in Chapters 7, 9, and 10 points to the importance of observational learning, modeling, and the influence of sociocultural modes and morals on determining motivation to drink. The effect of peer, family, and media models on shaping alcohol outcome expectancies clearly requires further investigation, particularly with regard to the prevention of maladaptive expectancies in young adults. Systematic attempts to vary both the direct and vicarious reinforcement effects (positive and negative) of drinking may clarify how alcohol expectancies can be modified.

The final chapter in this book attempts to integrate material presented in the foregoing ten chapters into an integrated model of incentive motivation, affective change, and alcohol use. In my view, Cox and Klinger have made a significant contribution to our understanding of why people drink. Their model is comprehensive, heuristic, and practical in its implications (the authors provide us with a very useful description of a motivational assessment and counseling program for use with problem drinkers). One of the assumptions of their model is that incentive motivation and effective change are basic to our understanding of why people drink. As Cox and Klinger state, "The motivation to drink, moreover, is closely tied to people's incentive motivation and the effective changes that they derive from their incentives."

Affective change appears to be at the core of reinforcement for drinking. In other writings, I have referred to alcohol as the "magic elixir," a potion capable of transforming "LEAD-LHCE" emotional states into the "golden glow" of intoxication. For many years it was assumed by reinforcement theorists in the alcohol field that the primary affective change motivating drinking was negative reinforcement, namely the reduction of tension or anxiety. Data pertaining to the validity of the tension-reduction hypothesis are reviewed by several authors (see Chapters 5, 6, and 7). In more recent years, greater attention has been paid to the positive reinforcement effects of drinking. In Chapter 5, West and Sutker refer to what they call the *mood enhancement* effects of alcohol—the increase in euphoria and enhancement of positive emotional states that many people seek from alcohol and other drugs. Research on the biochemical and brain mechanisms associated with the reinforcing effects of alcohol (reviewed by Hunt in Chapters 3 and 4) suggest that separate physiological mechanisms may be associated with these negative and positive effects. Other authors have discussed the biphasic or bivalent nature of alcohol's reinforcing effects. Initial positive effects such as enhanced mood are often followed by delayed, negative effects as dose increases and time passes. What is experienced as "positive" as a specific level on the ascending limb of the blood-alcohol level (BAL) curve may be experienced as "negative" for the same BAL on the descending limb (e.g., during alcohol withdrawal). Solomon has described this biphasic reaction in terms of opponent-process theory, in which affective changes caused by a drug such as alcohol are followed by compensatory "opponent-process" mechanisms that are in the opposite direction to the initial effects-presumably mediated by an innate homeostatic mechanism. Such opponent-process responses may be conditioned to drug cues, thereby triggering an oppositional compensatory response in the experienced drinker who is about to take a drink; such "conditioned withdrawal" reactions may motivate the drinker to seek relief from this state by further drinker (negative reinforcement). Brick has provided a review of this material in Chapter 7. Although further research is needed to clarify the underlying mechanisms involved in the biphasic response to alcohol, the implications for understanding motivational conflicts associated with alcohol use and abuse are clearly relevant.

The foregoing comments and ideas were stimulated by reading the excellent contributions to this volume. I found the material to be provocative and challenging, as I assume will be the experience for other readers. Motivational concepts are involved at all stages of understanding why people drink. Why do some people (and not others) initially experiment with the use of alcohol, and why do some (but not all) go on to become regular drinkers? Why do some regular drinkers develop problems or dependency on alcohol? Why do some people stop drinking whereas others continue? Why do some ex-drinkers relapse whereas others are able to maintain abstinence? Not all of these "why" questions are answered in this book, but readers will find much to satisfy and whet their motivational appetites. Although we still have many questions to answer regarding why people drink, there is no problem in understanding why people will want to read this book. With such positive outcome expectancies firmly in mind, read on!

ONE

ANIMAL MODELS FOR UNDERSTANDING ALCOHOL AS A REINFORCER

GAIL WINGER, Ph.D.

"It has been suggested that alcohol abuse is based, at least in part, on the positively reinforcing properties of ethanol" (Socaransky, Aragon, & Amit, 1985, p 361). It is on the basis of this suggestion that a chapter on the reinforcing effects of ethanol in animals is appropriately included in a book on why people drink. The correspondense between the positively reinforcing effects of intravenously delivered psychoactive drugs in animals and drug abuse in humans has been shown quite convincingly by comparing humans and animals on such measures as types of drugs voluntarily taken, patterns of drug taking, and effects of pharmacological or behavioral intervention on drug taking (Griffiths, Bigelow, & Henningfield, 1980). This demonstrated correspondence, plus the strong face validity of drug-reinforced responding in animals, has prompted extensive investigation into the reinforcing effects of drugs in animals, with the hope, and in some cases the realization, of a better understanding of the dynamics of drug abuse in humans.

Before examining data relevant to ethanol's reinforcing effects in animals, it is helpful to understand how the word "reinforcer" is used in this context. A reinforcer is a stimulus that, when presented as contingent on a particular response, leads to and maintains an increased rate

Support for the writing of this chapter was provided by UPHS Grants DA 00154 and DA 00254. Thanks are due Dr. J.H. Woods for editorial assistance.

of that response. This definition is taken from studies of operant behavior, the area of psychology that has been most concerned with describing the way in which response-contingent stimuli come to control behavior. Psychologists who study operant behavior typically use a discrete and measurable response such as lever pressing by an animal in an operant chamber. The study of such a simple response has a number of advantages. For one, the rate of responding can be measured very easily and can be related to independent variables such as magnitude of reinforcement or degree of deprivation. Furthermore, the historical use of rates of lever pressing has resulted in the accumulation of a large body of information on the effects of various manipulations of this measure; new experimental data obtained using the same measure can be easily compared with the existing body of data. For these reasons, data that utilize discrete, ethanol-contingent, lever-press responses to measure the reinforcing effects of ethanol are most useful and easy to interpret. The majority of studies described in this chapter measure ethanol's reinforcing effects by measuring rates of lever-press responses.

One of the thorniest issues for researchers who are interested in studying the reinforcing effects of ethanol in animals is to demonstrate that the property of ethanol that maintains animals' ethanol self-administration is relevant to that which maintains ethanol ingestion in humans. This issue is of particular concern for those who measure animals' preference for ethanol solutions since many strains of rats will consume low concentrations of ethanol in preference to water, but in patterns and amounts that apparently are related primarily to the gustatory, olfactory, or caloric properties of the liquid (see Cicero 1979, for review). Since it is commonly assumed that people drink ethanol for reasons other than its taste, smell, or value as a food, the animal model should drink for other reasons as well. The problem is to determine what properties of ethanol are critical to ethanol-maintained drinking in humans, and then require that these same properties maintain responding in animals. In other words, if we knew why people drink, we would know how better to establish a relevant measure of the reinforcing effect of ethanol in animals.

The reasons why people drink are so complex that it is not surprising that they are not fully understood. However, there is another aspect of human alcohol consumption that is not as difficult to determine, and more knowledge about it would aid a great deal in delineating the aspects of animal alcohol consumption that are relevant to humans. That is the question of *how* people drink. Careful descriptions of patterns of ethanol consumption, amounts of ethanol consumed, and the blood levels of ethanol that result from ethanol consumption by humans would be extremely useful. From these descriptions, additional questions could be asked: How do these measures differ among alcoholics? How do they differ among alcoholics, heavy drinkers, and social drinkers? How do they change when the concentration of ethanol in the drink changes? This type of information would increase our understanding of alcoholism, as well as enhance our ability to model alcoholism appropriately in animals. The small amount of data that has been obtained on how people drink is extremely interesting. Observations of patterns of experimental alcohol consumption in alcoholics (Mendelson & Mello, 1966; Bigelow, Griffiths, & Liebson, 1975) provide some of the best confirmation of the relevance of similar patterns of alcohol consumption in monkeys (Deneau, Yanagita, & Seevers, 1969; Woods, Ikomi, & Winger, 1971).

Determining whether factors that have been shown to modify ethanol consumption by humans will also modify such consumption by animals would also help to validate the methodology used in animals. Again, however, the data in humans are scanty. Bigelow and colleagues (1975) showed that intake of ethanol by alcoholic humans could be decreased by increasing the amount of work required to obtain the alcohol, by isolating the subject briefly when he or she worked and obtained ethanol, and by requiring minimal periods of time between opportunities to obtain ethanol. Vuchinich and Tucker (1983) found that responses by male college students with histories of moderate to heavy drinking that focused on obtaining ethanol could be decreased by making money available as an alternative reinforcer. Ethanol intake in humans can also be reduced by prior administration of such drugs as disulfiram (Antabuse) and calcium carbamide. Researchers who are trying to establish the reinforcing effect of ethanol in animals should attempt to manipulate variables similar to these manipulated in humans to help determine whether their data are relevant to human ethanol consumption.

Unfortunately, the criteria usually set up for such research rarely refer to experimental work with these effects in humans, but instead lean heavily on sequelae of chronic intake, such as tolerance and dependence (Cicero, 1979; Lester & Freed, 1973). It is quite clear from the literature on self-administration of opiates and central nervous system (CNS) stimulants, as well as ethanol, that physiological dependence is not necessary for the establishment of the reinforcing property of drugs. Thus this criterion is inappropriate when applied to the establishment of the reinforcing effects of ethanol. It has also been suggested that in order for an animal preparation to be relevant to humans, the animal should drink ethanol to the point of intoxication, and that this intoxication should be indicated by measured blood–ethanol concentrations (Cicero, 1979). This is probably an important emphasis—although, in the absence of similar measures in humans, it is difficult to know what blood levels are appropriate. This criterion can be taken one step further by adding that the animal should regulate its blood ethanol levels in some way, so that such procedures as altering the dose or concentration of ethanol, altering the work required to obtain the ethanol, or passively administering ethanol prior to the opportunity to consume ethanol should result in compensatory changes in behavior that result in similar final blood levels of ethanol. This recommendation has been applied to studies of the reinforcing effects of ethanol with interesting results (Karoly, Winger, Ikomi, & Woods, 1978), although, again, there are no similar data in humans to help establish the relevance of the blood measures.

Since there are no certain criteria to determine whether ethanol consumption in animals is relevant to the human condition, in studies of intake of oral ethanol in particular, judgment must frequently be made in individual experiments on the basis of amount ingested, blood ethanol levels, pattern of intake, observations of intoxicated behavior, or concentrations of ethanol consumed. Assessing the effect of the experimental manipulations on consumption of nonethanol fluids can also help to demonstrate whether any change in fluid preference is specific to ethanol. Thus one can often make a decision about whether the reinforcing property of ethanol, as measured in animals in a given experiment, is relevant to the property of ethanol that maintains ethanol ingestion in humans, but this decision may be subject to differences in opinion.

PROCEDURES FOR ESTABLISHING ETHANOL AS A REINFORCER

Many procedures have been used in attempts to establish ethanol as a reinforcer in experimental animals. Those discussed below represent the procedures that have been used most successfully or are interesting because they are new or have unusual promise. Some procedures that typically are included in reviews of methods to establish ethanol as a reinforcer are not included here. Specifically, studies of the effects of intracerebroventricular administration of various chemicals on the preference for ethanol and of the reinforcing effects of intragastrically administered ethanol are omitted because the results were difficult to interpret. Moreover, studies of schedule-induced ethanol drinking are not reviewed in any detail because the emphasis of most of these studies is on producing physiological dependence to ethanol rather than on establishing ethanol as a reinforcer.

Intravenous Self-Administration

Deneau, et al. (1969) were the first to demonstrate that ethanol could establish and maintain responding when delivered intravenously to rhesus monkeys. The procedure used was identical to that employed to determine the reinforcing effects of other psychoactive drugs. Indwelling intravenous catheters were implanted in the monkeys, who could respond on available levers and operate an infusion pump that resulted in the delivery of intravenous ethanol. Deneau and his co-workers reported that four of five monkeys initiated responding when ethanol was delivered as a result of the response, and three monkeys self-injected sufficient amounts to produce physiological dependence. A very erratic pattern of responding developed in these animals, with high rates of ethanol-reinforced responding followed by decreased rates of responding. During the periods of decreased ethanol administration, signs of ethanol withdrawal were observed.

The reinforcing effects of intravenous ethanol were further investigated by Winger and Woods (1973). As did Deneau et al., they found that not all animals spontaneously initiated ethanol-reinforced responding, but that those that did, showed episodic patterns of intake. If high rates of lever-pressing behavior were first established by making either cocaine or methohexital available, ethanol subsequently maintained responding in all tested animals. The reason some monkeys did not spontaneously self-administer ethanol was attributed to the fact that relatively high doses needed to be administered before ethanol came to serve as a reinforcer. Prior exposure to drugs that were more potent as reinforcers ensured sufficient behavior to produce intake of ethanol. The episodic nature of the intake patterns prevented the study of potential variables that could alter the pattern of ethanol self-administration. A more stable baseline resulted when the opportunity for self-administration was decreased from 24 to three hours each day. Under these conditions of limited access, daily intake was quite consistent, and, probably not coincidentally, the animals did not show signs of physiological dependence.

Woods, et al (1971) found that changing the dose/injection of ethanol led to changes in the number of ethanol injections taken. Similar effects were found when a dose of ethanol was administered prior to the opportunity to self-administer ethanol. The animals decreased the ethanol they self-administered on their own by an amount equal to the pretreatment dose. It thus appeared that the animals were closely regulating their intake in a way that suggested that pharmacological effects of the ethanol were maintaining the behavior. Indeed, when Karoly et al. (1978) measured blood ethanol levels, they found that the monkeys responded in such a way as to induce and maintain an ethanol blood level of approximately 400 mg percent.

The demonstration of the reinforcing effects of intravenous ethanol has not been as successful in the rat as in the rhesus monkey. Collins, Weeks, Cooper, Good, and Russell (1984) reported that ethanol was the only one of 18 psychoactive drugs that, when delivered intravenously, maintained behavior in the monkey but not in the rat. Sinden and Le Magnen (1982) reported the positive reinforcing effects of very low doses (0.001 g/kg) of ethanol when delivered intravenously in the rat, but Numan, Naparzewska, and Adler (1984) were unable to replicate this finding, and suggested that it may have been due to the use of a cylindrical chamber and a single response lever in the test. The capacity of low does of ethanol to stimulate behavior in general may have accounted for the results obtained with this apparatus.

Grupp (1981) found that, in the rat, as the number of responses required for an intravenous injection of cocaine increased, rates of responding increased as well; this relationship between response requirement and response rate did not hold for intravenous ethanol, calling into question the function of ethanol in this paradigm. Grupp and Stewart (1983) presented evidence that intravenous ethanol may actually be aversive in the rat. They observed that rats learned to jump a hurdle to *prevent* the intravenous administration of 200, 400, or 800 mg/kg ethanol. Rats also showed a decrease in frequency of entering a goal box if these doses of ethanol were administered in the goal box.

Numan (1981) reported that ethanol at a dose of approximately 0.1 g/kg per injection would serve as a reinforcer when delivered intravenously to rats, but only if the rats had first been given forced infusions of 9–16 g/kg/day ethanol for four to six days. Numan suggested that the prior forced infusions caused the rats to become physiologically dependent on ethanol, with the result that its reinforcing effects were enhanced by its capacity to relieve withdrawal. This suggestion must be considered in the light of other evidence that indicates that ethanol dependence does not lead to increase ethanol self-administration or selection (e.g., Tang, Kenny, & Falk, 1984; Allen, Fantom, & Wilson, 1982), and the study by Numan must be interpreted cautiously.

Food-Induced Drinking

The fact that food deprivation leads to increases in oral ethanol intake is one of the most consistent findings in the literature on voluntary ethanol consumption. Meisch and Thompson (1972) demonstrated that food deprivation alone could result in ethanol-maintained responding that exceeded water-maintained responding in rats. In fact, ethanol intake was sufficient at the higher concentrations to produce behavioral signs of intoxication. There are at least two obvious potential explanations for this effect: (1) food-deprived animals drink for the caloric properties of ethanol, and (2) ethanol has a faster onset of action in animals with empty stomachs. However, neither of these explanations can account entirely for the effect of food deprivation on ethanol ingestion. Animals deprived of food show higher rates of responding for intravenous drug delivery, thus disputing the "empty-stomach hypothesis." Subjects also show increased intake of orally available drugs that have no caloric value (Carroll, Stotz, Kliner, & Meisch, 1984; Carroll & Meisch, 1984). Although the mechanism of this effect has not been explained, food deprivation is used quite commonly as part of procedures that establish ethanol-maintained responding in animals.

The phenomenon of schedule-induced polydipsia, in which animals drink excessive amounts of available fluid when they receive small bits of food at prescribed intervals, develops with food deprivation as well (Falk, 1961). The procedures for producing polydipsia have been used to induce high-volume ethanol intake in rats, to the point of physiological dependence (e.g., Falk, Samson, & Winger, 1972; Samson & Falk, 1975). Meisch (1975) used schedule-induced polydipsia procedures in food-deprived rats to establish drinking of high volumes of ethanol solutions. Either water or ethanol solutions were available during the first six hours of a daily session; spaced food-pellet delivery, which typically resulted in increased fluid intake, occurred only during the last four hours of each session. Thus, during the first two hours, fluid-reinforced responding was measured in the absence of the conditions that generated high fluid intake.

Meisch found that rates of lever pressing were much higher during the initial two hours if ethanol solutions were available than if water was available. Moreover, when the intermittent food-delivery schedule was discontinued, 8, 16, or 32 percent ethanol maintained much higher rates of responding than did water. Thus Meisch clearly demonstrated the reinforcing effects of ethanol in this paradigm, both in terms of the patterns of responding and in the amount of ethanol consumed. In further studies in this same series, Meisch reported that the schedule-induction procedure was not necessary to establish ethanol as a reinforcer. Simply placing food in the operant chamber along with water resulted in the consumption of large quantities of water by food-deprived rats.

Substituting gradually increasing concentrations of ethanol for the water did not result in decreased fluid intake as long as the food was given during the session. In fact, during one-hour sessions, 8 percent ethanol maintained higher rates of responding than did water, thus demonstrating the reinforcing effects of ethanol under these conditions. In the final study of this series, animals first responded and received water when their limited food ration was available during the opportunity to drink. Once water-reinforced responding was established, food was given after rather than during the drinking session. The rate of water-reinforced responding decreased, since it had been maintained by the concurrent availability of food. When increasing concentrations of ethanol replaced the water, the rate of fluid-reinforced lever pressing increased and reached a maximum at an ethanol concentration of 8 percent. This series of studies by Meisch and colleagues demonstrated that the reinforcing effects of ethanol could be established not only after experience with ethanol consumption under conditions of schedule-induced polydipsia, but also in conditions in which food-deprived animals simply have experience with responding to receive fluid and do so because of a history of drinking in conjunction with eating.

The volume of ethanol solution consumed decreased as the concentration of ethanol increased, suggesting appropriate regulation by the animals of their ethanol consumption (Meisch & Beardsley, 1975). To rule out the possibility that this outcome was due to a more aversive taste of the higher concentrations, Henningfield and Meisch (1975) altered the dose of ethanol per delivery by increasing the volume rather than the concentration. A similar pattern of regulated intake was shown under conditions of increased volume.

The reinforcing effect of ethanol as a result of food-induced drinking has also been demonstrated in rhesus monkeys. Meisch and Henningfield (1977) used the food-induction method described above for rats to obtain drinking of intoxicating amounts of ethanol by monkeys. The animals were reduced to 80 percent of their free-feeding weight and given access to low concentrations of ethanol at the time their daily food ration was available. Large quantities of ethanol were consumed initially; the experimenters then gradually increased the concentration of ethanol. When the monkeys were drinking 100–200 ml of 8 percent ethanol on a regular basis, their food was made available after, rather than during, the period of ethanol availability. Consumption of large quantities of ethanol continued, with resulting blood ethanol levels of 100–200 mg percent. When water was substituted for the ethanol, fluid decreased markedly, demonstrating the reinforcing effects of ethanol. These effects were further evident when the fixed ratio value (number of responses required for delivery of ethanol) was increased. Local response patterns were very similar to those that develop when food is available on fixed ratio schedules, with the primary difference being that the rate of responding across a daily session was negatively accelerated. The quantity of ethanol consumed remained fairly constant across fixed ratio values that increased from one to sixteen (Henningfield & Meisch, 1976), indicating that the animals were regulating the amount of ethanol ingested.

Regulation of intake was also demonstrated by changing ethanol concentrations. Increasing the ethanol concentrations led to decreases in the volume of the solution consumed but increases in the amount of ethanol consumed. Blood alcohol levels were sometimes above 100 mg percent at the higher concentrations (Henningfield & Meisch, 1979). One of the three subjects showed a pattern of binge drinking that was particularly interesting in view of the fact that this pattern has been described in humans (Mendelson & Mello, 1966) and monkeys under conditions of intravenous ethanol-maintained responding (Woods et al., 1971). In an attempt to produce physiological dependence on ethanol with food-induced drinking, Henningfield and Meisch (1979) made ethanol and water available for 23 hours each day. Although high ethanol intake was maintained by frequent drinking bouts, no clear signs of withdrawal were observed when the ethanol was removed after ten days.

To determine whether food-deprived animals were consuming ethanol because of its caloric value, Henningfield and Meisch (1981) compared the amount of ethanol consumed under postsession feeding conditions with that consumed under presession feeding conditions. Feeding the monkeys before the opportunity to drink ethanol should decrease the ethanol intake, if it was maintained because of the calories it provides. When the monkeys were fed 15 minutes before the drinking sessions, they drank considerably more ethanol and only slightly more concurrently available water. Thus it was concluded that the caloric value of the ethanol was not responsible for maintained drinking in the paradigm of food-induced consumption of ethanol.

Because of the ease of inspiring food-induced ethanol consumption, and because of the large quantity of ethanol that is consumed with this procedure, other investigators have evaluated its ability to bring about ethanol consumption. Henningfield, Ator, and Griffiths (1981), for instance, utilized a food-induced drinking paradigm in baboons. The food-deprived baboons consumed relatively stable amounts of 8–32 percent ethanol. Intoxication developed during the three-hour sessions, as assessed both by behavioral observations and by assays of blood-alcohol concentrations. When both water and 8 percent ethanol were made available in the experimental paradigm, the baboons continued to drink large quantities of ethanol. Thus the food-induced drinking paradigm revealed the reinforcing property of ethanol in the baboon in much the same way it had previously in rats and rhesus monkeys.

Stewart and Grupp (1984) used a food-induced drinking procedure to produce high-volume ethanol consumption in food-deprived rats. They tested the animals for 60 minutes each in "drinking cages" where a single drinking tube and, initially, 5 g of food were placed. The solution available was water or ethanol on alternate days. They gradually increased the concentration of ethanol that was available to rats, along with their daily ration of food. Once drinking of an 8 percent ethanol solution was established, they fed the rats after, rather than during, the period of ethanol availability. Stewart and Grupp reported that, when the rats were deprived to 80 percent of their free-feeding weights, they drank ethanol in preference to water, and drank most rapidly during the initial 15 minutes of a 60-minute period of ethanol availability. When the rats were given free access to food, however, their intake of ethanol decreased significantly. Blood ethanol levels as high as 150 mg/100 ml were reached in the study. Elmer, Meisch, and George (1986) demonstrated the reinforcing effect of ethanol in food-deprived C57BL/6 mice, an ethanol-preferring strain of mice, using food-induced drinking to establish the drinking of ethanol. Blood ethanol levels of nearly 200 mg/100 ml were recorded in animals drinking ethanol when the food was given after the session.

The procedure of food-induced ethanol consumption thus appears simple to develop and can be used with different animal species. It seems to produce drinking of substantial amounts of ethanol, and the ethanol clearly becomes a reinforcer under these circumstances. One possible reason why the reinforcing effects of ethanol can be demonstrated in this procedure is that making fluid available along with food to food-deprived animals produces high volumes of fluid ingestion. If this fluid is ethanol in gradually increasing concentrations, the animals may adapt to its aversive taste and consume enough to "make contact" with its reinforcing effects. Ethanol drinking is maintained thereafter even if the food is no longer available during the opportunity to drink. This analysis of food-induced ethanol consumption suggests that other procedures that produce high intakes of ethanol should also eventuate in ethanol serving as a reinforcer. Consistent with this view, rats that drink large volumes of ethanol under conditions of schedule-induced polydipsia show a greater preference for ethanol over higher concentrations of sucrose than do rats without this exposure (Samson & Falk, 1974). Whether this reflects an increase in the positive reinforcing effects of ethanol is not certain. The fact that ethanol consumption decreases dramatically when the generating conditions of spaced food presentation are removed (Tang, Brown, & Falk, 1982) suggests that this procedure may not be as effective as simple food-induced drinking in producing long-term increases in ethanol preference.

Several other procedures that lead to high ethanol consumption in animals also do not clearly alter their preference for ethanol once the inducing conditions are removed (e.g., Black & Martin, 1972; Keehn, 1969; Martin & Myers, 1972; Senter & Persensky, 1968). Therefore, there may be more to the development of ethanol as a reinforcer than simply inducing high levels of ethanol ingestion through the manipulation of food deprivation and food availability. Also, using adaptation to the taste of ethanol and consumption of large amounts of ethanol to explain how ethanol comes to function as a reinforcer does not account for the fact that ethanol ingestion declines dramatically when the animals are given free access to food. It also is not clear that the inducing condition of food deprivation is relevant to the development of alcoholism in humans. Thus, although food-induced ethanol consumption has resulted in much interesting data on ethanol-reinforced responding in animals, it has also raised many questions.

Concurrent Schedules

Samson and his colleagues at the University of Washington have evaluated methods for establishing ethanol as a reinforcer. One procedure they used is a concurrent schedule of ethanol and either water or sucrose availability. The subjects were food-deprived rats. [The critical nature of food deprivation was demonstrated in a later study by Samson, Toliver, and Roehers (1983).] During daily 60-minute sessions, rats could gain access to a dipper of 5 percent ethanol by pressing one of two available levers, and gain access to a dipper of water by pressing the other lever. Under the basic schedule contingencies, eight responses on each lever resulted in the presentation of the appropriate fluid. Rates of responding on the lever associated with ethanol were higher than rates of responding on the water-associated lever, but this difference decreased when the animals were no longer deprived of food (Roehrs & Samson, 1982). When the water was replaced by different concentrations of sucrose, the rates of sucrose-reinforced responding increased and the rates of ethanol-reinforced responding decreased. However, when the response requirement on the sucrose-associated lever was increased from eight to 64, the rates of sucrose-reinforced responding decreased and the rates of ethanol-reinforced responding increased to levels as high as twice those that had developed when the choice had been between ethanol and water. When the response requirement on the sucrose-associated level was returned to the initial value of eight, rates of responding on this lever increased and rates on the ethanol-associated lever decreased. However, when water replaced the sucrose solution (with a response requirement of eight on both water- and ethanol-associated levers), the increased rate of ethanol-reinforced responding, established under conditions of high response requirements for sucrose, was maintained (Samson, Roehrs, & Tolliver, 1982).

Samson and Lindberg (1984) evaluated the generality of this phenomenon whereby rates of responding maintained by a nonpreferred solution could be increased by increasing the response requirement necessary for presentation of a more preferred solution. They used two concentrations of sucrose. As has been demonstrated with ethanol and sucrose solutions, when the response requirement on both levers was equal, rats responded more frequently on the lever associated with higher sucrose concentrations. When the response requirement on the lever associated with the higher concentration was increased, rates of responding maintained by the lower concentration of sucrose increased. The magnitude of the increase in responding maintained by low sucrose concentrations was not as great as that maintained by ethanol as shown in the earlier studies. Nevertheless, the investigators concluded that "part of the previously observed increase in ethanol responding was not necessarily due to some specific property of ethanol, but can occur for any given set of reinforcers presented in a concurrent situation when the more preferred of the pair becomes more difficult to obtained" (Samson & Lindberg, 1984, p 976).

This description of increases in ethanol-maintained responding consequent to restricted access to a more preferred stimulus has features in common with the phenomenon of schedule-induced polydipsia. Polydipsic intake of water, ethanol, or other palatable fluids that develops when food-deprived animals receive small pieces of food at regular, spaced intervals is also an example of increased fluid consumption when a more preferred stimulus is not available. Both schedule-induced polydipsia and the concurrent schedule procedures described by Samson and colleagues produce increased ingestion of solutions other than ethanol—that is, they are not inducers of ethanol ingestion specifically. Since drinking of ethanol by humans is usually thought to be maintained by some specific aspect of ethanol, procedures that produce nonspecific increases in fluid ingestion may not be relevant to the human condition of alcohol ingestion. If, however, humans increase their intake of ethanol because a preferred commodity is more difficult to obtain or is delayed, as suggested by Tucker, Vuchimich, and Harris (1985) and Cox and Klinger (Chapter 11), then schedule-induced polydipsia and concurrent access procedures could indeed be relevant to drinking by humans.

The next step would be to demonstrate that the behavioral mechanisms underlying the human consumption of ethanol are the same as those in experimental paradigms, discussed here, with the rat. Whether or not these procedures will prove to have behavioral relevance to the human alcoholic, they remain interesting because of their potential usefulness in establishing and evaluating the reinforcing property of ethanol in animals.

Sucrose-Induced Ethanol Consumption

The ubiquitous effect of food deprivation on ethanol consumption in animals has been a puzzling problem to researchers interested in measuring a reinforcing effect of ethanol that is relevant to its effects in humans. Although it has not been determined what the effects of food deprivation on drug taking are in humans, it is not commonly thought that consumption of drugs such as ethanol is related to food deprivation in the alcoholic human. Thus there have been frequent attempts to obtain ethanol-reinforced responding in food-satiated animals. Grant and Samson (1985a), for example, required food-satiated rats to lick a 5 percent ethanol solution in order to receive access to a dipper of sucrose. Once every five sessions, the sucrose solution was replaced with 5 percent ethanol so that the rats licked 5 percent ethanol to gain access to an additional 5 percent ethanol. After 20 sessions of ethanol-reinforced licking, the "lickometer" was removed and a response lever was inserted. Lever pressing was reinforced with a 5 percent ethanol solution and the response requirement for presenting the ethanol solution was increased gradually from one to eight. Once responding had stabilized under the fixed-ratio schedule, the ethanol concentration was increased to as high as 40 percent. Rats developed rates of ethanol-maintained responding indicative of a reinforcing effect of ethanol. Moreover, they continued to respond when either the response requirement or the concentration of ethanol was increased. At a concentration of 40 percent ethanol, in fact, rats consumed as much as 0.99 g/kg during a 30-minute session, and showed blood alcohol levels as high as 123 mg/100 ml. Absolute ethanol intake was lower at lower concentrations, but most rats had blood alcohol levels of over 100 mg/100 ml at concentrations of 10 percent or greater. The pairing of ethanol with sucrose was apparently able to overcome the aversive taste of ethanol and led to high consumption of ethanol in food-satiated rats.

To determine whether sucrose-induced ethanol consumption was specific to ethanol and related to its pharmacological properties, Grant and Samson (1985b) repeated the procedure, evaluating not only the reinforcing effects of ethanol, but also those of quinine. They found that concentrations of quinine that were aversive in other situations could maintain responding with the sucrose-induction procedure. Interestingly, rates of quinine-reinforced responding did not decline as the concentration of quinine was increased, although in the case of ethanol, as the concentration was increased, the rate of responding decreased. The authors indicated that, since response rates declined with increasing concentrations of ethanol but not quinine, the decreased rate of ethanol-reinforced responding may have been attributable to the pharmacological properties of the consumed ethanol that were not present in the quinine solution. This was further evidence that pharmacologically relevant amounts of ethanol were being consumed. It appears, however, as though the sucrose-induction procedure could lead to a variety of previously aversive fluids serving as reinforcers, and was not specific to ethanol. Although this lack of specificity does not necessarily mean that the procedure is not useful or relevant to human ethanol consumption, it does not mean that the behavioral process involved is more important than the nature of the fluid that is available. This process must be more thoroughly evaluated so that its possible relevance to human ethanol consumption can be determined.

In a similar method of producing ethanol consumption in free-fed rats, Samson (1986) first trained the animals to press a lever and obtain access to 20 percent sucrose. Once the response was learned, the response requirement was increased to four (FR4); the concentration of sucrose was gradually decreased to 0 percent while increasing concentrations of ethanol were added to the fluid. Eventually the rats could access 10 percent ethanol by responding on one lever and access water by pressing on another lever. The fluid available for responding on a given lever was alternated from session to session, and the rats selected the ethanol-associated lever more than 82 percent of the time. Rates of responding were higher on the ethanol-associated lever than on the water-associated lever, and ethanol consumption did not decrease when 1 percent sucrose replaced the water solution as the concurrently available fluid. When 5 percent sucrose was available concurrently with ethanol, rates of ethanol-maintained lever pressing decreased and rates of sucrose-maintained responding increased. When 40 percent ethanol was available concurrently with water, the rats consumed nearly 1 g/kg during the 30-minute sessions. Patterns of responding were indicative of reinforcing function of ethanol. Each of the tested concentrations of ethanol maintained high rates of responding early in the session; the higher the concentration, the more quickly the rats ceased responding. Home-cage preference for ethanol over water increased after the training procedure from a negligible selection of 5 percent ethanol to a nearly 50 percent selection of 10 percent ethanol. These data indicate that ethanol can serve as a reinforcer in free-fed rats; it remains unclear how this procedure differs from others that have not been able to maintain responding in animals in the absence of food deprivation, and whether this difference is relevant to ethanol consumption by humans.

Selective Breeding

The possibility that genetics plays an important role in human alcoholism was pointed out by the research of Goodwin (1973; also Chapter 2, this volume), who showed that the offspring of alcoholic parents were more likely to become alcoholic than the offspring of nonalcoholic parents. The issue of what exactly is inherited by the children of alcoholics has not been resolved (Crabbe, 1984), but the possibility that genetics may influence susceptibility to the reinforcing effects of ethanol must be entertained.

Work with animals on inherited susceptibility to various effect of ethanol has produced some of the most interesting data on animal–ethanol interactions in recent years. Some of the early work demonstrated that mice could be bred for their sensitivity to the sleep-inducing effects of ethanol (McClearn & Kakihana, 1973). The two strains, long sleep (LS) and short sleep (SS), were found to differ in their responses to a variety of alcohols, but to differ less in their responses to the effects of other sedative hypnotics (Erwin, Heston, McClearn, & Deteich, 1976: Dudek & Phillips, 1983). Mice have been bred as well for differential severity of ethanol withdrawal signs (Crabbe, Kosabud, & Young, 1983; McClearn, Wilson, Petersen, & Allen, 1982; McSwigan, Crabbe, & Young, 1984; Wilson, Erwin, Defries, Petersen, & Cole-Harding, 1984).

Rats have also been bred for differential sensitivity to ethanol. The biological marker in this research has often been the willingness to consume ethanol solutions (Eriksson, 1968; Li, Lumeng, McBride, & Waller, 1979; Tampier, Quintanilla, Contreras, Segovia-Requelma, & Mardones, 1984; Mardones & Segovia-Riquelme, 1983), a characteristic that may have relevance to the capacity of ethanol to serve as a reinforcer in these animals. The same questions arise about the relevance to humans of increased drinking of ethanol produced by selective breeding of animals as arise with increased voluntary ethanol consumption by other means. Attempts to answer these questions have been more extensive and the replies more convincing that those with many other approaches to voluntary ethanol consumption.

Li and colleagues (1979) developed two lines of rats, the alcohol preferring (P line), which exhibited preferences for ethanol solutions up to

14 percent or greater, and the alcohol nonpreferring (NP line), which did not show preference for alcohol solutions. Substantial amounts of alcohol were consumed by the P line of animals during the dark part of the day–night cycle, as indicated by measured blood ethanol levels. Intoxication, however, was rarely observed. Although Penn, McBride, Lumeng, Gaff, and Li, (1978) demonstrated that alcohol-preferring rats would press a lever to gain access to ethanol, it was not clear that the pharmacological effects of ethanol were responsible for the observed reinforcing effects. Further evaluation of the reinforcing effects of ethanol in the P strain of rats was carried out by determining whether intravenous administration of ethanol would alter the amount of ethanol consumed by these animals in a situation in which both ethanol and water were available. It was found that the oral intake of ethanol decreased and that of water increased in proportion to the amount of the ethanol that was administered intravenously. Furthermore, administration of 4-methylpyrazole, an agent that decreases the rate of ethanol metabolism, also produced decreases in ethanol intake and increases in water intake (Waller, McBride, Lumeng, & Li, 1982). Rats trained to press levers that resulted in the simultaneous presentation of drinking water and intravenous infusions of ethanol or saline showed increased rates of lever pressing when ethanol infusions were contingent on this behavior (Li et al., 1979). These data suggest that the reinforcing effect of ethanol in these rats was related to its pharmacological effects.

Perhaps the most definitive demonstration of the reinforcing effects of ethanol in the P line of rats was that of Waller, McBride, Gatto, Lumeng, and Li (1984). These investigators delivered ethanol intragastrically to rats contingent on the animals' drinking water flavored with either banana or almond. The P line of rats selected the flavor that resulted in ethanol infusions and, at a concentration of 40 percent ethanol, received as much as 9.4g/kg of ethanol each day. The NP line selected the flavor not resulting in ethanol infusions and received only about 0.7g/kg of 40 percent ethanol. The amount of intragastric 40 percent ethanol received by the P line of rats was higher than the amount the P line ordinarily drank, but at lower concentrations, the amount received intragastrically was very close to the amount consumed orally. Blood alcohol levels ranged from 92 to 415 mg/100 ml, which were higher than those measured in these animals when they simply drank ethanol. When the flavors associated with ethanol and water infusions were switched, the animals preferred flavors changed as well. The authors concluded that a "postabsorptive, pharmacological mechanism" underlay the preference of the P line of rats for ethanol.

Another program (Ericksson, 1968) led to the breeding of two other lines of rats that are analogous to those in Li's program: alcohol accepting (AA) and alcohol nonaccepting (ANA). The differential reinforcing effects of ethanol in these two lines has been evaluated via a food-induction procedure (Ritz, George, deFiebre, & Meisch, 1986), When food satiated, neither AA nor ANA rats responded at substantial rates on levers that gave them access to dippers of ethanol or water. However, when they were deprived to 75 percent of their free-feeding weights and, following their daily feeding, allowed to respond for ethanol of increasing concentrations, both lines responded at much higher rates on the ethanol-related lever and drank significant amounts of ethanol. The AA rats consumed higher volumes of ethanol during the drinking opportunities than did the ANA rats, and their blood ethanol levels were slightly higher as well. When the daily food allowance was given after rather than before access to water and 5.7 percent ethanol, the AA line demonstrated higher rates of responding on the lever associated with ethanol delivery than on the lever associated with water delivery. The ANA line, however, did not show an increased rate of responding on the ethanol-associated lever. Thus food-induced ethanol consumption developed in both lines of rats, but exposure to ethanol under these conditions resulted in ethanol-reinforced responding only in the alcohol-accepting rats when drinking was no longer induced by eating. Therefore, "at least under the environmental constraints outlined in this study, genotype is a critical factor in determining the reinforcing efficacy of ethanol" (Ritz et al., 1986). Similar results were reported using mice and comparing the reinforcing effects of ethanol in an ethanol-preferring strain (C57GL/6J) with that in an ethanol-avoiding strain (BALB/cJ) (Elmer, Meisch & George, 1987).

Studies such as these on the genetics of ethanol-reinforced responding in animals raise many questions of experimental and theoretical interest. For instance, will these alcohol-accepting and alcohol-preferring strains demonstrate the reinforcing effects of other drugs more readily than their nondrinking relatives? Are they different in their sensitivity to other acute or chronic effects of ethanol? How do the reinforcing effects of ethanol relate to "intoxication" in these different strains? These are some of the questions that may be studied using strains of rats or mice that differ in their sensitivity to the effects of ethanol and that result in maintained ethanol-reinforced responding.

The preliminary data from rats and mice suggest that sensitivity to the reinforcing effects of ethanol may be in part genetically determined. That is, some strains of rodents may be more likely to show increased rates of ethanol-contingent responding than other strains. This raises the interesting possibility that humans who become alcoholic have a genetic predisposition that results in their greater alcohol intake than do those who do not become alcoholic. Some of the genetically related factors that may predispose to alcoholism and that have been evaluated in humans are ethanol metabolism, personality or psychiatric disorders, and the response to acute doses of ethanol (Schuckit, Li, Cloninger, & Deteich, 1985). Among the most provocative results to date are those that indicate that the sons of alcoholic fathers have a less intense response to acute administration of ethanol than do young men without a family history of alcoholism (Schuckit, 1985b). Studies of these effects in different strains of rodents could provide evidence of the relevance of the rodent to humans as far as the genetic response to ethanol is concerned.

APPLICATION OF PROCEDURES THAT EVALUATE THE REINFORCING EFFECTS OF ETHANOL

Behavior Modification

Despite a large number of animal studies using behavioral procedures to induce ethanol intake, relatively few have been designed to use behavioral procedures to produce decrements in an established reinforcing effect of ethanol. One of the most interesting was carried out in rats, using the method of food-induced ethanol drinking described earlier. Drinking of 8 percent ethanol was first established in food-deprived rats in the presence of food, and then food was made available after the ethanol-drinking session. The experimental subjects could respond by pressing a lever and thus obtain access to a dipper of 8 percent ethanol. After each delivery of ethanol, further access was prevented for as long as 480 seconds. The rate of responding, and hence the number of presentations of the ethanol-filled dipper, decreased as a function of the length of delay between opportunities for ethanol-reinforced responding. The researchers suggest that the decreased response rate may be attributable to the delay-induced disruption of the normal burst pattern of ethanol-reinforced responding. "Perhaps ethanol is weakened as a reinforcer if bursts of drinking are prevented because, as a result, the local level of obtainable pharmacological effect is reduced" (Beardsley, Lemaire, & Meisch 1983, p. 846). The potential importance of imposing delays between opportunities to self-administer ethanol is emphasized by the finding that such delays can reduce alcohol intake in humans by nearly 50 percent (Bigelow et al., 1975).

Pharmacologic Interventions

CNS Depressants. Chlordiazepoxide has been used in a few studies to attempt to alter the reinforcing effects of ethanol. Beaman, Hunter, Dunn, and Reid (1984) evaluated the ability of chlordiazepoxide to modify rats' preference for sweetened ethanol solutions and found that their preference was unchanged by this drug. Roehrs, Yang, and Samson (1984) reported that chronic administration of several doses of chlordiazepoxide produced decrements in the intake of ethanol but no change in the intake of water. Three procedures were used to establish ethanol consumption: (1) schedule-induced drinking, producing high ethanol intakes; (2) food-induced drinking in food-deprived rats, producing moderate ethanol intakes; and (3) drinking of ethanol in free-feeding rats, producing low ethanol intakes. Chlordiazepoxide reduced ethanol consumption in both the schedule-induced and food-induced conditions, although not in proportion to the dose of chlordiazepoxide.

Samson and Grant (1985) investigated the effects of two doses of chlordiazepoxide on the consumption of ethanol by rats under conditions of concurrent access to ethanol and either water or a sucrose solution. They found that ethanol intake was reduced by both 15 and 20 mg/kg chlordiazepoxide if the alternative solution was water, but only by 20 mg/kg chlordiazepoxide if the alternative solution was sucrose. Thus the degree to which chlordiazepoxide reduced ethanol consumption depended on the nature of the other available fluid.

It is not surprising that chlordiazepoxide reduced consumption of ethanol, since both of these drugs are CNS depressants and could be expected to potentiate each other. It has not yet been demonstrated that chlordiazepoxide specifically reduces the reinforcing effects of ethanol in animals, or that it might be helpful in treating human alcohol abuse. Pilot experiments in rhesus monkeys self-administering intravenous ethanol suggested that benzodiazepines reduced ethanol-reinforced responding at the same dose that reduced food-reinforced responding, indicating a surprising lack of selectivity (Winger, unpublished observations). This outcome, combined with justifiable concerns that alcoholics might abuse benzodiazepines, indicates that benzodiazepines may not be appropriately included in a regimen for treating alcoholics.

Opioids and Opioid Antagonists. There have been a number of studies of the effects of opiates and opiate antagonists on ethanol ingestion. This research was generated in large part by theories that suggest that a common biochemical mechanism underlies both alcohol abuse and opiate abuse (e.g., Davis & Walsh, 1970). Altshuler, Phillips, and Feinhandler (1980) demonstrated that doses of 1, 3, or 5 mg/kg of the opiate antagonist naltrexone was able to decrease the rate of intravenous ethanol self-administration by rhesus monkeys. The effect was not immediate, but required that the antagonists be given for six consecutive days. Samson and Doyle (1985) reported that 20 mg/kg naltrexone reduced oral ethanol-reinforced responding in food-deprived rats given concurrent access to five percent ethanol and water. This dose of naltrexone did not alter the intake of sucrose in a similar paradigm. The fact that much higher doses of naltrexone were required to reduce ethanol-reinforced responding than those necessary to block the behavioral effects of opiates led these investigators to suggest that ethanol maintains behavior via mechanisms other than those involved in the opiate system.

A series of experiments by Reid and his colleagues demonstrated that the consumption of sweetened ethanol solutions was increased by the opiate antagonist diprenorphine and the opiate agonist morphine, and decreased by the opiate antagonist naltrexone (Reid & Hunter, 1984; Beaman et al., 1984; Hunter, Beaman, Dunn, & Reid, 1984). Although these investigators concluded that the opiate system was involved in the propensity of rats to drink ethanol, their procedures and results were far from clear, and further evaluation is necessary to determine the interaction between the opiate systems and the reinforcing effects of ethanol. The facts that the acute effects of ethanol are distinct from those of opiates and that the signs of withdrawal from ethanol are quite different than the signs of opiate withdrawal (Seevers, 1970) make it extremely unlikely that drugs that antagonize one system would be effective antagonists of the other. The data presented here notwithstanding, this is not an area of research that is likely to be profitable in terms of understanding and treating human alcohol abuse.

Social Interaction and the Reinforcing Effects of Ethanol

One of the accepted differences between humans and animals is that the social interactions of humans contribute very differently to their propensity to consume ethanol than do those of animals. Humans can condemn or support ethanol drinking by other humans in ways that cannot be modeled in animals. Nevertheless, the question of how ethanol intake can vary as a function of social interaction can be asked regarding animals, particularly the more social mammals such as monkeys. There has been a very limited amount of research on this interesting topic, but there is the promise of more to come. Crowley, Wersbard, Hydinger-MacDonald (1983) used a procedure of food-induced drinking in socially housed Macacca nemestrina to evaluate some social influences on ethanol consumption. They found that monkeys housed in small groups drank flavored, sweetened ethanol solutions that were presented along with their daily food ration. The reinforcing effect of ethanol was not established in this study, but these investigators have made the establishment of the reinforcing effects of ethanol their goal, and it will be interesting to see if they are able to accomplish it.

Kraemer and McKinney (1985) were interested in determining whether social separation would lead to increases in ethanol consumption among socially reared juvenile rhesus monkeys. They found that when the monkeys were intermittently housed in solitary cages, their intake of sweetened 6 percent ethanol solutions increased. The ethanol intake of some monkeys was considerably and dependably higher than the intake of other monkeys in the same individually housed circumstances, demonstrating individual differences in ethanol consumption. The investigators also found that the monkeys drank more ethanol when they were again group housed than they had previously, indicating that experience with ethanol under solitary conditions increased consumption of ethanol under social conditions.

CONCLUSIONS

The studies reviewed here demonstrate that, under certain conditions, ethanol does serve as a reinforcer in animals, and serves this function in a way that appears relevant to the human use and abuse of alcohol. This means, at a minimum, that research on the reinforcing effects of ethanol in animals has made considerable progress over the past 30 years, since a review by Lester (1966) indicated that no demonstration of a relevant reinforcing effect of ethanol in animals had been presented at that time. Knowing that the reinforcing properties of ethanol can be measured in animals gives us a handle on the question of why people drink—the condition of alcoholism is probably not due to human psychopathology, but can be understood in terms of reinforcement principles that govern most other aspects of normal human and animal behavior. The implication of this knowledge is that research on modification of behavior maintained by other reinforcers can be applied to behavior maintained by alcohol.

The ability of behavioral procedures, such as punishment, time out from reinforcement, or reinforcement of behavior incompatible with alcohol use, to decrease alcohol consumption can be evaluated in much the same way that they have been studied with other reinforcers. Some of these behavioral techniques have been used to reduce alcohol intake by human alcoholics or heavy drinkers in experimental situations (Bigelow et al., 1975; Vuchinich & Tucker, 1983), demonstrating that alcohol use in humans can be decreased by behavioral techniques that are well within our current capabilities. The use of behavioral principles in the treatment of alcoholics who live in the "real world," as opposed to an experimental laboratory, has provided some of the most successful results to date in dealing with this difficult disease. Azrin Sisson, Meyers, and Godley (1982) described an alcoholism treatment program that promotes consistent use of disulfiram in alcoholics by using reinforcement and punishment provided by significant other people in the alcoholic's environment. Since alcoholics who are taking disulfiram cannot safely drink ethanol, clients in the program showed dramatic decreases in alcohol consumption. Sisson and Azrin (1986) demonstrated that training wives or children of male alcoholics to reinforce their alcoholic relatives for not drinking and to punish them for drinking can produce decreases in their alcohol consumption and increases in their attendance in alcoholism treatment programs.

It is probably by supporting the idea that ethanol can be considered as acting as a reinforcing stimulus, and that its use or abuse can be best understood as behavior maintained by its consequences, that studies of the reinforcing effects of ethanol in animals have made their largest contribution to understanding "why people drink". This is true even though a large number of studies of voluntary ethanol drinking in animals have not been directly concerned with evaluating the drug's reinforcing effect. In other words, only a few of the many studies of voluntary ethanol drinking in animals have contributed to our understanding of why people drink, and it is not clear that our understanding of alcoholism in humans would be different, even if the data from these few studies were not available.

There are several reasons why studies in animals of behavior relevant to alcoholism have not been particularly productive. They include the following: (1) People who study ethanol's reinforcing effects in animals do not often pay close attention to studies of the reinforcing effects of ethanol in humans, to attempt to produce behavior that is maintained in the same way, and affected by similar manipulations. Many animal researchers have been more interested in obtaining an "animal model of alcoholism," and in meeting the criteria set up by themselves or other researchers for such a model, than in establishing ethanol as a reinforcer in such a way that it can be of help in understanding its reinforcing effects in humans. (2) Far too few researchers are studying the reinforcing effect of ethanol in humans, so there are insufficient data in humans for comparison with animals. (3) Ethanol is, both pharmacologically and behaviorally, a very difficult drug to work with. It has low potency as a reinforcer and unique taste qualities, as well as value as a food. It probably does not act through specific receptors, and there is therefore, little hope, recent data notwithstanding (Suzdak, Glowa, Crawley, Schwartz, Skolnick, & Paul, 1986), of developing specific antagonists for ethanol.

The lack of specific binding sites, plus the toxicity of alcohols other than ethanol, precludes the development of interesting structure–activity relationships. The excitement and promise of novel ethanol-like agonists or useful ethanol antagonists are thus largely lacking in the pharmacological study of ethanol and its use and abuse, and may account for the fact that the development of pharmacological therapy for alcoholism lags far behind that of similar therapy for opiate addiction. Experimental work on the reinforcing effects of opiates and central stimulants has been most interesting and of the most potential usefulness when evaluating pharmacological variables that might influence the reinforcing effects of the drugs or evaluating drugs that might have similar therapeutic use but less abuse potential. Since this approach cannot yet be applied to ethanol, it is not surprising to find that studies of the reinforcing effects of ethanol have had little influence on the development of new treatment strategies. There is some possibility that such drugs as benzodiazepines and barbiturates—which act through specific binding sites, have specific antagonists, and have many actions in common with ethanol—may be able to modify ethanol's reinforcing effects in a potentially useful way. Thus far this possibility seems quite remote.

Recent data on the effects of selective breeding on the reinforcing effects of ethanol offer the most promise of providing relevant information on the reasons why *some* people drink. If it can be determined that different strains of rodents are different primarily in their sensitivity to the reinforcing effects of ethanol, this may be an important step toward understanding the genetics of alcoholism. One of the most exciting aspects of much of this work is that studies in animals are closely coordinated with studies in humans, and in some cases with biochemical studies as well (Schuckit et al., 1985). Even more interchange of ideas and techniques between those working with animals and those working with people is desirable. Findings of different electrophysiological activity in the offspring of alcoholics (e.g., Elmasian, Neville, Woods, Schuckit, & Bloom, 1982; Schuckit, 1985a) for example, represent a type of study that could be applied to inbred lines of rats, and perhaps also to nonhuman primates that differ in their consumption of alcoholic beverages (e.g., Kramer & McKinney, 1985).

REFERENCES

Allen, D.L., Fantom, H.J., & Wilson, J.R. (1982). Lack of association between preference and dependence on ethanol. *Drug and Alcohol Dependence, 9*, 119–125.

Altshuler, H.L., Phillips, P.E., & Feinhandler, D.A. (1980). Alterations of ethanol self-administration by naltrexone. *Life Sciences, 26*, 679–688.

Azrin, N. H., Sisson, R.W., Meyers, R., & Godley, M. (1982). Alcoholism treatment by disulfiram and community reinforcement therapy. *Journal of Behavior Therapy and Experimental Psychiatry, 13*, 105–112.

Beaman, C.M., Hunter, G.A., Dunn, L.L., & Reid, L.D. (1984). Opioids, benzodiazepines and intake of ethanol. *Alcohol, 1*, 39–42.

Beardsley, P.M., Lemaire, G.A., & Meisch, R.A. (1983). Effects of minimum-interreinforcer interval on ethanol-maintained performance of rats. *Pharmacology Biochemistry and Behavior, 19*, 843–847.

Bigelow, G., Griffiths, R., & Liebson, I. (1975). Experimental models for the modification of human drug self-administration. *Federation Proceedings, 34*, 1785–1792.

Black, E.L., & Martin, G.L. (1972). Extinction of alcohol drinking in rats following acquisition of a fixed-ratio schedule of reinforcement. *Psychonomic Science, 29*, 152–154.

Carroll, M.E., & Meisch, R.A. (1984). Increased drug-reinforced behavior due to food-deprivation. In T. Thompson, P.B. Dews, & J.E. Barrett (Eds.), *Advances in Behavioral Pharmacology* (Vol. 4). New York: Academic Press, pp. 47–84.

Carroll, M.E., Stotz, D.C., Kliner, D.J., & Meisch, R.A. (1984). Self-administration of orally-delivered methohexital in rhesus monkeys with phencyclidine or pentobarbital histories: Effects of food deprivation and satiation. *Pharmacology Biochemistry and Behavior, 20*, 145–151.

Cicero, T.J. (1979). A critique of animal analogues of alcoholism. In E. Majchrowicz & E.P. Noble (Eds.), *Biochemistry and pharmacology of Ethanol* (Vol 2). New York: Plenum Press pp. 533–560.

Collins, R.J., Weeks, J.R., Cooper, M.M., Good, P.I., & Russell, R.R. (1984). Prediction of abuse liability of drugs using IV self-administration by rats. *Psychopharmacology, 82*, 6–13.

Crabbe, J.C. (1984). Pharmacogenetic strategies for studying alcohol dependence. *Alcohol, 1*, 185–191.

Crabbe, J.C., Kosobud, A., & Young, E.R. (1983). Genetic selection for ethanol withdrawal severity: Differences in replicate mouse lines. *Life Sciences, 33*, 955–962.

Crowley, T.J., Weisbard, C., & Hydinger-MacDonald, M.J. (1983). Progress toward initiating and maintaining high-dose alcohol drinking in monkey social groups. *Journal of Studies on Alcohol, 44*, 569–590.

Davis, V.E., & Walsh, M.J. (1970). Alcohol, amines, and alkaloids: A possible biochemical basis for alcohol addiction. *Science, 167*, 1005–1007.

Deneau, G.A., Yanagita, T., & Seevers, M.H. (1969). Self-administration of psychoactive substances by the monkey: A measure of psychological dependence. *Psychopharmacologia, 16*, 30–48.

Dudek, B.C., & Phillips, T.J. (1983). Locomotor stimulant and intoxicant properties of methanol, ethanol, tertiary butanol and pentobarbital in long-sleep and short-sleep mice. *Substance and Alcohol Actions Misuse, 4*, 31–36.

Elmasian, R., Neville, H., Woods, D., Schuckit, M., & Bloom, F. (1982). Event-related brain potentials are different in individuals at high and low risk for developing alcoholism. *Proceedings of the National Academy of Sciences, 79,* 7900–7903.

Elmer, G.I., Meisch, R.A., & George, F.R. (1986). Oral ethanol reinforced behavior in inbred mice. *Pharmacology Biochemistry and Behavior, 24,* 1417–1421.

Elmer, G.I., Meisch, R.A., & George F.R. (1987). Differential concentration-. response curves formal ethanol self-administration in C57Bl/6J and BALB/cJ mice. *Alcohol, 4,* 63–68.

Eriksson, K. (1968). Genetic selection for voluntary alcohol consumption in the albino rat. *Science, 159,* 739–740.

Erwin, B.G., Heston, W.D.W., McClearn, G.E., & Deitrich, R.W. (1976). Effects of hypnotics on mice genetically selectively bred for differential sensitivity to ethanol. *Pharmacology Biochemistry and Behavior, 4,* 679–683.

Falk, J.L. (1961). Production of polydipsia in normal rats by an intermittent food schedule. *Science, 133,* 195–196.

Falk, J.L., Samson, H.H., & Winger, G. (1972). Behavioral maintenance of high concentrations of blood ethanol and physical dependence in the rat. *Science, 177,* 811–813.

Goodwin, D.W., Schulsinger, F., Hermansen, L., Guze, S.B., & Winokur, G. (1973). Alcohol problems in adoptees raised apart from alcoholic biological parents. *Archives of General Psychiatry, 28,* 238–241.

Grant, K.A., & Samson, H.H. (1985a). Induction and maintenance of ethanol self-administration without food deprivation in the rat. *Psychopharmacology, 86,* 475–479.

Grant, K.A., & Samson, H.H. (1985b). Oral self-administration of ethanol in free feeding rats. *Alcohol, 2,* 317–321.

Griffiths, R.R., Bigelow, G.E., & Henningfield, J.E. (1980). Similarities in animal and human drug-taking behavior. In N.K. Mello (Ed.), *Advances in Substance Abuse* (Vol. 1). Greenwich, Conn: JAI Press, pp. 1–90.

Grupp, L.A. (1981). An investigation of intravenous ethanol self-administration in rats using a fixed ratio schedule of reinforcement. *Physiological Psychology;* 9, 359–363.

Grupp, L.A., & Stewart, R.B. (1983). Active and passive avoidance behavior in rats produced by IV infusions of ethanol. *Psychopharmacology, 79,* 318–321.

Henningfield, J.E., Ator, N.A., & Griffiths, R.R. (1981). Establishment and maintenance of oral ethanol self-administration in the baboon. *Drug and Alcohol Dependence* 7, 113–124.

Henningfield, J.E., & Meisch, R.A. (1975). Ethanol-reinforced responding and intake as a function of volume per reinforcement. *Pharmacology Biochemistry and Behavior, 3,* 437–441.

Henningfield, J.E., & Meisch, R.A. (1976). Ethanol as a positive reinforcer via the oral route for rhesus monkeys: Maintenance of fixed-ratio responding. *Pharmacology Biochemistry and Behavior, 4,* 473–475.

Henningfield, J.E., & Meisch, R.A. (1979). Ethanol drinking by rhesus monkeys with concurrent access to water. *Pharmacology Biochemistry and Behavior, 10,* 777–782.

Henningfield, J.E., & Meisch, R.A. (1981). Ethanol and water drinking by rhesus monkeys: Effects of nutritive loading. *Journal of Studies on Alcoholism, 42,* 192–201.

Hunter, G.A., Beaman, C.M., Dunn, L.L., & Reid, L.D. (1984). Selected opioids, ethanol and intake of ethanol. *Alcohol, 1*, 43–46.

Karoly, A.J., Winger, G., Ikomi, F., & Woods, J.H. (1978). The reinforcing property of ethanol in the rhesus monkeys. II. Some variables related to the maintenance of intravenous ethanol-reinforced responding. *Psychopharmacology, 58*, 19–25.

Keehn, J.D. (1969). "Voluntary" consumption of alcohol by rats. *Quarterly Journal on Studies on Alcohol, 30*, 320–329.

Kraemer, G.W., & McKinney, W.T. (1985). Social separation increases alcohol consumption in rhesus monkeys. *Psychopharmacology, 86*, 182–189.

Lester, D. (1966). Self-selection of alcohol by animals, human variation, and the etiology of alcoholism. *Quarterly Journal of Studies on Alcohol, 27*, 395–438.

Lester, D., & Freed, E.X. (1973). Criteria for an animal model of alcoholism. *Pharmacology Biochemistry and Behavior, 1*, 103–107.

Li, T.K., Lumeng, L., McBride, W.J., & Waller, M.B. (1979). Progress towards a voluntary oral consumption model of alcoholism. *Drug and Alcohol Dependence, 4*, 45–60.

Mardones, J., & Segovia-Requelme, N. (1983). Thirty-two years of selection of rats by ethanol preference: UChA and UChB strains. *Neurobehavioral Toxicology and Teratology, 5*, 171–178.

Martin, G.E., & Myers, R.D. (1972). Ethanol ingestion in the rat induced by rewarding brain stimulation. *Physiology and Behavior 8,*, 1151–1160.

McClearn, G.E., & Kakihana, R. (1973). Selective breeding for ethanol sensitivity in mice. *Behavioral Genetics, 3*, 409–410.

McClearn, G.E., Wilson, J.R., Petersen, D.R., & Allen, D.L. (1982). Selective breeding in mice for severity of the ethanol withdrawal syndrome. *Substance and Alcohol Actions Misuse, 3*, 135–143.

McSwigan, J.D., Crabbe, J.C., & Young, E.R. (1984). Specific ethanol withdrawal seizures in genetically selected mice. *Life Sciences, 35*, 2119–2126.

Meisch, R.A. (1975). The function of schedule-induced polydipsia in establishing ethanol as a positive reinforcer. *Pharmacological Reviews. 27*, 465–473.

Meisch, R.A., & Beardsley, P. (1975). Ethanol as a reinforcer for rats: Effects of concurrent access to water and alternate positions of water and ethanol. *Psychopharmacologia, 43*, 19–23.

Meisch, R.A., & Henningfield, J.E. (1977). Drinking of ethanol by rhesus monkeys: Experimental strategies for establishing ethanol as a reinforcer. *Advances in Experimental Medical Biology, 85B*, 443–463.

Meisch, R.A., & Thompson, T. (1972). Ethanol reinforcement: Effects of concentration during food deprivation. In O. Forsander & K. Eriksson (Eds.), *Biological Aspects of Alcohol Consumption*. Helsinki: Finnish Foundation of Alcohol Studies, pp. 71–75.

Mendelson, J.H., & Mello, N.K. (1966). Experimental analysis of drinking behavior of chronic alcoholics. *Annals of the New York Academy of Sciences, 133*, 828–845.

Numan, R. (1981). Multiple exposures to ethanol facilitate intravenous self-administration of ethanol by rats. *Pharmacology Biochemistry and Behavior, 15*, 101–108.

Numan, R., Naparzewska, A.M., & Adler, C.M. (1984). Absence of reinforcement with low dose intravenous ethanol self-administration in rats. *Pharmacology Biochemistry and Behavior, 21*, 609–615.

Penn, P.E., McBride, W.J., Lumeng, L., Gaff, T.M., & Li, T.-K. (1978). Neurochemical and operant behavioral studies of a strain of alcohol preferring rats. *Pharmacology Biochemistry and Behavior, 8*, 475–481.

Reid, L.D., & Hunter, G.A. (1984). Morphine and naloxone modulate intake of ethanol. *Alcohol, 1*, 33–37.

Ritz, M., George, F.R., deFiebre, C.M., & Meisch, R.A. (1986). Genetic differences in the establishment of ethanol as a reinforcer. *Pharmacology Biochemistry and Behavior, 24*, 1089–1094.

Roehrs, T.A., & Samson, H.H. (1981). Ethanol reinforced behavior assessed with a concurrent schedule. *Pharmacology Biochemistry and Behavior, 15*, 539–544.

Roehrs, T.A., & Samson, H.H. (1982). Relative responding on concurrent schedules: Indexing ethanol's reinforcing efficacy. *Pharmacology Biochemistry and Behavior, 16*, 393–396.

Roehrs, T., Yang, O., & Samson, H.H. (1984). Chlordiazepoxide's interaction with ethanol intake in the rat: Relation to ethanol exposure paradigms. *Pharmacology Biochemistry and Behavior, 24*, 849–853.

Samson, H.H. (1986). Initiation of ethanol reinforcement using a sucrose-substitution procedure in food- and water-sated rats. *Alcoholism: Clinical and Experimental Research, 10*, 436–442.

Samson, H.H., & Doyle, T.F. (1985). Oral ethanol self-administration in the rat: Effect of naloxone. *Pharmacology Biochemistry and Behavior, 22*, 91–99.

Samson, H.H., & Falk, J.L. (1974). Alteration of fluid preference in ethanol dependent animals. *Journal of Pharmacology and Experimental Therapeutics, 190*, 365–376.

Samson, H.H., & Falk, J.L. (1975). Schedule-induced physical dependence on ethanol. *Pharmacological Reviews, 27*, 449–464.

Samson H.H., & Grant, K.A. (1985). Chlordiazepoxide effects on ethanol self-administration: Dependence on concurrent conditions. *Journal of Experimental Analysis of Behavior, 43*, 353–364.

Samson, H.H., & Lindberg, K. (1984). Comparison of sucrose-sucrose to sucrose-ethanol concurrent responding in the rat: Reinforcement schedule and fluid concentration effects. *Pharmacology Biochemistry and Behavior, 20*, 973–977.

Samson, H.H., Roehrs, T.A., & Tolliver, G.A. (1982). Ethanol reinforced responding in the rat: A concurrent analysis using sucrose as the alternate choice. *Pharmacology Biochemistry and Behavior, 17*, 333–339.

Samson, H.H., Tolliver, G.A., & Roehrs, T.A. (1983). Ethanol reinforced responding in the rat: Relation of ethanol introduction to later ethanol responding. *Pharmacology Biochemistry and Behavior, 18*, 895–900.

Schuckit, M.A. (1985a). Genetics and the risk for alcoholism. *Journal of the American Medical Association, 254*, 2614–2617.

Schuckit, M.A. (1985b). Subjective response to alcohol in sons of alcoholics and controls. *Archives of General Psychiatry, 41*, 879–884.

Schuckit, M.A., Li, T.-K., Cloninger, C.R., & Deitrich, R.A. (1985). Genetics of alcoholism. *Alcoholism: Clinical and Experimental Research, 9*, 475–492.

Seevers, M.H. (1970). Differentiating characteristics of morphine and ethanol types of physical dependence: A critique of an hypothesis. *Science, 170*, 1113–1115.

Senter, R.J., & Persenky, J.J. (1968). Effects of environment on ethanol consumption in rats after conditioning. *Quarterly Journal of Studies on Alcohol, 29*, 856–862.

Sinden, J.D., & Le Magnen, J. (1982). Parameters of low dose ethanol intravenous self-administration in the rat. *Pharmacology Biochemistry and Behavior, 16*, 181–183.

Sisson, R.W., & Azrin, N.H. (1986). Family-member involvement to initiate and promote treatment of problem drinkers. *Journal of Behavioral Therapy and Experimental Psychiatry, 17*, 15–21.

Socaransky, S.M., Aragon, C.M.G., & Amit, Z. (1985). Brain ALDH as a possible modulator of voluntary ethanol intake. *Alcohol, 2*, 361–365.

Stewart, R.B., & Grupp, L.A. (1984). A simplified procedure for producing ethanol self-selection in rats. *Pharmacology Biochemistry and Behavior, 21*, 255–258.

Suzdak, P.D., Glowa, J.R., Crawley, J.N., Schwartz, R.D., Skolnick, P., and Paul, S.M. (1986). A selective imidazobenzodiazepine antagonist of ethanol in the rat. *Science, 234*, 1243–1247.

Tampier, L., Quintanilla, M.E., Contreras, S., Segovia-Requelme, N., & Mardones, J. (1984). Biological similarities and differences between rats genetically different in alcohol preference. *Alcohol and Alcoholism, 19*, 203–209.

Tang, M., Brown, C., & Falk, J.L. (1982). Complete reversal of chronic ethanol polydipsia by schedule withdrawal. *Pharmacology Biochemistry and Behavior, 16*, 155–158.

Tang, M., Kenny, J., & Falk, J.L. (1984). Schedule-induced ethanol dependence and phenobarbital preference. *Alcohol, 1*, 55–58.

Tucker, J.A., Vuchinich, R.E., & Harris, C.V. (1985). Determinants of substance abuse relapse. In *Determinants of Substance Abuse: Biological, Psychological, and Environmental Factors*. New York; Plenum Press, pp. 383–421.

Vuchinich, R.E., & Tucker, J.A. (1983). Behavioral theories of choice as a framework for studying drinking behavior. *Journal of Abnormal Psychology, 92*, 408–416.

Waller, M.B., McBride, W.J., Gatto, G.J., Lumeng, L., & Li, T.-K. (1984). Intragastric self-infusion of ethanol by ethanol-preferring and -nonpreferring lines of rats. *Science, 225*, 78–80.

Waller, M.B., McBride, W.J., Lumeng, L., & Li, T.-K. (1982). Effects of intravenous ethanol and of 4-methylpyrazole on alcohol drinking in alcohol-preferring rats. *Pharmacology Biochemistry and Behavior, 17*, 763–768.

Wilson, J.R., Erwin, V.G., Defries, J.C., Petersen, D.R., & Cole-Harding, S. (1984). Ethanol dependence in mice: Direct and correlated responses to ten generations of selective breeding. *Behavioral Genetics, 14*, 235–256.

Winger, G., & Woods, J.H. (1973). The reinforcing property of ethanol in the rhesus monkeys. I. Initiation, maintenance and termination of intravenous ethanol-reinforced responding. *Annals of the New York Academy of Sciences, 215*, 162–165.

Woods, J.H., Ikomi, F., & Winger, G. (1971). The reinforcing property of ethanol. In M.K. Roach, W.M. McIsaac, & P.J. Creaven (Eds.), *Biological aspects of alcohol*. Austin, Texas University of Texas Press, pp. 371–388.

TWO

GENETIC DETERMINANTS OF REINFORCEMENT FROM ALCOHOL

DONALD W. GOODWIN, M.D.

In some ways, alcoholism can still be considered a bad habit, as it has been for centuries. The phrase "bad habit" refers to repetitious, harmful, semireflexive behavior resulting from conditioning in "susceptible" individuals. With regard to drugs, "susceptibility" may be *specific* for certain drugs or *nonspecific*, that is, a person may be susceptible to abusing a number of drugs, perhaps only in certain classes (e.g., the sedative-hypnotics) or across classes (e.g., opiates, sedative-hypnotics, nicotine). Susceptibility may be partly inherited (under some degree of genetic control) or reflect purely psychosocial influences, or both.

This chapter is divided into three sections. The first part presents evidence for a genetic factor in alcoholism, focusing mainly on adoption studies. The next section considers how genetics and learned factors interact to produce alcohol problems. The chapter ends with a discussion of the roles of agent, host, and environment in producing addictions in general.

GENETIC FACTORS

Family studies of alcoholism consistently emphasize its high prevalence among the relatives of alcoholics (Cotton, 1979). In most studies, at least 25 percent of alcoholics' male relatives are also alcoholic. As a rule, these studies also show a higher than expected frequency of alcoholism among female relatives (between 5 and 10 percent). General population surveys indicate that 3–5 percent of male adults and 0.1–1 percent of female adults are alcoholic.

"Familial," of course, is not synonymous with genetic. One approach to separating "nature" from "nurture" in the etiology of alcoholism is to study people who were separated from their alcoholic biological relatives soon after birth and raised by nonalcoholic adoptive parents. In 1970 this writer and his colleagues began a series of adoption studies in Denmark, supported by the National Institute on Alcohol Abuse and Alcoholism (Goodwin, 1985). The studies were intended to investigate further the possibility that alcoholism has genetic roots; they have gone through three phases.

Phase One

Because men are more likely to develop drinking problems than are women, the study's first phase focused on 55 Danish males who had a biological parent with a hospital diagnosis of alcoholism and who had been adopted during the first few weeks of life by nonrelatives. The control group consisted of 78 age-matched men who were selected from a large pool of adoptees and whose biological parents had not suffered from alcoholism as far as we could determine. (It is possible that some of the control subjects had alcoholic parents, but we found no evidence of such a family history in the central neuropsychiatric registries maintained in Denmark.)

The average age of the total sample was 30 years, with a range of 23–45. The subjects and controls were interviewed by a psychiatrist, who did not know whether they were the sons of alcoholics or of presumed nonalcoholics; the study was blind from its inception until the data were analyzed. Experimenter bias, therefore, could not have been a factor in the study.

The results of this phase can be summarized as follows:

(1) Ten of the 55 probands (sons of alcoholics) were judged to be alcoholic according to specific criteria as well as a history of treatment for alcoholism. Of the 78 control subjects, four met the criteria for alcoholism, but none had received treatment. The difference was significant at the 0.02 level (χ^2, two tailed).

(2) The probands were no more likely to be heavy drinkers—defined as those who drank daily, with six or more drinks a day at least several

times a month—than were the control subjects: about 40 percent of each group were heavy drinkers. Thus having a biological parent who was alcoholic increased the likelihood of the sons being alcoholic, but did not increase the chance of his being classified as a heavy drinker.

(3) According to the complete psychiatric history obtained by the interviewer and the mental status examination performed, the probands were no more likely to have a diagnosis of depression, sociopathy, drug abuse, or other diagnosable psychiatric conditions than were the control subjects. Both groups had sizable numbers of individuals diagnosed as having various personality disturbances, but these vaguely described traits were as common among the control subjects as among the probands.

From these data it could be concluded that although the sons of alcoholics had no exposure to the alcoholic biological parent after the first few weeks of life, they were about four times more likely to be alcoholic than were sons of nonalcoholics. Moreover, they were likely to be alcoholic at a relatively early age (in their 20s) and to have a form of alcoholism serious enough to warrant treatment. Having a biological parent who was alcoholic apparently did not increase their risk of developing psychiatric disorders other than alcoholism, and did not predispose them to heavy drinking in the absence of alcoholism. The familial predisposition to alcoholism in this group was specific for alcoholism, not for various degrees of heavy drinking.

Phase Two

Some of the probands had brothers who had been raised by their alcoholic biological parents (most of the alcoholic parents were fathers). The 30 sons raised by their alcoholic biological parents also had a high rate of alcoholism compared with the rate of the control sample, which was composed of 78 nonadopted men raised by nonalcoholic parents. However, the rate of alcoholism was no greater among the sons raised by their alcoholic biological parents than was the rate observed in their brothers who were raised by nonalcoholic foster parents (about 18 percent in both groups).

We concluded from the study's first two phases that alcoholism was transmitted in families, and that the increased susceptibility to alcoholism occurred about equally in men raised by their alcoholic biological parents and men raised by nonalcoholic foster parents. In other words, if indeed there was a genetic predisposition to alcoholism, exposure to the alcoholic parent did not appear to augment this increased susceptibility.

Phase Three

The final phase involved studying the daughters of alcoholics, both those raised by foster parents and those raised by their alcoholic biological parents. The sample consisted of 49 probands (adopted daughters of alcoholics) and 48 control subjects (adopted daughters of presumed nonalcoholics). As in the first two phases, the interviews were blind, with no chance of biased results. The subjects were between the ages of 30 and 41, with a mean age of 35. The major findings were as follows:

(1) One of the probands was clearly alcoholic and another was a serious problem drinker who did not completely meet the criteria for alcoholism. Two of the control subjects were alcoholic. The three women diagnosed as alcoholic had all received treatment for their alcoholism.

Hence 4 percent of the women in both groups were either alcoholic or serious problem drinkers. The sample was too small to draw definite conclusions, but since the estimated prevalence of alcoholism among Danish women is about 0.1–1 percent. the data suggest that there may indeed be an increased prevalence of alcoholism in these two particular groups. Since nothing is known about the parents of the control subjects other than that no biological parent had a hospital diagnosis of alcoholism, it is possible that the two alcoholic control subjects had parents who had alcohol problems; the parents could not be located. However, it was interesting that both of the alcoholic control subjects had foster parents who were described as alcoholic, suggesting that environmental exposure to alcoholism may contribute to alcoholism in women but not in men.

(2) More than 90 percent of the women in both groups were abstainers or very light drinkers. This rate contrasted with the 40 percent of Danish male adoptees who were considered heavy drinkers.

(3) Family history studies have suggested that alcoholics often have male relatives who are alcoholic or sociopathic and female relatives who are depressed (Winokur, Reich, Rimmes, et al., 1970). In this study, we obtained complete psychiatric histories and performed mental status examinations. We found a low rate of depression among both groups of adopted women, with no more depression in the daughters of the alcoholics than in the control subjects. Among daughters of alcoholics raised by their alcoholic parents, the incidence of depression was significantly higher than it was among the control subjects. There was no evidence of increased susceptibility to other psychiatric disorders in the daughters of alcoholics, whether raised by foster parents or by their own alcoholic biological parents.

It therefore appears that alcoholism in women may have a partial genetic basis, but the sample size of our Danish study precluded any definitive conclusion. Since the great majority of the women were very mild drinkers, it is possible that social factors discouraging heavy drinking may suppress a genetic tendency, when one exists

We also discovered no evidence of a genetic predisposition to depression in the daughters of alcoholics. If such a predisposition exists, apparently environmental factors are required to make the depression clinically manifest. We found it impossible to determine whether the increased rate of depression among daughters raised by their alcoholic parents was due to environmental factors precipitating a genetic predisposition or due entirely to environmental factors.

It should be noted that some evidence indicates that women develop alcoholism at a later age than do men (Goodwin, 1981), and possibly not all these women in their 30s had all entered the age of risk for alcoholism. Further follow-up studies are needed to explore this possibility.

Review of Other Studies

Since the 1940s, four studies similar to our Danish series have been conducted. Roe (1944) obtained information about 49 foster children in the 20- to 40-year age group—22 of normal percentage and 27 with a biological parent described as a "heavy drinker." Among children with heavy-drinking parents, 70 percent were users of alcohol compared with 64 percent in the control parent group. In adolescence two children of alcoholic parents got into trouble because of drinking too much, compared with only one child in the "normal parentage" group.

Roe found that adopted children of heavy drinkers had more adjustment problems in adolescence and adulthood than did adopted children of nonalcoholic biological parents, but the differences were not significant, and neither group had adult drinking problems. She concluded that there was no evidence of hereditary influences on drinking.

This conclusion, however, can be questioned on several grounds. First, the sample was small. There were only 21 men of alcoholic parentage and 11 of presumed normal parentage. Since women, particularly at the time of the study, were at very low risk for alcoholism, Roe's discovery that they had no problem with alcohol was not unexpected.

Second, although the biological parents of the proband group were described as heavy drinkers, it is unclear how many would meet the diagnostic criteria for alcoholism. Most had a history of antisocial behavior, and apparently none had been treated for drinking problems. In contrast, all of the biological parents of the proband group in the Danish study had received a hospital diagnosis of alcoholism at a time when this diagnosis was rarely employed in Denmark.

Schuckit, Goodwin, and Winokur (1972) also studied a group of people reared apart from their biological parents; in many cases, either a biological parent or a "surrogate" parent had a drinking problem. The subjects were significantly more likely to have a drinking problem if their biological parent was considered alcoholic than if their surrogate parent was alcoholic.

In this study of 32 alcoholics and 132 nonalcoholics, most of whom came from broken homes, Schuckit and colleagues found that 62 percent of the alcoholics had an alcoholic biological parent compared with 20 percent of the nonalcoholics, a statistically significant difference. The association occurred irrespective of personal contact with the alcoholic biological parent. Simply living with an alcoholic parent appeared to have no relationship to the development of alcoholism.

Bohman (1978) studied 2,000 adoptees born between 1930 and 1949; he inspected official registers in Sweden for notations about alcohol abuse and criminal offenses attributed to the adoptees and their biological and adoptive parents. Registered criminal acts attributed to the biological parents did not predict criminality or alcoholism among the adopted sons. However, there was a significant correlation between registrations for abuse of alcohol among biological parents and the adopted sons. The higher the number of registrations for alcoholism on the records of the biological parents, the greater was the incidence of registration for alcohol abuse on the records of the adopted sons. Bohman's results support a genetic hypothesis for the development of alcoholism and closely parallel the results of the first phase of our Danish study.

Cadoret and Gath (1978) studied 84 adult adoptees (18 years or older) who had been separated at birth from, and had no further contact with, their biological relatives. Alcoholism was seen significantly more frequently among the adoptees whose biological background included a person with alcoholism than it did among adoptees without this biological background. Alcoholism did not correlate with any other biological parental diagnosis. Incidence of childhood conduct disorder was significantly higher among adoptees who later received a diagnosis of alcoholism or problem drinking.

The adoption studies of Bohman and of Cadoret and Gath produced results that closely resemble those found in our Danish adoption studies: alcoholism in the biological parents predicted alcoholism in their male offspring raised by unrelated adoptive parents but did not predict other psychiatric illness (such as sociopathy). In both the Danish studies and the Cadoret and Gath study, alcoholics had an increased incidence of childhood conduct disorder but no higher incidence of other psychopathology.

What Is Inherited?

In summary, perhaps the strongest evidence of a genetic factor in alcoholism is the evidence that alcoholism strongly runs in families, even when the children are separated from the alcoholic biological parents. If so, what is inherited?

Certain behaviors associated with drinking must be explained before it is known why serious drinking problems develop in perhaps one of 12 or 15 drinkers in western countries.

These core features must be explained: (1) loss of control, (2) tendency to relapse, and (3) tolerance. The following is an attempt to blend possible genetic with nongenetic factors in explaining them.

Indisputably, there is a wide range of innate variations in response to alcohol. This is true in humans as well as in every other species studied. Not only are there strain and species differences but there also differences among individuals. It is difficult to account for this variation other than ascribing it to innate, probably genetically controlled, influences.

Among humans the most conspicuous example of aversive effects from alcohol has been shown in Orientals. Studies have shown that small amounts of alcohol cause a cutaneous flush, nausea, and faintness in about three quarters of Orientals (Wolff, 1973). The Orient has a low rate of alcoholism, usually attributed to social factors. Now it appears that a large number of Orientals are physiologically intolerant of alcohol, and this, to some extent, protects them from alcoholism.

The biochemical basis for the flush and unpleasant reactions to alcohol has not been determined, but studies indicate a high frequency of atypical alcohol dehydrogenase and aldehyde dehydrogenase among Japanese. These coenzymes may alter the metabolism of alcohol, leading to increased formation of acetaldehyde, and this may explain the flush and other ill effects (such as nausea).

Other groups with relatively low alcoholism rates similarly may be protected by an innate sensitivity to alcohol. For example, fewer women are alcoholic than men, and one study reports that women have higher blood alcohol levels after a given amount of alcohol than do men (Jones & Jones, 1976). Informal surveys by the author suggest that a substantial proportion of women experience unpleasant physical effects after drinking modest amounts of alcohol (e.g., nausea and headache).

Anecdotal evidence also suggests that more Jews than non-Jews have adverse physical reactions to modest amounts of alcohol, which conceivably may contribute to the low prevalence of alcoholism among Jews. Systematic studies have not been conducted in either women or Jews, so this is still hypothetical.

In any case, it obviously is essential to be able to drink large quantities of alcohol to be alcoholic. Many people are protected from drinking these large amounts because of innate cutoff points that almost certainly are under genetic control. That genetic control is an important factor in drug metabolism generally has been demonstrated by numerous studies showing that identical twins metabolize a wide variety of drugs (including alcohol) at almost identical rates of metabolism (Vesell, Page, & Passananti, 1971). Whether the development of alcoholism is to some extent under genetic control remains conjectural.

It is widely believed that tolerance to alcohol is acquired mainly from "practice": the more a person drinks, the more he or she needs to drink to achieve the same effects. With opiates, this clearly is true. With alcohol, it is not so clear. Animals fail to show much tolerance to alcohol, even after repeated exposure. Also, young men with almost no prior drinking experience vary widely in their response to alcohol in experimental studies (D.W. Goodwin, unpublished data). Some show almost no effect, while others are quite intoxicated. Since this variability does not correlate with prior drinking history, the only other explanation is that innate biological factors are responsible.

To summarize, many people are more or less "protected" from becoming alcoholic because of genetically determined adverse physical reactions to alcohol. If anything is inherited in alcoholism, it may be a lack of intolerance for alcohol. (Parenthetically, it is interesting that Alcoholics Anonymous often refers to allergy as a factor in alcoholism, usually properly putting "allergy" in quotation marks. It now seems that allergy is indeed a factor in alcoholism, but it is the nonalcoholics who are allergic rather than the alcoholics).

How Genetic Factors Interact with Learned Factors

Here, in brief, is a hypothesis explaining one way in which genetic and experimental factors may interact to produce alcoholism.

1. As we saw in the preceding section, the potential alcoholic must be able to drink a lot (i.e., lack an intolerance for alcohol).

2. Some people experience more euphoria from alcohol than others do. This factor may also be under genetic control. Because euphoria is a positive reinforcer, presumably people who experience the most euphoria are the ones most likely to drink heavily.

3. Like most drugs of abuse, alcohol is quickly absorbed and eliminated; the effects occur rapidly and disappear rapidly. Experimental studies indicate that alcoholics experience dysphoric as well as euphoric effects from alcohol (Mello, 1975). Those who experience the most euphoria (because of genetic factors) quite possibly also experience the most dysphoria. The cure for the dysphoria is more alcohol. After a few drinks, such people may drink more to relieve the dysphoria than to restore the euphoria. In any case, during a single drinking period there may be two reinforcer mechanisms involved: production of euphoria and reduction of dysphoria. This peak-valley effect may explain loss of control. The height of the peak and the depth of the valley may be genetically controlled.

4. For reasons described above, alcohol in genetically susceptible individuals may be massively reinforcing. The reinforcement occurs during individual drinking periods as well as on "the morning after," when the "hair of the dog" swiftly relieves that formidable dysphoria known as a hangover. When binge drinking occurs, withdrawal symptoms (a superhangover) follow.

5. After long periods of abstinence, binge drinkers often relapse. This is one of the mysteries of alcoholism. If it is true that alcoholics continue heavy drinking mainly to curb dysphorant effects, and if it is true that alcohol is a relatively weak euphoriant compared, say, with cocaine or amphetamines, then why should a binge drinker start drinking again after experiencing horrendous effects from previous binges? Some alcoholics are sociopaths and their relapse may be explained as another instance of "not learning from experience." Most alcoholics, however, seem to learn from most experiences as well as the next person. Why then do alcoholics relapse?

Stimulus generalization may be the answer. As noted, alcohol in genetically susceptible individuals is a massively reinforcing agent. Both the positive (euphoriant) and negative (dysphoriant) effects resemble mood states and physical feelings experienced in sobriety. The terms "euphoriant" and "dysphoriant" are used here as shorthand for "positive reinforcer" and "negative reinforcer," respectively. The former may resemble any type of rewarding experience—for example, sex or the pleasure of receiving a gift. The latter may resemble hunger, fatigue, or feelings of loneliness, anxiety, and depression.

Through the process of stimulus generalization, the ups and downs introduced by alcohol become cued to a wide variety of internal states and external circumstances. Even heavy drinkers drink more on some occasions and in certain settings than in others. These occasions and settings become associated with both the highs and lows of drinking. They become conditioned stimuli, just as do the internal feelings that resemble the highs and lows of drinking.

Relapse may in part represent a conditioned response to these conditioned stimuli. Since relapse is usually erratic and unpredictable, quite likely a combination of "interoceptive" and "exteroceptive" conditioned stimuli are required to produce relapse. The necessary combination very likely differs between individuals, and in each individual from time to time. As Keller (1972) wrote:

> For any alcoholic there may be several or a whole battery of critical cues or signals. By the rule of generalization, any critical cue can spread like the tentacles of a vine over a whole range of analogs, and this may account for the growing frequency of bouts, or for the development of a pattern of continuous inebriation. An exaggerated example is the man who goes out and gets drunk every time his mother-in-law gives him a certain wall-eyed look.

The use of conditioning to explain alcoholism is not new. Ludwig and Wikler (1974) have described it in much detail. It remained a theory, and not an easy theory to test at that. Combined with the genetic data, it has the advantage of showing how genetic factors may interact with learning (conditioning) to produce problem drinking. As Ludwig and Wikler have pointed out, social and psychological "modifiers" obviously influence the "addictive cycle." For example, some studies indicate that alcoholics may differ from nonalcoholics in having a dominant mother and a weak, passive father (Barry, 1974). A host of other psychological and social modifiers have been described in the alcoholism literature; few would dispute the importance of some or all of these modifiers in promoting or discouraging the hypothetical genetic-conditioning sequence proposed above.

A MODEL FOR SUBSTANCE ABUSE

Assuming that the above hypothesis explaining alcoholism is valid, to what extent can it explain other forms of substance abuse? In an attempt to show features that alcoholism and other drug abuse have in common, the problem can be broken down into the traditional triad of agent, host, and environment.

Agent

Commonly abused psychotropic substances have, it is proposed some features in common. First, they are short acting. They are rapidly assimilated and rapidly eliminated. Nicotine by inhalation perhaps meets this definition better than any other compound widely used and abused today (and some believe nicotine is the most abused of readily available substances).

Historically, phenobarbital, a long-acting drug, was not considered addictive, but with the introduction of short and intermediate acting barbiturates in the 1930s, the addictive problem with this class of drugs soon became, apparent. Alcohol (which is rapidly absorbed and eliminated at rate of about 15 ml per hour), together with opiates, newer barbiturates and their analogues, amphetamines, and other short-acting stimulants rank among the most abused substances in the world.There is still some doubt about marijuana, which, if smoked, is rapidly assimilated but has metabolites with very long half-lifes. Its abuse potential in western countries still remains controversial, but all the other drugs listed have the common feature of being short acting.

Host

Genetic factors could operate in two ways to increase or decrease the possibility of a person becoming dependent on a substance or substances. First, many people are "protected" from abusing specific substance because they have aversive physiological and subjective reactions to the drug or drugs, even in small quantities. There are many anecdotal reports of individuals who can "never learn" to smoke cigarettes, drink alcohol, use sleeping pills, or tolerate amphetamines or opiates, and the reason appears to be genetic. In the case of alcoholism, many millions of people are thus protected; how many are protected from the use or abuse of other substances is not known.

A second means by which peak-and-valley drugs, such as described above, may produce dependence in "unprotected" individuals is probably also under genetic control. It involves varying degrees of positive reinforcement from the substance followed quickly by aversive effects, which can be relieved only by reuse of the substance that produced the reinforcement-aversive sequence in the first place.

For example, after many years of nonsmoking, the chain smoker, for whatever reason, lights up his or her first cigarette and is reinforced for doing so. From that point on, however, his or her need to smoke is based more on a "drug hunger" or craving produced by that first cigarette than on a desire to obtain whatever gratification the first cigarette produced. Thus begins the "addictive cycle," which, in the chain smoker, can be extremely difficult to overcome.

Enhancement of positive effects from smoking decreases over time, whereas relief from negative affect becomes more salient across time.

The initial reinforcing effect obviously is not the same for all commonly abused substances. The euphoria afforded by amphetamines and cocaine is apparently much stronger than that produced by alcohol, and the reinforcing mechanism that drives the cigarette habit clearly is not euphoria.

To recapitulate, a drug of abuse is one that quickly enters and leaves the body. It produces aversive effects during the aversive stage, which can be relieved only by reintroduction of that specific substance. (For example, a chocolate bar, Valium, or even a pipe does not truly substitute for a cigarette for the chain smoker who has started the addictive cycle.)

One last word about the host: however available the agent, and however susceptible the host, it must be remembered that the host is also born with other traits and susceptibilities. In the intricate byplay of genetic and environmental factors, forces may emerge that oppose or nullify tendencies to use or abuse a particular substance. These countervailing forces must always be taken into account in evaluating people at risk.

Environment

The agent obviously must be available, and this does not necessarily mean that it is the agent being legal and commercially available. Prices, legal ages of buyers, prevailing attitudes toward the substance, and a multitude of other social and cultural factors influence the use of the agent. There is no question but that availability, in the broadest sense, influences use. During the American prohibition, hospitalizations for drinking problems and cirrhosis rates dropped precipitously. This was also true during the second World War in such countries as France and England, where wine and beer were scarce, expensive, and even rationed.

SUMMARY

A susceptibility to alcoholism is unevenly distributed among people in the general population. This chapter attempts to explain part of this variation, applying information obtained from genetic studies of alcoholism and principles of conditioning.

The starting point is that alcoholism clusters in families. Whether this is due primarily to learning or to genetic factors was not known until the 1970s, when adoption studies were conducted that suggest that genetic factors play an important role. How do genetic factors increase susceptibility to addictive drinking? It is proposed that addiction-prone individuals experience biphasic effects from alcohol in which pleasant reinforcing affects are quickly followed by unpleasant affects. During a drinking episode the person drinks both to produce the pleasant affects and to abolish the unpleasant ones. This produces an "addictive cycle" and eventual "loss of control." Relapse can also be explained partly in terms of conditioned stimuli resistant to extinction and the phenomenon of stimulus generalization.

The development of alcoholism involves elements other than genetic vulnerability and conditioning. For example, many people are protected from alcoholism because they experience unpleasant effects after drinking even small amounts. Countervailing personality traits—innate and/or acquired—also may nullify other forces directed toward producing alcoholism. Finally, social custom, peer pressure, and availability of alcohol are influential in the development of alcoholism.

REFERENCES

Barry, H. (1974). Psychological factors in alcoholism. In B. Kissing and H. Begleiter (Eds), *The Biology of Alcoholism,* Vol. 3. New York: Plenum Press.

Bohman, M. (1978). Genetic aspects of alcoholism and criminality through material of adoptions. *Archives of General Psychiatry, 35,* 269–276.

Cadoret, R., & Gath, A. (1978). Inheritance of alcoholism in adoptees. *British Journal of Psychiatry, 132,* 252–258.

Cotton, N.S. (1979). The familial incidence of alcoholism: A review. *Journal of Studies on Alcohol,* 89–116.

Goodwin, D.W. (1981). *Alcoholism: The Facts.* New York: Oxford University Press.

Goodwin, D.W. (1985). Alcoholism and genetics: The sins of the fathers. *Archives of General Psychiatry, 42,* 171–178.

Jones, B.M., & Jones, M.K. (1976). Male and female intoxication levels for three alcohol doses or do women really get higher than men? *Alcohol Technology Report, 5,* 11–14.

Keller, M. (1972). On the loss-of-control phenomenon in alcoholism. *British Journal of Addiction, 67,* 153–166.

Ludwig, A.M., & Wikler, A. (1974). Craving and relapse to drink. *Quarterly Journal of Studies on Alcohol, 35,* 108 130.

Mello, N.K. (1975). A semantic aspect of alcoholism. AE LeBlanc HD Cappell dependence. *Biological and Behavioral Approaches to Drug* (Eds), Toronto: Addiction Research Foundation of Ontario.

Roe, A. (1944). The adult adjustment of children of alcoholic parents raised in foster homes. *Quarterly Journal of Studies on Alcohol, 5,* 378–393.

Schuckit, M.A. Goodwin, D.W., & Winokur, G. (1972). A half-sibling study of alcoholism. *American Journal of Psychiatry, 128,* 1132–1136.

Vesell, E.S., Page, J.F., & Passananti, G.T. (1971). Genetic and environmental factors affecting ethanol metabolism in man. *Clinical Pharmacological Therapy, 12,* 192.

Winokur, G., Reich, T., Rimmer J. et al. (1970). Alcoholism, Ill: Diagnosis and familial psychiatric illness in 259 alcoholic probands. *Archives of General Psychiatry, 23,* 104–107.

Wolff, P.H. (1973). Vasomotor sensitivity to ethanol in diverse mongoloid populations. *American Journal of Human Genetics, 25,* 193–199.

THREE

BIOCHEMICAL BASES FOR THE REINFORCING EFFECTS OF ETHANOL

WALTER A. HUNT, Ph.D

Ethanol is a simple molecule that, once absorbed, is distributed throughout the body and alters the function of a variety of organs. The consequences of these alterations may contribute to the reinforcing effects of ethanol, sometimes in unexpected ways. Together with the next two chapters, this chapter discusses possible biological mechanisms that might contribute to the various actions of ethanol on the brain, and how they, in turn, could influence the reinforcing properties of ethanol.

Although ethanol is metabolized in a fairly simple manner, the formation of a number of pharmacologically active substances is possible. These substances are either the direct products of the metabolism of ethanol or they are precursors for the potential formation of other novel substances. In this chapter, the possible role of these metabolic products in the reinforcing effects of ethanol is examined. However, we shall first address important experimental considerations that have bearing on the relevance and interpretation of reported results.

EXPERIMENTAL DESIGN

Elucidating the mechanisms underlying actions of any drug is often a complex undertaking. Mechanisms that might be proposed are often a result of studies using animals models (of Chapter 1), whose appropriateness can determine the potential validity of the mechanism. Consequently, when dealing with experimental models, satisfactory criteria need to be developed. When putative mechanisms are found, then a determination of whether they conform to these criteria can be made.

The following criteria should be satisfied for a biological mechanism underlying the reinforcing effects of ethanol to be valid. (1) The model being used must be able adequately to measure the reinforcing effects of ethanol. (2) Measurable blood-ethanol concentrations must be present after exposure to ethanol. (3) The appearance and disappearance of the reinforcing effects of ethanol should parallel the appearance and disappearance of ethanol in the blood. (4) Modification of a proposed mechanism of reinforcement must alter ethanol intake.

In biological studies, the usual method for assessing the reinforcing effects of ethanol is to measure ethanol preference. Animals are given either ethanol solutions as their only source of water (one-bottle test) or a choice of an ethanol solution or water alone (two-bottle test). The amount of ethanol consumed is, of course, recorded in both types of experiments. However, the measure of primary interest is the proportion of ethanol consumed relative to total fluid consumption.

Preference is difficult to study in the one-bottle design because of the inherent conflict induced. Animals have only two choices—either they drink the fluid or risk becoming dehydrated. In the two-bottle design, preference (or aversion) is more easily demonstrable because the animal has the choice of drinking either ethanol or the other fluid. If the two solutions are neither reinforcing nor aversive, animals will consume them at random, so that total fluid intake will be distributed evenly between both fluids, (i.e., 50 percent from each bottle). If the ethanol is more reinforcing than the other fluid, more than 50 percent of the total fluid intake will be from the bottle containing the ethanol solution. Conversely, if the ethanol is aversive, less than 50 percent of the fluid consumed is ethanol. It should be noted that when high concentrations of ethanol are presented, the volume of fluid consumed may be reduced, but the actual amount consumed may be the same or increased. Consequently, in many cases, data may have to be considered in terms of the amount of ethanol consumed rather than the volume. Since the effects of ethanol on the brain are presumed to be relevant to the reinforcing effects of ethanol, taste preferences or aversions and possible habits of drinking from a bottle in the same position also should be controlled.

A more ideal way to measure ethanol preference may be through experiments in which animals have to work for ethanol. Human alcoholics have to make some effort to obtain alcoholic beverages. Situations in which animals work for ethanol provide a more valid test of their motivation to drink than do situations in which ethanol is readily available, as in free-choice, two-bottle experiments.

The use of different genetic strains that freely consume varying amounts of ethanol is another way used to study ethanol preference in biological experiments. This approach is based on the assumption that ethanol preference is genetically determined. Most animals generally find ethanol aversive and do not willingly drink excessive amounts. However, considerable variability in ethanol consumption exists among animals within a species and among strains of the same species. This variability can be used as the basis for breeding strains that consume either large or small amounts of ethanol. Such animal models have been used on the premise that the genetic compositions of two strains, say, "drinkers" and "nondrinkers," are indentical except for differences in the genes that influence ethanol consumption. However, in addition to these genetic factors that relate directly to mechanisms of reinforcement of ethanol, other attributes, whose expression also is genetically determined could play a role in the differences in ethanol consumption between strains. They include the perceived taste of ethanol by an animal, the sensitivity of the brain to ethanol, and the rate of metabolism of ethanol. Indeed, they may play a major role in the amount of ethanol an animal will consume.

Any acute effects of ethanol consumption in humans are associated with measurable amounts of ethanol in the blood. For ethanol to have a reinforcing effect due to its action on the brain, measurable amounts of consumed ethanol must reach the brain. Once consumed, ethanol is absorbed and distributed throughout the body, with the concentration in the blood reflecting the concentration in the brain. To maintain elevated blood-ethanol concentrations, ethanol intake must be at a rate that exceeds the rate at which it is metabolized. Determining blood ethanol concentrations at appropriate times during an experiment is the best way to assess whether sufficient amounts of ethanol have been consumed to reach the brain.

The depressant effect of ethanol follows the appearance and disappearance of ethanol in the brain. The reinforcing properties of ethanol should generally follow this course. Other factors, however, such as consuming ethanol in anticipation of its actions and residual effects after ethanol elimination may modify the time course of the reinforcing effects of ethanol.

Once the putative mechanisms underlying the reinforcing effects of ethanol have been indentified, these mechanisms can be manipulated in order to see whether the reinforcing effects of ethanol are altered. In biological experiments, this approach could include administering drugs or applying lesions to parts of the brain. For example, if the reinforcing properties of ethanol involved the release of some substance in the brain, inhibiting the actions of this substance or destroying its source should block the reinforcing effects of ethanol.

ACETALDEHYDE

Ethanol is metabolized predominantly in the liver by a two-step enzymatic process. Initially, ethanol is converted to acetaldehyde by the enzyme alcohol dehydrogenase, then to acetate by another enzyme, aldehyde dehydrogenase. Acetate is ultimately metabolized to carbon dioxide and water. The conversion of ethanol to acetaldehyde is an important step because the maximum rate of conversion is attained at relatively low concentrations of ethanol (50–100 mg/dl). Thus, at higher concentrations, the rate of ethanol metabolism is constant no matter how high they become, making detoxification a slow process.

Acetaldehyde concentrations are normally low after ethanol consumption. However, in some human populations, such as Orientals, that are genetically deficient in the enzyme aldehyde dehydrogenase, drinking alcoholic beverages induces a "flushing response" characterized by facial flushing, vasodiation, tachycardia, nausea and vomiting. This reaction occurs as a consequence of high blood acetaldehyde concentrations, and is also the cause of the adverse response experienced by alcoholics who drink ethanol after being treated with disulfiram (Antabuse). By becoming ill, alcoholics associate drinking ethanol with feeling sick.

The producton of acetaldehyde after consuming alcoholic beverages, even in low concentrations, has been thought to play a role in the reinforcing properties of ethanol. Although acetaldehyde in high concentrations is aversive, a long-lasting production of small concentrations may be important as a positive reinforcer and may depend on where the acetaldehyde is synthesized, as described below.

Infusions of acetaldehyde into the ventricles of the brain have been shown in several studies to increase the amount of ethanol consumed. When 10μg of acetaldehyde were infused into the ventricles of rats every 15 minutes for five days, the animals, when given a choice between an ethanol solution or water, drank significantly more ethanol (Myers & Veale, 1969). In addition, when rats were presented with different concentrations of ethanol, the concentrations at which the ethanol solutions became aversive increased from 9 percent to 20 percent. However, total intake of ethanol was less than 2 g/kg/day and no signs of intoxication were observed.

In another set of experiments, rats could obtain infusions of 64 μg of acetaldehyde by pressing a lever (Brown, Amit, & Smith, 1980). During the 11-day experiment, the animals responded more frequently for infusions of acetaldehyde solutions than for solutions not containing acetaldehyde. Those animals receiving acetaldehyde subsequently consumed more ethanol (ranging from concentrations of 9 percent to 21 percent) during a four-day period than controls. Mean intake per day was 4.5 g/kg, and no signs of intoxication were recorded. In addition, animals would not self-administer ethanol (Brown, Amit, & Rockman, 1979).

Infusion of acetaldehyde intraventricularly led to the development of a conditioned place preference (Smith, Amit, & Splawinsky, 1984). This conclusion was based on the observation that when animals were placed in a box in which one wall was unpainted and the opposite wall was painted, they preferred the wall where they received infusions of acetaldehyde.

An increase in ethanol consumption also was observed when rats could obtain acetaldehyde infusions intraperitoneally (Myers, Ng, & Singer, 1984a). This effect on ethanol consumption was greatest when the animals were food deprived (Myers, Ng, Marzuki, Myers, & Singer, 1984; Myers, Ng, & Singer, 1982). The effect of acetaldehyde on ethanol consumption may involve the release of natural opioid peptides in the brain since treatment with the opiate antagonist naloxone reduced in a dose-dependent manner the self-infusion of acetaldehyde (Myers, Ng, & Singer, 1984b).

The concentrations of most substances in the body are a function of their rates of enzymatic synthesis and degradation. Accordingly, the concentration of acetaldehyde depends largely on the activities of alcohol and aldehyde dehydrogenases. If the activities of these enzymes are altered by drugs, or if they vary from animal to animal, any resulting changes in the concentrations of acetaldehyde should influence ethanol preference. For example, when aldehyde dehydrogenase was inhibited with calcium cyanamide, an elevation in acetaldehyde concentrations was found after ethanol ingestion (Eriksson & Deitrich, 1980; Sinclair & Lindros, 1981; Sinclair, Lindros, & Terho, 1980). Rats subsequently drank very little ethanol (less than 1 g/kg/day) as compared with controls (3–5 g/kg/day). When 4-methylpyrazole, an alcohol dehydrogenase inhibitor that reduces acetaldehyde concentrations after ethanol ingestion, was administered, the action of cyanamide was partially antagonized (Sinclair & Lindros, 1981). On the other hand, 4-methylpyrazole alone had no effect on ethanol consumption. This finding suggests that only elevated acetaldehyde concentrations are aversive.

Since the synthesis of the enzymes responsible for ethanol metabolism is under genetic control, the variability of enzymatic activities within and between species might influence the concentrations of acetaldehyde attained after ethanol administration. If the concentraion of acetaldehyde plays a role in ethanol preference, correlations between enzymatic activities and ethanol consumption might be found. Several studies have addressed this possibility, generally with strains of mice or rats that show different preferences for ethanol. These strains either have natural differences in ethanol preference or were bred specifically to have either high preference or low preference.

One strain is C57BL mice that freely consume more ethanol than do other strains of mice such as DBA, and have lower blood acetaldehyde concentrations after ethanol ingestion (Schlesinger, Kakihana, & Bennett, 1966). Hepatic alcohol dehydrogenase activity is significantly higher in C57BL mice than in DBA mice. However, the blood-ethanol concentrations after a given dose and rate of ethanol metabolism are not different between the strains (Wilson, 1967). Similar results were found with AA (ethanol preferring) and ANA (ethanol nonpreferring) rats, strains specifically bred for differences in ethanol preference (Eriksson, 1973; Koivula, Koivusalo, & Lindros, 1975). Correlations between ethanol preference and hepatic aldehyde dehydrogenase activity have also been found. Consistent with lower blood acetaldehyde concentrations, aldehyde dehydrogenase activity is higher in the C57BL mice and AA rats, the ethanol-preferring strains (Koivula et al., 1975; Sheppard, Albersheim, & McClearn, 1970). However, in another study no differences in brain aldehyde dehydrogenase activities were found between AA and ANA rats (Inoue, Rusi, & Lindros, 1981).

Another factor concerning the ethanol preference of the different genetic strains of rodents may be their sensitivity to the actions of ethanol. It is possible that this sensitivity may influence how much ethanol the animals will drink. When the sensitivities of ethanol-preferring C57BL mice and AA rats were compared with the nonethanol-preferring DBA mice and ANA rats, the ethanol-preferring animals were significantly less intoxicated by a dose of ethanol, as measured by the tilt-plane test for motor incoordination, even though the blood-ethanol concentrations were equivalent (Malia, 1978; Sheppard et al., 1970). Consequently, if animals find intoxication aversive, the preferring animals may be able to consume more ethanol before becoming intoxicated.

Chronic administration of ethanol can alter the activities of alcohol and aldehyde dehydrogenases, changes that may influence the concentration of acetaldehyde in the blood. In one study in which ethanol was administered for 14 days, alcohol dehydrogenase activity was elevated in the brain (Raskin & Sokoloff, 1974) but not in the liver (Raskin & Sokoloff, 1972a). In another study, aldehyde dehydrogenase activity also was higher in the brain after 60 days of ethanol treatment but was lower in the liver (Amir, 1978). These results suggestd that chronic consumption of ethanol leads to progressively lower acetaldehyde concentrations in the brain but possibly higher concentrations in the blood. Studies with alcoholics support this possibility. In some laboratories, when blood acetaldehyde concentrations were compared in alcoholics and nonalcoholics after ethanol consumption, the concentrations were found to be elevated in alcoholics (Korsten, Matsuzaki, Feinman, & Lieber, 1975; Lindros, Stowell, Pikkarainen, & Salaspuro, 1980; Schuckit & Rayses, 1979; Truitt, 1971). A more recent study challenged this finding, however, by not detecting any difference in blood acetaldehyde concentrations between alcoholics and nonalcoholics (Eriksson & Peachy, 1980).

The exact manner in which acetaldehyde exerts a positive reinforcing effect after ethanol ingestion is not clear. One possibility is that acetaldehyde interacts with processes in the brain that underlie reward. A few studies have examined the effect of acetaldehyde on catecholamines and indoleamines, two transmitters that may be related to the reinforcing effects of ethanol (see Chapter 4). The administration of both acetaldehyde and disulfiram has been reported to reduce norepinephrine concentrations (Duritz & Truitt, 1966) and to elevate catecholamine synthesis (Svensson & Waldeck, 1973) and serotonin concentrations (Fukumori, Minegishi, Satoh, Kitagawa, & Yanaura, 1980) in the brain. However, these effects were not related to the increased locomotor activity and electroencephalographic changes observed after ethanol administration (Erickson, Lau, Schulz, & Matchett, 1975; Mikeska & Klemm, 1979; Svensson & Waldeck, 1973). Thus, these findings suggest that the physiological changes may not be related to the mechanisms by which acetaldehyde is reinforcing.

From the results reviewed so far, elevated blood-acetaldehyde concentrations appear to play a role in some of the aversive effects of ethanol. Whether acetaldehyde in the brain contributes to the positive reinforcing effect of ethanol, as the previous described experiments in which acetaldehyde was infused into the brain suggest, depends largely on the amount of acetaldehyde that accumulates in the brain after ethanol is consumed.

Since ethanol is metabolized mainly in the liver, the source of most of any acetaldehyde would be in this organ. Although acetaldehyde is quickly metabolized to acetate, some acetaldehyde can pass into the bloodstream. The concentrations of acetaldehyde found in the blood have varied widely in different laboratories, partly as a result of methodological differences among studies (Eriksson, 1980). The accuracy of the analysis of acetaldehyde depends on the degree to which it is formed by the nonezymatic oxidation of ethanol, binds to erythrocytes, and decomposes in blood samples before analysis.

When measured in blood, acetaldehyde concentrations after ethanol administration have been reported to be as high as 400 μM (see review of Lindros, 1978). Such a high concentration has not been found in brain because acetaldehyde does not readily cross the blood-brain barrier. Blood-acetaldehyde concentrations above 250 μM are needed to observe any appreciable amounts in the brain (Sippel, 1974). The best estimate of brain-acetaldehyde concentrations is less than 20 μM (Sippel, 1974; Tabakoff, Anderson, & Ritzman, 1976; Eriksson & Sippel, 1977; Westcott, Weiner, Shultz, & Myers, 1980).

The source of acetaldehyde in the brain does not necessarily have to originate in the blood. The brain, of course, could metabolize ethanol to acetaldehyde, but little alcohol dehydrogenase activity has been detected there (Raskin & Skoloff, 1972b). Furthermore, little acetaldehyde can be detected in the cerebrospinal fluid of intoxicated alcoholics (Lindros & Hillbom 1979). On the other hand, the enzyme catalase, which will convert ethanol to acetaldehyde through a reaction with hydrogen peroxide, has been detected in the rat brain (Cohen, Sinet, & Heikkila, 1980). The presence of this enzyme might suggest the possibility that higher concentrations of acetaldehyde are localized in specific areas rather than uniformly distributed throughout the brain. Significant effects on the brain might result. This possibility has yet to be demonstrated.

Since the concentrations of acetaldehyde in the brain after ethanol ingestion are so low, it is difficult to see how it could play a role in the positive reinforcing effects of ethanol consumption. This conclusion raises doubt about the relevance of those studies in which acetaldehyde was infused into the brain and increased ethanol consumption observed. It is possible, however, that rather than acetaldehyde exerting a direct effect on the reinforcing effects of ethanol administration, infusions of acetaldehyde into the brain provide the necessary precursor for the synthesis of novel substances that themselves promote ethanol consumption. In the next section, we discuss this possibility in detail.

ABERRANT NEUROTRANSMITTERS

Tetrahydroisoquinolines

Acetaldehyde, like many aldehydes, chemically is a very reactive substance. It can react with a variety of moieties, the most important of which for this discussion are the biogenic amines. During the metabolism of the catecholamines and indoleamines, aldehyde intermediates are formed and, along with acetaldehyde, can react with the amines to produce more complex molecules.

It has been suggested that ethanol and acetaldehyde enhance the reaction of aldehyde intermediates of biogenic amine metabolism and acetaldehyde with the parent amines to form a class of compounds called tetrahydroisoquinolines (TIQS) (Cohen & Collins, 1970; Davis & Walsh, 1970; Davis, Walsh & Yamanaka, 1970; Walsh, Davis & Yamanaka, 1970). Because one of the TIQS, tetrahydropapaveroline (THP), is a precursor of morphine in plants (Battersby, 1961), hypotheses have been presented to link ethanol and opiate dependence (Davis & Walsh, 1970). Basically, these hypotheses state that ethanol consumption leads to the synthesis of alkaloids with opiate-like activity that ultimately induce an opiate-like dependence.

A number of mechanisms have been proposed for the synthesis of TIQs. Figure 3-1 shows one possible pathway involving dopamine metabolism. Dopamine is oxidized to the unstable dopaldehyde, which can, in turn, condense with dopamine to an unstable Schiff-base intermediate, then cyclize to form THP (Weiner, 1978). Also, acetaldehyde produced from the metabolism of ethanol can condense with dopamine to form salsolinol. Similar reactions presumably can occur with norepinephrine and serotonin, two of the other biogenic amines. Reactions between acetaldehyde and enkephalins, naturally occurring opioids, to form alkaloids have been suggested (Summers & Lightman, 1981).

With regard to the reinforcing properties of ethanol, the most intriguing experiments with TIQs have involved demonstrating an apparently permanent preference for ethanol after TIQs were administered to animals that do not normally prefer ethanol. Whether TIQs were infused once a day or continuously into the ventricles of the brains of rats or monkeys, their consumption of ethanol increased dramatically to 8-17 g/kg/day. These animals displayed signs of ethanol intoxication and had blood-ethanol concentrations as high as 200 mg/dl (Melchior & Myers, 1977; Myers, McCaleb, & Ruwe, 1982; Myers & Melchior, 1977). During the day, when blood-ethanol concentrations of the animals were lowest, an enhanced susceptibility to audiogenic seizures was found, suggesting that the animals had become physically dependent on the ethanol. Ethanol consumption remained high for as long as nine months after the TIQ infusions were discontinued. In further experiments, THP was found to be the most effective of the TIQs in inducing high ethanol consumption and increased drinking after only a few days of THP treatment (Myers & Oblinger, 1977). A single dose or systemic injections of THP were ineffective. Derivatives of beta-carbolines, con-

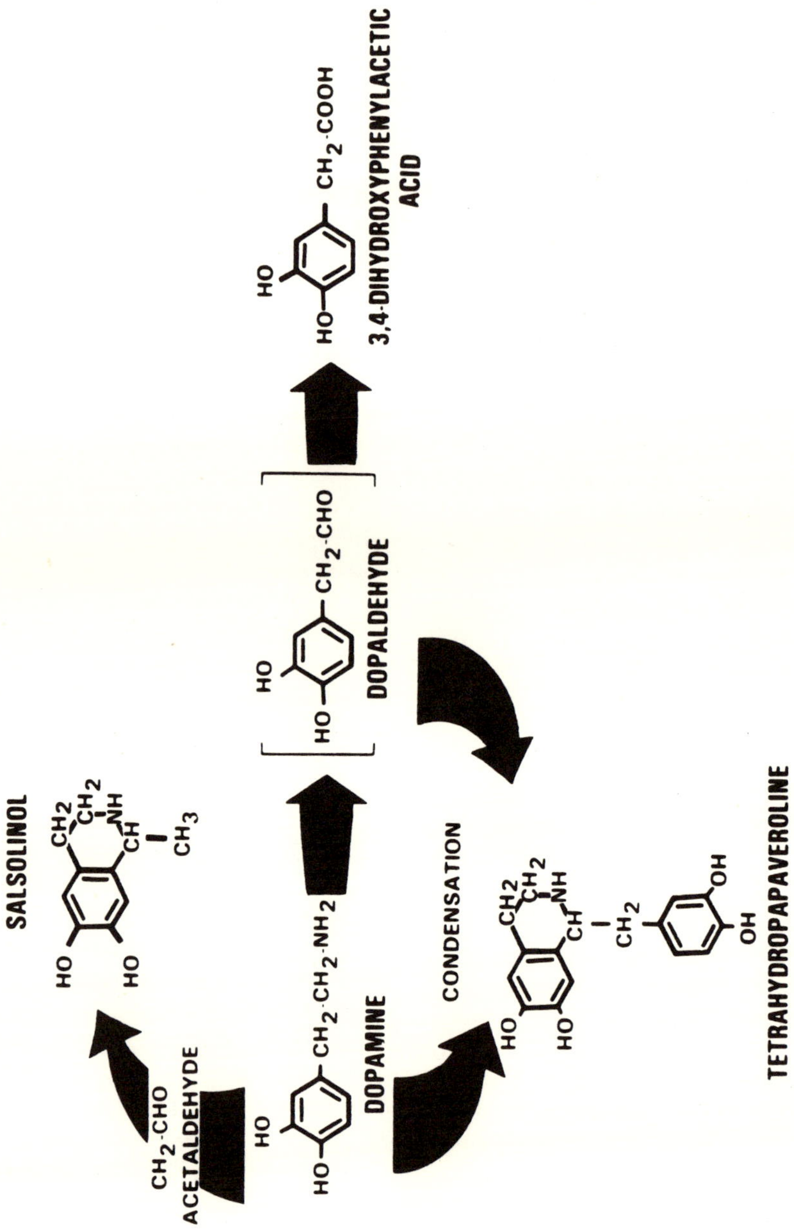

Figures 3-1.
The metabolism of dopamine to tetrahydroisoquinolines. Not all possible reactions are show[n]. [Reproduced from Hunt (1983).]

densation products of aldehydes and indoleamines such as serotonin, were also capable of inducing ethanol consumption in rats (Myers & Melchior, 1977; Tuomisto, Airaksinen. Peura, & Eriksson, 1982).

Attempts to replicate these results in other laboratories have not always been successful. One study was able to show increased ethanol consumption only when THP was continually infused into the ventricles, but there was no evidence of withdrawal signs after discontinuing treatment (Duncan & Deitrich, 1980). Other studies were unable to find any increase in ethanol consumption after TIQ administration. (Sinclair & Myers, 1982; Smith, Brown, & Amit, 1980). Even in the laboratory in which the initial observations of TIQ-induced drinking were made, ethanol consumption was later reported to be less than 5 g/kg/day (Sinclair & Myers, 1980). It appears, therefore, that the exact conditions under which TIQ administration will induce high ethanol consumption have not been fully determined.

A role for endogenous opioids has been implicated in the actions of TIQs. As discussed earlier, the positive reinforcing effects of intraventricularly infused acetaldehyde can be blocked by prior administration of the opiate antagonist naloxone. Similar responses have been observed regarding TIQ-induced drinking. When naloxone was administered to animals that drank ethanol, their consumption significantly decreased (Myers & Critcher, 1982). Morphine injections also reduced ethanol intake (Critcher, Lin, Patel, & Myers, 1983). Although the effects of the two drugs may appear to be contradictory, it could be argued that each drug reduces ethanol consumption by different means. For example, naloxone may reduce intake by blocking the reinforcing effect of the ethanol, whereas morphine may itself provide reinforcement, thereby reducing the desire to drink ethanol for further reinforcement. In any case, an effect on opioid receptors is likely to be indirect since TIQs have a low affinity for opioid receptors (Lucchi, Bosio Spano, & Trabucchi, 1981).

As with acetaldehyde, the role of TIQs in ethanol preference depends on the synthesis of sufficient concentrations to exert an action. The studies discussed so far were pharmacological in nature in that exogenous substances were administered. For TIQs to have a role in the reinforcing effects of ethanol, measurable amounts must be produced after ethanol consumption. To date this has been difficult to demonstrate for a variety of theoretical and analytical reasons. TIQs are formed as condensation products from reactions between aldehydes and amines. As with any chemical reaction, the availability and concentrations of the substrates, and the rates at which synthesis and degradation occur determine the concentrations of the products. In addition, the concentrations of one or more of these precursors must increase after ethanol consumption.

In the case of TIQs, the availability of suitable amines might not be a problem, With high concentrations of amines such as found in the adrenal medulla, profusion with high concentrations of acetaldehyde (23 mM) induces detectable formation and subsequent release of TIQs (Greenberg & Cohen, 1973). These TIQs can be taken up by nerve terminals and released when the nerves are stimulated (Mytilineou, Cohen, & Barrett, 1974), suggesting that TIQs may act as false transmitters, substituting themselves for the naturally occurring transmitters (Cohen, 1976). In the brain, high concentrations of various biogenic amines can be found in a number of areas, such as the caudate nucleus (dopamine and serotonin) and the hypothalamus (norepinephrine). However, the availability of aldehydes and the stability of any TIQs formed are another matter, and have been the basis of disputes as to whether TIQs should form at all in the brain.

An attempt has been made to calculate the maximum concentrations of TIQs expected after ethanol consumption using reported concentrations of dopamine and acetaldehyde in the brain and the rates of formation and degradation of TIQs (Weiner, 1981). Considering that acetaldehyde concentrations are low and catecholamine concentrations are high in localized regions of the brain, very little TIQs would be expected to be found there. However, the calculated concentrations of less than 1 ng/g are generally below the limits of detection possible with most analytical methods.

In addition to expecting very low concentrations of TIQs, they are also metabolized quickly in the brain, with half-lives of less than 20 minutes (Melchior, Mueller, & Deitrich, 1980). Therefore, we must consider the possibility that the TIQs are metabolized to other products that also are active substances. The most immediate metabolites of TIQs are likely to be O-methylated derivatives (Collins & Origitano, 1983; Origitano & Collins, 1980). These derivatives might be expected because TIQs are good substrates for catechol-O-methyltransferase (COMT), a major enzyme involved in the metabolism of catecholamines (Collins, Cashaw, & Davis, 1973). Consequently, attempts to detect TIQs must take these metabolic possibilities into account.

Attempts to detect TIQs by different approaches after acute and chronic ethanol administration have produced variable results. So far no reports have claimed an ability to detect TIQs in the brain after a single dose of ethanol, although in one study in which animals were pretreated with the drug pyrogallol, a COMT inhibitor, salsolinol could be found after only one dose (Collins & Bigdeli, 1975). Furthermore, when [3H]-dopamine was injected intraventricularly, ethanol treatment did not lead to the conversion of dopamine to THP, salsolinol, or O-methylated salsolinol (Shier, Koda, & Bloom, 1983).

If TIQs play a role in the reinforcing effects of ethanol, it is possible that chronic ethanol administration is required for enough TIQs to be synthesized so that they can be measured. Results of studies testing this possibility have been variable. No detectable salsolinol or THP concentrations have been found in the brain after six to eight days of ethanol administration (O'Neill & Rahwan, 1977; Turner, Baker, Algeri, Frigerio, & Garattini, 1974). However, 150 days after rats had consumed an ethanol solution as their sole source of fluid, salsolinol concentrations were increased in the dopamine-rich areas of the caudate nucleus (1.1 nmol/g) and limbic forebrain (0.25 nmol/g) (Sjoquist, Liljequist, & Engel, 1982). These values are much higher than the theoretically maximum values discussed earlier (Weiner, 1981). Salsolinol and its O-methylated metabolites were also elevated in the urine of detoxifying alcoholics, an effect that dissipated as ethanol was eliminated from the body (Collins, Nijm, Borge, Teas, Goldfarb, 1979

Considering the high concentrations of salsolinol observed in the brain and urine after long-term ethanol administration, two points need to be addressed. Expected concentrations of TIQs have been calculated from a few existing reports on the concentrations of acetaldehyde in the brain and the rates of formation and metabolism of TIQs. It is possible that one or more of these factors has not been determined precisely and may contribute to erroneous estimates of TIQ concentrations. Another alternative is that the TIQs being measured are not derived from neural sources, especially TIQs in urine. Numerous studies have determined that much lower concentrations of acetaldehyde exist in the brain in than blood. Consequently, blood acetaldehyde may be condensing with catecholamines in other organs and released into the blood.

Beta-Carbolines

The last area of consideration is one that is still quite speculative, but could have relevance to the reinforcing effects of ethanol. Ethanol consumption can relieve anxiety, an effect that might contribute to excessive drinking. Some recent research into the underlying mechanisms of anxiety has centered on a class of substances called beta-carbolines.

Derivatives of beta-carbolines can be formed from the condensation of acetaldehyde with indoleamines, such as serotonin. These substances exert a number of behavioral effects, including the induction of convulsions and anxiety (Braestrup, Honore, Nielsen, Petersen, & Jensen,

1984; Stephens, Kehr, Schneider, & Schmiechen, 1984). Since beta-carbolines have been reported to increase the consumption of ethanol (Myers & Melchior, 1977; Tuomisto et al., 1982), it is possible that an accumulation of beta-carbolines accompanying ethanol consumption leads to increased anxiety. This increase may perpetuate further consumption of ethanol to relieve the anxiety.

Specific mechanisms could underlie this possibility and involve the same receptors on which the benzodiazepines (e.g., diazepam) act. The benzodiazepines are a class of tranquilizers that relieve anxiety and also have anticonvulsant and sedative actions. Another class of substances that includes the beta-carbolines also acts on the benzodiazepine receptors (Gee, Ehlert, & Yamamura, 1983), but instead of relieving anxiety as the benzodiazepines do, the beta-carbolines induce it (Stephens et al., 1984).

Ethanol appears to interact with the receptors mediating the effects of benzodiazepines (see review by Hunt, 1983b). This interaction may play a role in the stress-relieving effect of ethanol. During chronic ethanol consumption, it is possible that the accumulation of beta-carbolines counteracts this effect of ethanol, increases the level of anxiety, and then promotes further consumption of ethanol in an attempt to relieve the anxiety. This cyclical process may perpetuate excessive drinking. To date, however, there is no evidence to support this hypothesis.

SUMMARY AND CONCLUSIONS

This chapter has reviewed the possibility that metabolic products that might accumulate after ethanol consumption contribute to the reinforcing effects of ethanol. We saw that there is no direct evidence to demonstrate conclusively that acetaldehyde or aberrant neurotransmitters, such as TIQ or beta-carbolines, are involved. None of the criteria for a valid biological mechanism underlying the reinforcing effects of ethanol has been satisfied. Moreover, there are a number of theoretical and methodological problems with our present knowledge in this area.

Most of the studies presented in this chapter are pharmacological in that the metabolites were administered to animals. The doses used may or may not have any relevance to possible concentrations synthesized in vivo after ethanol consumption.

The ability of metabolic products to play a role in the reinforcing effects of ethanol obviously depends on their being present in the body in sufficient concentrations to be effective. Although acetaldehyde and aberrant neurotransmitters have been found in the periphery, little if any of them have been found in the brain. In the case of TIQs, however, the active substances could be as yet unidentified metabolites.

Most of the studies that we reviewed used ethanol preference as an index of the reinforcing effects of ethanol. Although this index can provide useful information, it is unsatisfactory for assessing ethanol's reinforcing effects. Animals rarely drink enough ethanol to obtain measurable blood-ethanol and presumably brain-ethanol concentrations. Without evidence of ethanol in the brain, the relevance of ethanol preference to human drinking behavior is doubtful.

The idea that the formation of novel substances can lead to high levels of ethanol consumption has important implications in understanding the reinforcing effects of ethanol. Normally we think that people have a choice whether or not to drink ethanol (Chapter 11). However, if certain metabolic products accumulate and significantly contribute to excessive ethanol consumption, individuals may find it difficult to regulate their drinking because of an altered biological condition over which they have no control. If specific substances could be identified that maintain high ethanol consumption, drugs could be developed to interrupt the action of these substances, thus providing a new mode of treatment for alcoholism.

REFERENCES

Amir, S. (1978). Brain aldehyde dehydrogenase: Adaptive increase following prolonged ethanol administration in rats. *Neuropharmacology, 17*, 463–467.

Battersby, A.R. (1961). Alkaloid biosynthesis. *Quarterly Reviews, 25*, 259–286.

Braestrup, C., Honore, T., Nielsen, M., Petersen, E.N., & Jensen, L.H. (1984). Ligands for benzodiazepine receptors with positive and negative efficacy. *Biochemical Pharmacology, 33*, 859–862.

Brown, Z.W., Amit, Z., & Rockman, G.E. (1979). Intraventricular self-administration of acetaldehyde, but not ethanol, in naive laboratory rats. *Psychopharmacology (Berlin), 64*, 271–276.

Brown, Z.W., Amit, Z., & Smith, B. (1980). Intraventricular self-administration of acetaldehyde and voluntary consumption of ethanol in rats. *Behavioral and Neural Biology, 28*, 150–155.

Cohen, G. (1976). Alkaloid products in the metabolism of alcohol and biogenic amines. *Biochemical Pharmacology, 25*, 1123–1128.

Cohen, G., & Collins, M. (1970). Alkaloids from catecholamines in adrenal tissue: Possible role in alcoholism. *Science, 167*, 1749–1751.

Cohen, G., Sinet, P.M., & Heikkila, R. (1980). Ethanol oxidation by rat brain *in vivo*. *Alcoholism: Experimental and Clinical Research, 4*, 366–370.

Collins, A.C., Cashaw, J.L., & Davis, V.E. (1973). Dopamine-derived tetrahydroisoquinoline alkaloids—Inhibitors of neuroamine metabolism. *Biochemical Pharmacology, 22*, 2337–2348.

Collins, M.A., & Bigdeli, M.G. (1975). Tetrahydroisoquinolines *in vivo*. I. Rat brain formation of salsolinol, a condensation product of dopamine and acetaldehyde, under certain conditions during ethanol intoxication. *Life Science, 16*, 585–602.

Collins, M.A., Nijm, W.P., Borge, G.F., Teas, G., & Goldfarb, C. (1979). Dopamine-related tetrahydroisoquinolines: Significant urinary excretion by alcoholics after alcohol consumption. *Science, 206*, 1184–1186.

Collins, M.A., & Origitano, T.C. (1983). Catecholamine-derived tetrahydroisoquinolines: O-methylated patterns, and regional brain distribution following intraventricular administration in rats. *Journal of Neurochemistry, 41*, 1569–1575.

Critcher, E.C., Lin, C.I., Patel, J., & Myers, R.D. (1983). Attenuation of alcohol drinking in tetrahydrosioquinoline-treated rats by morphine and naltrexone. *Pharmacology, Biochemistry, and Behavior, 18*, 225–229.

Davis, V.E., & Walsh, M.J. (1970). Alcohol, amines, and alkaloids: A possible biochemical basis for alcohol addiction. *Science, 167*, 1005–1007.

Davis, V.E., Walsh, M.J., & Yamanaka, Y. (1970). Augmentation of alkaloid formation from dopamine by alcohol and acetaldehyde *in vitro*. *Journal of Pharmacology and Experimental Therapeutics, 174*, 401–412.

Duncan, C., & Dietrich, R.A. (1980). A critical evaluation of tetrahydroisoquinoline-induced ethanol preference in rats. *Pharmacology, Biochemistry, and Behavior, 13*, 265–281.

Duritz, G., & Truitt, E.B., Jr. (1966). Importance of acetaldehyde in the action of ethanol on brain norepinephrine and 5-hydroxytryptamine. *Biochemical Pharmacology, 15*, 711–721.

Erickson, C.K., Lau, A.S., Schulz, J.D., & Matchett, J. A. (1975). A time-course and dose-response study of the relationship between brain acetaldehyde, norepinephrine, and locomotor activity after ethanol in mice. In K.O. Lindros & C. P.E. Eriksson (Eds.), *Finish Foundation for Alcohol Studies, 23*, 177–186.

Eriksson, C.J.P. (1973). Ethanol and acetaldehyde metabolism in rat strains genetically selected for their ethanol preference. *Biochemical Pharmacology, 22*, 2283–2292.

Eriksson, C.J.P. (1980). Problems and pitfalls in acetaldehyde determinations. *Alcoholism: Clinical and Experimental Research, 4*, 22–29.

Eriksson, C.J.P., & Deitrich, R.A. (1980) Evidence against a biphasic effect of acetaldehyde on voluntary ethanol consumption in rats. *Pharmacology, Biochemistry, and Behavior, 13* (suppl. 1), 291–296.

Eriksson, C.J.P., & Peachy, J.E. (1980). Lack of difference in blood acetaldehyde of alcoholics and controls after ethanol ingestion. *Pharmacology, Biochemistry, and Behavior, 13* (suppl. 1), 101–105.

Eriksson, C.J.P., & Sippel, H.W. (1977). The distribution and metabolism of acetaldehyde in rats during ethanol oxidation—I. The distribution of acetaldehyde in liver, brain, blood, and breath. *Biochemical Pharmacology, 26*, 241–247.

Fukumori, R., Minegishi, A., Satoh, T., Kitagawa, H., & Yanaura, S. (1980). Changes in the serotonin and 5-hydroxyindoleacetic acid contents in rat brain after ethanol and disulfiram treatments. *European Journal of Pharmacology, 61*, 199–202.

Gee, K.W., Ehlert, F.J., & Yamamura, H.I. (1983). Differential effects of *gamma*-aminobutyric acid on benzodiazepine receptor subtypes labeled by [3H]propyl *beta*-carboline-3-carboxylate in the rat brain. *Journal of Pharmacology and Experimental Therapeutics, 225*, 132–137.

Greenberg, R.S., & Cohen, G. (1973). Tetrahydroisoquinoline alkaloids: Stimulated secretion from the adrenal medulla. *Journal of Pharmacology and Experimental Therapeutics, 184*, 119–128.

Hunt, W.A. (1983a). Ethanol and the central nervous system. In B. Tabakoff, P.B. Sutker, & C. L. Randall (Eds), *Medical and Social Aspects of Alcohol Abuse*. New York: Plenum Press, pp. 133–163.

Hunt, W.A. (1983b). The effect of ethanol on GABAergic transmission. *Neuroscience and Biobehavioral Reviews, 7*, 87–95.

Inoue, K., Rusi, M., & Lindros, K.O. (1981). Brain aldehyde dehydrogenase activity in rat strains with high and low ethanol preferences. *Pharmacology, Biochemistry, and Behavior, 14*, 107–111.

Koivula, T., Koivusalo, M., & Lindros, K.O. (1975). Liver aldehyde and alcohol dehydrogenase activities in rat strains genetically selected for their ethanol preference. *Biochemical Pharmacology, 24*, 1807–1811.

Korsten, M.A., Matsuzaki, S., Feinman, L., & Lieber, C.S. (1975). High blood acetaldehyde levels after ethanol administration. Difference between alcoholic and non-alcoholic subjects. *New England Journal of Medicine, 292*, 386–389.

Lindros, K.O. (1978). Acetaldehyde—Its metabolism and role in the actions of alcohol. In Israel, F.B. Glaser, H. Kalant, R.E. Popham, W. Schmidt, & R.G. Smart (Eds.) *Research Advances in Alcohol and Drug Problems*, Vol. 4, New York: Plenum Press, pp. 111–176.

Lindros, K.O., & Hillbom, M.E. (1979). Acetaldehyde on cerebrospinal fluid: Its near-absence in ethanol-intoxicated alcoholics. *Medical Biology, 57*, 246–247.

Lindros, K.O., Stowell, A., Pikkarainen, P., & Salaspuro, M. (1980). Elevated blood acetaldehyde in alcoholics with accelerated ethanol elimination. *Pharmacology Biochemistry and Behavior, 13* (suppl. 1), 119–124.

Lucchi, L., Bosio, A., Spano, P.F., & Trabucchi, M. (1981). Action of ethanol and salsolinol on opiate receptor function. *Brain Research, 232*, 506–510.

Malia, A. (1978). Intoxicating effects of three aliphatic alcohols and barbital on two rat inbred strains of mice. *Pharmacology, Biochemistry, and Behavior, 8*, 197–201.

Melchior, C.L., Mueller, A., Dietrich, R.A. (1980). Half-lives of salsolinol and tetrahydropapaveroline hydrobromide following intracerebroventricular injection. *Biochemical Pharmacology, 29*, 657–658.

Melchior, C.L, & Myers, R.D. (1977). Preference for alcohol evoked by tetrahydropapaveroline (THP) chronically infused in the cerebral ventricle of the rat. *Pharmacology Biochemistry and Behavior, 7*, 19–35.

Mikeska, J.A., & Klemm, W.R. (1979). Evidence against a role of acetaldehyde in electroencephalographic signs of ehtanol-induced intoxication. *Science, 203*, 276–279.

Myers, R.D., & Critcher, E.C. (1982). Naloxone alters alcohol drinking induced in the rat by tetrahydropapaveroline (THP) infused ICV. *Pharmacology Biochemistry and Behavior, 16*, 827–836.

Myers, R.D., McCaleb, M.L., & Ruwe, W.D. (1982). Alcohol drinking induced in the monkey by tetrahydropapaveroline (THP) infused into the cerebral ventricle. *Pharmacology Biochemistry and Behavior, 16*, 995–1000.

Myers, R.D., & Melchior, C.L. (1977). Alcohol drinking: Abnormal intake caused by tetrahydropapaveroline in brain. *Science, 196*, 554–556.

Myers, R.D., & Oblinger, M.M. (1977). Alcohol drinking in the rat induced by acute intracerebral infusion of two tetrahydroisoquinolines and a *beta*-carboline. *Drug and Alcohol Dependence, 2*, 469–483.

Myers, R.D., & Veale, W.L. (1969). Alterations volitional alcohol intake produced in rats by chronic intraventricular infusions of acetaldehyde, paraldehyde or methanol. *Archives Internationales de Pharmacodynamie et de Therapie, 180*, 100–113.

Myers, W.D. Ng, K.T., Marzuki, S., Myers, R.D., & Singer, G. (1984). Alternation of alcohol drinking in the rat by peripherally self-administered acetaldehyde. *Alcohol, 1*, 229–236.

Myers, W.D., Ng, K.T. & Singer, G. (1982). Intravenous self-administration of acetaldehyde in the rat as a function of schedule, food deprivation, and photoperiod *Pharmacology Biochemistry and Behavior, 12*, 807–811.

Myers, W.D., Ng, K.T., & Singer G. (1984a). Ethanol preference in rats with a prior history of acetaldehyde self-administration. *Experientia, 40*, 1008–1010.

Myers, W.D., Ng, K.T., & Singer G. (1984b). Effects of naloxone and buprenorphine on intravenous acetaldehyde self-injection in rats. *Physiology and Behavior, 33*, 449–455.

Mytilineou, C., Cohen, G., & Barrett, R. (1974). Tetrahydroisoquinoline alkaloids: Uptake and release by adrenergic nerves in vivo. *European Journal of Pharmacology, 25*, 390–401.

O'Neill, P.J., & Rahwan, R.G. (1977). Absence of formation of brain salsolinol in ethanol-dependent mice. *Journal of Pharmacology and Experimental Therapeutics, 200*, 306–313.

Origitano, T.C., & Collins, M.A. (1980). Confirmation of an unexpected brain O-methylated pattern for the dopamine-derived tetrahydroisoquinoline, salsolinol. *Life Sciences, 26*, 2061–2065.

Raskin, N.H., & Sokoloff, L. (1972a). Ethanol-induced adaptation of alcohol dehydrogenase activity in rat brain. *Nature (New Biology London), 236*, 138–140.

Raskin, N.H., & Sokoloff, L. (1972b). Enzymes catalyzing ethanol metabolism in neural and somatic tissue of the rat. *Journal of Neurochemistry, 19*, 273–282.

Raskin, N.H., & Sokoloff, L. (1974). Changes in brain alcohol dehydrogenase activity during chronic ethanol ingestion and withdrawal. *Journal of Neurochemistry, 22*, 427–434.

Schlesinger, K.R., Kakihana, R., & Bennett, E.L. (1966). Effects of tetraethylthiuramdisulfide (Antabuse) on the metabolism and consumption of ethanol in mice. *Psychosomatic Medicine, 28*, 514–520.

Schuckit, M.A., & Rayses, V. (1979). Ethanol ingestion: Differences in blood acetaldehyde concentrations in relatives of alcoholics and controls. *Science, 203*, 54–55

Sheppard, J.R., Albersheim, P., & McClearn, G. (1970). Aldehyde dehydrogenase and ethanol preference in mice. *Journal of Biological Chemistry, 245*, 2876–2882.

Shier, W.T., Koda, L.Y., & Bloom, F.E. (1983). Metabolism of [3H]dopamine following intracerebroventricular injection in rats pretreated with ethanol or chloral hydrate. *Neuropharmacology, 22*, 279–286.

Sinclair, J.D., & Lindros, K.O. (1981). Suppression of alcohol drinking with brain aldehyde dehydrogenase inhibition. *Pharmacology, Biochemistry, and Behavior, 14,* 377–383.

Sinclair, J.D., Lindros, K.O., & Terho, K. (1980). Aldehyde dehydrogenase inhibitors and voluntary ehtanol drinking in rats. In R.G. Thurman (Ed.), *Alcohol and aldehyde metabolizing systems*—IV, New York: Plenum Press, pp. 481–487.

Sinclair, J.D. & Myers, R.D. (1982). Cerebroventricular tetrahydropapaveroline infusions and ethanol consumption in the rat. *Substance and Alcohol Actions/Misuse, 1,* 209–221.

Sippel, H.W. (1974). The acetaldehyde content in rat brain during ethanol metabolism. *Journal of Neurochemistry, 23,* 451–452.

Sjoquist, B., Liljequist, S., & Engel, J. (1982). Increased salsolinol levels in rat striatum and limbic forebrain following chronic ethanol treatment. *Journal of Neurochemistry, 39,* 259–262.

Smith, B.R., Amit, Z., & Splawinsky, J. (1984). Conditioned place preference induced by intraventricular infusions of acetaldehyde. *Alcohol, 1,* 193–195.

Smith, B.R., Brown, Z.W., & Amit, Z. (1980). Chronic intraventricular administration of tetrahydroisoquinoline alkaloids: Lack of effect on voluntary ethanol consumption in the rat. *Substance and Alcohol Actions/Misuse, 1,* 209–221.

Stephens, D.N., Kehr, W., Schneider, H.H., & Schmiechen, R. (1984). *Beta*-carbolines with agonistic and inverse agonistic properties at benzodiazepine receptors of the rat. *Neuroscience Letters, 47,* 333–338.

Summers, M.C. & Lightman, S.L. (1981). A reaction of acetaldehyde with enkephalins and related peptides. *Biochemical Pharmacology, 30,* 1621–1627.

Svensspn T.H., & Waldeck, B. (1973). Significance of acetaldehyde in ethanol-induced effects on catecholamine metabolism and motor activity in the mouse. *Psychopharmacologia (Berlin,) 31,* 229–238.

Tabakoff, B., Anderson, R.A., & Ritzmann, R.F. (1976). Brain acetaldehyde after ethanol administration. *Biochemical Pharmacology, 25,* 1305–1309.

Truitt, E.B., Jr. (1971). Blood acetaldehyde levels after alcohol consumption by alcoholic and non-alcoholic subjects. In M.K. Roach, W.M. McIsaac, & P. J. Creaven (Eds.), *Biological Aspects of Alcohol Advances in Mental Science,* Vol. 3. Austin: The University of Texas Press, pp. 212–223.

Tuomisto, L., Airaksinen, M.M., Peura, P., & Eriksson, C.J. P. (1982). Alcohol drinking in the rat: Increases following intracerebroventricular treatment with tetrahydro-*beta*-carbolines. *Pharmacology Biochemistry and Behavior, 17,* 831–836.

Turner, A.J., Baker, K.M., Algeri, S., Frigerio, A., & Garattini, S. (1974). Tetrahydropapaveroline: Formation *in vivo* and *in vitro* in rat brain. *Life Sciences, 14,* 2247–2257.

Walsh, M.J., Davis, V.E., & Yamanaka, Y. (1970). Tetrahydropapaveroline: An alkaloid metabolite of dopamine *in vitro Journal of Pharmacology and Experimental Therapeutics, 174,* 388–400.

Weiner, H. (1978). Relationship between 3,4-dihydroxyphenylacetaldehyde levels and tetrahydropapaveroline formation. *Alcoholism: Clinical and Experimental Research, 2,* 127–131.

Weiner, H. (1981). Possible steady-state concentrations of tetrahydroisoquinolines in brain after the consumption of ethanol. *Federation Proceedings, 40,* 2082–2085.

Westcott, J.Y., Weiner, H., Schultz, J., & Myers, R.D. (1980). *In vivo* acetaldehyde in the brain of the rat treated with ethanol. *Biochemical Pharmacology, 29,* 411–417.

Wilson, E.C. (1967). Ethanol metabolism in mice with levels of hepatic alcohol dehydrogenase. In R.P. Maickel (Ed.), *Biochemical factors in alcoholism.* New York: Pergamon Press, pp. 115–124.

FOUR

BRAIN MECHANISMS THAT UNDERLIE THE REINFORCING EFFECTS OF ETHANOL

WALTER A. HUNT, Ph.D.

Ethanol has a variety of effects on the brain resulting from its interaction with excitable membranes (Hunt, 1985). These effects alter the basic processes by which neurons generate and propagate electrical potentials and by which information is transferred throughout the brain. Since the ongoing processes in the brain that underlie reinforcement might be influenced by the presence of ethanol, an examination of the possible involvement of these processes in the reinforcing effects of ethanol is warranted. Basically, in order to understand how consuming ethanol can be reinforcing, it is necessary to know how ethanol interacts with various mechanisms in the brain.

In this chapter, the various actions of ethanol on the brain are reviewed with emphasis on the mechanisms of reinforcement. The actions covered include general interactions of ethanol with membranes, processes involved in neural excitation and in synaptic transmission, and specific mechanisms of reinforcement.

MECHANISMS OF REWARD

Ethanol-seeking behavior is based on a learned association between taking a drug and the positive feelings that result, and is an inappropriate expression of an important survival mechanism. The ability of many animal species to survive depends largely on the animal's being able to recognize and respond in a suitable manner to beneficial and threatening stimuli in the environment. The positive or negative consequences of the responses to these stimuli provide the catalyst for learning these responses. In order for these consequences to be effective reinforcers, neural mechanisms that mediate reinforcement are activated. It is possible that ethanol, as well as other abused drugs, interacts in some way with these mechanisms to make consumption of the drugs pleasurable.

The neural mechanisms of reward have been examined extensively. Studies of these mechanisms began in earnest with the observations that when electrodes were placed in certain areas of the brain, animals responded for electrical impulses to those areas, that is, they self-stimulated (Olds & Milner, 1954). Animals presumably self-stimulate because they find such stimulation beneficial or, more anthropomorphically, because the stimulation makes them "feel good." In principle, the pleasurable feelings associated with the consumption of addictive drugs is presumably the reason why people take them.

Attempts to find one specific locus in the brain that mediates reinforcement have been unsuccessful. Indeed, stimulation of many areas of the brain, ranging from the prefrontal cortex to the brain stem, will initiate self-stimulation (Phillips, 1984). It appears that the area of the brain that mediates reward of a particular behavior depends on the sensory input, motor activity, and emotional expression associated with that behavior.

In order to assess what specific mechanisms play a role in reinforcement, a number of studies have been undertaken to identify specific neurotransmitters (the chemical substances that relay electrical information from one neuron to another) that might be possible mediators of reward. The most promising candidates are the catecholamines, especially dopamine, and the endogenous opioids. Dopamine is found in several areas of the brain, including the nucleus accumbens, caudate nucleus, and prefrontal cortex. Although stimulation of any of these areas will initiate self-stimulation, the nucleus accumbens in particular seems to be an important site that mediates reward.

Administration of some of the stimulant drugs, such as amphetamine and cocaine, will cause animals to self-administer these drugs. Evidence has been accumulated suggesting that dopaminergic mechanisms in the nucleus accumbens and the ventral tegmentum (the source of dopaminergic cell bodies located in the brain stem and projecting to the nucleus accumbens) underlie the reinforcing effects of stimulant drugs (see review by Wise & Bozarth, 1984). Experiments have been conducted in which dopaminergic transmission was modified by lesioning these two areas or by using dopaminergic agonists and antagonists to determine whether the reinforcing effects of amphetamine or cocaine could be altered. Dopaminergic agonists, which enhance transmission, increased the self-administration of the drugs, while dopaminergic antagonists and lesions of the dopamine fibers reduced self-administration.

It is generally accepted that morphine and heroin interact with specific receptors in the brain. The study of these receptors led to the discovery that the brain has its own endogenous opioids that are involved with its normal functioning. In addition, these endogenous opioids seem to interact with dopaminergic neurons (Vincent & Hokfelt, 1982; Watson, Khachaturian, Akil, Coy, & Goldstein; 1982). Such an interaction might suggest that the actions of opiates are ultimately, by way of dopaminergic fibers, similar to amphetamine and cocaine. However, in experiments where dopaminergic terminals in the nucleus accumbens were destroyed, animals still self-administered heroin, Self-administration of cocaine was not affected, suggesting that opiates can be reinforcing in the absence of dopaminergic neurons (Pettit, Ettenberg, Bloom, & Koob, 1984).

What this brief discussion of reward mechanisms suggests is that ethanol may exert its reinforcing properties by interacting with the neuronal pathways leading to the ventral tegmentum and the nucleus accumbens, similar to other abused drugs. As we shall see in the following, ethanol, because of its diverse actions, could very well modify the activity of neurons in these and other pathways whose activation induces self-stimulation.

EFFECTS OF ETHANOL ON MEMBRANES AND MEMBRANE FUNCTION

In order to understand how ethanol might activate the mechanisms of reinforcement, a basic understanding of how ethanol interacts with the brain is essential. It is generally accepted that ethanol exerts its actions on the brain through an interaction with excitable membranes (see review by Hunt, 1985). Since it has a simple molecular structure, ethanol probably does not act through specific receptors as do most other drugs. Rather, ethanol has certain properties that particularly contribute to the degree to which it partitions into membranes

Ethanol is soluble in both fat and water, although not to the same extent. In fact, a large number of other alcohols, having actions similar to ethanol, induce intoxication in animals in doses that are related to the ability of the alcohols to dissolve into the fat of membranes (McCreery & Hunt, 1978). As the fat solubility of the alcohol increases, its potency to induce intoxication also increases. At the turn of the century, the initial discovery of this relationship, using a smaller sample of alcohols, led to the development of the Meyer-Overton theory of general anesthesia, which states that the potencies of general anesthetics are directly related to their lipid solubilities (Meyer, 1901; Overton, 1901). Further refinements of the Meyer-Overton theory by Mullins (1954) and Ferguson (1939) suggested that anesthesia is attained when the concentration of the anesthetic in the membrane reaches a particular and biologically effective point.

More recently, ethanol has been shown to dissolve in and to expand membranes (Seeman, 1974). Furthermore, the actions of ethanol appear to be related to a disordering of the lipids that compose membranes. Advances in our understanding of ethanol-membrane interactions have been made using molecular probes with moieties attached that can be studied by electron paramagnetic resonance (EPR) spectroscopy and fluorescence spectrophotometry. These probes can report on the microenvironment in which they reside and can indicate whether the intrinsic fluidity of the membrane is altered by the presence of ethanol.

The basic studies using molecular probes have demonstrated that ethanol can disorder or "fluidize" membranes in a concentration-dependent manner (Chin & Goldstein, 1977; Harris & Schroeder, 1981). Using probes that localize at different depths of the membrane, Chin & Goldstein (1981) found that ethanol disorders the lipid core of the membrane rather than areas near its surface. Also, the disordering effect of ethanol can be reduced if the temperature of the membrane preparation is lowered or cholesterol is added to the membrane, two actions that make membranes more rigid (Chin & Goldstein, 1981).

Lipids within membranes are largely structural. Consequently, physiological consequences of lipid disordering in the brain must involve the functional entities in membranes that regulate the various processes of neural activity. In fact, a number of such entities require the presence of lipids in a presumed ideal organization for optimal activity. These entities include ion channels, enzymes, and neurotransmitter receptors.

The electrical activity of neurons is generated by the movements of ions through membranes. This is accomplished through the generation and propagation of impulses and involves the transient movement of sodium ions into the neuron, followed by the movement of potassium ions out of the neuron (Hodgkin & Huxley, 1952). Once an electrical impulse reaches the end of a neuron, it can be transmitted to another neuron only through the release of a chemical mediator that diffuses to a receptor on the next neuron. The interaction of the transmitter with its receptor leads to changes in electrical current that modify the excitability of the neuron. The stimulus for the release of the transmitter is the movement of calcium ions into the synaptic terminal through pores, or channels, in the membrane.

Ethanol appears to modify the movements of both sodium and calcium into neurons, especially when they are activated with potassium ions or neurotoxins that open channels. It inhibits the inward movement of both sodium and calcium ions in a concentration-dependent manner (Mullin & Hunt, 1985; Harris & Bruno, 1985; Leslie, Barr, Chandler, & Farrar, 1983). Other alcohols exert similar effects with potencies proportional to their lipid solubilities.

The movement of sodium and calcium ions can be determined by measuring the flow of electrical currents carried by these ions. Using appropriate electrophysiological techniques, the effects of ethanol on ionic movements have been examined in a number of invertebrate and vertebrate preparations. In the giant axon from squid and neurons from the sea mollusc *Aplysia,* ethanol was found to reduce the inward movement of sodium and calcium currents (Armstrong & Binstock, 1964; Moore, Ulbricht, & Takata, 1964; Bergmann, Klee, & Faber, 1974). Vertebrate preparations have been used to study the sensitivity of both processes involved in the transmission of electrical impulses from one neuron to another (presynaptic) and in the initiation of electrical impulses (postsynaptic). It appears that presynaptic processes are more sensitive to the effects of ethanol than are postsynaptic ones (Durand, Corrigall, Kujtan, & Carlen, 1981).

A number of enzymes important in synaptic processes and located in neural membranes depend on the lipid environment for optimal activity, including the sodium- and potassium-activated adenosine triphosphatase (Na-K ATPase), responsible for maintaining sodium gradients, and adenylate cyclase, responsible for converting adenosine triphosphate (ATP) to adenosine- 3',5'-cyclic monophosphate (cyclic AMP), a second messenger (Hobbs & Albers, 1980; Lefkowitz, Limbard, Mukherjee, & Caron, 1976). Ethanol in a concentration-dependent manner inhibits in vitro Na-K ATPase (Israel, Kalant, & Laufer, 1965) and stimulates adenylate cyclase activities (Rabin & Molinoff, 1981; Hoffman & Tabakoff, 1982). It is not yet known whether ethanol disorders the lipid environment of these enzymes or exerts its effect directly on the enzymes.

The neurotransmitter receptors are generally insensitive to ethanol (see Hunt, 1985). However, ethanol has been reported to interact with two receptor systems that may have some relevance to its reinforcing effects. They are the gamma-aminobutyric acid (GABA) and opioid receptors. The GABA receptor is part of a complex that also binds one class of tranquillizers, the benzodiazepines (Olsen, 1981). Ethanol has been reported to enhance the binding of both GABA and benzodiazepines to their receptor sites (Ticku & Burch, 1980; Davis & Ticku, 1981). Since the benzodiazepines are used to relieve anxiety, an interaction of ethanol with the GABA-receptor complex suggests that ethanol may be reinforcing, in part, because it relieves stress. The opioid receptors may also play a role in the reinforcing effects of ethanol. The action of ethanol on these receptors will be discussed later in this chapter.

The point of this discussion is that the disordering effect of ethanol is nonspecific and it probably acts in a qualitatively similar manner in membranes throughout the brain. Quantitative differences, however, may occur, and may be related to the dose-dependent effects of ethanol (stimulatory effects at lower doses and depressant effects at higher doses), as well as to the different areas of the brain involved. Any of these actions of ethanol may influence the mechanisms of reinforcement in the brain.

EFFECTS OF ETHANOL ON NEUROTRANSMITTERS

Important regulators of electrical activity in the brain are the neurotransmitters, chemical substances released from nerve endings when they are stimulated electrically. Some of the transmitters have been implicated in the mechanisms of reward, and it might well be that ethanol consumption is reinforcing because of its effect on these mechanisms. In fact, studies conducted over the past 15 years have revealed complex alterations after ethanol administration in the activity of various neurotransmitters, especially the catecholamines (Hunt & Majchrowicz, 1979; Hunt, 1981). Because dopamine apparently has a role in mechanisms of reward, we first examine the possible involvement of catecholamines in the reinforcing effect of ethanol.

Catecholamines

Low doses of ethanol appear to be stimulative when given to humans presumably because ethanol acts to release their inhibitions. The stimulation is manifested as increased social interactions, feelings of euphoria, and reduced tension (see Hunt, 1983). These responses probably reflect some aspects of the reinforcing effort of ethanol. In experimental animals, however, this is difficult to assess. One approach may be to study certain general behavioral changes that might reflect a stimulatory response to ethanol administration.

Ethanol in low doses increases locomotor activity in a number of species, especially in mice, and the possible involvement of catecholamines, particularly dopamine, has been investigated. Enhanced locomotor activity observed after low doses of ethanol is possibly mediated by dopaminergic pathways. The evidence was derived from two experimental approaches. One approach was to reduce the concentrations of dopamine in the brain or the ability of dopamine to interact with its receptor. The other approach examined the activity of dopaminergic neurons using biochemical and physiological techniques. Ethanol-induced locomotion can be blocked when animals are pretreated with either alpha-methyl-p-tyrosine (Carlsson, Engel, & Svensson, 1972), an inhibitor of catecholamine synthesis; low doses of dopaminergic agonists that reduce dopamine release (Carlsson, Engel, Strombom, Svensson, & Waldeck, 1974); or dopaminergic antagonists (Matchett & Erickson, 1977). Neurochemical studies have indicated that low doses of ethanol increase the utilization and release of dopamine, especially in the caudate nucleus and nucleus accumbens (Carlsson & Lindqvist, 1973; Carlsson, Magnusson, Svensson, & Waldeck, 1973; Darden & Hunt, 1977; Hunt et al, 1985; Murphy, McBride, Lumeng, & Li, 1983). The firing rate of nigrostriatal neurons has also been reported to be increased after ethanol in low doses (Mereu, Fadda, & Gessa, 1984). All these studies suggest that stimulation of dopaminergic pathways is associated with the enhanced locomotor activity observed after ethanol consumption.

Several studies have addressed the role of dopamine in voluntary ethanol consumption by manipulating the amount of catecholamines that can interact with their receptors. Such manipulations can alter the quantity of the ethanol consumed. However, no clear involvement of dopamine has been found. For example, when the catecholaminergic neurons were destroyed with the neurotoxin 6-hydroxydopamine or catecholamines were depleted with alpha-methyl-p-tyrosine, ethanol consumption decreased (Ahlenius, Carlsson, Engel, Svensson, & Sodersten, 1973; Kiianmaa, Andersson, & Fuxe, 1979; Myers & Melchior, 1975). Conversely, when animals were pretreated with amphetamine, which stimulates the release of catecholamines, ethanol consumption increased (Potthoff, Ellison, & Nelson, 1983). Unfortunately, since both dopaminergic and noradrenergic neurons were affected by these treatments, it was not possible to determine which transmitter was related to the changes in ethanol consumption.

Using drugs that are most specific to dopaminergic pathways, ethanol intake was found to be reduced when dopaminergic activity was suppressed with gamma-butyrolactone (Fadda, Argiolas, Melis, De Montis, & Gessa, 1983). Pretreatment with dopaminergic antagonists or with 6-hydroxydopamine and desmethylimipramine, which selectively depletes dopamine and not norepinephrine, had no effect on ethanol consumption (Brown & Amit, 1977; Brown, Gill, Abitbol, & Amit, 1982; Corcoran, Lewis, & Fibiger, 1983; Potthoff et al., 1983). Furthermore, selective depletion of norepinephrine concentrations reduced ethanol consumption (Amit, Brown, Levitan, & Ogren, 1977; Brown, Amit, Levitan, Ogren, & Sutherland, 1977; Davis, Smith, & Werner, 1978; Davis, Werner, & Smith, 1979). These results suggest that norepinephrine rather than dopamine is the catecholamine mediating the reinforcing effect of ethanol.

The basic problem with studies involving ethanol preference was discussed in Chapter 3 and concerns the amount of ingested ethanol that actually reaches the brain. Rodents do not consume more than a few grams per kilogram over a 24-hour period and only negligible concentrations of ethanol in the blood would be expected. Thus the relevance of these observations to human drinking is unclear because the consumption of ethanol by humans is accompanied by measurable blood-ethanol concentrations. Indeed, when noradrenergic antagonists were tested for efficacy in reducing the intoxicating effects of ethanol, little or no effect was found, including the mood states of the subjects (Alkana, Parker, Cohen, Birch, & Noble, 1976; 1977; Mendelson, Rossi, Bernstein, & Kuehnle, 1974). On the other hand, a more recent paper reported that the dopaminergic agonist bromocriptine significantly reduced ethanol intake by heavy social drinkers and alcoholics (Borg, 1983).

Serotonin

Accumulating evidence suggesting that serotonergic mechanisms play a role in the reinforcing effects of ethanol has been obtained by manipulating the interaction of serotonin with its receptor. In the earliest reports, serotonin synthesis was inhibited by pretreating animals with p-chlorophenylalanine or p-chloroamphetamine, tryptophan hydroxylase inhibitors. In these experiments, drug-pretreated animals consumed less ethanol (Frey, Magnussen, & Kaergaard Nielsen, 1970; Veale & Myers, 1972). However, the effect of these drugs may not have been specific to ethanol, since fluid intake in general was reduced (Stein, Wayner, & Tilson, 1977). Animals pretreated with tryptophan-rich diets consumed more ethanol (Sprince, Parker, Smith, & Gonzales, 1972).

More recent reports have provided opposite results. When serotonergic terminals were destroyed with 5,6-dihydroxytryptamine, ethanol preference was enhanced (Ho, Tsai, Chen, Begleiter, & Kissin, 1974; Myers & Melchior, 1975). Similarly, when animals were pretreated with 5-hydroxytryptophan (5-HTP) or pargyline to elevate serotonin concentrations in the brain, ethanol consumption was suppressed (Sanders, Collins, & Wesley, 1976; Zabik, Liao, Jeffreys, & Maickel, 1978). Furthermore, the effect of 5-HTP could be antagonized if its conversion to serotonin was blocked (Geller, Hartmann, & Messiha, 1981). Also, it is possible that the increased ethanol consumption induced by the chemical lesions was mediated though a lower cholinergic activity, since treatment with a cholinesterase inhibitor antagonized the effect (Ho et al., 1974).

Specific inhibitors of serotonin uptake have been examined for their efficacy in reducing ethanol consumption (Amit, Sutherland, Gill, & Ogren, 1984). Treatment with drugs such as zimeldine significantly reduced consumption (Rockman, Amit, Carr, Brown, & Ogren, 1979), although the effect does not seem to be through enhanced serotonergic activity, since blockade of the receptors or prior depletion of serotonin did not block the action of the drugs on ethanol consumption (Amit et al., 1984; Rockman, Amit, Brown, Bourque, & Ogren, 1982). However, inhibiting norepinephrine uptake with desmethylimipramine blocked the action of zimeldine, suggesting that zimeldine treatment might lead to a functional norepinephrine deficiency (Rockman, Amit, Carr, & Ogren, 1979). The possibility of a zimeldine-induced noradrenergic deficiency leading to a reduction in ethanol intake is consistent with results of studies suggesting that increased ethanol consumption can result from noradrenergic hyperactivity.

There have been a few clinical studies on the efficacy of zimeldine to block the effects of ethanol. Pretreatment with zimeldine has been found to reduce ethanol consumption by alcoholics (Naranjo, Lawrin, Addison, Roach, Harrison, Sanchez-Craig, & Sellers, 1983) and to counteract the disruptive effect of ethanol on information processing and memory (Linnoila, Johnson, Dubyoski, Ross, Buchsbaum, Potter, & Weingartner, 1983).

Benzodiazepines

One of the many psychological theories concerning the underlying basis of excessive consumption of ethanol is the tension-reduction hypothesis (see Chapter 6). This hypothesis states that (1) ethanol reduces tension and (2) organisms drink to reduce their tension.

Although the hypothesis has generated much research, it is clear that not only can ethanol reduce tension under some circumstances, but it can have negative emotional consequences as well. The tension-reduction hypothesis is the subject of Chapters 5 and 6 in this volume.

Some biological evidence on the actions of ethanol tends to support the tension-reduction hypothesis. Research performed over the last few years, shows that anxiety is mediated through receptors on which the benzodiazepine tranquillizers act. The benzodiazepines are used clinically to relieve anxiety. However, it has been postulated that endogenous substances induce anxiety through an interaction on another site of the benzodiazepine receptor. Putative endogenous substances, such as the beta-carbolines and a recently isolated polypeptide in the brain, bind to the benzodiazepine receptors and induce anxiety (Costa, Corda, & Guidotti, 1983; Gee, Ehlert, & Yamamura, 1983; Stephens, Kehr, Schneider, & Schmiechen, 1984).

As indicated earlier, ethanol enhances the binding of benzodiazepines with their receptor sites. Ethanol accomplishes this indirectly by interacting with another site on the receptor complex (Ticku & Davis, 1981) and presumably stimulates the brain's own anxiety-relieving system. In addition, there are cross-tolerance and cross-dependence between ethanol and the benzodiazepines (Woo & Greenblatt, 1979), suggesting common mechanisms of action. These data, then, suggest that ethanol reduces anxiety because it acts like a benzodiazepine.

Behavioral experiments have not conclusively demonstrated that ethanol relieves anxiety. Experimentally, tests have been used to study anxiety in which animals were punished for engaging in normal consummatory activities, such as drinking water (Lal & Emmett-Oglesby, 1983). Such activities were then suppressed. Benzodiazepines counteracted this suppression of behavior caused by punishment. Ethanol, in some studies, was found to have an effect similar to that of the benzodiazepines (Cook & Davidson, 1973; Glowa & Barrett, 1976; McMillan & Leander, 1975; Vogel, Frye, Wilson, Kuhn, Koepke, Mailman, Mueller, & Breese, 1980), whereas in other studies no effect was observed (Barry, Wagner, & Miller, 1963; Geller, Croy, & Ryback, 1974).

The effect of benzodiazepines on ethanol preference has also been examined. If ethanol relieves anxiety in a manner similar to the benzodiazepines, administration of benzodiazepines would be expected to reduce ethanol preference. Such an effect has been reported, but its occurrence appears to depend on the experimental design. When benzodiazepines were given concurrently with ethanol (Chan, Leong, & Schanley, 1983) or were administered chronically to animals with a previously developed preference for ethanol (Zakusov, Lyubimov, Yavorasku, & Folin, 1979), ethanol intake was reduced. But if animals were chronically treated with ethanol and received only intermittent injections of benzodiazepines, no alteration in ethanol consumption was observed (Chan et al., 1983). On the other hand, animals that self-administered ethanol after being force-fed ethanol continued to consume ethanol after cessation of the force feeding if benzodiazepines then were administered, whereas without the treatment, ethanol intake decreased (Deutsch & Walton, 1977). This decrease in consumption was not observed in another study (Ferko, Bobyock, & Chernick, 1979).

EFFECTS OF ETHANOL ON OPIOID SYSTEMS

Morphine and other opiates exert their actions on specific receptors in the brain that are normally acted upon by endogenous peptides with opioidlike activity. The various actions of opiates are mediated by a number of different opioid receptors that specifically bind different opiate drugs and peptides (Snyder, 1984). One of these subtypes, the delta-receptor, binds naturally occurring enkephalins and mediates the euphoric effects of opiates, possibly through receptors in the limbic system, including those in the nucleus accumbens (Chang, Hazum, & Cuatrecasas, 1980). Through an interaction with these systems, ethanol may exert actions that lead to euphoria, thereby promoting further ethanol consumption.

A possible link between ethanol and opiate dependence was proposed in 1970, based on the idea that the ingestion of ethanol could lead to the formation of aberrant alkaloids having opiatelike activity (see Chapter 3). Given the nonspecific effects of ethanol discussed earlier in this chapter, mechanisms involving the endogenous opioids may be modified by the presence of ethanol itself.

To date, most experiments addressing the possible effect of ethanol on opioid mechanisms have used indirect approaches, although some studies, report a direct interaction of ethanol with opiate receptors. At physiologically compatible concentrations of ethanol, the binding of opioid ligands is increased by about 20 percent (Levine, Hess, & Morley, 1983; Tabakoff & Hoffman, 1983). Higher concentrations of ethanol inhibit binding (Hiller, Angel, & Simon, 1981, 1984; Tabakoff & Hoffman, 1983). These data suggest that ethanol consumption might enhance the actions of endogenously released opioids.

Other studies have examined the effectiveness of antagonists of the actions of morphine to block the actions of ethanol. Opiate antagonists, such as naloxone or naltrexone, have been reported to block increased locomotion stimulated by low doses of ethanol (Kiianmaa, Hoffman, & Tabakoff, 1983; Middaugh, Read, & Boggan, 1978) and to reduce ethanol preference (Reid & Hunter, 1984). However, the antagonists reduced self-selection of ethanol only after several days of treatment (Altshuler, Phillips, & Feinhandler, 1980) and had no effect on the ability of animals to discriminate between ethanol and saline (Altshuler, Applebaum, & Shippenberg, 1981; Chipkin, Stewart, & Channabasavaiah, 1980) or on ethanol-induced changes in mood in humans (Ewing & McCarty, 1983).

An effort has been made to correlate the concentrations of endogenous opioids in the brain with ethanol preference. This approach is based on the premise that ethanol consumption may result from the lack of these opioids and represents the organism's attempt to provide some level of psychological "well-being" otherwise afforded by naturally occurring opioids (Blum, Briggs, Elston, & DeLallo, 1980). When two strains of mice, one ethanol-preferring and the other ethanol-nonpreferring, were compared, the ethanol-preferring animals and significantly less met-enkephalin, a naturally occurring opioid, in their brains than the nonpreferring ones (Blum, Elston, DeLallo, Briggs, & Wallace, 1983). These data suggest that abnormally low amounts of opioids contribute to excessive ethanol consumption.

The possibility that an opioid deficiency may underlie ethanol dependence has also been investigated (Blum, et al, 1980). The hypothesis that has been advanced suggests that ethanol consumption increases after chronic administration because naturally occurring opioids are depleted and that drinking ethanol activates opioid mechanisms in the brain to compensate for this loss. This hypothesis is analogous to theories of opiate dependence. It has been suggested that with opiate administration, the opioid receptors are excessively stimulated, resulting in a reduced synthesis of the natural opioids, which are then depleted (Kosterlitz & Hughes, 1975). After withdrawal, a functional deficiency of the opioids occurs. Subsequent opiate administration compensates for this deficiency. If ethanol dependence involves a functional opioid deficiency, several experimental approaches could be taken to test this possibility.

An opioid deficiency might be produced by lowering the concentrations of the endogenous opioids or by interfering with the ability of opioids to interact with their receptors. Chronic ethanol administration leads to a reduction in met-enkephalin concentrations in some areas of the brain (Hong, Majchrowicz, Hunt, & Gillin, 1981; but studies to date that addressed opioid-receptor interactions have shown conflicting results. Both increases and decreases in opioid binding have been observed, depending on the species, area of the brain examined, and the experimental design (Charness, Gordon, & Diamond, 1983; Hoffman, Urwyler, & Tabakoff, 1982; Hynes, Lochner, Bemis, & Hymson,

1983; Lucchi, Bosio, Spano, & Trabucchi, 1981; Lucchi, Rius, Uzumaki, Govoni, & Trabucchi, 1984; Pfeiffer, Seizinger, & Herz, 1981). On the other hand, morphine can suppress an ethanol withdrawal syndrome (Blum, Wallace, Schwertner, & Eubanks, 1976), and ethanol given chronically can suppress a morphine withdrawal syndrome (Jones & Spratto, 1977). Furthermore, animals specifically bred for their sensitivity to ethanol intoxication are also more sensitive than other animals to ethanol- and morphine-induced hypothermia and analgesia (Mayer, Khanna, Kim, & Kalant, 1983) and show more severe ethanol and morphine withdrawal syndromes (Horowitz & Allan, 1982).

These data do not point conclusively to a role of opioid mechanisms in the reinforcing properties of ethanol. No direct evidence is available linking alterations in the release of opioids in the brain to the effects of ethanol. Changes in plasma concentrations of opioids have been reported, however. Ethanol administration to normal human volunteers has been reported to increase plasma opioid activity (Naber, Soble, & Pickar, 1981). In addition, plasma met-enkephalin concentrations were found to be lower in chronic alcoholics and in children whose mothers were alcoholics (Govoni, Bosio, Di Monda, Fazzari, Spano, & Trabucchi, 1983). Although these changes are consistent with the hypotheses developed here, such effects do not directly address changes in the brain.

SUMMARY AND CONCLUSIONS

From the results discussed in this chapter, it is not clear that any specific mechanism can be identified as a single process underlying the reinforcing effects of ethanol. In fact, since ethanol acts on membranes in a relatively nonspecific manner, a variety of mechanisms relevant to reinforcement may be involved. Of course, determining which changes are particularly important has not been easy.

In chapter 3, four criteria for the study of the reinforcing effects of ethanol were discussed. These criteria included a valid animal model, measurable blood-ethanol concentrations after ethanol consumption, a relationship between blood-ethanol concentrations and the reinforcing effects of ethanol, and alterations of ethanol intake by modifying proposed mechanisms of reinforcement. As with the metabolic by-products of ethanol consumption discussed in that chapter, no proposed mechanism for the reinforcing effects of ethanol satisfies all of these criteria. However, some promising leads have developed.

Serotonergic mechanisms appear to be involved in the reinforcing effects of ethanol, a conclusion that is based mainly on studies using pharmacological manipulations. Several reports have suggested that the activity of serotonergic neurons determines the level of ethanol consumption. An inhibitor of serotonin uptake, zimeldine, is currently being tested for its efficacy in reducing ethanol intake, although its utility in treating alcoholism has not been established. Why ethanol intake is reduced by zimeldine is unknown. In fact, it is not clear that inhibition of serotonin uptake is responsible in itself for the reduced ethanol consumption. Some evidence suggests that zimeldine may induce a functional norepinephrine deficiency. As indicated earlier, however, beta-adrenergic antagonists do not antagonize the mood changes induced by ethanol in humans. Moreover, noradrenergic and serotonergic mechanisms have not been implicated in the mechanisms of reward.

On the basis of the available evidence, there are no clear physiological reasons to explain why people drink. Data have failed to demonstrate a direct relationship between the end point being studied and any pharmacological effect of ethanol on the brain. The small differences in ethanol consumption in experimental animals after various manipulations are difficult to relate to compulsively high rates of ethanol intake by alcoholics.

Future research on the biological mechanisms underlying the reinforcing effects of ethanol needs to be more concerned with experimental details. Since ethanol is not freely available to alcoholics, models should be used in which animals work for ethanol. Also, animals must consume enough ethanol to maintain measurable blood-ethanol concentrations and to become intoxicated. Finally, with the introduction of newer drugs with greater specificity, a more precise determination of the mechanisms of ethanol reinforcement might be possible. The knowledge obtained through further, more complete studies could lead to more effective treatments of addictive drinking.

REFERENCES

Ahlenius, S., Carlsson, A., Engel, J., Svensson, H, & Sodersten, P. (1973). Antagonism by *alpha*-methyl-p-tyrosine of the ethanol-induced stimulation and euphoria in man. *Clinical Pharmacology and Therapeutics, 14,* 586–591.

Alkana, R.L., Parker, E.S., Cohen, H.B., Birch, H., & Noble, E.P. (1976). Reversal of ethanol intoxication in humans: An assessment of the efficacy of propranolol. *Psychopharmacology, 51,* 29–37.

Alkana, R.L., Parker, E.S., Cohen, H.B., Birch, H., & Noble, E.P. (1977). Reversal of ethanol intoxication in humans: An assessment of the efficacy of L-DOPA, aminophylline, and ephedrine. *Psychopharmacology, 55*, 203–212.

Altshuler, H.L., Applebaum, E., & Shippenberg, T.S. (1981). The effects of opiate antagonists on the discriminative stimulus properties of ethanol. *Pharmacology, Biochemistry and Behavior, 14*, 97–100.

Altshuler, H.L., Phillips, P.E., & Feinhandler, D.A. (1980). Alteration of ethanol self-administration by naltrexone. *Life Sciences, 26*, 679–688.

Amit, Z., Brown, Z.W., Levitan, D.E., & Ogren, S.O. (1977). Noradrenergic mediation of the positive reinforcing properties of ethanol: I. Suppression of ethanol consumption in rats following dopamine-*beta*-hydroxylase inhibition. *Archives Internationales de Pharmacodynamie et de Therapie, 230*, 65–75.

Amit, Z., Sutherland, E.A., Gill, K., & Ogren, S.O. (1984). Zimeldine: A review of its effects on ethanol consumption. *Neuroscience and Biobehavioral Reviews, 8*, 35–54.

Armstrong, C.M., & Binstock, L. (1964). The effects of several alcohols on the properties of the squid giant axon. *Journal of General Physiology, 48*, 265–277.

Barry, H., III., Wagner, S.A., Miller, N.E. (1963). Effects of several drugs on performance in an approach-avoidance conflict. *Psychological Reports, 12*, 215–221.

Bergmann, M.C., Klee, M.W., & Faber, D.S. (1974). Different sensitivities to ethanol of early transient voltage clamp currents of *Aplysia* neurons. *Pfuegers Arhchives of Physiology, 348*, 139–153.

Blum, K., Briggs, A.H., Elston, S.F.A., & DeLallo, L. (1980). Psychogenetics of drug seeking behavior. *Substance and Alcohol Actions/Misuse, 1*, 255–257.

Blum, K., Elston, S.F.A., DeLallo, L., Briggs, A.H., & Wallace, J.E. (1983). Ethanol acceptance as a function of genotype amounts of brain [Met]enkephalin. *Proceedings of the National Academy of Sciences, 80*, 6510–6512.

Blum, K., Wallace, J.E., Schwetner, H.A., & Eubanks, J. D. (1976). Morphine suppression of ethanol withdrawal in mice. *Experientia, 32*, 79–81.

Borg, A. (1983). Bromocriptine in the prevention of alcohol abuse. *Acta Psychiatrica Scandanavica, 68*, 100–110.

Brown, Z.W., & Amit, Z. (1977). The effects of selective catecholamine depletions by 6-hydroxydopamine on ethanol preference in rats. *Neuroscience Letters, 5*, 333–336.

Brown, Z.W., Amit, Z., Levitan, D.E., Ogren, S.O., & Sutherland, A. (1977). Noradrenergic mediation of the positive reinforcing properties of ethanol. II. Extinction of ethanol drinking behavior in laboratory rats by inhibition of dopamine-*beta*-hydroxylase. Implications for treatment procedures in human alcoholics. *Archives Internationales de Pharmacodynamie et de Therapie, 230*, 76–82.

Brown, Z.W., Gill, K., Abitbol, M., & Amit, Z. (1982). Lack of effect of dopamine receptor blockade on voluntary ethanol consumption in rats. *Behavioral and Neural Biology, 36*, 291–294.

Carlsson, A., Engel, J., Strombom, U., Svensson, T.H., & Waldeck, B. (1974). Suppression by dopamine agonists of the ethanol-induced stimulation of locomotor activity and brain dopamine synthesis. *Naunyn-Schmiedeberg's Archives of Pharmacology, 283*, 117–128.

Carlsson, A., Engel, J., & Svensson, T.H. (1972). Inhibition of ethanol-induced excitation in mice and rats by *alpha*-methyl-p-tyrosine. *Psychoparmacologia (Berlin), 26*, 307–312.

Carlsson, A., & Lindqvist, M. (1973). Effect of ethanol on the hydroxylation of tyrosine and tryptophan in rat brain *in vivo. Journal or Pharmacy and Pharmacology, 25*, 437–440.

Carlsson, A., Magnusson, T., Svensson, T.H., & Waldeck, B. (1973). Effect of ethanol on the metabolism of brain catecholamines. *Psychopharmacologia (Berlin), 30*, 27–36.

Chan, A.W.K., Leong, F.W., & Schanley, D.L. (1983). Influence of chlordiazepoxide on alcohol consumption in mice. *Pharmacology, Biochemistry and Behavior, 18*, 797–802.

Chang, K.-J, Hazum, E., & Cuatrecasas, P. (1980). Multiple opiate receptors. *TINS*, July, 160–162.

Charness, M.E., Gordon, A.S., & Diamond, I. (1983). Ethanol modulation of opiate receptors in cultured neural cells. *Science, 222*, 1246–1248.

Chin, J.H., & Goldstein, D.B. (1977). Effects of low concentrations of ethanol on the fluidity of spin-labeled erythrocytes and brain membranes. *Molecular Pharmacology, 13*, 435–441.

Chin, J.H. & Goldstein, D.B. (1981). Membrane disordering action of ethanol: Variation with membrane cholesterol content and depth of the spin label probe. *Molecular Pharmacology, 19*, 425–431.

Chipkin, R.E., Stewart, J.M., & Channabasavaiah, K. (1980). The effects of peptides on the stimulus properties of ethanol. *Pharmacology, Biochemistry and Behavior, 12*, 93–98.

Cook, L., & Davidson, A. B. (1973). Effects of behaviorally active drugs in a conflict-punishment procedure in rats. In S. Garattini, E. Mussini, L.O. Randall (Eds.), *The benzodiazepines*. New York: Raven Press, pp. 327–345.

Corcoran, M.E., Lewis, J., & Fibiger, H.C. (1983). Forebrain norepinephrine and oral self-administration of ethanol by rats. *Behavioral Brain Research, 8*, 1–21.

Costa, E., Corda, M.G., & Guidotti, E. (1983). On a brain polyeptide functioning as a putative effector for the recognition sites of benzodiazepine and *beta*-carboline derivatives. *Neuropharmacology, 22*, 1481–1492.

Darden, J.H., & Hunt, W.A. (1977). Reduction of striatal dopamine release during an ethanol withdrawal syndrome. *Journal of Neurochemistry, 29*, 1143–1145.

Davis, W.C., & Ticku, M.J. (1981). Ethanol enhances [3H]-diazepam binding at the benzodiazepine-GABA receptor-ionophore complex. *Molecular Pharmacology, 20*, 289–294.

Davis, W.M., Smith, S.G., & Werner, T.E. (1978). Noradrenergic role in the self-administration of ethanol. *Pharmacology, Biochemistry, and Behavior, 9*, 369–374.

Davis W.M., Werner, T.E., & Smith, S.G. (1979). Reinforcement with intragastric infusions of ethanol: Blocking effect of FLA-57. *Pharmacology, Biochemistry, and Behavior, ll*, 545–548.

Deutsch, J.A., & Walton, N.Y. (1977). Diazepam maintenance of alcohol preference during alcohol withdrawal. *Science, 198*, 307–309.

Durand, D., Corrigall, W.A., Kujtan, P., & Carlen, P.L. (1981). Effects of low concentrations of ethanol on CAl hippocampal neurons *in vitro. Canadian Journal of Physiology and Pharmacology, 59*, 979–984.

Ewing, J.A., & McCarty, D. (1983). Are the endorphins involved in mediating the mood effects of ethanol? *Alcoholism: Clinical and Experimental Research, 7,* 271–275.

Fadda, F., Argiolas, A., Melis, M.R., De Montis, G., & Gessa, G.L. (1983). Suppression of voluntary ethanol consumption in rats by *gamma*-butyrolactone. *Life Sciences, 32,* 1471–1477.

Ferguson, J. (1939). The use of chemical potentials as indices of toxicity. *Proceedings of the Royal Society of London. Series B, 127,* 387–404.

Ferko, A.P., Bobyock, E., & Chernick, W.S. (1979). A study on diazepam and postwithdrawal drinking of ethanol solutions in rats. *Toxicology and Applied Pharmacology, 50,* 355–363.

Frey, H.-H., Magnussen, M.P., & Kaergaard Nielsen, C. (1970). The effect of p-chloroamphetamine on the consumption of ethanol by rats. *Archives Internationales de Pharmacodynamie et de Therapie, 183,* 165–172.

Gee, K.W., Ehlert, F.J., & Yamamura, H.I. (1983). Differential effects of *gamma*-aminobutyric acid on benzodiazepine receptor subtypes labeled by [3H]propyl-*beta*-carboline-3-carboxylate in the rat brain. *Journal of Pharmacology and Experimental Therapeutics, 225,* 132–137.

Geller, I., Croy, D.J., & Ryback, R.S. (1974). Effects of ethanol and sodium pentobarbital on conflict behavior of goldfish (*Carassius auratus*). *Pharmacology, Biochemistry, and Behavior, 2,* 545–548.

Geller, I., Hartmann, R.J., & Messiha, F.S. (1981). Blockade of 5-HTP reduction of ethanol drinking with the decarboxylase inhibitor, Ro 4–4602. *Pharmacology, Biochemistry and Behavior, 15,* 871–874.

Glowa, J.R., & Barrett, J.E. (1976). Effects of alcohol on punished and unpunished responding of squirrel monkeys. *Pharmacology, Biochemistry, and Behavior, 4,* 169–173.

Govoni, S., Bosio, A., Di Monda, E., Fazzari, G., Spano, P.F., & Trabucchi, M. (1983). Immunoreactive met-enkephalin plasma concentrations in chronic alcoholics and in children born from alcoholic mothers. *Life Sciences, 33,* 1581–1586.

Harris, R.A., & Bruno, P. (1985). Effects of ethanol and other intoxicant-anesthetics on voltage-dependent sodium channels of brain synaptosomes. *Journal of Pharmacology and Experimental Therapeutics, 232,* 401–406.

Harris, R.A., & Schroeder, F. (1981). Ethanol and the physical properties of brain membranes: Fluorescence properties. *Molecular Pharmacology, 20,* 128–137.

Hiller, J.M., Angel, L.M., & Simon, E.J. (1981). Multiple opiate receptors: Alcohol selectively inhibits binding to *delta* receptors. *Science, 214,* 468–469.

Hiller, J.M., Angel, L.M., & Simon, E.J. (1984). Characterization of the selective inhibition of the *delta* subclass of opioid binding sites by alcohols. *Molecular Pharmacology, 25,* 249–255.

Ho Hobbs, A.L., & Albers, R.W. (1980). The structure of proteins involved in active membrane transport. *Annual Reviews of Biophysics and Bioengineering, 9,* 259–291.

Hodgkin A.L., & Huxley, A.F. (1952)). A quantitative description of membrane current and its application to conduction and excitation in nerve. *Journal of Physiology, 117,* 500–544.

Hoffman, P.L., & Tabakoff, B. (1982). Effects of ethanol on Arrhenius parameters and activity of mouse striatal adenylate cyclase. *Biochemical Pharmacology, 31,* 3101–3106.

Hoffman, P.L., Urwyler, S., & Tabakoff, B. (1982). Alterations in opiate receptor function after chronic ethanol exposure. *Journal of Pharmacology and Experimental Therapeutics, 222,*, 182–189.

Ho, A.K.S., Tsai, C.S., Chen, R.C.A., Begleiter, H., & Kissin, B. (1974). Experimental studies on alcoholism I. Increased in alcohol preference by 5,6-dihydroxytryptamine and brain acetylcholine. *Psychopharmacologia (Berlin), 40* 101–107.

Hong, J.S., Majchrowicz, E., Hunt, W.A., & Gillin, J.C. (1981). Reduction in cerebral methionine-enkephalin content during the ethanol withdrawal syndrome. *Substance and Alcohol Actions/Misuse 2,* 233–240.

Horowitz, G.P., & Allan, A.M. (1982). Morphine withdrawal in mice selectively bred for differential sensitivity to ethanol. *Pharmacology, Biochemistry, and Behavior, 16,* 35–39.

Hunt, W.A. (1981). Neurotransmitter function in the basal ganglia after acute and chronic ethanol treatment. *Federation Proceedings, 40,* 2077–2081.

Hunt, W.A. (1983). Ethanol and the central nervous system. In B. Tabakoff, P.B. Sutker, and C.L. Randall (Eds.), *Medical and social aspects of alcohol abuse.* New York: Plenum Press, pp. 133–163.

Hunt, W.A. (1985). *Alcohol and biological membranes.* New York: Guilford Press.

Hunt W.A., Dalton, T.K., Majchrowicz, E., & Mullin, M.J. (1985). Regional differences in dopamine metabolism after acute and chronic ethanol administration. *Federation Proceedings, 44* 1484.

Hunt, W.A., & Majchrowicz, E. (1979). Alterations in neurotransmitter function after acute and chronic treatment with ethanol. In E. Majchrowicz and E.P. Noble (Eds.), *Biochemistry and pharmacology of ethanol,* Vol. 2. New York: Plenum Press. pp. 167–185.

Hynes, M.D., Lochner, M.A., Bemis, K.G., & Hymson, D.L. (1983). Chronic ethanol alters the receptor binding characteristics of the *delta* opioid receptor ligand, D-ala2-D-Leu5 enkephalin in mouse brain. *Life Sciences, 33,* 2331–2337.

Israel, Y, Kalant, H., & Laufer, I. (1965). Effects of ethanol on Na, K, Mg-stimulated microsomal ATPase activity. *Biochemical Pharmacology, 14,* 1803–1814.

Jones, M.A., & Spratto, G.B. (1977). Ethanol suppression of naloxone-induced withdrawal in morphine-dependent rats. *Life Sciences, 20,* 1549–1556.

Kiianmaa, K., Anderson, K., & Fuxe, K. (1979). On the role of ascending dopamine systems in the control of voluntary ethanol intake and ethanol intoxication. *Pharmacology, Biochemistry, and Behavior, 10* 603–608.

Kiianmaa, K., Hoffman, P.L., & Tabakoff, B. (1983) Antagonism of the behavioral effects of ethanol by naltrexone in BALB/c, C57BL/6, and DBA/2 mice. *Psychopharmacology, 79,* 291–294.

Kosterlitz, H.L., & Hughes, J. (1975). Some thoughts on the significance of enkephalin, the endogenous ligand. *Life Sciences, 17* 91–96.

Lal, H., & Emmett-Oglesby, M.W. (1983). Behavioral analogues of anxiety: Animal models. *Neuropharmacology, 22,* 1423–1441.

lefkowitz, R.J., Limbard, L.E., Mukherjee, C., & Caron, M. G. (1976). The *beta*-adrenergic receptor and adenylate cyclase. *Biochimica et Biophysica Acta, 457,* 1–39.

Leslie, S.W., Barr, E., Chandler, J., & Farrar, R.P. (1983). Inhibition of fast- and slow-phase depolarization-dependent synaptosomal calcium uptake by ethanol. *Journal of Pharmacology and Experimental Therapeutics, 225* 571–575.

Levine, A.S., Hess, S., & Morley, J.E. (1983). Alcohol and the opiate receptor. *Alcoholism: Clinical and Experimental Research, 7,* 83–92.

Linnoila, M., Johnson, J., Dubyoski, T., Ross, R., Buchsbaum, M., Potter, W.Z., & Weingartner, H. (1983). Effects of amitriptyline, desipramine, and zimeldine, alone and in combination with ethanol, on information processing and memory in health volunteers. *Acta Psychiatrica Scandanavica, suppl. 308, 68,* 175–181.

Lucchi, L., Bosio, A., Spano, P.F., & Trabucchi, M. (1981). Action of ethanol and salsolinol on opiate receptor function. *Brain Research 232,* 506–510.

Lucchi, L., Rius, R.A., Uzumaki, H., Govoni, S., & Trabucchi, M. (1984). Chronic ethanol changes opiate receptor function in rat striatum. *Brain Research, 293,* 368–371.

Matchett, J.A., & Erickson, C.K. (1977). Alteration of ethanol-induced changes in locomotor activity by adrenergic blockers in mice. *Psychopharmacology, 52,* 201–206.

Mayer, J.M., Khanna, J.M. Kim, C., & Kalant, H. (1983). Differential pharmacological responses to ethanol, pentobarbital, and morphine in rats selectively bred for ethanol sensitivity. *Psychopharmacology, 81* 6–9.

McCreery, M.J. & Hunt, W.A. (1978). Physicochemical correlates of alcohol intoxication. *Neuropharmacology, 17,* 451–461.

McMillan, D.E, & Leander, J.D. (1975). Drugs and punished responding: Effects of drugs on responding suppressed by response-dependent and response-independent electric shock. *Archives Internationales de Pharmacodynamie et de Therapie, 213,* 22–27.

Mendelson, J.H., Rossi, A.M., Bernstein, J.G., & Kuehnle, J. (1974). Propranolol and behavior of alcohol addicts after acute alcohol ingestion. *Clinical Pharmacology and Therapeutics, 15* 571–578.

Mereu, G., Fadda, F., & Gessa, G.L. (1984). Ethanol stimulates the firing rate of nigral dopaminergic neurons in unanesthetized rats. *Brain Research, 292,* 63–69.

Meyer, H. (1901). Zur Theorie der Alkolnarkoso: Der Einfuss wechselnder Temperatur auf Wirkungsstarke and Theilungscoefficient der Narcotica. *Naunyn-Schmiedeberg's Archiv fur Experimentelle Pathologie und Pharmacokologie, 46,* 338–346.

Middaugh, L.D., Read, E., & Boggan, W.O. (1978). Effects of naloxone on ethanol induced alterations of locomotor activity. *Pharmacology, Biochemistry, and Behavior, 9,* 157–160.

Moore, J.W., Ulbricht, W., & Takata, M. (1964). Effect of ethanol on the sodium and potassium conductances of the squid axon membrane. *Journal of General Physiology, 48* 279–295.

Mullin, M.J., & Hunt, W.A. (1985). Actions of ethanol on voltage-sensitive sodium channels: Effects on neurotoxin-stimulated sodium uptake in synaptosomes. *Journal of Pharmacology and Experimental Therapeutics, 232,* 413-419.

Mullins, L.J. (1954). Some physical mechanisms of narcosis. *Chemical Reviews, 54,* 289–323.

Murphy, J.M., McBride, W.J., Lumeng, L., & Li, T.-K. (1983). Monoamine and metabolite levels in CNS regions of the P line of alcohol-preferring rats after acute and chronic ethanol treatment. *Pharmacology, Biochemistry, and Behavior, 19* 849 856.

Myers, R.D., & Melchior, L. (1975). Alcohol drinking in the rat after destruction of serotonergic and catecholaminergic neurons in the brain. *Research Communications in Chemical Pathology and Pharmacology, 10,* 363–378.

Naber, D. Soble, M.G., & Pickar, D. (1981). Ethanol increases opioid activity in plasma volunteers. *Pharmacopysychiatry, 14,* 160–161.

Naranjo, C.A., Lawrin, M., Addison, D., Roach, C.A., Harrison, M., Sanchez-Craig, M., & Sellers, E.M. (1983). Zimeldine decreases alcohol consumption in non-depressed heavy drinkers. *Clinical Pharmacology and Therapy, 33,* 241.

Olds, J., & Milner, P.M. (1954). Positive reinforcement produced by electrical stimulation of septal area and other regions of the rat brain. *Journal of Comparative Physiological Psychology, 47,* 419–427.

Olsen, R.W. (1981). GABA-benzodiazepine-barbiturate receptor interactions. *Journal of Neurochemistry, 37,* 1–13

Overton, E. (1901). *Studien ueber die narkose zugleich ein beitrag zur allgemeinen pharmakologie.* Jena: Verlag von Gustav Fischer.

Pettit, H.O., Ettenberg, A., Bloom, F.E., & Koob, G.F. (1984). Destruction of dopamine in the nucleus accumbens selectively attenuates cocaine but not heroin self-administration in rats. *Psychopharmacology, 84,* 167–173.

Pfeiffer, A., Seizinger, B.R., & Herz, A. (1981). Chronic ethanol imbibition interferes with *delta-*, but not with mu-opiate receptors. *Neuropharmacology, 20,* 1229–1232.

Phillips, A.G. (1984). Brain reward circuitry: A case for separate systems. *Brain Research Bulletin, 12* 195–201.

Potthoff, A.D., Ellison, G., & Nelson, L. (1983). Ethanol intake increases during continuous administration of amphetamine and nicotine, but not several other drugs. *Pharmacology, Biochemistry, and Behavior, 18,* 489–493.

Rabin, R.A., & Molinoff, P.B. (1981). Activation of adenylate cyclase by ethanol in mouse striatal tissue. *Journal of Pharmacology and Experimental Therapeutics, 216,* 129–134.

Reid, L.D., & Hunter, G.A. (1984). Morphine and naloxone modulate intake of ethanol. *Alcohol, 1,* 33–37.

Rockman, G.E., Amit, Z., Carr, G., & Ogren, S.O. (1979). Attenuation of ethanol intake by 5-hydroxytryptamine uptake blockade in laboratory rats. I. Involvment of brain 5-hydroxytryptamine in the meditation of the positive reinforcing properties of ethanol. *Archives Internationale de Pharmacodynamie et de Therapie, 241,*, 245–259.

Rockman, G. E., Amit, Z., Carr, G., & Ogren, S. D. (1979). Attenuation of ethanol intake by 5-hydroxytryptamine uptake blockade in laboratory rats: II. Possible interaction with brain norepinephrine. *Archives Internationale de Pharmacodynamie et de Therapie, 241,* 260–265.

Rockman, G. E., Amit, Z., Brown, Z. W., Bourque, C., & Ogren, S.O. (1982). An investigation of the mechanisms of action of 5-hydroxytryptamine in the suppression of ethanol intake. *Neuropharmacology, 21,* 341–347.

Sanders, B., Collins, A.C., & Wesley, V.H. (1976). Reduction of alcohol selection by pargyline in mice. *Psychopharmacologia, 46,* 159–162.

Seeman, P. (1974). The membrane expansion theory of anesthesia: Direct evidence using ethanol and a high-precision density meter. *Experientia, 30,* 759–760.

Snyder, S.H. (1984). Drug and neurotransmitter receptors in the brain. *Science, 224* 22–31.

Sprince, H., Parker C.M., Smith, G.G., & Gonzales, L.J. (1972). Alcoholism: Biochemical and nutritional aspects of brain amines, aldehydes, and amino acids. *Nutrition Reports International, 5,* 185–200.

Stein, J.M., Wayner, M.J., & Tilson, H.A. (1977). The effect of para-chlorophenylalanine on the intake of ethanol and saccharin solutions. *Pharmacology, Biochemistry, and Behavior, 6,* 117–122.

Schulz, R., Wüster, M., Duke, T., & Herz, a. (1980). Acute and chronic ethanol treatment changes endorphin levels in brain and pituitary. *Psychopharmacology, 68,* 221–227.

Stephens, D.N., Kehr, W., Schneider, H.W., & Schmiechen, R. (1984). *Beta*-carbolines with agonistic and inverse agonistic properties at benzodiazepine receptors of the rat. *Neuroscience Letters, 47* 333–338.

Tabakoff, B., & Hoffman, P. (1983). Alcohol interactions with brain opiate receptors. *Life Sciences, 32,* 197–204.

Ticku, M.J., & Burch, T. (1980). Alterations in GABA receptor sensitivity following acute and chronic ethanol treatments. *Journal of Neurochemistry, 34,* 417–423.

Ticku, M.J., & Davis, W.C. (1981). Evidence that ethanol and pentobarbital enhances [3H]-diazepam binding at the benzodiazepine-GABA receptor-ionophore complex indirectly. *European Journal of Pharmacology, 71,* 521–522.

Veale, W.L., & Myers, R.D. (1970). Decrease in ethanol intake in rats following administration of p-chlorophenylalanine. *Neuropharmacology, 9,* 317–326.

Vincent, S.R., Hokfelt, T., Christensson, I., & Teronius, L. (1982). Dynorphin-immunoreactive neurons in the central neurons system of the rat. *Neuroscience Letters, 33,* 185–190.

Vogel, R.A., Frye, G.D., Wilson, J.H., Kuhn, C.M., Koepke, K.M., Mailman, R.B., Mueller, R.A., & Breese, G.R. (1980). Attenuation of the effects of punishment by ethanol: Comparisons with chlordiazepoxide. *Psychopharmacology, 71,* 123–129.

Wetson, S.J., Khachatarian, H., Akil, H., Coy, D., & Goldstein, A. (1982). Comparison of the distribution of dynorphin systems and enkephalin systems in brain. *Science, 218,* 1134–1136.

Wise, R.A., & Bozarth, M.A. (1984). Brain reward circuitry: Four circuit elements "wired" in apparent series. *Brain Research Bulletin, 12,* 203–208.

Woo, E., & Greenblatt, D.J. (1979). Massive benzodiazepine requirements during acute ethanol withdrawal. *American Journal of Psychiatry, 136,* 821–823.

Zabik, J.E., Liao, S.S., Jeffreys, M., & Maickel, R.P. (1978). The effects of DL-5-hydroxytryptophan on ethanol consumption by rats. *Research Communications in Chemical Pathology and Pharmacology, 20,* 69–78.

Zakusov, V.V., Lyubimov, B.I., Yavorsku, A.N., & Folin, V.I. (1979). Effect of phenazepam on ethanol intake in rats. *Bulletin of Experimental Biology and Medicine, 88,* 708–711.

FIVE

ALCOHOL CONSUMPTION, TENSION REDUCTION AND MOOD ENHANCEMENT

JEFFREY A. WEST, Ph.D., and
PATRICIA B. SUTKER, Ph.D.

Throughout history, drinking behaviors have been explained by conceptualizations of alcohol as a palliative agent with reinforcing properties, especially as regards mood states. In large part, drinking phenomena have been related to the hypothesis that alcohol alters affect in a reinforcing manner and is consumed because of this property. Beliefs that alcohol ameliorates dysphoria and reduces tension are reflected in the self-reports of various groups of drinkers, but the extent of these effects has been found to be related to individual drinking patterns. For example, Cahalan (1970) discovered that heavy or problem drinkers reported greater stress reduction from alcohol than did light or nonproblem drinkers. Such notions have been expressed formally as the tension reduction (TR) hypothesis by Conger (1956), who suggested that alcohol reduces tension and that organisms consume alcohol as a consequence of this effect.

The preparation of this chapter was supported by Research Grant AA 05673 awarded to the second author by the National Institute on Alcohol Abuse and Alcoholism. The authors express their appreciation to Albert N. Allain, Jr., for his assistance in the preparation of this manuscript.
Request for reprints may be mailed to Patricia B. Sutker, Chief, Psychology Service, VAMC, 1601 Perdido St., New Orleans, LA 70146.

The belief that alcohol consumption relieves tension has stimulated research efforts for the past 40 years. Although a simple construct, the TR hypothesis has been conceptualized in various ways and tested in diverse animal and human experimental paradigms. It has been hypothesized that external stressors and/or negative mood states comprise antecedent conditions or discriminative stimuli for alcohol consumption, which are negatively reinforced by the alleviation of psychological distress following drinking. Consumption of alcohol, however, may also induce euphoria and thus be positively reinforcing. The latter hypothesis has received comparatively little experimental attention. Both accounts predict enhancement of perceived mood following alcohol ingestion, but they suggest that different antecedent events may be important in determining drinking. Whether positive or negative reinforcing effects of alcohol are more salient in a given situation varies across persons and during the course of drinking histories (Cox, 1987).

Studies relating negative life events to alcohol consumption suggest that alcoholics drink to alleviate their distressed mood. A majority of relapsed alcoholics sampled by Marlatt and Gordon (1980) indicated that they resumed drinking in response to psychologial stressors, which presumably involved negative emotional states. The relationship between negative affect and alcohol abuse is also indicated by findings that alcoholism is frequently associated with affective disorder, and the two conditions seem to exacerbate each other (Hesselbrock, Meyer, & Keener, 1985; Schuckit, 1985). In fact, it has been hypothesized that some types of alcoholism represent a form of primary depression (Winokur, Clayton, & Reich, 1969), and secondary depression has been diagnosed in a large proportion of primary alcoholics (Cadoret & Winokur, 1974). Certain individuals with bipolar affective disorder show significant abuse of alcohol (Reich, Davies, & Hemmilhoch, 1974). Similarly, anxiety disorders, including agoraphobia (Mullaney & Trippett, 1979), social phobia (Smail, Stockwell, Canter, & Hodgson, 1984), and posttraumatic stress disorder (LaCoursiere, Godfrey, & Ruby, 1980), have been associated with problem drinking.

Mood factors have been identified as antecedents and consequences of drinking among nonproblem as well as problem drinkers. Of recent interest has been a description of the biphasic nature of acute alcohol intoxication, including the time-limited mood-enhancing properties of alcohol (Sutker, Tabakoff, Goist, & Randall, 1983). Thus information about alcohol-mood interactions can be seen as contributing to an understanding of the etiology, maintenance, and consequences of alcohol use and abuse in heterogeneous drinking groups and as having application to the treatment and prevention of alcohol-related problems. Among other possibilities, alcohol may be viewed as a mood-elevating agent, one offering relief from negative affect, including anxiety and depression, and one associated with other transitory or chronic mood state changes.

The purpose of this chapter is to summarize extant findings descriptive of relationships between alcohol consumption and mood states. Of primary interest is the TR hypothesis and the wealth of experimental data generated by animal and human studies testing this notion. Although perhaps of limited value as an explanatory construct, the TR hypothesis continues to influence the design of experimental studies and to underlie clinical accounts of drinking motives. It constitutes a time-preserved explanation of alcohol consumption, despite its simplistic nature and equivocal experimental support (Freed, 1978; Langenbucher & Nathan, 1983; Sher, 1984; Wilson, 1982). A second interest is the recent study of euphorigenic or mood-enhancement effects of drinking, which may be especially important in the absence of preexisting tension-related states. Rather than duplicate comprehensive literature reviews, we shall concentrate on recent tests of hypotheses related to tension reduction and on studies exploring relationships between alcohol consumption and antecedent and consequent affective states. Although the research discussed may have relevance to chronic alcohol ingestion, the acute effects of intoxication are of primary interest.

ALCOHOL AND TENSION REDUCTION

Animal Investigations

Animal experimentation has figured prominently in focusing attention on the tension reduction model of alcohol consumption. Some of the earliest experimental work testing the TR hypothesis was performed by animal researchers in the late 1940s and the 1950s using approach/avoidance conflict paradigms. For example, Masserman and Yum (1946) found that the "neurotic tension" displayed by hungry cats following repeated exposure to a situation of conflict between food and aversive electric shock or air blasts was reduced by ingestion of an available admixture of alcohol. Animals showed stronger goal-oriented behavior under conflict following alcohol consumption and developed a preference for foods with the admixture. In another early study, Conger (1951) demonstrated that alcohol injections in rats restored goal-orienting and eating behaviors that had been disrupted by shocking the animals as they approached food.

Conger's (1956) work has been seen as an impetus for systematic study of the TR hypothesis. Grounded in Hullian theory, he argued that drinking reinforces drive-reducing properties. Principal support for this notion was derived from demonstrations that alcohol consumption reduced avoidance responses and disruptions of goal-directed behaviors typically observed in rats and other animals under conditions of approach–avoidance conflict. Conger suggested that drinking was reinforced because alcohol reduced fear and tension engendered by the conflict. Since Conger's classic paper, studies of the effects of alcohol on conflict have continued to provide support for the TR hypothesis. For example, recent experiments with various species have quantified with precision the restorative effects of alcohol on operant response rates previously suppressed by punishment (e.g., Vogel et al., 1980). Full discussion of animal experiments, however, falls beyond the scope of this chapter, and the reader is referred to a series of reviews by Cappell and his associates (Cappel, 1975; Cappell & Greeley, 1986; Cappell & Herman, 1972).

In a widely cited critique of the TR hypothesis, Cappell and Herman (1972) described various categories of studies testing the TR hypothesis. These studies investigated the effect of alcohol on escape and avoidance, conditioned suppression, extinction and partial reinforcement, and stress-related disruptions such as induced audiogenic seizures in rats. The reviewers assumed that the variety of aversive procedures under scrutiny in these experiments involved negative emotional substrates such as anxiety, fear, frustration, and ambivalence, all of which could be construed as tension-related sources of motivation for behavior. The studies were designed to explore the effects of beverage or intravenous (IV) alcohol on animal responses under the stressful conditions. Cappell and Herman concluded that much of the evidence on the tension-reducing effects of alcohol was negative, equivocal, or contradictory, with the exception of conflict experiments such as those of Conger (1951) and Barry and Miller (1965).

Taking a different view of the approach–avoidance literature, Brown and Crowell (1974) argued that if alcohol consumption reduces anxiety, it should increase the tendency to approach a bivalent goal. However, this would increase rather than decrease an approach–avoidance conflict, because movement toward a bivalent goal necessarily intensifies the conflict. Thus, according to this analysis, alcohol consumption in the earlier studies on approach–avoidance conflict could not have been reinforced by reduced tension. In reexamining the applicability of extant data to the TR hypothesis, Hodgson, Stockwell, and Rankin (1979) distinguished between active and passive and one-way and two-way avoidance responses and argued that these are not equally motivated by fear or anxiety. Only passive avoidance achieved by inhibition of responding was reasoned to be affected by alcohol in a manner consistent with the TR model. They concluded that a restricted range of investigations among those reviewed by Cappell and Herman (1972) are germane to the TR model, and that these affirm the hypothesis. As additional support, Hodgson et al. (1979) summarized a series of rat experiments (Gray, 1976; Gray & Ball, 1970) that suggested that high-voltage hippocampal theta rhythms, associated reliably with conditions engendering anxiety and frustration, were inhibited following acute alcohol administration.

The Brown and Crowell (1974) and Hodgson et al. (1979) papers called attention to a central difficulty in execution and interpretation of TR research. That is, they raised questions about integrating a body of findings derived from methodologically diverse experimental designs having questionable relevance to the TR model. Although important methodological criticisms also have appeared in the literature (e.g., Freed, 1967), in large part the divergent conclusions of these and other reviewers have reflected differences in intrepretation and assumptions regarding the relevance of experimental results. Typically, the TR hypothesis has been formulated in a simplistic and nonspecific manner that has promoted latitude in defining the key constructs of "tension" and "tension reduction." This oversimplification has contributed to the absence of consensus evident in reviews of this literature. The actions of alcohol on behavior, even for time-limited periods under carefully controlled conditions, vary across different situations in which tension has been presumed to be induced.

In the years following Conger's (1956) formulations, animal research exploring the TR hypothesis continued, in the hope of finding explanations for human drinking. In fact, findings with animals initially were generalized to human drinkers without direct verification. Thus, in most cases, it was assumed that the behavioral effects of alcohol consumption could be attributed exclusively to pharmacological actions of the drug. In recent years, these practices have been challenged in the human literature. Although the effects of alcohol on such responses as avoidance, escape, and conditioned suppression remain a focus for study (e.g., Bammer & Chesher, 1982; Cunningham & Brown, 1983; Skurdal, Eckardt, & Brown, 1975), the relevance of this literature is controversial, and its application to the TR hypothesis is limited by methodological and interpretative difficulties. Typically, later animal research has tested more circumscribed predictions formulated from the TR hypothesis or alternative explanations than did earlier work, and the scope of this research has been broadened to include more specific tests of the TR model.

Of primary interest for the present discussion are data gathered from experimental conflict procedures applied to animal drinking paradigms. Anisman and Waller (1973), for example, conducted five experiments in which presumed stress resulting from inescapable and unavoidable shock produced increased alcohol self-selection in rats, an effect consistent with the TR hypothesis. Interestingly, however, animals did not increase their consumption of alcohol when a conflict situation was created by delivering shock exclusively in the cage areas where food was available—a finding that appears to be inconsistent with the TR hypothesis. The authors suggested that the degree of control over shock afforded and/or the availability of coping responses other than alcohol consumption may have mediated the amount of alcohol selected. As will be described subsequently, similar conclusions have been offered by investigators of human drinking.

Gathering additional data with the conflict paradigm, Mansfield and his associates (Mansfield, 1979; Mansfield, Eaton, Cunningham, & Brown, 1977) demonstrated that moderate doses of alcohol weaken conflicting response tendencies in an avoidance–avoidance conflict situation. Based in part upon this work, Brown, Mansfield, and Skurdaal (1980) offered support for an alternative account of the effects of alcohol on tension-related conflict behavior. In a departure from the classic TR model, which assumes that alcohol reduces conflict by selectively weakening fear-motivated avoidance, these investigators hypothesized that alcohol reduces the capacity of the weaker of any two competitive tendencies to interfere with the stronger. Although, under some conditions, this hypothesis leads to predictions identical to those of Conger (1956), in cases such as avoidance–avoidance paradigms it does not. Brown et al. (1980) reported the results of several studies in which inebriated rats approached a bivalent region more closely than did control animals; however, when placed in the apparatus at a point where the tendency to avoid was stronger than the tendency to approach, the alcohol-dosed rats retreated farther from the bivalent goal than did those saline-dosed—a finding not predicted by the TR hypothesis as originally formulated by Conger (1956). The authors considered several mechanisms to account for these interference-reduction effects, including the possibility that alcohol interferes with the ability to attend simultaneously to sets of cues affecting incompatible responses, such that only more salient or powerful cues are functionally effective in influencing behavior.

At present, conflict studies appear to offer the most robust experimental support in the animal literature for a specialized TR model. Researchers have demonstrated that alcohol intoxication can modify responses that are presumed to be motivated by tension in situations that produce conflicting response tendencies. As noted, Hodgson et al. (1979) have argued that such a paradigm (i.e., involving passive avoidance of fear-arousing stimuli) offers a reasonable test of the TR hypothesis. However, the majority of the conflict studies discussed here, though consistent with the TR model, have failed to rule out alternative mechanisms that could produce similar results. For example, Glowa and Barrett (1976) showed that alcohol increased low rates of operant responding in squirrel monkeys not only when these rates reflected suppression by punishment or conflict (the finding apparently supporting the TR hypothesis), but also when they did not result from such suppression. These results raise the possibility that a TR mechanism is unnecessary to explain the body of findings on conflict.

As in other areas of research on drug abuse, animal studies are valuable for exploring mechanisms such as tension reduction that may underlie the consumption of alcohol. The limitations of animal experimentation have been described well by Hodgson et al. (1979), who chose simply to consider whether such research indicates that alcohol can reduce tension under certain conditions. Animal research has been judged only tenuously relevant to human patterns of consumption, because the important role of mediating cognitive processes in humans cannot be assessed in animals (Wilson, 1982). Yet, animal work affords an opportunity to investigate under controlled conditions some of the basic conditioning processes with which cognitive and other variables could interact to determine alcohol consumption among humans. Although many of the findings generated by animal studies strongly suggest that alcohol alters tension-related behaviors, few data address adequately the question of whether nonhuman organisms drink alcohol because it reduces tension. The animal literature reflects controversy on the issue, but much of the work suggests that the negatively reinforcing effects of alcohol in reducing tension may be overshadowed by other controlling factors.

Human Investigations

Influenced by both the animal literature and clinical lore, researchers have tested formulations of the TR hypothesis among human subjects using a variety of design strategies. These studies range from cross-sectional interview and survey investigations to analogue drinking paradigms devised to explore acute and chronic intoxication. Interestingly, aspects of analogue drinking situations have often failed to mimic conditions fundamental to actual drinking conditions, and thus the work has been critized on some of the same grounds as have the animal studies reviewed above, for example, questionable relevance to human drinking in context. Nevertheless, valuable data describing drinking behaviors and their emotional correlates have been generated in the laboratory among both alcoholic and nonproblem drinking samples. In many of these studies, indices of affective responses have included self-report ratings on checklists or inventories, continuous self-report monitoring of various states, behavioral ratings of affective states, and psychophysiological measures of stress-related phenomena. As in the animal literature, much of the research has addressed that aspect of the TR model that posits that alcohol alters tension- or stress-related responses. There has been less extensive testing of the notion that beverage alcohol is consumed as a consequence of its tension reduction effects.

Methodological Considerations. It is impossible to consider the research designed to explore the TR hypothesis without acknowledging some of the methodological shortcomings common across studies. These include problems related to nonrepresentative subject samples, neglected individual difference factors such as drinking histories and familial histories of alcoholism, inadequately justified dependent variables, disparate drinking contexts in laboratory paradigms, poorly controlled placebo, expectancy and instructional effects, and imprecisely specified doses, blood–alcohol concentrations (BACs), and dependent variables. It has been observed that dependent measures assumed to reflect similar substrates typically have shown low to moderate correlations, suggesting that separate response systems are influenced by divergent sets of variables (cf. Lang, 1969). Some measures of depression and anxiety have shown reductions in negative affect or arousal under drinking-related conditions in which others do not. This difference in itself has served as a focus for experimental investigation (e.g., Steffen, Nathan, & Taylor, 1974), which has thus far yielded little theoretical resolution. In any case, the methodological limitations charaterizing the TR literature on human subjects have been well summarized by Collins and Marlatt (1983), Higgins (1976), and Wilson (1982) and need not be reiterated here, except as related to more recent developments.

If the methodological problems deserve notice, advances in design strategy over the past few years should also be mentioned. Although we are still far from a generalized understanding of the relationships between alcohol and tension reduction, there is evidence that researchers have recognized and begun to address some of the deficiencies noted above. Examination of published work since the critical reviews of the 1970s suggests that there has been a worthwhile expansion of types of subject populations and drinking contexts. Some investigators have turned away from the use of college male samples, and there have been attempts to identify and investigate individual differences that interact with drinking behaviors and risk for alcohol abuse. Development of a wider range of dependent variables and the use of multivariate methodology to assess different response systems have enhanced the quality and sophistication of recent studies. Greater attention has also been directed toward dose and time variables that influence the effects of consuming alcohol in any given context.

Among other significant improvements has been the attempt to control for the influence of strong subject expectations regarding the effects of alcohol consumption on mood and behavior. Although a few researchers used IV administration and other procedures to lessen nonpharmacological influences on subjects in intoxication experiments (e.g., Mayfield & Allen, 1967), it was not until application of the completely balanced-placebo design that systematically varied expectancy conditions were investigated in studies involving alcohol and stress. The balanced-placebo approach was described by Lyerly, Ross, Krugman, and Clyde (1964) and advanced by Marlatt and his colleagues, who pioneered studies examining alcohol/expectancy effects on various response systems including affective variables (Marlatt & Rohsenow, 1980). The various studies executed to clarify nonpharmacological mediating variables influencing initiation and response to drinking behaviors sometimes have found expectation of intoxication to exert greater impact on affective expression than actual alcohol consumption, at least at mild dose levels (see Chapter 8 in this volume). This finding can be seen as consistent with the TR hypothesis, if the latter is extended to include actions beyond those attributed to pharmacology.

Problem-Drinker and Alcoholic Samples. The effects of alcohol on mood states have been examined in acute and chronic intoxication paradigms among samples representing several drinking groups. Early studies targeted alcoholic subjects, because they were expected to exhibit maximal drinking effects such as relief from high levels of anxiety and depression. Fleetwood (1955) provided tentative support for the notion that alcoholics derive greater relief from dysphoria than do nonalcoholics as a consequence of intoxication. In contrast, most subsequent early reports suggested the opposite (e.g., Diethelm & Barr, 1962). The majority of studies of alcoholics in chronic drinking situations have shown eventual deterioration in mood states, with increased self-reported anxiety and depression confirmed by observational data (McGuire, Stein, & Mendelson, 1966; McNamee, Mello, & Mendelson, 1968; Mendelson, LaDou, & Solomon, 1964; Nathan & O'Brien, 1971; Nathan, Titler, Lowenstein, Solomon, & Rossi, 1970). These studies used drinking periods of four to 24 days and generally found adverse effects on mood within 72 hours after the onset of drinking. In some cases, transient euphoric reactions or reductions in dysphoria were described during the first 24 hours of drinking.

Mello and Mendelson (1970) and Tamerin and Mendelson (1969) reported increased anxiety and depression among chronic alcoholic men, even though the men expected positive effects. Similarly, Nathan and O'Brien (1971) found marked increases in anxiety and depression among male alcoholics after 24 hours of drinking, but they observed decreases in predrinking levels of anxiety and depression during the first 12–24 hours of consumption. These findings were replicated by Allman, Taylor, and Nathan (1972) and Nathan, Goldman, Lisman, and Taylor (1972) among alcoholic men but were not extended to women. Tracey and Nathan (1976) allowed four alcoholic women access to alcohol over a 12-day period. Unlike their male counterparts described in earlier studies, the women reported less depression, anger, fatigue, and confusion during drinking and showed consumption patterns more typical of male problem drinkers than of alcoholics. The women exhibited minimal early and maintenance drinking and consumed roughly half the alcohol quantities recorded among men in the same experimental paradigm (Nathan & O'Brien, 1971). Unlike male counterparts, the women in the Tracey and Nathan study worked consistently to earn the opportunity to socialize. Although they differed individually in response to alcohol consumption, they were unanimous in reporting less depression during drinking and in expecting alcohol to ease feelings of depression, anxiety, and loneliness. These and other sex-specific differences in self-selection of and response to beverage alcohol among groups characterized by different drinking patterns are discussed separately in this chapter.

Studies of mood state changes among alcoholics under conditions of acute intoxication have yielded mixed findings. For example, Majczack (1967) found euphoria, dysphoria, and no affective change to predominate across different individuals three hours following drinking. Van der Spuy (1972) concluded that acute intoxication led to increased tension in alcoholics, although he found individual variations and described what he observed to be temporary and superficial reduction of tension. Vanderpool (1969) showed that alcohol lowered stress tolerance and feelings of self-esteem, whereas Mayfield and Allen (1967) described a direct association between acute intoxication and palliative short-term mood changes. To control for expectancy effects, subjects in the latter study received alcohol by IV drip and were unaware of the identity of the infused drug. Although alcohol enhanced mood in alcoholics, the magnitude of this effect was less than for the nonproblem drinkers and depressed individuals who were also examined in the study. Interestingly, the depressed affect of the latter subjects was said to have improved dramatically during intoxication, whereas alcoholics derived the least relief from negative mood states of any of the groups included.

Similar patterns of negative reinforcement have been reported with acute and chronic opiate administration, and it may prove advantageous to compare the effects of such drug use with those of alcohol intoxication. Of interest are the double-blind studies of the subjective effects of unblocked heroin use reported by Meyer and Mirin (1979). These researchers concluded that the acute effect of heroin injections among long-term opiate addicts was that of tension relief. Subjects reported greater relaxation immediately after each heroin dose, although they also felt saddened. Mood response was correlated with frequency of administration, with those injecting the drug more frequently reporting themselves as happier and more elated. These findings were interpreted to be consistent with the earlier reports of Wikler (1952), Haertzen and Hooks (1969), and Martin et al. (1973), who administered morphine or methadone chronically to opiate addicts and found increased depression, irritability, anger, and social withdrawal over time. Because the opiate addicts in the Meyer and Mirin (1979) investigations showed powerful acute effects of heroin injections superimposed on negative mood sets throughout the series of chronic administrations, these researchers suggested that it was the acute tension-relieving effects of heroin rather than its long-standing euphorigenic properties that seemed to account for continued use.

In the alcohol studies reviewed above, subjects were identified by history of drinking behaviors and consumption was treated as an independent variable. Using a different approach to assess relationships between drinking behaviors and stress, Higgins and Marlatt (1973, 1975) pioneered an experimental analogue situation in which subjects were led to believe that the focus of the study was that of taste-testing beverages. In the first study, they exposed male alcoholics and social drinkers recruited by community advertisements to a stress-inducing manipulation that incorporated threat of low or high electric shock and measured the amount of alcohol consumed during the taste-testing procedure. Alcoholic subjects consumed more than twice as much alcohol during taste testing than did social drinkers, but the amount of alcohol ingested was not related to the anxiety manipulation or scores on a measure of trait anxiety. In the later study, Higgins and Marlatt (1975) found that manipulation of social anxiety, involving evaluation of individual interpersonal attractiveness, influenced wine tasting among heavy social drinking college students, with greater amounts of alcohol consumed by men subjected to interpersonal threat. The authors hypothesized that the nature of the stressors used—that is, social versus nonsocial—accounted for discrepant findings across the studies.

Miller, Hersen, Eisler, and Hilsman (1974) investigated operant drinking behaviors among alcoholic and social drinkers exposed to social stress. Introduced after subjects had learned to perform simple operant responses for bourbon and water, the stress manipulation consisted of a 15-minute harangue detailing the personal shortcomings of participants. A pulse-rate measure confirmed that both subgroups were equally aroused by this procedure. Results supported the hypothesis that alcoholics demonstrate stress-induced drinking behaviors more readily and to a greater extent than do social drinkers. Whereas alcoholics increased their operant response rate following the social stress manipulation, nonalcoholics decreased their rate. Miller et al. (1974) interpreted their findings in terms of differences in availability and response strength of additional coping mechanisms (i.e., other than drinking) in the two populations. In response to social provocation, social drinkers appeared to demonstrate adaptive behavioral alternatives to drinking, whereas alcoholics worked for and consumed alcohol in increasing amounts.

Although the research reviewed thus far has focused on measures of anxiety, other arousal states have been manipulated in experimental investigations of stress-induced drinking. Both pleasure-inducing and aversive procedures have been evaluated with respect to their effect on alcohol consumption. For example, Marlatt, Kosturn, and Lang (1975) used procedures similar to those described by Higgins and Marlatt (1973; 1975), except that anger rather than fear constituted the principal independent variable. Equal numbers of heavy social drinking undergraduate men and women participated, and anger was elicited by a confederate who provoked subjects verbally as they attempted to solve anagrams. As an added manipulation, some subjects were given the opportunity to retaliate by administering what they believed to be electric shocks to their provocateur. All subjects subsequently participated in a taste-testing session. Findings indicated that those who were insulted and given no chance to shock the confederate consumed significantly more alcohol than subjects who were insulted and had the opportunity to retaliate.

The findings of the Marlatt et al. (1975) study indicate that consuming alcohol might allow people to cope in stressful situations, depending upon their characteristics and the coping options available to them. Support for this notion was provided by Strickler, Tomaszewski, Maxwell, and Suib (1979), who found that the amount of alcohol that subjects consumed prior to a stressful public speaking experience varied as a function of the availability of alternative techniques for reducing stress.

Unfortunately, conclusions drawn from Marlatt and colleagues (1975) must be tempered by the finding that control subjects who were not insulted consumed alcohol in amounts intermediate to but not significantly different from provoked subjects who could and could not retaliate. It is unclear whether the results were influenced by the unresolved anger manipulation, the opportunity to retaliate against a stressor, or both. The description of provoked subjects as "angry" reflects only a plausible inference because mood states were not assessed. Factors that influenced drinking by control subjects who imbibed significant amounts of alcohol remain obscure. The authors suggested that these subjects may have been moderately stressed themselves as a result of working on the unsolvable anagram task. Future investigations might well follow up on the questions raised by this study to further our understanding of relationships among anger, coping, and drinking behaviors, especially as they apply to adult heavy drinkers of both sexes.

High-Risk Drinking Groups. Investigators have attempted to identify subgroups of drinkers according to vulnerability for developing drinking problems. There is little agreement as to which variables place drinkers at risk, but those that seem to play a role include family history of alcoholism (Goodwin, 1985; Chapter 2 in this volume; Schuckit, 1983, 1985), certain personal characteristics and types of psychopathology (Cox, 1986; Sher & Levenson, 1982; Sutker, Brantley, & Allain, 1980), learning and environmental factors (Nathan & Hay, 1984; Nathan & Niaura, 1985), and cultural factors that promote heavy drinking (Waddell & Everett, 1980; Westermeyer, 1985). One type of investigation in this area has focused on comparative differences in the extent to which alcohol consumption can modify stress reactions across individuals. In these stress-response-dampening (SRD) studies, subjects are exposed to a stress manipulation before consuming a fixed alcohol dose, and the effects of subsequent intoxication on various self-report and psychophysiological measures are examined.

Sher and Levenson (1982) used such a paradigm in an attempt to identify individuals who experience relatively high SRD effects and for whom reinforcement from drinking would be particularly potent. In two studies, male social drinkers with no history of alcohol problems were assessed on personality characteristics thought to relate to risk for alcoholism. High-risk subjects scored above the median on the MacAndrew Alcoholism Scale and/or below the median on the Socialization Scale of the California Psychological Inventory; remaining subjects served as low-risk controls. After alcohol consumption, high-risk subjects showed greater reductions in affective and cardiovascular responses to experimentally induced physical and social stressors than did low-risk controls. Thus high-risk men may be those who obtain more powerful reinforcement and greater SRD effects from drinking than do others, and subsects of the drinking population, including outgoing, impulsive, antisocial persons scoring in the high-risk direction on these instruments, may be more apt to show tension-reducing effects. Such results are consistent with recent studies of drinking and personality (Cox, 1985) and with Cahalan's (1970) finding that problem drinkers report greater stress reduction from alcohol than do their light-drinking counterparts. The Sher and Levenson (1982) finding represents a valuable addition to prior work, because high- and low-risk subjects did not differ in current consumption patterns or family history of alcoholism, and SRD differences were predictable solely on the basis of independent psychometric criteria.

Lipscomb, Nathan, Wilson, and Abrams (1980) reasoned that individual differences in alcohol tolerance, which has been widely assumed to be a causal factor in alcoholism, might predict differences in susceptibility to SRD effects following alcohol ingestion. After consuming either a high or a low dose of alcohol, male subjects classified as either high or low in tolerance on the basis of performance on a body-sway task during intoxication attempted to converse with a female confederate whose nonresponsive behavior was intended to engender anxiety during the interaction. Surprisingly, high- and low-tolerance subjects did not differ in self-reported prior drinking patterns. Pulse-rate and skin-conductance indices indicated that high-tolerance subjects showed greater increases in anxiety at the low dose than low-tolerance drinkers and that the men administered high doses of alcohol became less anxious during the stressful social interaction than those consuming low doses. These findings suggest that alcohol is less effective as a tension reliever for high-tolerance persons because more alcohol is required to achieve equivalent reductions of anxiety. The investigators speculated that these findings reflect effects of initial alcohol reactivity differences across individuals and that a mutually accelerating tolerance and consumption relationship may develop in certain people who demonstrate relatively low responsivity to the ameliorative effects of alcohol.

Thus, among drinkers, those who experience greater alcohol tension-reducing or euphoric effects that encourage increased drinking may be at higher risk for alcoholism. Other high-risk drinkers may be those more tolerant to alcohol and less affected by acute intoxication, and thus more able to consume large quantities. It is possible that such effects are influenced by heredity; for example, alcohol preferences and responses may be genetically determined in mice (Randall & Lester, 1975; Tabakoff, Ritzmann, Raju, & Deitrich, 1980; Tabakoff & Ritzmann, 1979; Chapter 1 in this volume). To explore the issue of inherited differences, Schuckit and his colleagues (Schuckit, 1980a, 1980b;

Schuckit & Rayses, 1979) have undertaken comparisons of responses to acute intoxication between college men with and without a family history of alcoholism, matched on demographics, height/weight ratio, and drinking history. The two groups were found to differ in subjective feelings of intoxication following alcohol consumption as well as in physiological responses to the drug. However, results did not reveal different rates of alcohol absorption or elimination (Schuckit, 1983). These findings suggest that important differences in susceptibility to SRD and other effects of intoxication may be inherited, but additional research is required to elucidate the nature and mechanisms of such differences and their role in affecting individual risk for the development of drinking problems.

Nonproblem Drinkers. With the emphasis on the empirical assessment of the antecedents and consequences of drinking behaviors came an explosion of studies investigating acute and chronic intoxication among nonproblem drinking samples. These studies assumed that motives underlying alcohol consumption and responses to intoxication are similar among nonproblem, early problem, and problem drinkers and, therefore, that investigating nonproblem drinking will help us to understand factors underlying problem drinking. Among the important research efforts testing the TR model of alcohol consumption are those that incorporated the balanced-placebo design to assess the relative contributions of subject expectancies and pharmacological actions. One of the first studies using the balanced-placebo design to test the TR hypothesis with nonproblem drinkers was that of Polivy, Schueneman, and Carlson (1976), who exposed male subjects to high- and low-shock threat. This stress manipulation was successful in engendering anxiety, and alcohol reduced anxiety significantly more than did placebo. An unexpected finding, however, was that subjects who thought that they had consumed alcohol reported experiencing more anxiety than those who did not expect intoxication. If the pharmacological and expectancy effects of alcohol consumption are antagonistic with respect to tension reduction under some conditions, as suggested by these results, this may explain in part the inconsistent pattern of support for TR models from human studies that confounded these two factors.

Subsequent balanced-placebo studies have yielded mixed results regarding the relative importance and nature of expectancy effects on response to drinking. Levenson, Sher, Grossman, Newman, and Newlin (1980), for example, examined the separate effects of alcohol consumption and expectation on psychophysiological and self-report measures prior to stress and on the magnitude of response to stress using a between-subjects design. Two separate stress conditions were employed—threat of shock and videotaping of a self-disclosing speech. Those subjects consuming alcohol were administered a relatively high experimental dose. A pronounced pattern of prestress psychophysiological arousal was found, with alcohol consumption reducing the psychophysiological response to stress. These subjects reported feeling more cheerful and less anxious. Unlike the Polivy et al. (1976) results, there was no evidence of effects associated with alcohol expectation. This finding may be attributable to the potency of pharmacological actions or to the failure of the expectancy manipulation at the higher alcohol dose levels used in this study relative to earlier balanced-placebo research.

Sutker, Allain, Brantley, and Randall (1982) tested the hypothesis that acute intoxication, or the expectation of intoxication, would reduce negative affect in male and female social drinkers. Negative affect was induced before alcohol consumption by threatening subjects with electric shock for incorrect responses during a learning task that appeared inevitably to involve errors. The effectiveness of this manipulation was verified by self-report and psychophysiological data. Results indicated that a complex interaction between alcohol expectancy, the beverage consumed, and the sex of the subject determined affective responses. That is, women who expected and received alcohol showed higher levels of anxiety and arousal than women who did not expect but received alcohol. In fact, women in the latter group reported significantly less anxiety following beverage consumption than did all other groups. Men who expected and received alcohol showed the lowest levels of anxiety by the end of the experiment. Results of this and the previously described balanced-placebo studies indicate that the effects of expectancy on alcohol response are rarely straightforward and may be mediated by the interaction of multiple variables.

Several studies by Wilson and his co-workers used the balanced-placebo design to examine pharmacological and expectancy effects of alcohol on anxiety in social situations. Wilson and Abrams (1977) studied male social drinkers in a situation involving a brief but intense interaction and engendered social stress. The men who believed they had consumed alcohol showed less physiological response to the stressor than those who believed they had consumed tonic, regardless of the drink actually consumed, but the two groups did not differ in self-reported or observational ratings of anxiety. Using a parallel design with female subjects, Abrams and Wilson (1979) found that women who believed they had consumed alcohol showed more intense physiological indications of anxiety than did women who thought they had ingested tonic. Wilson, Abrams, and Lipscomb (1980) also found that the effects of alcohol on anxiety were influenced by the amount consumed. The greater the amount of alchol ingested by undergraduate male social drinkers in this study, the less anxious the subjects appeared on objective physiological measures of arousal. In contrast, self-reported anxiety did not show a significant dose effect.

Keane and Lisman (1980) tested the TR hypothesis with socially anxious and nonanxious subjects in two studies. In the first study, socially shy men were requested to consume alcohol or placebo, were given varied instructional sets regarding alcohol effects on facility of social interaction, and were asked to interact with a female confederate. Self-report, observational, and psychophysiological measures indicated that those who consumed alcohol performed less skillfully and reported more negative self-statements during social interactions than did comparably anxious men who consumed placebo. Seemingly unaware of the impact of alcohol, they rated their interpersonal performances as no less skilled than men who did not consume alcohol. Replicating this effort with nonanxious men, these investigators found that alcohol impaired behavioral performance and self-reported ratings in a dose-related manner; however, the nonanxious men who did not consume alcohol saw themselves as performing better than those who did. Although findings were interpreted as offering no evidence of tension reduction in either experiment, they suggested a potentially important difference between socially anxious and nonanxious men. Shy men failed to evaluate their performance appropriately when intoxicated.

In another study involving socially anxious and nonanxious men, Holroyd (1978) examined drinking behaviors at a contrived beer party conducted after a stress manipulation in which some subjects received a negative social evaluation. Equal groups of men scoring high and low on measures of social anxiety participated. Contrary to expectations, anxious subjects and those subjected to stressful evaluation consumed less beer and produced lower BACs than did nonanxious subjects or those who received positive evaluations. Although this finding raises important questions about stress-induced drinking in nonalcoholic populations, its generality is obscured by the absence of a comparison group of nonevaluated subjects. Unlike other research described in this section, Holroyd's (1978) study did not include expectancy manipulations. Nevertheless, considered in conjunction with the discrepant results of Higgins and Marlatt (1975), the findings of Keane and Lisman (1980) and Holroyd (1978) highlight the complexity of interactions between social stressors, person variables, and alcohol self-administration, and suggest the need for clarification in this area.

Subsamples of Drinking Women. Women are underrepresented among heavydrinking and alcoholic samples in the American public (Fillmore, 1984), and attention has been called to the paucity of research studies devoted to drinking problems among female subsets of the population (Jones & Jones, 1976a). Within the past ten years, researchers have initiated investigations of drinking contexts, patterns, and responses, as well as long-term consequences among groups of moderate and heavy drinking women (Hill, 1984; Vannicelli, 1984). Of primary importance has been the notion that negative affective states, particularly anxiety and depression, underlie drinking in women more than in men (Mulford, 1977). At least two early reports indicated that alcoholic women reported increased drinking during the premenstrual and menstrual cycle phases to manage higher levels of tension and depression (Belfer, Shader, Carroll, & Harmatz, 1971; Podolsky, 1963). Recently, sex-role conflicts and reactive drinking associated with changing social roles have been foci for study. Of primary interest to this chapter are studies that explore negative affective states as precursors or consequences of acute and chronic alcohol intoxication among women with varying drinking histories.

Early animal work showed that ovariectomized female mice and rabbits were more sensitive than intact females to the pharmacological actions of alcohol, and these differences were attenuated by injection of exogenous estrogen (Goldberg & Stortebecker, 1943; Stortebecker, 1939). Erikkson (1969) reported that alcohol consumption in female rats decreased during certain phases of the estrus cycle and subsequent to ovariectomy, but recent studies have found no differences in alcohol sensitivity among female mice as a function of ovariectomy or estrus cycle (Randall, Lochry, Moseley, & Sutker, 1981). In part, these animal studies have stimulated research with humans investigating sex differences in alcohol pharmacokinetics, physiological and psychological responses to acute alcohol intoxication across the menstrual cycle, and effects of acute intoxication on hypophyseal and gonadal hormone levels at discrete menstrual cycle stages. Alcohol effects on female endocrinological, reproductive, and sexual functioning are beyond the scope of this chapter, and the reader is referred to Hill (1984), Mendelson, Mello, & Ellingboe (1981), and Wilsnack (1984).

Jones and Jones (1976b) reported that alcohol response may differ depending on sex and circulating levels of gonadal hormones. They found that women tested premenstrually reached significantly higher peak BACs than men and showed significantly faster absorption but not elimination rates. Women tested during the premenstruum also produced higher peak BACs and faster alcohol absorption rates than those tested during menstruation and before and after ovulation. These results were not supported by Sutker, Tabakoff, Goist, and Randall (1983), who used a design that minimized potential influences of fluctuating gonadal hormones and hypothesized associated emotional changes. Women reached significantly higher peak BACs than men, with no differences in time to reach peak, and results were explained in large part by male-female differences in body water content. Because the compartment for distribution of alcohol in women is smaller than that for men, women should be expected to receive a higher pharmacologically effective dose. This conclusion was supported by Goist and Sutker (1985), who found no sex differences in alcohol absorption and elimination times or in peak BACs when alcohol doses were based on anthropometric estimates of total body water compared with those based on body weight, which produced significantly higher peak BACs in women than in men.

Recently, Sutker, Goist, and King (in press) explored relationships between alcohol pharmacokinetics and gonadal hormone levels in normally cycling, nonproblem drinking women. Intraindividual differences in rates of absorption and elimination and peak BACs were investigated with two alcohol doses at three discrete points in the menstrual cycle: early follicular (days 2–7), ovulatory (day 14), and midluteal (days 20–25) phases. Levels of progesterone, estradiol-B luteinizing hormone (LH), and follicle-stimulating hormone (FSH) were determined by radioimmunoassay from blood samples drawn before alcohol consumption. Alcohol pharmacokinetics differed across cycle phases, with differences in elimination times and areas under the curve (AUCs) but not in absorption or peak BACs. Comparisons of menstrual-cycle phases reveal shorter elimination times and smaller AUCs during the midluteal phase compared with the average of the early follicular and ovulatory phases, which did not differ from each other. Results were consistent for both moderate and high alcohol doses, with changes in elimination associated with midluteal elevated levels of progesterone, increased ratios of progesterone to estradiol, and lowered FSH levels.

In a companion investigation, Sutker, Goist, and Allain (1986) found that men were relatively consistent on measures of alcohol pharmacokinetics across six alcohol administration sessions, whereas women showed faster alcohol metabolism associated with the midluteal phase of the menstrual cycle compared with early follicular and ovulatory phases. In addition, there was evidence of sex-specific differences in mood responses to acute intoxication. Increased levels of anxiety and depression during intoxication were found among women during the early follicular phase as compared with the other phases of the cycle, but baseline negative affect did not differ across phases. This suggests that alcohol intoxication may exacerbate preexisting negative moods, such as those often reported during menstruation. Changes in mood states during intoxication were found to be a complex function of sex and dose, although both men and women showed evidence of anxiety reduction on the ascending limb of the BAC curve as well as greater anxiety and depression during the later phase of intoxication. These findings indicate that both physiological and emotional responses to alcohol intoxication represent highly complex phenomena, depending on sex, dose, and time on the BAC curve.

Sutker, Tabakoff, Goist, and Randall (1983) investigated self-reported mood states recorded at baseline, absorption, and elimination phases and observed significant mood state changes across the course of acute intoxication. Positive mood states such as vigor and elation increased during absorption, whereas fatigue, depression, and anxiety were reported to increase during elimination. This biphasic effect of alcohol on moods and sensations may account for some of the inconsistences and disputes in the literature regarding tension reduction. Acute alcohol intoxication in relatively normal, nonproblem drinkers appears to be associated with positive effect during the ascending limb of the BAC and with negative moods during alcohol elimination. Failure to find sex differences in alcohol metabolism and more general mood states and sensations may have been associated with testing during post-menstrual phases. Further study is required to clarify the effects of alcohol intoxication on mood states and behavioral parameters at discrete points in the menstrual cycle and to determine whether sex influences affective and behavioral responses to alcohol intoxication and prompting drinking.

If the precursors of alcoholic drinking are assumed to be similar to those for less maladaptive consumption, it is relevant to investigate whether greater drinking or altered consumption rates coincide with negative mood states such as anxiety and depression in nonalcoholic drinking women. Further, if negative mood states are temporally combined with certain menstrual-cycle phases, changes in alcohol consumption patterns might be observed among this population. Using self-monitoring methods in three carefully selected samples of nonproblem drinking women and men, Sutker, Libet, Allain, and Randall (1983) found that normally cycling women reported significantly more negative moods, more solitary drinking, and greater tendencies to drink to relieve tension and depression at menstruation than at other times in the cycle, for example, ovulatory and premenstrual phases. These cyclic patterns were not observed among men or within a subset of women maintained on oral contraceptives. Results suggested that sex differences in drinking behaviors and alcohol responses may occur and be tied to psychological and/or physiological changes associated with the menstrual cycle.

Several studies have investigated predictions derived from the TR hypothesis in groups of female drinkers. Eddy (1979) reasoned that because problem drinking women have reported tension-reduction motives for alcohol consumption, it could be hypothesized that women would exhibit decreased anxiety after alcohol consumption in a stressful public speaking situation and that problem-drinking women would show greater anxiety reduction than their nonproblem-drinking counterparts. As predicted, Eddy found that problem drinkers showed greater anxiety reduction on a self-report measure than nonproblem drinkers when alcohol was consumed. These findings are consistent with results reported by Tracey and Nathan (1976), who found that female alcoholics experienced reductions in negative mood states with alcohol consumption on an acute and chronic basis. However, heart rate and independent behavioral ratings of speech disturbance data also collected by Eddy (1979) yielded a complex of discrepant interactions that were not readily interpretable in relation to TR predictions.

Looking across the studies described, we can conclude that the usual affective consequences of mild, acute, experimental intoxication in social drinkers of both sexes are short-term improvements in mood states, with subsequent deterioration at increased dose levels and during later intoxication phases. The literature is consistent in supporting this general picture, but there are experimental findings that limit the generalizability of the conclusion. To consider one important influence, the context in which drinking occurs is related to potential mood state changes, as demonstrated by the few studies that have manipulated drinking context as an independent variable. Lindman (1982), for example, exposed male social drinkers serving as their own controls to a social situation of their choosing and to a solitary laboratory situation. Subjects experienced greater euphoric effects and consumed significantly more alcohol under social conditions than under the laboratory alcohol condition, which was described as aversive. Similar findings have been reported by McClelland, Davis, Kalin, and Wanner (1972). Clearly then, it is critical to identify the environmental and contextual correlates of specific mood state changes associated with acute and chronic intoxication in varied drinking samples.

ALCOHOL AND MOOD ENHANCEMENT

It has been argued that pleasure is a basic emotional substrate associated with the consequences of drinking (e.g., Russell & Mehrabian, 1975), but the positive impact of alcohol intoxication has been less the focus of research attention in all categories of drinkers than have dysphoric consequences or negatively reinforcing effects such as tension reduction. As yet, only a small number of studies have investigated the possibility that alcohol consumption is motivated or influenced by mood-enhancing effects. However, the hypothesis that mood enhancement exerts an important influence on alcohol appetitive behaviors seems highly plausible if one considers the wealth of data generated in the area of learning to describe relationships between reinforcement and behavior. For instance, the immediacy with which a reinforcing consequence follows responding has been found to be an important determinant of its control over behavior. Studies of acute and chronic intoxication in problem and nonproblem drinkers show that alcohol produces transient positive changes in mood, particularly at low doses and during the early phases of intoxication (Davis, 1971; Menaker, 1967; Nathan & O'Brian, 1971; Nathan, Titler, Lowenstein, Solomon, & Rossi, 1970; Sutker et al., 1983; Tamerin & Mendelson, 1969; Williams, 1966). The immediate enhancement of positive affect may serve to reinforce alcohol consumption despite the inevitable delayed punishing effects. Moreover, human studies suggest that problem and nonproblem drinkers experience discrepant mood effects within and across drinking occasions, with pleasant or euphoric responses occurring inconsistently. Intermittent reinforcement produces behavior patterns that are relatively resistant to extinction as compared with those reinforced on a continuous schedule. Thus the fact that intoxication effects are varied, unpredictable, and only sometimes pleasurable may be helpful in explaining the durability of drinking behaviors over time despite their aversive consequences.

Alcoholic and Problem-Drinking Samples

Researchers have studied pleasurable or positive responses to intoxication in various drinking subgroups to identify unique parameters of reinforcement associated with problem drinking. For example, Senter, Heintzelman, Dorfmueller, and Hinkle (1979) reasoned that the euphoric effects of drinking may be more exaggerated among persons who become alcohol dependent than for those who do not. To test this hypothesis, the authors compared descriptions of alcohol-induced experiences generated by alcohol-addicted and nonaddicted men and women recruited from treatment programs and working populations. Men and women labeled as alcoholics tended to rate their best intoxication experiences as more euphoric than did nonalcoholics, and were more likely to recall the detailed circumstances and consequences of their initial drinking experience. In contrast, fewer nonalcoholics recalled their initial drinking exposure, and those who did rated the experience in more neutral terms. Alcoholics also described their worst intoxication experiences as more unpleasant and as occurring later in life.

Despite obvious methodological limitations, these findings emphasize the need for exploring individual differences in initial sensitivity to alcohol and in changes in affective responses to alcohol over time. They are also consistent with the authors' a priori hypothesis that alcoholics respond to alcohol with more initial pleasure and later pain than do nonalcoholics. Problem drinkers may evaluate, remember, or otherwise respond differently than nonalcoholics to similar drinking experiences, and the psychopharmacological effects of alcohol may serve different functions among different drinking groups. Related points were raised by Russell and Bond (1980), who hypothesized that alcoholics believe that drinking will both enhance pleasant feelings and counteract unpleasant mood states, whereas nonproblem drinkers view mild intoxication as improving pleasant affect but exacerbating unpleasant affect. These researchers studied inpatient alcoholic and nonproblem drinking college men and women who viewed highly pleasant and unpleasant slides and rated drinking desires while imagining personal involvement in the pictured situations. Compared with student drinkers, alcoholics scored significantly higher on desire to drink while experiencing unpleasant emotional states, a result supporting the experimental hypothesis.

Although this fascinating hypothesis is worthy of systematic scrutiny, several problems are posed for investigators attempting to ferret out differences in early and long-term cognitive and affective responses to alcohol. Not the least is that of comparing groups of practiced or chronologically older drinkers with those who have had less extensive alcohol-related experiences. The retrospective method for reporting drinking circumstances is problematic, and collection of longitudinal data is preferable. Ideally, one could measure responses to early intoxication, expectancies about alcohol effects, and responses to intoxication at later points in the drinking history among individuals who ultimately will fall into various drinking groups—light to heavy or alcoholic drinkers, for example. With this procedure, responses to acute intoxication could be studied in varied drinking situations using time-sampling strategies. On a practical level, however, researchers are often faced with more limited options, such as assessing affective responses to chronic intoxication among hospitalized alcoholics or exploring responses to acute intoxication among nonalcoholic subgroups, including college students who show varying patterns of habitual drinking.

At least one of the chronic intoxication studies discussed previously offers evidence that euphoric effects may function to sustain alcohol consumption among alcoholic drinkers. Two of the four alcoholic women in the Tracey and Nathan (1976) study reported reliable enhancement of positive moods under conditions of intoxication by self-administered alcohol. This is in contrast to the majority of reported outcomes with men, including other findings from Nathan's laboratory (e.g., Nathan & O'Brien, 1971). The uniqueness of these results might be attributed to the sex of the subjects or to their more controlled and less exaggerated drinking patterns, or both. The authors argued that maintaining relatively tight control of chronic drinking may serve to enhance mood or facilitate enhancement effects as well as to mediate against the more commonly observed dysphoric consequences of chronic consumption. In any case, data reflecting emotional responses to acute and chronic intoxication in male and female drinkers with varied consumption patterns over repeated occasions must be collected to clarify these issues.

Avery, Overall, Calil, and Hollister (1982) addressed the issue of mood enhancement in alcoholics during acute intoxication. These investigators studied affective change shown by detoxified male alcoholics and nonalcoholics during two hours of ad lib drinking in a simulated bar. Participants were instructed to consume their beverage of choice in a manner that would maximize their feelings of comfort, pleasure, and intoxication. Subjects rated their own moods prior to, during, and after drinking, and their behavior was rated by observers at hourly intervals. Alcoholics consumed significantly more alcohol than nonalcoholics, reached significantly higher BACs, and reported little relief from baseline dysphoria while intoxicated. They showed enhanced self-reported positive mood states, maniclike symptoms, and increased desires to drink. Simultaneous increases were found on measures of dysphoria, including anger and depression. Similar mood-enhancement effects were found among nonalcoholics, but they failed to show concomitant rises in dysphoria.

Avery el al. (1982) concluded that the magnitude of positive affective responses to alcohol is similar for alcoholics and nonalcoholics and that there is little support for the hypothesis that alcoholics derive special euphoria from drinking. However, several factors complicate interpretation of their findings. Alcoholic and nonalcoholic subjects differed significantly in their baseline level of dysphoria, and the alcoholics drank a larger quantity of alcohol and showed higher levels of intoxication. Perhaps the conservative conclusion is that members of both groups mediated their drinking behaviors in such a manner as to derive acute and mood-enhancement effects, but it is noteworthy that the dysphoria of the alcoholic subjects was exacerbated by drinking. This study underscores the necessity of considering multivariate models of drinking and intoxication, especially with regard to subject samples that differ in drinking histories, alcohol tolerance, age, and predrinking emotional states.

Nonproblem Drinker Samples

Most drinkers believe that alcohol is a powerful mood enhancer, just as they expect it to be a tension reducer. Of six independent factors extracted by Brown, Goldman, Inn, and Anderson (1980) to describe drinking-related expectancies of college student drinkers, five involved effects related to pleasure. It is probable that these widespread beliefs influence both patterns of consumption and actual responses to drinking. Reports of social drinkers have also suggested the importance of positive mood effects over other drinking benefits, as illustrated by findings that college students reported a greater desired to drink in pleasant as compared with unpleasant settings and while experiencing positive moods (Russell & Bond, 1979).

At least two studies have explored mood enhancement among nonproblem drinkers administered mild doses of alcohol. Using a balanced-placebo design, McCollam, Burish, Maisto, and Sobell (1980) assessed affective responses of male undergraduates during ascending and descending limbs of the BAC curve. Alcohol consumption produced increments in self-rated positive affect and physiological sensations, decrements in ratings of depression, and no significant impact on anxiety. Most ratings of physiological sensations were higher during the ascending than descending limb of the BAC, and drinkers were described as feeling and behaving in a more intoxicated manner while their BACs were rising. In a similar study, Connors and Maisto (1979) found that acute intoxication in moderate to heavy drinking male college students was associated with positive affective changes and alterations in physiological sensations. The rate of alcohol consumption was found to influence mood response, and faster drinking rates were associated with higher levels of anxiety and hostility. Results were interpreted to support the hypothesis that alcohol consumption acts to enhance positive moods rather than to reduce negative or tension states under nonthreatening circumstances. Moreover, the results of this and the McCollam et al. (1980) study demonstrate mood-enhancement effects separate from those attributed to cognitive expectancies.

Drawing upon Schachter's (1964) theory of emotions, Vuchinich, Tucker, and Sobell (1979) investigated the notion that alcohol-induced emotional changes depend upon the cognitive label applied by the drinker to the physiological effects of intoxication on a given occasion. Such labels were hypothesized to derive from the immediate environmental context as distinguished from expectancy effects originating in beliefs about the pharmacological effects of alcohol. In a factorial balanced-placebo design, nonproblem drinking college men were informed or not informed about physical sensations typically resulting from drinking, told to expect an alcoholic or a fictitious nutritious beverage, and were administered alcoholic or nonalcoholic drinks. Before and after these manipulations, participants were exposed to humorous recorded stimuli, and their laughter and self-reported affective states were monitored. Among specific hypotheses tested was the prediction that, of uninformed subjects who expected a nonalcoholic beverage, those who became intoxicated from alcohol would misattribute state changes to salient contextual cues. Observer ratings indicated that the behavioral expression of mirth was determined solely by drinker expectations of alcohol effects, whereas postconsumption changes in self-reported moods were influenced by prior mood states and, to a lesser extent, by actual alcohol administration. Thus the hypothesis that cognitive labeling mediated affective and behavioral effects of moderate alcohol intoxication was not supported.

A few studies have examined the effects that induced depressive mood exerts on drinking behaviors. Pihl and Yankofsky (1979), for example, employed a procedure in which heavy and light social drinking college men were led to believe that they had performed well or poorly on a measure of intelligence. Subjects who received uncomplimentary feedback did show increase self-reported anxiety and depression. Subsequent to receiving feedback, subjects participated in a taste-testing task allegedly designed to study relationships among intelligence, taste sensitivity, and alcohol preference. Contrary to predictions, more alcohol was consumed by men who had received complimentary feedback and showed positive changes in affect following the incentive manipulation. A subsequent analysis dividing subjects into those showing relatively more and relatively less negative affect after incentive manipulation indicated that more alcohol was consumed by those who were less depressed and anxious.

These results stand in contrast to those of Higgins and Marlatt (1975) described previously and to findings generated in two experiments with female social drinkers conducted by Noel and Lisman (1980). The latter studies employed a paradigm developed for investigations of learned-helplessness phenomena in which depression was engendered by requiring subjects to attempt to solve problems that actually were unsolvable. The effectiveness of this manipulation was verified by mood measures. In accord with a negative reinforcement account, women characterized by elevated levels of depression consumed more beer than did controls during a version of the taste-testing procedure. Their consumptive increase did not apply to ginger ale available concurrently. Thus stress-induced alcohol consumption was shown to be separate from increased drinking per se, such as might result from arousal in general.

Attempting to distinguish between aversive motivation and that arising from other types of arousal, Gabel, Noel, Keane, and Lisman (1980) compared rates of alcohol self-administration by undergraduate male nonalcoholics who viewed erotic, neutral, and unpleasant stimuli in a within-subjects design. On separate occasions, participants viewed slides of sexual activity, emotionally neutral scenes, and mutilated accident victims. Self-reports showed increased sexual arousal during the first and increased fear during the last presentation, and physiological measures confirmed that the mutilation and sexual scenes were arousing initially. These manipulations were followed by a wine taste-testing session for half of the subjects, and the remaining participants performed an operant task to obtain alcohol. More alcohol was consumed after viewing erotic slides than under other conditions, with no differences in wine consumed following exposure to neutral or injury scenes. Operant rates did not vary as a function of condition. Neither sustained autonomic arousal nor self-reported anxiety was associated with maximum consumption. The authors interpreted their findings as inconsistent with the TR hypothesis but compatible with Russell and Mehrabian's (1975) notion that social drinkers employ alcohol in moderation to enhance pleasant mood states.

This brief summary of research related to the mood-enhancing functions of alcohol reflects the complexity inherent in attempting to pinpoint possible affective precursors and responses to alcohol intoxication. Of perhaps greatest interest are the potential differences in emotional antecedents to drinking between alcoholic and nonproblem drinkers, the varying responses to acute and chronic intoxication among groups defined by drinking severity, the role of specific emotional sets in influencing responses to alcohol, and possible sex-specific differences in emotional cues to drinking and in affective responses during intoxication. Identifying drinking groups at high risk for alcohol abuse who differ from those at low risk will shed light on the etiology and progression of drinking disorders, and specifically on the mechanisms that sustain early problem drinking or prompt drinking relapse among alcoholic drinkers. Further, if coping versus pleasure motives for intoxication can be separated across drinking situations and time, our knowledge of alternative strategies for treating these problems will be broadened.

DISCUSSION AND CONCLUSIONS

Our understanding of the reinforcing properties of alcohol has been advanced by animal and human experiments devised to test predictions generated from the TR and other mood-related models of alcohol consumption. Given the conglomerate of emerging findings, the task of considering alcohol consumption, tension reduction, and mood enhancement is one demanding an ever-broadening and integrative perspective. Researchers have addressed criticisms of single-factor TR theory publicized a decade ago, and recent studies reflect greater attention to experimental methodology and appreciation of the complexity of the issues under scrutiny. Contemporary efforts assume that the pharmacological and psychological effects of alcohol consumption are multivariate and that tension reduction and mood enhancement are among the potentially reinforcing consequences of intoxication to be incorporated into an integrative model that explains motivation for alcohol consumption. As yet, the literature offers few concrete conclusions, and the more promising hypotheses that have been proposed have not been explored thoroughly.

For example, success has been modest in predicting TR or SRD effects associated with specific types of stressors or in reconciling discrepant findings regarding the potentially stressful impact of threatening stimuli devised to engender anxiety or other discomfort, for example, social versus nonsocial threats. Similarly, there is little support for the hypothesis that drinkers characterized by higher levels of state or trait anxiety and dysphoria are more likely to use or abuse alcohol to ameliorate negative affect. However, there are many suggestions that individuals differ in their capacity to derive palliative effects from alcohol. Such findings may be valuable in stimulating definitive work describing relationships among stressful stimuli, tension reduction, and consumptive patterns for groups defined by drinking histories, familial alcoholism, and other variables thought to place people at greater alcoholism risk.

Despite past inconsistent findings, it is likely that researchers will continue to design studies to test implications of TR accounts. For this research to prove fruitful, the focus of inquiry must be expanded and the methodology conceptualized more carefully. Until recently, the TR hypothesis has been approached as a central explanatory account of drinking behaviors. In the future, the objective of work will be to delineate the conditions under which TR and related mechanisms may initiate or sustain drinking behaviors among carefully defined subject samples and under well-specified circumstances. The task for researchers will then be to describe relevant variables and their effects and to order them within a theoretical structure having predictive utility. For example, much remains to be clarified as regards self-selection of beverage alcohol in contrived and natural situations and the multivaried responses to intoxication under defined conditions. Of possible benefit may be application of single-subject behavioral analyses of alcohol consumption that continues in the presence of advancing intoxication and progressive mood alteration

On balance, the limited data available suggest that mood enhancement may be a promising area for alcohol research, especially that used to compare various drinking history groups, such as moderate versus heavy drinkers or alcoholic versus heavy drinkers. On the one hand, studies by Connors and Maisto (1980), McCollam et al. (1981), and Tracey and Nathan (1976), among others, suggest that pleasurable affective consequences of intoxication may function as positive reinforcers for drinking behaviors. A second trend can be discerned in studies reported by Gabel et al. (1980) and Pihl and Yankofsky (1979), which provided support for positive mood states and associated conditions as antecedents influencing consumption. An advantage of the latter approach is that it permits hypotheses that are more readily analyzed functionally. That is, one can engender positive mood states and determine the effects on drinking, but it is difficult or impossible to manipulate the affective consequences of consuming alcohol to determine their functional relation to subsequent drinking.

Research incorporating expectancy manipulations has broadened our understanding of factors involved in drinking and mood alteration. Several of these studies suggest that alcohol serves to reduce anxiety or tension but that cognitive variables or expectancies can interfere with or intensify tension reduction under certain circumstances or among subsets of subjects. One of the problems with most of the studies of expectancy effects is that personal expectancies about the effects of various degrees of intoxication in different drinking situations are not assessed or manipulated adequately. Subjects may be led to expect that they will consume a certain type of alcoholic beverage, but their individual expectations regarding the consequences of this consumption usually are not probed. At least two studies (Noel & Lisman, 1980; Vuchinich et al., 1979) have attempted to address this issue by direct manipulation of subject expectancies of the specific effects of intoxication in unfamiliar contexts. Unfortunately, these experiments did not demonstrate strong expectancy effects, and this limitation should be remediated in future work.

Controversy aside, the view that people drink because alcohol reduces tension retains widespread popular appeal, and clinical lore attributes motivation for problem and other drinking behaviors to presumed effects on negative mood states. Alternatively, positive mood state antecedents and/or euphoric responses to intoxication appear to play a role in developing and maintaining drinking behaviors in at least some individuals. We have summarized research showing that positive or negative affective states may precipitate alcohol consumption or determine responses to intoxication and that practiced drinking behaviors may influence affective precursors and responses to intoxication. Clearly, no unitary or constant motive prompts drinking, whether within individuals, among narrowly defined groups, or across situations. We have seen also that alcohol intoxication may lead to increased negative affect rather than tension reduction. It is then left to behavioral researchers to continue attempts to chart the affective, cognitive, and behavioral antecedents of drinking and the responses after acute and chronic intoxication, taking into account events in the environment, drinking contexts, and personal characteristics of the drinkers themselves. This research has obvious implications for explaining the etiology and progression of alcoholic and other problem drinking. Fascinating in their own right, such studies will enhance our knowledge of appetitive and aversive motivation and the parameters of pleasure-seeking and coping behaviors.

REFERENCES

Abrams, D.B., & Wilson, G.T. (1979). Effects of Alcohol on social anxiety in Women: Cognitive versus physiological processes. *Journal of Abnormal Psychology, 88,* 161–173.

Allman, L.R., Taylor, H.A., & Nathan, P.E. (1972). Group drinking during stress: Effects on drinking behavior, affect and psychopathology. *American Journal of Psychiatry, 129,* 669–678.

Anisman, H., & Waller, T.G. (1974). Effects of inescapable shock and shock-produced conflict on self selection of alcohol in rats. *Pharmocology Biochemistry and Behavior, 2,* 27–33.

Avery, D.H., overall, J.E., Calil, H.M., & Hollister, L.C. (1982). Alcohol-induced euphoria: Alcoholics compared to nonalcoholics, *International Journal of the Addictions, 17,* 823–845.

Bammer, G., & Chester, G.B. (1982). An analysis of some effects of alcohol on performance in a passive avoidance task. *Psychopharmacology, 77,* 66–73.

Barry, H., III, & Miller, N.E. (1965). Comparison of drug effects on approach, avoidance, and escape motivation. *Journal of Comparative and Physiological Psychology, 59,* 18–24.

Belfer, M.L., Shader, R.I., Carroll, M., & Harmatz, J.S. (1971). Alcoholism in women. *Archives of General Psychiatry, 25,* 540–544.

Brown, J.S., & Crowell, C.R. (1974). Alcohol and conflict resolution: A theoretical analysis. *Quarterly Journal of Studies on Alcohol, 35,* 66–85.

Brown, J.S., Mansfield, J.G., & Skurdal, A.J. (1980). An interference-reduction theory of the effects of ethanol on conflict behavior. *Physiological Psychology, 8,* 423–432.

Brown, S.A., Goldman, M.S., Inn, A., & Anderson, L. (1980). Expectations of reinforcement from alcohol: Their domain and relation to drinking patterns. *Journal of Counsulting and Clinical psychology, 48,* 419–426.

Cadoret, R., & Winokur, G. (1974). Depression in alcoholism. *Annals of the New York Academy of Sciences, 233,* 34–39.

Cahalan, D. (1970). *Problem drinkers.* San Francisco: Jossey-Bass.

Cappell, H. (1975). An evaluation of the tension models of alcohol consumption. In R.J. Gibbins, Y. Israel, H. Kalant, R.E. Popham, W. Schmidt, & R.G. Smart (Eds.), *Research advances in alcohol and drug problems,* Vol. 2. New York: Wiley.

Cappell, H.,, & Greeley, J. (1987). Alcohol and tension reduction: An update on research and theory. In H.T. Blane & K.E. Leonard (Eds.), *Psychological theories of drinking and alcoholism.* New York: Guilford Press.

Cappell, H., & Herman, C.P. (1972). Alcohol and tension reduction: A review. *Quarterly Journal of Studies on Alcohol, 33,* 33–64.

Collins, R.L., & Marlatt, G. A. (1983). Psychological correlates and explanations of alcohol use and abuse. In B. Tabakoff, P.B. Sutker, & C.L. Randall (Eds.), *Medical and social aspects of alcohol abuse.* New York: Plenum Press.

Conger, J.J. (1951). The effects of alcohol on conflict behavior in the white rat. *Quarterly Journal of Studies on Alcohol, 12,* 1–29.

Conger, J.J.)1956). Reinforcement theory and the dynamics of alcoholism. *Quarterly Journal of Studies on Alcohol, 17,* 296–305.

Connors, G.J., & Maisto, S.A. (1979). Effects of alcohol, instuctions, and consumption rate on effect and physiological sensations. *Psychopharmacology, 62,* 261–266.

Cox, W.M. (1985). personality correlates of substance abuse. In M. Galizio & S.M. Maisto (Eds.), *Determinants of substance abuse: Biological, psychological, and environmental factors.* New York: Plenum Press.

Cox, W.M. (1987). Personality theory and research. In H.T. Blane & K. E. Leonard (Eds.), *Psychological theories of drinking and alcoholism.* New York: Guilford Press.

Cunningham, C.L., & Brown, J.S. (1983). Escape from fear under alcohol: Fear inhibits alcohol-enhanced responding. *Physiological Psychology, 11,* 18–86.

Davis, D. (1971). Mood changes in alcoholic subjects with programmed and free choice experimental drinking. In N.K. Mello & J.H. Mendelson (Eds.), *Recent advances in studies of alcoholism: An interdisciplinary Symposium.* Washington: U.S. Government Printing Office.[PO] Diethelm, O., & Barr, R.M. (1962). Psychotherapeutic interviews and alcohol intoxication. *Quarterly Journal of Studies on Alcohol, 23,* 243–251.

Eddy, C.C. (1979). The effects of alcohol on anxiety in problem-and nonproblem-drinking women. *Alcoholism: Clinical and Experimental Research, 3,* 107–114.

Erikkson, K. (1969). Effects of ovariectomy and contraceptive hormonics on voluntary alcohol consumption in the albino rat. *Japanese Journal of Studies on Alcohol, 4,* 1–5.

Ferster, C., & Skinner, B.F. (1957). *Schedules of Reinforcement..* New York: Appleton-Century-Crofts.

Fillmore, K.M. (1984). "When angels fall": Women's drinking as cultural preoccupation and as reality. IN S.C. Wilsnack & L.J. Beckman (Eds.), *Alcohol problems in women: Antecedents, consequences, and intervention.* New York: Guilford Press.

Fleetwood, M.F. (1955). Biochemical experimental investigations of emotions and chronic alcoholism. in O. Diethelm (Ed.), *Etiology of Chronic alcoholism.* Springfield, III.: Charles C. Thomas.

Freed, E.X. (1967). The effect of alcohol upon approach-avoidance conflict in the white rat. *Quarterly Journal of Studies on Alcohol, 28,* 236–254.

Freed, E.X. (1978). Alcohol and mood: An updated review. *International Journal of the Addictions, 33,* 172–200.

Gabel, P.C., Noel, N.E., Keane, T.M., & Lisman, S.A. (1980). Effects of sexual versus fear arousal on alcohol consumption in college males. *Behavior Research and Therapy, 18,* 519–526.

Glowa, J.R., & barrett, J.E. (1976). Effects of alcohol on punished and unpunished responding of squirrel monkeys. *Pharmacology Biochemistry and Behavior, 4,* 169–173.

Goist, K.C., Jr., & Sutker, P.B. (1985). Acute alcohol intoxication and body consumption in women and men. *Pharmacology Biochemistry and Behavior, 22,* 811–814.

Goldberg, L., & Storebecker, T.P. (1943). The antinarcotic effect of estrone on alcohol intoxication. *Acta Physiologica Scandinavica, 5,* 289–296.

Goodwin, D.W. (1985). Genetic determinants of alcoholism. In J.H. Mendelson & N.K. Mello (Eds.), *The diagnosis and treatment of alcoholism* (2nd ed.). New York: McGraw-Hill.

Gray, J.A. (1976). The behavioural inhibition system: A possible substitute for anxiety. In M.P. Feldman & A. Broadhurst (Eds.), *Theoretical and experimental basis of the behaviour therapies.* London: Wiley.

Gray, J.A., & Ball, G.G. (1970). Frequency-specific relations bewteen hippocampal theta rhythm, behaviour and amobarbital action *Science, 168,* 1246–1248.

Haertzen, C.A. & Hooks, N.T. (1969). Changes in personality and subjective experience associated with the chronic administration and withdrawal of opiates. *Journal of Nervous Mental Disease, 148,* 606–614.

Hesselbrock, M.N., Meyer, R.E., & Keener, J.J. (1985). Psychopathology in hospitalized alcoholics. *Archieves of General Psychiatry, 42,* 1050–1055.

Higgins, R.L. (1976). Experimental investigations of tension reduction models of alcoholism. In G. Goldstein & C. Neuringer (Eds.), *Empirical Studies of Alcoholism.* Cambridge, Mass.: Ballinger.

Higgins, R.L., & Marlatt, G.A. (1973). Effects of anxiety arousal on the consumption of alcohol by alcoholics and social drinkers. *Journal of Consulting and Clinical Psycology, 41,* 426–433.

Higgins, R.L., & Marlatt, G.A. (1975). Fear of interpersonal evaluation as a determinant of alcohol consumption in male social drinkers. *Journal of Abnormal Psychology, 84,* 644–651.

Hill, S.Y. (1984). Vulnerability to the biomedical consequences of alcoholism and alcohol-related problems among women. In S.C. Wilsnack & L.J. Beckman (Eds.), *Alcohol problems in women: Antecedents, consequences, and intervention.* New York: Guilford Press.

Hodgson, R.J., Stockwell, T.R., & Rankin, H.J. (1979). Can alcohol reduce tension? *Behaviour Research and Therapy, 17,* 459–466

Holroyd, K.A. (1978). Effects of social anxiety and social evaluation on beer consumption and social interaction. *Journal of Studies on Alcohol, 39,* 737–744.

Jones, B.M., & Jones, M.K. (1976a). Alcohol effects in women during the menstrual cycle. *Annals of the New York Academy of Sciences, 273,* 576–587.

Jones, B.M., & Jones, M.K. (1976b). Women and alcohol: Intoxication, metabolism and the menstrual cycle. In M. Greenblatt & M.A. Schuckit (Eds.), *Alcoholism Problems in women and children.* New York: Grune & Stratton.

Keane, T.M., & Lisman, S.A. (1980), Alcohol and social anxiety in males: behavioral, cognitive, and physiological effects, *Journal of Abnormal psychology, 89,* 213–223.

Lang, P.J. (1969). The mechanics of desensitization and the laboratory study of human fear. In C.M. Franks (Ed.), *Behavior Thferaphy: Appraisal and Status.* New York: McGraw-Hill.

LaCoursiere, R.B., Godfrey, K.E., & Ruby, L.M. (1980). Traumatic neurosis in the etiology of alcoholism: Viet Nam combat and other trauma. *American Journal of Psychiatry, 137,* 966–968.

Langenbucher, J., & Nathan, P.E. (1983). The "wet" alcoholic: One drink—then what? In W.M. Cox (Ed.), *Identifying and Measuring Alcoholic personality Characteristics.* San Francisco: Jossey-Bass.

levenson, R.W., Sher, K.J., Grossman, L.M., Newman, J., & Newlin, D.B. (1980). Alcohol and stress response dampening: Pharmacological effects. *Journal of Abnormal Psychology, 89,* 528–538.

Lindbeck, V.L. (1972) The woman alcoholic: A review of the literature. *International Journal of the Addictions, 7,* 567–580.

Lindman, R. (1982). Social and solitary drinking: Effects on consumption and mood in male social drinkers. *Physiology and Behavior, 28,* 1098–1095.

Lipscomb, T.R., Nathan, P.E., Wilson, G.T., & Abrams, D.B. (1980). Effects of tolerance on the anxiety-reducing function of alcohol. *Archives of General Psychiatry, 37,* 577–582.

Lisansky, E.S. (1957). Alcoholism in women: Social and psychological concomitants: I. Social history data. *Quarterly Journal of Studies on Alcohol, 18,* 588–623.

Lisman, S.A., Keane, T.M., & Noel, N.E. (1983). Feeling depressed, angry, shy, sexually aroused?—Why not have a drink? In L.A. Pohorecky & J. Brick (Eds.), *Stress and Alcohol Use.* New York: Elsevier.

Lyerly, S.B., Ross, S., Krugman, A.D., & Clyde, D.J. (1964). Drugs and placebo. *Journal of Abnormal and Social Psychology, 68,* 321–327.

Majczak, A. (1967). O nastrojach w przebiegu alkoholizowania sie czlowieka [On mood changes during alcoholization in humans]. *Probl Alkzmu, Warsaw, 15,* 4–6. (From *Quarterly Journal of Studies on Alcohol,* 1968, *35,*, 733.)

Mansfield, J.G. (1979). Dose-related effects of ethanol on avoidance conflicts behavior in the rat. *Psychopharmacology, 66,* 67–71.

Mansfield, J.G., Eaton, N.K., Cunningham, C.L., & Brown, J.S. (1977). Ethanol and avoidance-avoidance conflict in the rat. *Physiological Psychology, 5,* 197–203.

Marlatt, G.A. (1976). Alcohol, stress, and cognitive control. In I.G. Sarason & C.D. Spielberger (Eds.). *Stress and Anxiety,* Vol III. New York: Hemisphere.

Marlatt, G.A., & Gordon, J. (1980). Determinants of relapse: Implications for behavior change. in P.O. Davidson & S.M. Davidson (Eds.), *Behavioral Medicine: Changing Health Lifestyle.* New York: Brunner/Mazel.

Marlatt, G.A., Kosturn, C.F., & Lang, A.R. (1975). Provocation to anger and opportunity for retaliation as determinants of alcohol consumption in social drinkers. *Journal of Abnormal Psychology, 84,* 652–659.

Marlatt, G.A., & Rohsenow, D.J. (1980). cognitive processes in alcohol use: Expectancy and the balanced placebo design. In N.K. Mello (Ed.), *Advances in Substance Abuse: Behavioral and Biological Research.* Greenwich, Conn.: JAI Press.

Martin, W.R., Jasinski, D.R., Haertzen, C.A., Kay, D.C., Jones, B.E., Mansky, P.A., & Carpenter, R.W. (1973). Methadone—A reevaluation. *Archives of General Psychiatry,* 28, 286–295.

Masserman, J.H., & Yum, K.S. (1946). An analysis of the influence of alcohol on experimental neuroses in cats. *Psychosomtic Medicine, 8,* 36–52.

Mayfield, D.G. (1968). Psychopharmacology of alcohol: II. Affective tolerance in alcohol intoxication. *Journal of Nervous and Mental Disease, 146,* 322–327.

Mayfield, D., & Allen, D. (1967). Alcohol and affect: A psychopharmacological study. *American Journal of Psychiatry, 123,* 1346–1351.

McClelland, D.C., Davis, W.N., Kalin, R., & Wanner, W. (1972). *The Drinking Man.* New York: Free Press.

McCollam, J.B., Burtish, T.G., Maisto, S.A., & Sobell, M.B. (1980). Alcohol's effects on physiological arousal and self-reported affect and sensations. *Journal of Abnormal Psychology, 89,* 224–233.

McGuire, M.T., Stein, S., & Mendelson, J.H. (1966). Comparative psychosocial studies of alcoholic and nonalcoholic subjects undergoing experimentally induced ethanol intoxication. *Psychosomatic Medicine, 28,* 13–26.

McNamee, H.B., Mello, N.K., & Mendelson, J.H. (1968). Experimental analysis of drinking patterns of alcoholics: Concurrent psychiatric observations. *American Journal of Psychiatry, 124,* 1063–1069.

Mello, N.K., & Mendelson, J.H. (1970). Experimentally induced intoxication in alcoholics: A comparison of programmed and spontaneous drinking. *Journal of Pharmacology and Experimental Therapeutics, 173,* 101–116.

Menaker, T. (1967). Anxiety about drinking in alcoholics. *Journal of Abnormal Psychology, 72,* 43–49.

Mendelson, J.H., LaDou, J., & Solomon, P. (1964). Experimentally induced chronic intoxication and withdrawal in alcoholics. Part III: Psychiatric findings. *Quarterly Journal of Studies on Alcohol, 25,* (suppl. 2), 40–52.

Mendelson, J.H., Mello, N.K., & Ellingboe, J. (1981). Acute alcohol intake and pituitary gonadal hormones in normal human females. *Journal of Pharmacology and Experimental Therapeutics, 218,* 23–26.

Meyer, R.E., & Mirin, S.W. (1979). *The Heroin Stimulus: Implications for a Theory of Addiction.* New York: Plenum Press.

Miller, P.M., Hersen, M., Eisler, R.M., & Hilsman, G. Effects of social stress on operant drinking of alcoholics and social drinkers. *Behavior Research and Therapy, 12* 76–72.

Mulford, H.a. (1977), Women and men problem drinkers: Sex diferences in patients served by Iowa's community alcoholism centres. *Journal of Studies in Alcohol, 38,* 1624–1639.

Mullaney, J.A., & Trippett, C.J. (1979). Alcohol dependence and phobias: Clinical description and relevance. *British Journal of Psychiatry, 135,* 565–573.

Nathan, P.E., Goldman, M.S., Lisman, S.A., & Taylor, H.A. (1972). Alcohol and alcoholics: A behavioural approach. *Transactions of the New York Academy of Sciences, 34,* 602–607.

Nathan, P.E., & Hay, W.M. (1984). Alcoholism: Psychopathology, etiology, and treatment. In H.E. Adams & P.B. Sutker (Eds.), *Comprehensive Handbook of Psychopathology.* New York: plenum Press.

Nathan, P.E., & Niaura, R.S. (1985). Behavioral assessment and treatment of alcoholism. In J.H. Mendelson & N.K. Mello (Eds.), *The diagnosis and Treatment of Alcoholism* (2nd ed.). New York: McGraw-Hill.

Nathan, P.E., & O'Brien, J.S. (1971). An experimental analysis of the behavior of alcoholics and nonalcoholics during prolonged experimental drinking: A necessary precusor of behavior therapy? *Behavior Therapy, 2,* 455–476.

Nathan, P.E., Titler, N.A., Lowenstein, L.M., Solmon, P., & Rossi, A. M. (1970). Behavior analysis of chronic alcoholism. *Archives of General Psychiatry, 22,* 419–430.

Noel, N.E., & Lisman, S.A. (1980). Alcohol consumption in college females following exposure to unsolvable problems: learned helplessness or stress induced drinking? *Behaviour Research and Therapy, 18,* 429–440.

Pihl, R.O., & Yankofsky, L. (1979). Alcohol consumption in male social drinkers as a function of situationally induced depressive affect and anxiety. *Psychopharmacology, 65,* 251–257.

Podolsky, E. (1963). the woman alcoholic and premenstrual tension. *Journal of the American Medical Women's Association, 18* 816–818.

Polivy, J., Schueneman, A.L. & Carlson, K. (1976). Alcohol and tension reduction: Cognitive and physiological effects. *Journal of Abnormal Psychology, 85,* 595–600.

Rabdall, C.L., & Lester, D. (1975). Cross-fostering of DBA and C57BL mice: Increase in voluntary consumption of alcohol by DBA weanlings. *Journal of Studies on Alcohol, 36,* 973–980.

Randall, C.L., Lochry, E.A., Mosely, J.W., & Sutker, P.B. (1981). Alcoholic sensivity in female mice: Effect of ovariectomy. *Pharmacology Biochemistry and Behavior, 15,* 191–195.

Reich, L.H., Davies, R.K., & Hemmilhoch, J.M. (1974). Excessive alcohol use in manic depressive illness. *American Journal of Psychiatry, 131,* 83–84.

Rohsenow, D.J. (1983). Drinking habits and expectncies about alcohol's effects for self versus others. *Journal of Consulting and Clinical Psychology, 52* 752–756.

Russell, J.A., & Bond, C.R. (1979). Beliefs among college students on settings and emotions conducive to alcohol and marijuana use. *International Journal of the Addictions, 14,* 977–986.

Russell, J.A., & Bond, C.R. (1980). Individual differences in beliefs concerning emotions conducive to alcohol use. *Journal of Studies on Alcohol, 41,* 753–759.

Russell, J.A., & Mehrabian, A. (1975). The mediating role of emotions in alcohol use. *Journal of Studies on Alcohol, 36,* 1508–1536.

Schacter, S. (1964). the interaction of cognitive and physiological determinants of emotional state. *Advances in Experimental Social Psychology, 1,* 49–80.

Schuckit, M.A. (1980a). Biological markers: Metabolism and cute reactions to alcohol in sons of alcoholics. *Pharmacology Biochemistry and Behavior, 13,* (suppl 1), 9–16.

Schuckit, M.A. (1980b). Self-rating of alcohol intoxication by young men with and without family histories of alcoholism. *Journal of Studies on Alcohol, 41,* 242–249.

Schuckit, M.A. (1983). the genetics of alcoholism. In B. Tabakoff, P. B. Sutker, & C.L. Randall (Eds.), *Medical and Social Aspects of Alcohol Abuse.* New York: Plenum Press.

Schuckit, M.A. (1985). The clinical implications of primary diagnostic groups among alcoholics. *Archieves of General Psychiatry, 42,* 1043–1049.

Schuckit, M.A., & Rayses, V. (1979). Ethanol ingestion: Differences in blood acetaldehyde concentrations in relatives of alcoholics and controls. *Science, 203* 54–55.

Senter, R.J., Heintzelman, M., Dorfmueller, M., & Hinkle, H. (1979). A comparative look at ratings of the subjective effects of beverage alcohol. *Psychological Record, 29* 49–56.

Sher, K. (1984). Alcohol and stress. *Behavioural Medicine Abstracts, 5,* 80–82.

Sher, K.J., & Levenson, R.W. (1982). Risk for alcoholism and individual differences in the stress-response-dampening effect of alcohol. *Journal of Abnormal psychology, 91,* 350–367.

Skurdal, A.J., Eckardt, M.J., & Brown, J.S. (1975). The effects of alcohol on escape learning and on regular and punished extinction in a self-punitive situation with rats. *Physiological Psychology, 3,* 29–34.

Smail, P., Stockwell, T., Canter, S. & Hodgson, R. (1984). Alcohol dependence and phobic anxiety states: I. A prevalence study. *British Journal of Psychiatry, 144,* 53–57.

Steffen, J.J., Nathan, P.E., & Taylor, H.A. (1974). Tension-reducing effects of alcohol: Further evidence and some methodological considerations. *Journals of Abnormal Psychology, 83,* 542–547.

Stortebecker, T.P. (1939). Hormones and resistance: An acute antinarcotic and antitoxic effect of the estrogenic hormones. *Acta pathologica et Microbiological Scandinavica, 16* (Suppl. 41).

Strickler, D.P., Tomaszewski, R., Maxwell, W.A., & Suib, M.R. (1979). The effects of relaxation instructions on drinking behavior in the presence of stress. *Behavior Research and Therapy, 17,* 45–51.

Sutker, P.B., Allain, A.N., Brantley, P.J., Randall, C.L. (1982). Acute autonomic intoxication, negative affects, and autonomic arousal in women and men. *Addictive Behaviors, 7,* 17–25.

Sutker, P.B., Archer, R.P. Brantley, P.J., & Kilpatrick, D.G. (1979). Alcoholics and opiate addicts: Comparison of personality characteristics. *Journal of Studies on Alcohol, 40,* 635–644.

Sutker, P.B., Brantley, P.J., & Allain, A.N. (1980). MMPI response patterns and alcohol consumption in DUI offenders. *Journal of Consulting and Clinical Psychology, 48,* 350–354.

Sutker, P.B., Goist, K.C., Jr., & Allain, A.N. (1986). *Acute alcohol intoxication: Sex comparisons on pharmacokinetic and mood measures.* Manuscript submitted for publication.

Sutker, P.B., Goist, K.C., Jr., & King, A.R. (in press). Acute alcohol intoxication in women: relationship to dose and menstrual cycle phase. *Alcoholism: Clinical and Experimental Research.*

Sutker, P.B., Libet, J.M., Allain, A.N., & Randall, C.L. (1983). Alcohol use, negative mood states, and menstrual cycle phases. *Alcoholism: Clinical and Experimental Research, 7,*327–331.

Sutker, P.B., Tabakoff, B., Goist, K.C., Jr., & Randall C.L. (1983). Acute alcohol intoxication, mood states and alcohol metabolism in women and men. *Pharmacology Biochemistry and Behavior, 18,* 349–354.

Tabakoff, B., & Ritzmann, R. F. (1979). Acute tolerance in inbred and selected lines of mice. *Drug and Alcohol Dependence, 4,* 87–90.

Tabakoff, B., Ritzman, R.F., Raju, T.S., & Dietrich, R.A. (1980). Characterization of acute and chronic tolerance in mice selected for inherent differences in sensitivity to ethonol. *Alcoholism: Clinical and Experimental Research, 4,* 70–73.

Tamerin, J.S., & Mendelson, J.H. (1969). The psychodynamics of chronic inebriation: Observations of alcoholics during the process of drinking in an experimental group setting. *American Journal of Psychiatry, 125,* 886–899.

Tracey, D.A., & Nathan, P.E. (1976). Behavioural analysis of chronic alcoholism in four women. *Journal of Consulting and Clinical Psychology, 44,* 832–842.

Vanderpool, J.A. (1969). Alcoholism and self-concept. *Quarterly Journal of Studies on Alcohol, 30,* 59–77.

van der Spuy, H.I. (1972). The influence of alcohol on the mood of the alcoholic. *British Journal of Addiction, 67,* 225–265.

Vannicelli, M. (1984). Treatment outcome of alcoholic women: The state of the art in relation to sex bias and expectancy effects. In S.C. Wilsnack & L.J. Beckman (Eds.), *Alcohol Problems in Women: Antecedents, Consequences, and Intervention.* New York: Guilford Press.

Vogel, R.A., Frye, G.D., Wilson, J.H., Kuhn, C.M., Koepke, K.M., Mailman, R.B., Mueller, R.A., & Breese, G.R. (1980). Attenuation of the effects of punishment by ethanol: Comparisons with chlordiazepoxide. *Psychopharmacology, 71,* 123–129.

Vuchinich, R. E., Tucker, J.A., & Sobell, M.B. (1979). Alcohol, expectancy, cognitive labelling, and mirth. *Journal of Abnormal Psychology, 88,* 641–651.

Waddell, J.O., & Everett, M.W. (Eds.) (1980). *Drinking behavior among Southwestern Indians: An anthropological perspective.* Tucson: University of Arizona Press.

Westermeyer, J. (1985). Substance abuse and psychopathology: Sociocultural factors. In A.I. Alterman (Ed.), *Substance Abuse and Psychopathology.* New York: Plenum Press.

Wikler, A. (1952). A psychodynamic study of a patient during self-regulated readdiction to morphine. *Psychiatric Quarterly, 26,* 270–293.

Williams, A.F. (1966). Social drinking. anxiety, and depression. *Journal of Personality and Social psychology, 3,* 689–693.

Wilsnack, S.C. (1984). Drinking, sexuality, and sexual dysfunction in women. In S.C. Wilsnack & L.J. Beckman (Eds.), Alcohol Problems in Women: Antecents, Consequences, and Intervention. New York: Guilford Press.

Wilson, G.T. (1982). Alcohol and anxiety: Recent evidence on the tension reduction theory of alcohol use and abuse. *Advances in the Study of Communications and Affect, 7,* 117–141/

Wilson, G.T., & Abrahams, D. (1977). Effects of alcohol on social anxiety and physiological arousal: Cognitive versus pharmacological processes. *Cognitive Therapy and Research, 1,* 195–210.

Wilson, G.T., Abrams, D.B., & Lipscomb, T.R. (1980). Effects of intoxication levels and drinking pattern on social anxiety in men. *Journal of Studies on Alcohol, 41,* 250–261.

Winokur, G., Clayton, P.J., & Reich, T. (1969). *Manic Depressive Illness.* St. Louis: Mosby.

SIX

THE TENSION-REDUCTION HYPOTHESIS:

A Reanalysis of Some Crucial Early Data

JAMES W. LANGENBUCHER, Ph.D., and PETER E. NATHAN, Ph.D.

The aim of this chapter is to examine, once again, the validity of the tension-reduction hypothesis (TRH). As is noted below, this hypothesis has been influential in generating a range of hypotheses concerning the antecedent and consequent conditions of alcoholic drinking. Despite its apparent utility in this regard, however, the validity of the TRH continues to be hotly debated. In an effort to add light to this debate, we have reanalyzed some crucial early data from chronic alcohol administration studies of human beings; in our view, these data, from 15 studies, enable a reasoned assessment of the validity of the TRH that appears to hew closer to the data than any prior judgment in this regard.

Chapter 5 on alcohol consumption, tension reduction, and mood enhancement has a broader purpose, for which it considers a much more diverse research literature, than our chapter. To quote its authors West and Sutker their aim is "to summarize extant findings descriptive of relationships between alcohol consumption and mood states." To this end, these authors consider the results of animal as well as human studies, focusing their attention on the acute effects of intoxication, in contrast to our review, which is devoted solely to chronic alcohol administration studies of human beings. In other words, these two chapters, which consider the validity of the TRH, deal with different aspects of the hypothesis—and do so from different research vantage points.

Together they provide a thorough exploration of recent data on the validity, and utility, of the TRH.

THEORIES OF ALCOHOLIC DRINKING

The idea that alcoholics drink because beverage alcohol possesses euphoriant or emotionally palliative properties is one deeply rooted in our folklore; it is also supported by a variety of empirical studies both of social drinkers and alcoholics (eg., Holloway, 1969; Tamerin, Weiner, & Mendelson, 1970; Wanberg, 1969).

Not surprisingly, this conviction is a core feature of two complementary bodies of theoretical and empirical work that seek to explain the development and maintenance of alcoholic drinking. The first is the so-called unitary disease model of alcoholism proposed by the foremost student of alcoholism of his time, E.M. Jellinek (1952, 1960), and elaborated by Glatt (1967, 1974), Keller (1972), and, most recently, Vaillant (1983). The second is the tension-reduction hypothesis presaged by the contributions of Masserman and Yum (1946), Dollard and Miller (1950), and others, but brought into focus in the classic monograph by Conger (1956).

The Unitary Disease Model

The unitary disease model includes the following tenets: (1) alcoholics differ from nonalcoholics in terms of psychological predisposition, nutritional status, or allergic sensitivity to alcohol; (2) these differences lead to disease-process-like psychological and/or biochemical changes that are progressive, irreversible, and predisposing to the development of craving (Jellinek, 1960) and loss of control (Glatt, 1967; Jellinek, 1960); and (3) the disease of alcoholism is remediable in every case by the sole expedient of lifelong abstinence. These views have been extensively criticized elsewhere (eg., Caddy, 1978; Chafetz, 1966; Cox, 1983; Horn & Wanberg, 1969; Marlatt, 1976; Mello, 1975; Nathan & Lisman, 1976; Pattison, 1976; Pattison, Sobell, & Sobell, 1977). Clearly, the tenor of the times no longer gives this model unqualified support. For example, the discussion of alcohol abuse and dependence in the American Psychiatric Association's (1980) *Diagnostic and Statistical Manual of Mental Disorders*, third edition (DSM-III), clearly departs from many of the assumptions of Jellinek's unitary disease model. The prevailing current view seems to have benefited from a sensitivity to such alternative approaches as that of Pattison et al. (1977), who view alcohol abuse and dependence as a variety of syndromes located on a continuum of pathology. In contrast to a unitary disease, the multiple syndromes of alcoholism presumably differ in etiology, onset, course, and prognosis; are variable over time with respect to the dimensions and consequences of drinking; and are maintained by a multitude of factors.

Despite its inadequacies, the unitary disease model has had a powerful influence on the study of alcohol's effects on alcoholics. First, the model posits that, in at least two "species" of alcoholism, *alpha alcoholism* (prealcoholic drinking, one of the early stages of *gamma alcoholism*), and *epsilon alcoholism* (periodic binge drinking), drinking occurs in part because it helps the drinker to escape from an aversive emotional climate such as depression, anxiety, insomnia, or pain. This position, supported by the retrospective reports of alcoholics (referenced above), has helped to spur much research. However, the model has also led, paradoxically, to an antiempirical bias against inquiry into alcohol's effects on alcoholic subjects—due largely to opposition to giving alcohol to alcoholic research subjects (Adesso, 1980); this is the second, and perhaps more important, form of the influence of this model.

The Tension-Reduction Hypothesis

Conger's (1951, 1956) tension-reduction hypothesis—and etiologic model—enjoys substantially more support than the unitary disease model by many alcoholism researchers. The TR model calls on principles of respondent learning and related experimental findings from alcohol research on infrahuman species to explain the development and maintenance of human alcohol problems (Conger, 1951, 1956). Conger's theory is simple, reasonably congruent with clinical lore (and with the experimental evidence available to Conger 30 years ago), and eminently testable. In essence, the theory presumes that alcoholic drinking is a product of escape learning; alcoholics drink because they have been negatively reinforced for drinking in the face of life stress. Drinking behavior is negatively reinforced because it leads to a reduction in aversive emotional states (e.g., anxiety, fear, depression). Put another way, the TR model holds that alcoholics drink because drinking relieves negative emotional states, which we variously define as anxiety, depression, fear, and so on.

Taken together, the unitary disease model and the TRH have produced testable hypotheses concerning the antecedent and consequent conditions of alcoholic drinking. Beginning in 1964 (Mendelson,

LaDou, & Solomon, 1964), these hypotheses began to be tested in both acute and chronic alcohol administration studies of human beings. The major hypotheses tested in these studies were derived from both models. They were, simply, that (1) alcoholics will drink more in the presence of stressors, and (2) their consumption of alcohol will attenuate their experience of the negative emotional states associated with the stressors. Subsequent to the development of the research reviewed in this chapter, alternative theoretical models of alcoholism (e.g., cognitive social learning theory, family systems) developed; however, it was these early models, which remain influential, that guided the development of this empirical research line.

CHRONIC ADMINISTRATION STUDIES: AN OVERVIEW

The experiments reviewed here involve examination of the behavioral effects of chronic administration of alcohol to humans; in our view, these studies have been most influential in the crucial task of hypothesis testing. The first investigation of this kind was conducted by a ten-person research team assembled by Jack H. Mendelson. Results were published in a 126-page supplement to the *Quarterly Journal of Studies on Alcohol* in 1964.

In most of the chronic administration studies reviewed below, volunteers from correctional or treatment facilities were restricted to a controlled environment, such as a hospital ward or a laboratory with live-in facilities, for lengthy periods, during which alcohol intake was monitored and dependent measures were taken. Besides Mendelson, Mello, and colleagues, who completed chronic administration studies at the Massachusetts General Hospital in Boston and, later, Saint Elizabeth's Hospital in Washington, D.C., chronic administration research has been published by Nathan and colleagues. The latter group of researchers worked at Boston City Hospital from 1967 to 1970 and, from 1970 to the present time, at the Alcohol Behavior Research Laboratory, Rutgers University. Several independent researchers, geographically dispersed, have also reported on chronic administration studies; most have contributed only one or two studies to the field, while the Mendelson/Mello and Nathan groups each published substantially more. Most chronic administration research was completed during the 1960s and early 1970s; for the most part, the behavior of live-in subjects was observed for periods of up to ten weeks.

Several features of the chronic administration experiment are attractive. Chronic administration studies permit exquisite control over subjects and their drinking. Alcohol can be administered *ad libitum*, according to a fixed schedule, or as a reward for an operant response. Periods of isolation and social contact can be imposed and their effects on drinking assessed. Subjects can be observed and measures taken on a 24-hour basis during predrinking, drinking, and withdrawal periods.

Even more important, in the eyes of some critics of acute administration studies, is that chronic administration studies permit the observation of behavior before, during, and after not simply a single episode of drinking but a period of weeks or months in a social and physical environment to which the subjects have presumably become habituated. Mendelson, Nathan, and the others clearly believed that chronic drinking under these conditions more closely approximates the heavy, prolonged drinking maintained by alcoholics in their natural environments.

Chronic administration studies also have significant drawbacks. To begin with, they are enormously expensive in terms of staff resources and appropriate facilities. Few researchers have access to either staff or facilities suitable for the long-term behavioral, experimental, and medical management of alcoholics undergoing experimental intoxication. Moreover, alcoholic subjects appropriate for such a demanding regimen are rare: They must show "hard signs" of alcohol dependence and yet be free of concurrent medical and psychiatric complaints. They must also be willing to accept only modest reimbursement on a live-in basis for several weeks. This coincidence of subject characteristics has resulted in the recruitment of many chronic administration subjects from correctional facilities, with the concurrent subject characteristics—low socioeconomic status (SES), high sociopathy, unstable family and employment histories, etc.—usually associated with this unique environment.

In fact, through the first decade of this tradition's history, the majority of subjects came to their research setting from jail. To make the tradition's findings even more specific to a unique group of subjects, nearly all of them were recruited from a single source, the Massachusetts Correctional Institution at Bridgewater (MCI-Bridgewater). Both Mendelson and Mello, as well as Nathan, drew most of their subjects from MCI-Bridgewater.

REVIEW OF CHRONIC ADMINISTRATION STUDIES

Our method of review differs from other reviews of this literature (e.g., Adesso, 1980, 1985; Cappell & Herman, 1972; Freed, 1978; Chapter 5, this volume; Pihl & Smith 1983; Pohorecky, 1981) in two respects. First, although like Pihl and Smith (1983) we classify each study as supportive, nonsupportive, or ambiguous with regard to the TRH, we are sensitive to the liabilities of this kind of microanalysis and also explicate each experiment in considerable detail, so as to bring the reader as close as possible to the original source material. In this way, a principal shortcoming of the "box score" approach to microanalysis—its artificiality and arbitrariness—can be leavened by permitting the reader to make some independent judgment of the same data on which we have made our decisions.

Second, since some believe that the findings of this experimental tradition are less a function of objective reality than of the methods selected to study it, we have chosen to evaluate—or "grade"—each study according to its status on ten dimensions of methodologic adequacy. Each study is rated on each dimension on a scale from 1 to 5. The ultimate aim of this assessment is evaluation of the extent to which a study's findings will be *generalizable*. Intermediate aims include *reliability* of measurement, potential *utility* of results, and *methodological adequacy* of study designs. At the same time, it should be clear that this rating system is both subjective and imprecise; at best, it can only provide a rough index of the degree to which the 15 studies so rated approximate the aims of the rating.

The first evaluation dimension has to do the study's sample size. The study reviewed in this survey that had the largest sample size, 61 subjects (Alterman, Gottheil, & Crawford, 1975), takes precedence here and, accordingly, receives a score of 5. Another study by the same research team, with 25 subjects (Gottheil, Murphy, Skoloda, & Corbett, 1972), receives a score of 4; other studies with smaller sample sizes receive lower scores, while five studies with four or fewer subjects receive a score of 1.

The second evaluation dimension relates to source of subject recruitment. The disadvantages of recruiting subjects from jails, in terms of limited generalizability of results, have been noted above; accordingly, the five studies reviewed here that did so receive a score of 1. By contrast, two researchers recruited subjects directly from the community at large; these studies receive a score of 5. Studies that recruited subjects from general hospitals and Veterans Administration medical centers and, in one case, both the community and a jail, occupy the middle ground and receive intermediate scores.

The third evaluation dimension refers to the environment in which the subjects lived and drank for the duration of the experiment. Two studies were conducted in an inpatient psychiatric unit, a restricted and unnatural environment that receives a 1. Six studies conducted in the general medical or rehabilitation units of a hospital receive a score of 2. The remainder of the studies, all carried out in self-contained laboratory units, appear to merit scores of 3. Had a chronic administration experiment taken place in an actual drinking setting, such as a bar or private home, it would have merited a higher score.

The fourth evaluation dimension relates to the length of time subjects were restricted to the experimental setting and so deprived of familiar persons and settings. The presumption here is that those studies that employed the briefest quarantine periods merit the highest scores on this variable because subjects' behavior would be more clearly a function of real rather than laboratory-induced events and phenomena.

The fifth evaluation dimension considers whether subjects had to violate a period of abstinence from alcohol in order to participate in the experiment. This dimension relates to Marlatt's (1978) concept of the abstinence violation effect, which is presumed to influence the behavior of recently abstinent alcoholics newly returned to drinking in profound ways. Interestingly, all chronic administration studies recruited abstinent alcoholics and, as a consequence, had to induce them to violate abstinence. Thus all studies reviewed receive a score of 1 on this dimension.

The sixth evaluation dimension has to do with choice of control group. Eleven studies employing the convenient but less than ideal design in which subjects serve as their own controls receive a score of 1. Another study (McGuire, Stein, & Mendelson, 1966), which used nonalcoholic jailed sex offenders for controls, receives a score of 2. Yet another (Nathan & O'Brien, 1971) used carefully matched nonalcoholics, which merits the score of 3. The study that used the most appropriate controls (Alterman et al., 1975; Gottheil et al., 1972) employed alcoholic participants who abstained on an *ad lib* basis for the duration of the study, a practice that receives the score of 4. Given, however, the dual nature of the hypothesis under study—stress drives drinking and drinking relieves distress—even greater merit would attach to a study that used matched groups of stressed and nonstressed alcoholic subjects.

The seventh evaluation dimension relates to how alcohol was administered to subjects in the 15 studies evaluated here. Two studies used "programmed" doses of alcohol at preset intervals, and receive a score of 1, because this manner of administration is grossly artificial and unnatural. Two other studies employed both programmed and "free access" methods, for which a score of 2 is assigned. Seven studies employed an "operant" procedure, which required subjects to earn alcohol credits by pressing a response key repeatedly; this procedure merits a score of 3. The remaining studies allowed subjects generally free access to beverage alcohol; they receive a score of 4. A superior method would allow subjects free but socially appropriate and controlled access to alcohol, as in the natural drinking environment.

The eighth evaluation dimension is the extent to which subjects' own decisions controlled alcohol intake. Understandably, the two studies that programmed drinking receive a score of 1. The two studies with both programmed and free access drink-delivery methods receive a score of 3. Most other studies reviewed, which utilized either free access or operant methods, allowed their subjects free choice over drinking—but the subtle experimental demand imposed by the presence of uniformly heavy-drinking subjects in these studies requires that they receive a score of 4. By contrast, the Alterman et al. (1975) and Gottheil et al. (1972) studies, in which large numbers of subjects themselves initiated and maintained abstinence at their own option while others drank, merit the maximum score of 5.

The ninth evaluation dimension relates to dependent measures employed in the studies reviewed. The least adequate methods, for which a score of 1 is given, were unstructured interviews and casual staff observations of behavior on the experimental unit. A study that employed an unvalidated Q-sort for mood merits a score of 2. Studies that relied primarily on one of the several forms of the Mood Adjective Checklist (MACL) or a similar instrument deserve a score of 3. Two studies were clearly superior in choice of measures; they receive a maximum score of 5. The first (Steffen, Nathan, & Taylor, 1974) programmed the frequent assessment of both subjective discomfort and electromyographic activity in subjects' frontalis muscles, the only instance of a psychophysiological measure of stress among the studies reviewed in this section. The second (Tracey & Nathan, 1976) administered a series of standardized psychological instruments on a regular basis.

The final evaluation dimension concerns whether and how stress was manipulated experimentally in these studies. Given that stress is so often antecedent to drinking by alcoholics in the real world, the experimental manipulation of stress in studies of this kind is necessary to permit escape from the logical fallacy of arguing from an effect (e.g., drinking causes changes in subjective tension) to the cause (e.g., the experience of tension causes drinking). Surprisingly, though, only one study (Allman, Taylor, & Nathan, 1972) programmed a stress manipulation; accordingly, it receives a score of 5. The remainder of studies reviewed receive a score of 1.

The Studies and Their Scores

Mendelson, Ladou, and Solomon (1964). This study was the first to examine the long-term consequences of alcoholic drinking under carefully controlled conditions. Its findings, which contravened the then-prevailing view that alcohol reduces tension in alcoholic drinkers, and its methods, which involved a whole new approach to the study of the behavior of drinking alcoholics, loom large in the alcoholism literature to the present day.

Although its viability as a test of the TRH is questionable, as we note below, this experiment nonetheless caused many other researchers, including some of Mendelson's co-workers, to question the viability of the hypothesis, as they themselves explored it later.

Mendelson and his colleagues recruited ten subjects from MCI Bridgewater. All were males, 30 to 45 years old, of low SES, and unmarried or estranged from their spouses. They had six- to 32-year histories of chronic spree drinking, and all had experienced withdrawal symptoms in the past. Because all were incarcerated at the time of their selection for the study, their last drink had been between ten and 37 days before the beginning of the research. The experimental protocol imposed another three days of abstinence during the "control" or pre-drinking phase of the experiment.

The inclusion of an abstinent control period at the beginning of the chronic alcohol administration studies reviewed here was to become a standard feature of these studies. Although the rationale of this design decision, to provide a sober baseline against which subsequent intoxicated behavior could be compared, was reasonable, it also raises a significant question. Why should a highly unusual circumstance for alcoholics—prolonged abstinence from alcohol—be utilized as a control procedure, a benchmark, to permit comparison with the future performance of men who will be, and are, typically intoxicated?

During the drinking phase of this experiment, alcohol was administered on a fixed schedule. Each subject consumed a dose of 86-proof Bourbon whiskey every four hours, including 2:00 a.m. and 6:00 a.m., for 24 consecutive days. On the first day of drinking, six ounces of whiskey, one ounce every four hours, were consumed. On the second day, 12 ounces of whiskey were given. Doses rose incrementally to the fifth day, when 30 ounces of whiskey, five ounces every four hours, were administered. The last dosage level was maintained for 14 days, and then raised to 40 ounces of whiskey per day for the final six days of drinking.

The planned drinking schedule, however, was not actually followed by every subject. In fact, only one subject had the fortitude to follow it exactly: "It can be seen that all the subjects did not adhere to the regimen as scheduled. This was primarily due to the development of gastritis with nausea and vomiting by some subjects" (p.10).

Subjects' blood alcohol concentrations (BACs) ranged from about 50 mg% at the outset of the study to 100–150 mg% during the middle phase to as high as 350 mg% during the final days of the study. At the very high levels, subjects suffered substantial debilitation: "During marked intoxication the subjects were quite unstable in walking and would frequently stumble or fall over large objects within the ward . . . They spent most of their time either sleeping or in a state of mild stupor" (p. 12).

Measures of affect taken during drinking consisted of mental-status examinations and unstructured staff observations of subject behavior on the ward. By and large, they were casual and prone to bias. No affective changes were noted during the early stages of drinking, with the exception of one subject who manifested "mild depression tendencies" during the predrinking phase and thereafter became more depressed. During the middle phase of the study (when 30 ounces of whiskey a day were being given), this subject became more depressed. Another actually developed psychotic symptoms, whereupon his dose of alcohol was reduced to 20 ounces a day. Morale among other subjects remained high and conviviality increased during this phase of the study. Nonetheless, "almost uniformly, the anxiety levels of the subjects, as determined by the mental status examinations, tended to increase . . . . Associated with the heightened anxiety was a tendency toward more compulsive drinking behavior. The subjects drank their beverage faster . . . and occasionally requested more whiskey" (p. 46).

During the final study phase (with consumption set at 40 ounces per day), "anxiety . . . was characterized by feelings of tension and apprehension induced by minor stresses which previously had not seemed to bother the subjects" (p. 46). The only mention of depression in the report on this study was the following:

> Associated with anxiety was an element of despondency, with overt symptoms of depression. There was ... an emergence of psychopathological symptoms. Two subjects exhibited overt passive–aggressive and aggressive behavior ... in the form of lying and minor thefts. One subject tried to get into bed with other subjects. One began to wander off the ward. Three became suspicious and showed moderate paranoid tendencies. (pp. 46–47)

These, then, were the findings that first cast serious doubt on the validity of the tension-reduction hypothesis. Not surprisingly, Pihl and Smith (1983) considered these results nonsupportive of the TRH. We agree. *Our methodologic ranking* finds the use of ten subjects (score = 3) recruited from a jail (1), quarantined for 30 days (2) on a neurological unit (2), who violated abstinence (1) to serve as their own controls (1), exercised no volitional control (1) over programmed doses of alcohol (1), and were studied with casual dependent measures (1) under no stress manipulation (1) to result in a score of 14. This score places the study 15th in methodologic adequacy of the 15 chronic administration studies published.

McGuire, Stein, and Mendelson (1966). These researchers set out to conduct a controlled replication and extension of Mendelson's 1964 study. Four male alcoholics and four male nonalcoholics were recruited from MCI-Bridgewater for the study. The alcoholic subjects were 39 to 43 years old, of low SES, and unmarried or estranged from their wives. They had histories of spree drinking ranging from ten to 23 years, had experienced withdrawal symptoms, and had been abstinent from alcohol for a period of two months prior to the beginning of the study. The four nonalcoholics were roughly matched for SES, but differed from the alcoholic subjects in other important respects. All were sex offenders in active psychiatric and rehabilitative treatment at the time of the study. One was a teetotaler; the other three were social drinkers. All had been abstinent from alcohol for 15–24 months before the study.

The experimental and control groups were studied in different facilities—the sex offenders in the hospital ward of their prison, and the alcoholics in a psychiatric unit of Massachusetts General Hospital (MGH). Because of limited space at MGH, they were studied in two separate groups of two subjects each. A six-day control period began each study.

The schedule for drink administration (a dose of alcohol every four hours around the clock) was similar to that of Mendelson et al. (1964), although the total dose was lower (28 ounces of 86-proof whiskey a day) and drinking lasted for only four days. Measures to assess mood were also similar; they included observation of ward behavior and daily nondirective interviews, both by members of the research team.

Like the 1964 study, the results of McGuire et al. (1966) are equivocal with regard to the tension reduction hypothesis. McGuire et al. found: "Those subjects who predicted that they would not be affected by the alcohol showed no increase in anxiety during the drinking phase.... The other subject showed an increase in anxiety. Pleasure increased for the entire group during the early phase of drinking" (p. 20). These authors also reported an increase in subjects' subjective "masculinity" and "sexual power" as well as in hostility. However, "no significant degree of depression was observed during the first 3 days of drinking, but it appeared on the ... last day" (p. 20). Unexpectedly, it was the nonalcoholic subjects whose behavior during intoxication most resembled that of the alcoholic *S*s in Mendelson's 1964 study: "[These] subjects reported an increase in feelings of anxiety.... There was a uniform depression about their plight and their inability to escape from it.... All experienced some nausea. Two subjects vomited" (p.20). Like Mendelson's alcoholics, these subjects were expected to drink very substantial quantities of alcohol; the result often was nausea and vomiting—and complaints of "their plight and their inability to escape from it."

By contrast, the alcoholic subjects in this research tended not to report increases in anxiety during the study's drinking phase, and experienced depression only on the fourth and last day of drinking, when they knew that abstinence would be reimposed on the following day.

Pihl and Smith (1983) omitted this study from their review. We find the results ambiguous and classify them in that way. *Our methodologic ranking* finds that McGuire's selection of eight subjects (score = 2) from jail (1), who lived for ten days (4) in a psychiatric unit or prison ward (1), who violated abstinence (1) to participate in a study in which the control group consisted of jailed sex offenders (2), who exercised no volitional control (1) over programmed doses of alcohol (1), and who were studied with casual dependent measures (1) under no stress manipulation (1) merits a summary score of 15. Accordingly, in methodologic adequacy this study ranks 13.5 among the 15 chronic administration studies published according to our evaluation system.

McNamee, Mello, and Mendelson (1968). This study, the last of Mendelson's inpatient research in Boston, was designed as another variant of the original, 1964 study. A sample of 12 male alcoholics was recruited from the MCI-Bridgewater and screened as before by these researchers. All subjects were between 30 and 45 years old, of low SES, and unmarried or estranged from their wives. Each reported at least a five-year history of chronic spree drinking, had experienced withdrawal symptoms in the past, and had been abstinent from alcohol for a minimum of two weeks prior to the beginning of the experiment. Like the McGuire et al. study (1966), this research was conducted in an MGH inpatient psychiatric unit.

The procedure for drink administration in this experiment was a departure from the programmed drinking imposed on subjects in its predecessors. Instead, McNamee and his colleagues adopted the operant paradigm developed for other purposes by Mello and Mendelson (1965). This method required subjects to press a response key repeatedly during the drinking phase of the experiment to obtain alcohol. As we note below, Nathan was so impressed by the measurement potential offered by this method that he chose to highlight the operant method of drink administration in a number of the studies done by his group. The rationale chosen by McNamee, Mello, and Mendelson for use of the operant paradigm in this research included the following

> This technique was similar to a real life situation in that the subject could control both the amount and rate of his alcohol intake.... Since alcohol is not usually available to most alcoholics without some expenditure of effort or money, it seemed realistic to require the subject to perform a simple operant task to obtain his alcohol. (p. 1065)

The introduction of the operant method gave subjects substantially more control over their own alcohol use; hence we judge it to have enhanced the value of this research. Nonetheless, it is also clear that, in the real world, the temporal and psychological relationships among work, money, and drinking are not nearly as clear and direct as in the operant paradigm used here. Money is not immediately available at the conclusion of work and beverage alcohol is not purchased immediately after money has been acquired. In other words, the operant paradigm that came to be favored by the chronic administration researchers for a time is, in our opinion, an imperfect analogue of the circumstances that typically regulate alcoholic drinking. As noted later in this chapter, a better analogue may well be one that allows free access to alcohol.

Like its two predecessors, McNamee's study was divided into three phases—a preexperimental control phase, a drinking phase, and a withdrawal phase. The drinking phase lasted seven days. Again, as before, nondirective interviews were conducted daily, with information from them supplemented by staff observation of subjects' behavior on the ward.

McNamees' results appear at first glance to be unequivocal. "A marked increase in anxiety and depression occurred in nine subjects during the second or third day... and grew more intense the longer the subjects drank. There appeared to be a correlation between the amount of alcohol consumed and the severity of the anxiety and depression" (p. 1066). McNamee et al. also noted apparent increases in hostility, guilt, resentment, demandingness, and assertiveness during the drinking phase of this study. Given that these behaviors are consistent with those of persons newly confined to prison or a psychiatric inpatient unit, it was well that these authors observed that "all [of the subjects] were slightly anxious and apprehensive. They attributed this apprehension to adjusting to the new environment and to their doubts regarding their ability to perform the experimental task" (p. 1066).

The following additional observation of subjects' behavior suggests that dysphoria increased toward the end of the drinking phase of the study, probably because of the subjects' awareness of the upcoming withdrawal period and their return to MCI-Bridgewater. It is also clear that subjects used alcohol as a vehicle for tension reduction: "Toward the termination of the drinking phase, most of the subjects showed considerable ambivalence about the cessation of drinking. Most increased ... consumption during the last 24 hours" (p. 1067).

In their review, Pihl and Smith (1983) classified the work of McNamee and colleagues as nonsupportive of the TRH. Our analysis of these data, however, leads us to conclude that the results are more accurately viewed as ambiguous. We find that McNamee's choice of 12 subjects (3) from jail (1), who were quarantined for about ten days (4) on a psychiatric unit (1), who violated abstinence (1) to serve as their own controls (1), and who exercised considerable volitional control (4) over an operant drink procedure (3), but were studied with casual dependent measures (1) under no stress manipulation (1) results in a summary score of 20. This score places the study 12th in methodologic adequacy among the 15 chronic administration studies reviewed in this paper.

Tamerin and Mendelson (1969). This study was designed in order "to understand these observable phenomena [the affective consequences of alcoholic drinking] within the context of a psychodynamic structural theory" (p. 887). The first of three studies to be completed by Mendelson's group at St. Elizabeth's Hospital in Washington, D.C., this study was also the first of two in which John Tamerin, a psychoanalytically oriented psychiatrist, was a coinvestigator.

The authors recruited four male alcoholics, 37 to 46 years old, from the wards of the hospital. Two of the men were married; all had a 20 to 29-year history of alcoholism. Subjects were abstinent during an initial, 14-day control phase. Like subjects in virtually all chronic administration studies, these subjects entered the experiment with ambivalence: "All of the subjects expressed feelings that their drinking patterns were detrimental and that they wanted to modify them" (p. 887).

Two different procedures for administering drinks were used during the five phases of the experiment. Phases and drink-administration methods included, in turn, a 14-day abstinent control period, a 21-day drinking phase (during which subjects consumed standard doses of alcohol at four-hour intervals), a ten-day withdrawal phase, a second 21-day drinking phase (during which subjects could exchange unearned credits for up to 33 ounces of 86-proof beverage alcohol a day), and a ten-day withdrawal phase. Dependent measures were taken during "nondirective and essentially exploratory interviews."

During the early stages of drinking, the subjects were described as experiencing increased relaxation and elation and decreased inhibition, although details on these effects were not specified. As drinking progressed, subjects were reported to experience increasing remorse, self-depreciation, guilt, depression, emotional liability, and anxiety. These mood changes were explained, in part, as follows: "Subjects were often filled with remorse and self-depreciation, which was heightened by the guilt they felt for having reinitiated drinking in the first place" (p. 889). This explanation appears to represent an example of what Marlatt (1978) terms the abstinence violation effect. Its impact on these alcoholics' behavior seems to have been considerable.

Though the authors of this report ultimately conclude that "prolonged drinking was characterized by progressive depression, guilt, and psychic pain . . . " (p. 897), the implication that these negative mood stages derived from pharmacological properties of alcohol alone is unsupported by data. In fact, the effects of the alcohol appear to have been perfectly consistent with the TRH:

> As defenses broke down, subjects were often flooded with affects of depression and anxiety which at times reached panic proportions. These findings could be controlled temporarily only by drinking more. When the immediate effect of the alcohol wore off . . . the painful feelings would return. . . . This intense psychic pain led to more drinking which, in fact, did diminish the painful feelings temporarily. (pp. 893–894)

Said another way, tension drove drinking, drinking relieved tension, in this study. It seems clear that the results of this study are supportive of the TRH, even though Pihl and Smith (1983) classified them as ambiguous. Methodologically, we find that Tamerin's selection of four subjects (1) from a hospital population (2), who lived for 66 days (1) in a hospital impatient unit (2), violated abstinence (1) to serve as their own controls (1), exercised some volitional control (3) over a split protocol of programmed and free access drinking (2), and were studied with casual dependent measures (1) with no stress manipulation (1) yields a summary score of 15. Accordingly, this study, with the experiment by McGuire et al. (1966), ranks 13.5 in methodologic adequacy of the 15 chronic administration studies reviewed here.

Tamerin, Weiner, and Mendelson (1970) Mendelson and his colleagues published several more chronic administration studies that are not reviewed here because they did not deal directly with the affective consequences of alcoholic drinking. Tamerin et al. (1970), the study reviewed here, is the last of the research from Mendelson's group that will be examined in detail. It was the second study of its kind to be conducted at St. Elizabeth's Hospital, and took as its foci (1) alcoholics' predrinking expectancies about their affective states while drinking, (2) the extent to which these expectancies were confirmed during subsequent drinking, and (3) the extent to which alcoholics, after withdrawal from alcohol, recall their affective experiences while intoxicated. This set of interrelated intents was derived from a paradoxical finding from Mendelson's earlier chronic administration studies: Given that alcohol seems to exert a negative impact on alcoholics' moods, and given as well that alcoholics predictably consume alcohol despite this negative consequence, then it is necessary to specify how alcoholics expect to benefit from drinking and, when they do not, how it is that they fail to recall this disappointing outcome when they are again sober.

Thirteen males, 26 to 48 years old, with ten to 29-year histories of alcoholism, were recruited from the wards of St. Elizabeth's. No data on length of subjects' abstinence from alcohol prior to the experiment or on the duration of the preexperimental control phase are given. Depending on the subject, the drinking phase lasted from 14 to 60 days. During this phase, subjects had free access to one quart of 100-proof whiskey per day (though data as to actual quantities consumed are not provided). Whether and how BACs were monitored during the study are not furnished. Given this lack of detail, substantial "guess work" is involved in the methodological analysis of this study.

Importantly, however, this study included a new dependent measure that was designed to supplement interview data and staff observations on subjects' affective behavior. This measure was a modified Q-sort consisting of 45 self-descriptive statements that subjects were to sort according to their sober and intoxicated selves. The instrument covered five domains: aggression, sexuality or closeness, dysphoria, responsibility, and activity/passivity. Unfortunately, the measure was given only once during each of the study's four phases-control, early drinking, late drinking, and withdrawal.

The findings of the study are consistent with the bulk of earlier work by this research group. During intoxication, subjects reported an increase in aggression, sexual feelings, dysphoria, and activity, and a decrease in feelings of responsibility. During withdrawal, subjects rated their intoxicated selves as somewhat more anhedonic than they had rated themselves while they were actually intoxicated. (This finding tends to disconfirm the view that alcoholics are amnestic for the mood deterioration they are said to experience during intoxication.)

Pihl and Smith (1983) did not include this study in their review. The incompleteness of the study report's descriptions of method and results is troublesome, but we consider its findings as nonsupportive of the TRH. Tamerin's selection of 13 subjects (3) from a hospital ward (2), who remained between 14 and 60 days (2) on a hospital ward (2), violated abstinence (1) in order to serve as their own controls (1), exercised some volitional control (4) over their free access to alcohol (4), and were studied with a Q-sort (2) under no stress manipulation (1) results in a summary score of 22 for this experiment. The study ranks tenth among the 15 studies ranked here.

Nathan, Zare, Ferneau, and Lowenstein (1970) This was the first experiment of its kind published by Nathan (who, at the time, directed the Alcohol Study Unit at Boston City Hospital) and his group. Unlike Mendelson's subjects, who lived for the course of their experiments in medical and psychiatric inpatient units where they were generally not segregated from the regular patients in treatment there, Nathan's subjects lived in a specially designed, self-contained laboratory capable of housing four subjects in private quarters. This unit was equipped with private bedrooms, a day room, a bathroom, a kitchen, and other amenities that, although located in a hospital, did much to diminish the hospital atmosphere. Thus the physical setting of the Nathan group's chronic administration studies represents a substantial improvement over the settings of most other experiments in the field

Another methodologic advance achieved by Nathan and his co-workers was their decision to utilize formal psychological instruments to measure dependent variables. These instruments, whose results at times yielded results appropriate for statistical analysis, included the Wittenborn Psychiatric Rating Scale (WPRS), and several forms of the Mood Adjective Checklist (MACL). Nathan also gathered and reported frequent alveolar breath analyses of his subjects' blood–alcohol concentrations during experimental drinking.

Other features of the work of the Nathan group bear comment. First, following the procedure of Mello and Mendelson (1965) and McNamee et al. (1966), Nathan allowed his subjects the opportunity to gain access to alcohol by emitting operant responses. In all but one of the studies by this group, subjects had to press a manipulandum repeatedly to earn points worth measured quantities of beverage alcohol. Second, subjects were customarily exposed to alternating periods of isolation and social interaction; these periods were not intended as stress manipulations but as a means to weigh the differential reinforcement value of alcohol and socialization. (Subjects had to expend points for relief from isolation as well as beverage alcohol.) Finally, the work of this group is somewhat more varied than that of Mendelson and his colleagues across studies with regard to measures, procedures, recruitment policies, etc.

The first study by this group (Nathan et al., 1970b) examined the behavior of eight male alcoholics recruited from MCI-Bridgewater. The men were between 33 and 45 years old, with alcoholic histories of from five to 31 years. Six of the men had experienced withdrawal symptoms in the past, and the other two had had alcoholic blackouts. Their SES was varied. Seven of the eight were unmarried, and all had been abstinent from alcohol for 14 days prior to the beginning of the experiment.

The experiment consisted of two 30-day trials, with four men participating in each trial. Each trial was further divided into three phases: (1) a six-day abstinent control phase, during which subjects could earn points later to be exchanged for alcohol or socialization (see below) by working at an operant task; (2) an 18-day drinking phase, during which subjects could purchase alcohol or socialization with their points and work to earn more points; and (3) a six-day withdrawal phase. All three phases were further divided into three-day periods during which subjects were alternately isolated (confined to their private rooms) or allowed to socialize. Subjects could "break isolation" by spending points for time out of their rooms during the isolation period.

The major dependent measure was a Q-sort version of the McNair and Lorr (1964) MACL, consisting of 21 cards designed to assess seven areas of functioning, which included vigor/activity, confusion, depression/dejection, anger/hostility, anxiety/tension, fatigue/inertia, and friendliness. This instrument was administered once each day; the WPRS was administered at three-day intervals only during the second 30-day trial. Blood alcohol concentrations were monitored by Breathalyzer three times daily, but the psychological measures were taken only once daily, making it impossible precisely to correlate BAC with mood.

Nathan and his colleagues obtained mixed results with regard to the affective consequences of alcoholic drinking. While subjects in trial I became more sociable after drinking began, those in trial II did not. On the MACL, subjects in trial I reported statistically significant increases in anxiety, depression, and hostility during drinking; during trial II, though, subjects did not show the same effects. Instead they maintained quite stable moods throughout the study.

By spending their earned points for beverage alcohol, Nathan's subjects were given the opportunity to control their own rates of consumption; the manner in which they did so was closely monitored. To this end, Nathan et al. (1970b) reported the following: "All [subjects] peaked at or beyond a [BAC] of 200 mg per 100 cc during the first days of drinking, then returned to a zero blood alcohol reading one or more times during the remainder of drinking.... The subjects *drank less as drinking progressed than when it first began*" (p. 94, emphasis added). Other studies by the Nathan group (e.g., Nathan et al., 1970a; Nathan & O'Brien, 1971) showed a similar pattern. But recall that, in three of the five studies by Mendelson's group, a drinking schedule quite different from the one preferred by Nathan's subjects was imposed (i.e., subjects were to consume doses that either did not vary or increased incrementally to a peak near the end of the drinking phase). Thus the dysphoria experienced by subjects in Mendelson's experiments seems at least partly to have been schedule induced.

This study was not evaluated by Pihl and Smith (1983). We classify the results as ambiguous, since one group of subjects showed neither affective improvement nor decay and the other group showed both improvement and decay. Methodologically, we note that Nathan's selection of eight subjects (2) from a jail (1), who lived for 24 days (3) in a hospital-based laboratory (3), violated abstinence (1) to serve as their own controls (1), exercised substantial volitional control (4) over operant access to alcohol (3), and were assessed with the MACL and WPRS (3) under no stress manipulation (1) results in a summary score of 22 for this experiment. It ranks as tenth of the 15 chronic administration studies evaluated here.

Nathan, Titler, Lowenstein, Solomon, and Rossi (1970). For this second study conducted by Nathan and his co-workers, 12 male alcoholics were recruited from MCI-Bridgewater. All were between 31 and 45 years of age, with alcoholic histories ranging from six to 31 years. All had experienced withdrawal symptoms in the past. All were unmarried, and most were semiskilled laborers. These subjects had been abstinent for 12–23 days prior to the beginning of the experiment, which was conducted in the Alcohol Study Unit at Boston City Hospital.

Because of limited space on this unit, the study was conducted as three separate trials, each involving four subjects. Each trial began with a six-day control period during which subjects could work at their operant tasks to earn points that could be exchanged for alcohol during a subsequent phase. Each trial ended with a six-day withdrawal period. The duration of the drinking phases, however, varied from six days in trial I to 12 days in trial II to 18 days in trial III.

As before, the sole measure of affective change was the MACL, which was administered at three-day intervals during trials I and II and daily during trial III. Each phase of each trial was divided into alternating three-day periods of isolation and socialization.

The affective changes obtained in this study were more robust than those obtained by Nathan et al. (1970b). In two of the trials, a significant increase in anxiety/tension was reported during the drinking phase; there was a tendency for this increase to continue into the withdrawal phase. In other words, the increase in anxiety appears to have been more closely associated with the duration of the experiment than with drinking per se. Nevertheless, during all three trials, there were also significant increases in depression/dejection and anger/hostility, which were confined to the drinking phase. These mood changes began several hours to a few days after the onset of drinking. These findings led the authors to the following conclusion: "The data... suggest that chronic alcoholics do feel more anxious, depressed, hostile and less vigorous when they are drinking than when they are not doing so" (p. 425).

Pihl and Smith (1983) did not evaluate this study. We find these results to be straightforward and nonsupportive of the TRH. Methodologically, we note that Nathan's selection of 12 subjects (3) from jail (1), who were quarantined from 12 to 24 days (4) in a hospital laboratory (3), violated abstinence (1) to serve as their own controls (1), exercised some substantial control (4) over their operant access to alcohol (3), and were studied with the MACL (3) under no stress manipulation (1) results in a summary score of 24. This study ranks seventh among the 15 chronic administration studies reviewed here.

Nathan and O'Brien (1970). Like McGuire et al. (1966), Nathan and O'Brien (1970) compared alcoholics and nonalcoholics undergoing experimental intoxication on (1) drinking pattern, (2) the affective consequences of drinking, and (3) the effects of social and isolated drinking. Eight males—four alcoholics and four nonalcoholics—were recruited from MCI-Bridgewater. They were between 37 and 49 years of age, with alcoholic histories of from seven to 28 years. All had experienced withdrawal symptoms in the past. All were unmarried and of low SES; all had been abstinent from alcohol for 15–28 days prior to the beginning of the study.

The four matched control subjects were much more carefully selected than were McGuire and colleagues' (1966) nonalcoholic controls, who were imprisoned sex offenders. By contrast, Nathan and O'Brien recruited their nonalcoholic men over the course of several months from "bars, flophouses and social clubs in the South End of Boston," the area in which their alcoholic subjects normally lived.

These alcoholic and nonalcoholic subjects were studied in separate trials. Each trial consisted of a nine-day abstinent control phase, an 18-day drinking phase, and a six-day withdrawal phase; each phase was further divided into alternating periods of isolation and socialization. As in previous experiments by this group, subjects had the opportunity to purchase alcohol, relief from social isolation, or both with points earned by operant responding. Two measures of affective change were used. The MACL was administered twice daily, and the WPRS was taken at three-day intervals.

The results of the experiment are generally consistent with those previously reported by this research group. On only two of the MACL scales, depression/dejection and vigor/activity, did the alcoholic drinkers show increases after they began drinking. The nonalcoholic men did not evince these changes. That is, even though the nonalcoholic men were exposed to an experimental milieu identical in every respect to that experienced by the alcoholic subjects (except that they elected to consume less alcohol), they showed no affective changes when drinking, whereas the alcoholic men became more depressed and less vigorous. By contrast, on the WPRS, both groups showed an increase in pathology after they began drinking. Although the alcoholics showed more pathology than the nonalcoholics, this difference was already apparent before the men began to drink:

> [O]n seven of the nine WPRS subscales, the alcoholic and nonalcoholic groups differed significantly. On each of these seven subscales, the behavior of the alcoholic subjects was judged to be more pathological than that of the nonalcoholic subjects, irregardless of whether the behavior was judged before, during, or after drinking.(p. 469)

Pihl and Smith (1983) classified this study as nonsupportive of the TRH. We classify the results as ambiguous. Methodologically, we find that Nathan and O'Brien's selection of eight subjects (2) from both jail and the community (4), who lived for 27 days (3) in a hospital laboratory (3), violated abstinence (1) in order to serve in an experiment in which the control group consisted of carefully matched nonalcoholics (3), exercised some volitional control (4) over their operant access to alcohol (3), and were studied with formal psychological instruments (3) under no stress manipulation (1) results in a summary score of 27 for this experiment. It ranks 5.5 among the 15 chronic administration studies reviewed here.

Allman, Taylor, and Nathan (1972). This experiment was the first to be conducted by Nathan and his colleagues after their move to the Alcohol Behavior Research Laboratory (ABRL) at Rutgers University. The ABRL, which was and is a self-contained laboratory with private live-in facilities, is a duplicate in most respects of the Alcohol Study Unit at Boston City Hospital.

Allman et al. (1972) incorporated an important methodological advance. An experimenter-controlled stressor was included as an independent variable in the design of the experiment. Although it has been argued (Cappell & Herman, 1972; Freed, 1978) that a true test of the TRH must include such a manipulation in order to avoid the logical fallacy of arguing from an effect (tension reduction) to a cause (tension-induced drinking), the Allman et al. experiment is the only chronic administration experiment with this feature. Unfortunately, it also has the dubious distinction of having examined the behavior of only three subjects.

Three male alcoholics were recruited from the alcohol rehabilitation unit at a nearby Veterans Administration hospital. All three were 46 years old; two were unmarried and the other was separated from his wife. Their alcoholic histories ranged from 15 to 25 years; all had previously experienced withdrawal symptoms. All had been abstinent from alcohol for 14 days prior to the start of the experiment.

The study was divided into three phases, including a four-day abstinent control phase, a 21-day drinking phase, and an eight-day withdrawal period. Each phase was additionally divided into alternating periods of isolation and socialization. Subjects could earn points either by working at their operant panels or by participating in a social activity with the other subjects. Except for the latter feature, the design of this experiment is characteristic of Nathan's earlier work. An additional difference, however, involved the imposition of a social stressor twice during the drinking phase and once during the withdrawal phase. The stressor was a communication to subjects on four consecutive days that their performance on the two tasks by which they earned points had deteriorated; because the performance of each individual was to be used to calculate a group average that could qualify the men for a cash bonus at the conclusion of the study, none would qualify if the poor performance continued. Nonstress periods lasting four days alternated with the stress periods. During the nonstress periods, subjects were told that they were performing adequately and would probably qualify for the cash bonus. Mood changes were measured by the MACL, which was administered twice daily, and the WRPS, completed once a day.

The authors' description of mood changes in the alcoholic subjects during drinking phases is sketchy. Moreover, the effects that were reported were both weak and confounded by intersubject variability. The authors found "a marked change in Subject l's mood, a moderate change in Subject 2's mood, and a minimal change in Subject 3's mood . . . during the first stress period after four days of drinking. The subjects reported, to varying degrees, increased levels of depression, tension, fatigue and confusion . . ." (p. 675). Positive moods appeared to rebound during the nonstress drinking periods: "The second drinking/stress periods yielded similar changes in mood that were, however, of lesser magnitude. Comparable mood changes were not observed during nonstress/drinking periods" (p. 675). Interestingly, although the earlier work of both Nathan and Mendelson suggested an increase of tension/anxiety during drinking, MACL anxiety scores (as well as anger and depression scores) in this study did not increase significantly during 21 days of drinking—but they did increase during the withdrawal phase of the study. Most important, however, was that subjects' moods, which deteriorated when the men were faced with the loss of a cash bonus, improved while they continued to drink after the threat was removed. Moreover, consumption of alcohol appeared to reduce stress even more effectively when the stressor was applied a second time.

Pihl and Smith classified these results as ambiguous. While we do not consider them clear-cut, they do seem to balance in favor of the TRH. Methodologically, we find that Allman's et al.'s selection of three subjects (1) from a VA hospital (3), who lived for 25 days (3) in a laboratory (3), violated abstinence (1) to serve as their own controls (1), exercised some volitional control (4) over their operant access to alcohol (3), and were studied with formal psychological instruments (3) in a study that included a stress manipulation (5) results in a summary score of 27 for this experiment. It ranks 5.5 among the 15 chronic administration experiments reviewed here.

Goldman, Taylor, Carruth, and Nathan (1973). This ABRL study was designed to examine the impact of small group process (i.e., the "bottle gang") on drinking by alcoholics. Specifically, the effects of group and individual decision making on the social and individual behavior of a group of alcoholics were examined in this experiment.

Four male alcoholics were recruited from the Lyons Veterans Administration Hospital. The men were 35 to 51 years old, with alcoholic histories ranging from 15 to 35 years. All were unmarried and of low to medium SES. All had experienced withdrawal symptoms in the past, and all had been abstinent from alcohol for 14–19 days prior to the beginning of the study.

The experiment lasted 25 days and was divided into seven phases. During five of the phases (a total of 17 days), alcohol was available following either individual or group decisions to drink; alternating two-day periods of isolation and socialization were also a feature of the research design. Mood changes were assessed by daily MACLs and a short form of the WPRS.

The authors observe that their findings regarding the affective consequences of their subjects' drinking were consistent with their prior research: "As in previous studies, [MACL] data showed that . . . the subjects' mood changed in the direction of greater discomfort during drinking, increasing with rising [BAC]" (p. 816). In fact, the results do not appear to have been so straightforward. While a significant increase in depression was observed during drinking, no data showing mood decay as "increasing with rising BAC" were reported. Unfortunately, mood changes were not monitored frequently enough to establish their correlation, if any, with BAC. In other words, it seems that Nathan's group, as had Mendelson's group before them, assumed without justification that their subjects' BACs steadily increased during the study when, in fact, they did not. Nonetheless, the illusion of a uniform, replicated, and linear relationship between alcoholics' BACs and the intensity of their negative moods has become a part of the literature, in part because of these conclusions.

Subjects in this study reported more intense anger and depression during *ad lib* drinking (based on individual decisions) than during drinking based on group decisions and subjects showed greater disturbance during this drinking phase. However, subjects experienced greater affective disturbance at the beginning of the experiment, during the abstinent control period, than at its conclusion, in the withdrawal period. This finding is not damaging to the TRH.

Pihl and Smith (1983) did not include this study in their review. In general, its results do not support the TRH, but the improvement in disturbed behavior from the control to the withdrawal phases complicates matters. Nevertheless, we consider the results to be nonsupportive of the TRH. Methodologically, we find that Goldman's et al. selection of four subjects (1) from a VA hospital (3) who lived in a laboratory for 20 days (3), violated abstinence (1) to serve as their own controls (1), exercised some volitional control (4) over their operant access to alcohol (3), and were measured with formal psychological instruments (3) under no stress manipulation results in a summary score of 23 for this experiment. It ranks eighth out of the 15 chronic administration studies reviewed here.

Steffen, Nathan, and Taylor (1974). In the introduction to this study, the authors raise some objections to the means by which moods were assessed in earlier experiments and suggest that an "objective" measure of tension be used to supplement self-report data. To this end, these authors decided to measure electromyographic activity (EMG) of the frontalis muscles of their subjects' foreheads regularly during the course of this study. This is the only chronic administration experiment to assess mood psychophysiologically. This study also was the only experiment conducted by the Nathan group in which alternating periods of isolation and socialization were not a feature of the design. It was one of the simplest and yet most informative in the long series of experiments conducted by Nathan and colleagues.

Besides choice of dependent measures, the Steffen et al. (1974) study has an additional feature to recommend it: The four male alcoholics who participated were recruited directly from the general community, and not from a jail or hospital. The men were 28-to 45-years-old and had alcoholic histories of from four to 19 years. All were unmarried or estranged from their spouses and all were unemployed after being educated through grade 12. No data on prior withdrawal symptoms or the duration of preexperimental abstinence are given.

Subjects were given free-access to drinking during a single 12-day period. The self-report instrument to assess mood was not the standard MACL but the Subjective Units of Disturbance Scale or SUDS developed by Wolpe (1969). The SUDS, popularly called a "fear thermometer" and actually constituting a primitive method of *magnitude estimation*, simply requires that subjects assign a number between zero (total relaxation) and 100 (stark panic) to best describe subjective state.

EMG, SUDS, and BAC data were taken at two-hour intervals during the subjects' waking days, so that BAC, subjective distress, and the psychophysiological measure of tension could be intercorrelated.

Steffen et al. (1974) highlight the difficulty inherent in conducting chronic administration research in which human subjects are exposed to aversive experimental procedures, including long periods of time on high doses of alcohol. Two of the study's original four subjects were experimental failures. One suffered from convulsions and another refused to comply with the EMG procedure. One of these men was replaced outright and the abbreviated data of the other were included in the report.

The results of the experiment suggest the need for analysis beyond that undertaken by its authors. During the experiment, there were a total of 40 drinking days, so that 40 zero-order correlations between BAC as the independent variable and EMG and SUDS scores as the dependent variables could be computed. In the case of BAC and SUDS correlations, 26 of these correlations were positive and eight reached statistical significance, prompting the authors to comment that "the prevailing relation between blood alcohol level and subjective units of disturbance was one of increasing blood alcohol level and increasing subjective units of disturbance" (p. 545). What might escape notice here, however, is the fact that, although 26 of these correlations were positive, 14 were negative (and two of the latter were significant), indicating only that, in some subjects on some days, alcohol and a reduction in subjective distress coincided. Contradictory results were obtained when BACs were correlated with the EMG measure of tension: 29 of these relationships were negative, of which 11 were satistically significant. In other words, in psychophysiological terms, alcohol was associated with tension reduction!

The contradictory EMG and SUDS results are a mystery. Could Lang's (1971) notion of *desynchrony* between cognitive and physiological response systems account for the discrepancy, or might *demand characteristics* (Orne, 1962) have subtly shaded the subjects' self-reports in favor of the experimenters' bias while EMG results, as measures of an autonomic activity, remained insensitive to this influence? Unfortunately, no other study has involved the methods of Steffen and co-workers or illuminated their findings.

In their review, Pihl and Smith (1983) classified these findings as ambiguous. The point is arguable. Further analysis of the correlation arrays indicates that the observed preponderance of positive correlation between BACs and SUDS scores, 26 of 40 correlation, does not differ significantly from the expected value of 20/40 (X^2 = 3.6, t = 1.897,p = n.s.), while the observed preponderance (29/40) of negative corelations between BAC and EMG does differ significantly from the expected value (X^2 = 8.1., t=2.846, $p\langle oO.05$ one-tailed). Nevertheless, we will follow Pihl and Smith (1983), and classify the results as ambiguous. Methodologically, we find that Steffen et al's. selection of four subjects (1) from the community (5) who were quarantined for about 12 days (4) in a laboratory (3), violated abstinence (1) to serve as their own controls (1), exercised some volitional control (4) over their free access to alcohol (4), and were measured with sophisticated instruments (5) under no stress manipulation (1) results in a summary score of 29 for this experiment. It ranks third in methodologic adequacy among the 15 chronic administration studies reviewed here.

Tracey and Nathan (1976). This study was the last chronic administration study to be reported by Nathan and his group. It raises further questions about prior data that attacked the validity of the TRH. The study was designed to redress the fact that "the female alcoholic has been neglected in . . . empirical studies despite a substantial body of anecodotal literature which suggests that female alcoholics differ from their male counterparts on several important dimensions" (p. 832). This was the first and only experiment in which female alcoholics were exposed to chronic drinking conditions.

Four female alcoholics were recruited from the community through newspaper advertisements. The women were between 38 and 50 years of age and had alcoholic histories of from ten to 18 years. All were of moderate SES; three were married, the other divorced. Duration of pre-experimental abstinence from alcohol is not given, but the experiment was initiated with a six-day abstinent control period.

The study programmed three phases, including a six-day control phase, a 12-day drinking phase, and a four-day withdrawal phase. As in most of Nathan's experiments, subjects were able to purchase alcohol or relief from social isolation with points earned by working at an operant panel and each phase of the experiment was further divided into alternating periods of isolation and socialization. Characteristically, affective change was measured by the MACL, which was given twice every third day, and by the WPRS, which was administered at three-day intervals. An addition was the Beck Depression Inventory (BDI), which was given twice every third day.

The findings of the study are strong and, interestingly, directly opposed to the bulk of both Nathan's and Mendelson's previous findings:

> Overall, subjects reported they became less depressed, angry, fatigued and confused after drinking began. Individually, Subjects 3 and 4 reported uniformly positive effects of drinking; both experienced less tension, anger, depression, fatigue and confusion and more vigor and friendliness after drinking began... [E]very subject's mean Beck score decreased significantly once drinking began... (p.839)

Pihl and Smith (1983) failed to included this study in their review. We classify the results as supportive of the TRH. We find that Tracey and Nathan's recruitment of four subjects (1) from the community (5), who lived for a period of 18 days (4) in a laboratory (3), violated abstinence (1) to serve as their own controls (1), exercised some volitional control (4) over thier operant access to alcohol (3), and were studied with an array of dependent measures (5) under no stress manipulation (1) results in a summary score of 28 for this experiment. The study ranks fourth among the 15 chronic administration studies evaluated for methodologic adequacy in this review.

Davis 1971. This study constituted the first contribution by an investigator other than Mendelson or Nathan to the chronic administration literature. It was conducted, like the later research by Mendelson's group, at St. Elizabeth's Hospital in Washington, D.C. It bears a striking resemblance to the study by Tamerin and Mendelson (1969), in which drinkers were exposed to two conditions for alcohol administration: programmed and free-access drinking. While Tamerin and Mendelson exposed each of their subjects to both conditions, Davis (1971) arranged separate trials in which subjects either were put on programmed (n = 9) schedules or permitted free access (n = 8).

Seventeen male alcoholics were recruited from an alcohol treatment center. The men were between 27 and 50 years old, with histories of chronic spree drinking ranging from nine to 30 years. All had experienced withdrawal symptoms in the past. Five were married. Six were black.

Programmed drinking included five phases: (1) an eight-day control phase; (2) a five-day drinking phase, during which subjects consumed 2⅔ ounces of 100-proof beverage alcohol every four hours; (3) a five-day withdrawal phase; (4) a second five-day drinking phase, during which subjects consumed 4⅓ ounces of beverage alcohol every four hours; and (5) a final five-day withdrawal phase. The free-access experiment consisted of three phases: (1) an eight-day control period; (2) a five-day drinking phase, during which subjects had access to as much as 24 ounces of 100-proof beverage alcohol per day; and (3) a five-day withdrawal period. In both experiments, the sole measure of affective change was a 68-item Q-sort version of the Lorr and McNair (1964)

MACL. This instrument, a longer version of the MACL than that used by the Nathan group, measures nine domains of affect, including depression, carefree friendliness, hostility, anxiety, confusion reduction, guilt, fatigue, and miscellaneous. During the programmed drinking and free-access trials, the MACL was administered three times daily and four times daily, respectively.

The results of both trials, reported in great detail, reveal mixed results with regard to the effects of alcohol on mood. For example, in the programmed drinking experiment, two of the nine subjects became more depressed as drinking progressed, but another subject became both less depressed and less anxious, and still another showed no change in mood even after the dosage was raised to 4⅓ ounces every four hours. During this high-dose period, subjects' average depression scores were lower than during the abstinent control phase. With regard to anxiety, programmed-drinking subjects were, on the whole, less carefree and more fatigued after drinking began. In the free-access trial, too, there were great differences among subjects in their affective responses. On the whole, they were less carefree and friendly, and more confused and hostile, after drinking began.

Pihl and Smith (1983) did not include this study in their review. We consider the results nonsupportive of the TRH. We also find that Davis' selection of 17 subjects (3) from a treatment facility (2), who lived between 18 and 28 days (4) on a hospital ward (2), violated abstinence (1) to serve as their own controls (1), exercised variable volitional control (3) over both programmed and free access to alcohol (2), and were studied with a formal dependent measure (3) under no stress manipulation (1) results in a summary score of 22 for this experiment. Accordingly, the study ranks tenth among the 15 chronic administration studies reviewed here.

Gottheil, Murphy, Skoloda and Corbett (1972). This was the first of two studies conducted by a research team at the Veterans Administration Medical Center in Coatesville, Pa. Like Mendelson, Nathan, and Davis, these investigators studied the affective consequences of alcoholic drinking. There were important differences in their approach, however. Most important, Gottheil and his colleagues, who were clinicians, were interested (like others at that time) in nonabstinent treatment goals. As a consequence, their subjects were recruited "not as subjects for a drinking study but as patients for a new and experimental treatment program" (p. 328). The Fixed Interval Drinking Decision (FIDD) program was developed as a primary treatment vehicle at the Coatesville VA Center. Participants in the program, patients on the inpatient alcohol unit of the hospital, could choose to drink at regular intervals or to abstain.

Gottheil and his team collected data on mood changes as a regular part of the protocol.

Numerous other design innovations were introduced by this team. Because their inpatient unit hosted large numbers of subjects, their *N*s are the largest reported in the literature. Their subjects were of quite varied background and included a number of married professional men. Most important, however, was the inclusion in the study of subjects who remained abstinent of their own volition for the course of the experiment but nevertheless participated along with men who chose to drink heavily. This had two consequences. First, the behavior of drinking alcoholics could be compared directly with that of excellent control subjects, namely, alcoholics who chose to remain abstinent. Second, the presence of abstinent men rendered drinking by other subjects wholly volitional, with no implicit demand to drink.

Twenty-five male FIDD patients participated in this study. Their average age was 41, and they had been problem drinkers for an average of 11.5 years. Most had experienced withdrawal symptoms in the past. Seven of the men were black. Eight were married and lived with their wives. SES was variable.

The study consisted of three phases, including (1) a seven-day abstinent control phase, (2) a 28-day drinking phase, and (3) a seven-day withdrawal phase. The drinking phase actually involved about 20 drinking days, since alcohol was unavailable on weekends, on holidays, and when patients had appointments scheduled elsewhere in the hospital. On weekdays, however, subjects could choose to abstain or to drink up to two ounces of 80-proof beverage alcohol every four hours from early morning to late evening—and they could further choose to begin or terminate their use of alcohol at any time. As it turned out, nine of the men abstained throughout the experiment and another nine ceased drinking spontaneously during the experiment.

Two measures of affective change were taken. The first, the Situational Discomfort Scale (SDS), required subjects to respond on a five-point bipolar scale to 17 adjectives (e.g., "nervous," "angry," "worrying"). This measure was taken three times a day. The second measure, a self-esteem scale, was administered weekly.

Subjects' drinking patterns varied widely. Whereas some chose to abstain entirely, four other subjects drank daily, and one drank to the allowable limit throughout the experiment. The discomfort scores of those who chose to drink revealed an interesting pattern. The few heaviest drinkers showed a decrease in discomfort during the first week, followed by a rise: Then, by the end of the drinking phase, their discomfort scores had essentially returned to baseline levels. Self-esteem scores did not change during the experiment. The more numerous moderate drinkers, who consumed a daily average of 12 ounces of 80-proof beverage alcohol or less, showed a steady and progressive decline in discomfort during the drinking phase. This group also experienced improved self-esteem.

Pihl and Smith did not review this study. While its results were somewhat mixed, on balance they favor the TRH. Selection of 25 subjects (4) from a VA hospital (3), who had to live for 35 days (2) in a hospital ward (2), violated abstinence (1) to serve in an experiment with a control group consisting of spontaneous alcoholic abstainers (4), and were studied with formal dependent measures (4) under no stress manipulation (1) results in a summary score of 30 for this experiment. The study ranks 1.5 among the 15 chronic administration studies reviewed here. This rank is matched only by the second and final report of the Gottheil team, which follows.

Alterman, Gottheil, and Crawford (1975). This study was similar in most respects to Gottheil et al. (1972). Sixty-one FIDD patients, an unprecedented number of subjects, participated. Their average age was 42, and they had been problem drinkers for an average of ten years. All had experienced blackouts and/or withdrawal symptoms in the past.

The procedure was identical in most respects to that of the earlier experiment, with a seven-day abstinent control period followed by a 28-day drinking phase, during which subjects could choose to drink or abstain at hourly intervals. The Situational Discomfort Scale was administered three times daily, at 9:00 a.m. (before alcohol was available), at 1:00 p.m., and at 9:00 p.m. (when alcohol administration ceased for the day and subjects were presumably at or near peak BAC).

Eighteen of the 61 men drank heavily during the study; the others either drank less or not at all. This variety of drinking patterns, as well as the taking of mood measures both when subjects were sober and when they were intoxicated, turned out to be crucial:

> These findings demonstrate that drinkers experienced less discomfort during the 1st week of drinking and more discomfort during the following 3 weeks of drinking. These results appear to confirm earlier findings that the beneficial effect of alcohol consumption on mood is a transitory effect that is ultimately replaced by dysphoria. However, this interpretation of our findings was brought into question when comparisons of several control conditions in our study were made.... The effect of increased or decreased discomfort... did not appear to be directly related to the amount of alcohol in the body. This conclusion was supported by our finding that *differences in discomfort occurring between nondrinking and drinking periods were reflected equally in drinkers and nondrinkers*. We, therefore, concluded that the systematic changes in discomfort that occurred for drinkers and non-

> drinkers... could not be attributed to the physiological effects of alcohol. (p. 1036, emphasis added)

These results are antithetical to both the TRH and the main body of chronic administration research, in that neither tension reduction nor tension induction was demonstrated. More than anything else, and as the emphasized phrase above indicates, these results point up the hazard of using subjects as their own controls.

Pihl and Smith (1983) overlooked these results; we find them ambiguous. Methodologically, we find that Alterman et al.'s selection of 61 subjects (5) from a VA hospital (3), who lived for 35 days (2) on a hospital ward (2), violated abstinence (1) to serve in an experiment in which the control group consisted of spontaneous alcoholic abstainers (4), exercised absolute volitional control (5) over their free access to alcohol (4), and were studied with a single formal instrument (3) under no stress manipulation (1) results in a summary score of 30 for this experiment. The study ranks 1.5 among the 15 chronic administration studies reviewed by us.

Assessment of the Chronic Administration Literature

The experiments reviewed above, 15 that span nearly one and one-half decades, cannot be summarized in a few paragraphs. In like fashion, their results defy ready summarization. As a partial consequence of the differences among these studies in aims, design and methodology, and results, they do not easily lend themselves to a simple answer to the question of the validity of the TRH.

Our approach to the complexity and diversity of this data source is to undertake a multidimensional analysis of 15 chronic administration studies. In this context, our analysis goes beyond the simple question, "Does/does not this study lend support to the validity of the tension-reduction hypothesis?" Instead, it examines data on both the adequacy of methodology and the direction of findings as they relate jointly to the TRH's validity.

The first part of this analysis is shown in Table 6-1. This table summarizes the ten properties of each experiment evaluated above. The second part of our analysis is shown in Table 6-2. Here the year of each study's publication, its summary score for methodological quality, and the classification of its results are shown. We have ranked the score of each study on each of these variables to be able to calculate a nonparametric statistic, Spearman's rho, to test the direction and strength of the relationships between a study's year of publication, its methodological quality, and its findings with regard to the validity of the TRH.

Table 6-1

CHRONIC ADMINISTRATION STUDIES—METHODOLOGICAL CHARACTERISTICS

AUTHOR(S) YR. PUB.	*NO. SUBJ.*	*(SCORE)*	*SUB. SOURCE*	*(SCORE)*	*QUARANTINE*	*(SCORE)*	*SETTING*	*(SCORE)*
Mendelson et al. (1964)	10	(3)	Jail	(1)	30 days	(2)	Neuro ward	(2)
McGuire et al. (1966)	8	(2)	Jail	(1)	10 days	(4)	Psych ward/ Pris ward	(1)
McNamee et al. (1968)	12	(3)	Jail	(1)	10 days	(4)	Psych ward	(1)
Tamerin & Mendelson (1969)	4	(1)	Hospital	(2)	66 days	(1)	Hosp ward	(2)
Tamerin et al (1970)	13	(3)	Hospital	(2)	14–60 days	(2)	Hosp ward	(2)
Nathan et al. (1970a)	12	(3)	Jail	(1)	12–24 days	(4)	Hosp lab	(3)
Nathan et al. (1970b)	8	(2)	Jail	(1)	24 days	(3)	Hosp lab	(3)
Nathan & O'Brien (1971)	8	(2)	Jail/community	(4)	27 days	(3)	Hosp lab	(3)
Allman et al. (1972)	3	(1)	VA hospital	(3)	25 days	(3)	Indep lab	(3)
Goldman et al. (1973)	4	(1)	VA hospital	(3)	20 days	(3)	Indep lab	(3)
Steffen et al. (1974)	4	(1)	Community	(5)	12 days	(4)	Indep lab	(3)
Tracey & Nathan (1976)	4	(1)	Community	(5)	18 days	(4)	Indep lab	(3)
Davis (1971)	17	(3)	Hospital	(2)	13–23 days	(4)	Hosp ward	(2)
Gottheil et al. (1972)	25	(4)	VA hospital	(3)	35 days	(2)	Hosp ward	(2)
Alterman et al. (1975)	61	(5)	VA hospital	(3)	35 days	(2)	Hosp ward	(2)

AUTHOR(S) YR. PUB.	*ADMINISTRATION*	*(SCORE)*	*DEP. MEASURES*	*(SCORE)*	*STRESS MANIP.*	*(SCORE)*
Mendelson et al. (1964)	Programmed	(1)	Casual	(1)	No	(1)
McGuire et al. (1966)	Programmed	(1)	Casual	(1)	No	(1)
McNamee et al. (1968)	Operant	(3)	Casual	(1)	No	(1)
Tamerin & Mendelson (1969)	Programmed—free	(2)	Casual	(1)	No	(1)
Tamerin et al. (1970)	Free access	(4)	Q-sort	(2)	No	(1)

Nathan et al. (1970a)	Operant	(3)	MACL	(3)	No	(1)
Nathan et al. (1970b)	Operant	(3)	MACL, WPRS	(3)	No	(1)
Nathan & O'Brien (1971)	Operant	(3)	MACL, WPRS	(3)	No	(1)
Allman et al. (1972)	Operant	(3)	MACL, WPRS	(3)	Yes	(5)
Goldman et al. (1973)	Operant	(3)	MACL, WPRS	(3)	No	(1)
Steffen et al. (1974)	Free access	(4)	EMG, SUDS	(5)	No	(1)
Tracey & Nathan (1976)	Operant	(3)	MACL, WPRS, BDI	(5)	No	(1)
Davis (1971)	Programmed—free	(2)	MACL	(3)	No	(1)
Gottheil et al. (1972)	Free access	(4)	SDS, self-esteem	(4)	No	(1)
Alterman et al. (1975)	Free access	(4)	SDS	(3)	No	(1)

AUTHOR(S) YR. PUB.	*ABST. VIOL.*	*(SCORE)*	*CONTROL GRPS.*	*(SCORE)*	*VOLITION*	*(SCORE)*
Mendelson et al. (1964)	Yes	(1)	Own control	(1)	None	(1)
McGuire et al. (1966)	Yes	(1)	Sex offenders	(2)	None	(1)
McNamee et al. (1968)	Yes	(1)	Own control	(1)	Substantial	(4)
Tamerin & Mendelson (1969)	Yes	(1)	Own control	(1)	Some	(3)
Tamerin et al. (1970)	Yes	(1)	Own control	(1)	Some	(3)
Nathan et al. (1970a)	Yes	(1)	Own control	(1)	Some	(3)
Nathan et al. (1970b)	Yes	(1)	Own control	(1)	Some	(3)
Nathan & O'Brien (1971)	Yes	(1)	Nonalcoholics	(3)	Substantial	(4)
Allman et al. (1972)	Yes	(1)	Own control	(1)	Substantial	(4)
Goldman et al. (1973)	Yes	(1)	Own control	(1)	Substantial	(4)
Steffen et al. (1974)	Yes	(1)	Own control	(1)	Substantial	(4)
Tracey & Nathan (1976)	Yes	(1)	Own control	(1)	Substantial	(4)
Davis (1971)	Yes	(1)	Own control	(1)	Variable	(3)
Gottheil et al. (1972)	Yes	(1)	Abstainers	(4)	Perfect	(5)
Alterman et al. (1975)	Yes	(1)	Abstainers	(4)	Perfect	(5)

Table 6-2

CHRONIC ADMINISTRATION STUDIES—METHODS AND OUTCOMES

AUTHOR(S) YR. PUB.	*YEAR RANK*	*QUALITY*	*QUALITY RANK*	*FINDINGS*	*FINDINGS RANK*
Mendelson et al. (1964)	15	14	15	Nonsupportive	12.5
McGuire et al. (1966)	14	15	13.5	Ambiguous	7
McNamee et al. (1968)	13	20	12	Nonsupportive	12.5
Tamerin & Mendelson (1969)	12	15	13.5	Supportive	2.5
Tamerin et al. (1970)	10	22	10	Nonsupportive	12.5
Nathan et al. (1970a)	10	24	7	Nonsupportive	12.5
Nathan et al. (1970b)	10	22	10	Ambiguous	7
Nathan & O'Brien (1971)	7.5	27	5.5	Ambiguous	7
Allman et al. (1972)	5.5	27	5.5	Supportive	2.5
Goldman et al. (1973)	4	23	8	Nonsupportive	12.5
Steffen et al. (1974)	3	29	3	Ambiguous	7
Tracey & Nathan (1976)	1	28	4	Supportive	2.5
Davis (1971)	7.5	22	10	Nonsupportive	12.5
Gottheil et al. (1972)	5.5	30	1.5	Supportive	2.5
Alterman et al. (1975)	2	30	1.5	Ambiguous	7

Comparison 1: rho (year/quality) = 0.886, *p*/0.005
Comparison 2: rho (year/findings) = 0.418, *p*/0.10
Comparison 3: rho (quality/findings) = 0.460, *p*/0.05

The results of this analysis can be summarized as follows:

It is reassuring to note that the correlation between a study's year of publication and its methodological quality is positive and highly significant: rho = 0.886, $p \leq 0.005$. This appears to reflect the developing maturity of our field.

Interesting as well is the trend linking year of publication of a study and the degree to which it lends support to the validity of the TRH: rho = 0.418 $p \leq 0.10$.

Most interesting, perhaps, is the relationship demonstrated in Table 6-2 between the methodological adequacy of a study and the degree to which its findings support the validity of the TRH: rho = 0.460, $p \leq 0.05$. The greater the methodologic adequacy of a study, the stronger is its support for the view that consumption of beverage alcohol is associated with improvement in the emotional state of the alcoholic drinkers. As noted earlier, this idea is consistent with both clinical lore and the beliefs of alcoholics themselves. In this instance, the empirical data appear to support both clinical lore and folk lore.

REFERENCES

Adesso, V.J. (1980). Experimental studies of human drinking behavior. In H. Rigter & J.C. Crabbe, Jr. (Eds.) *Alcohol Tolerance and Dependence.* New York: Elsevier /North Holland, (pp. 335–391).

Adesso, V.J. (1985). Cognitive factors in alcohol and drug use.

Galizio & S.A. Maisto (Eds.), *Determinants of Substance Abuse.* New York : Plenum Press, (pp. 179–208).

Allman, L.R., Taylor, H.A., & Nathan, P.E.(1972). Group drinking during stress: Effects on drinking behavior, affect, and psychopathology. *American Journal of Psychiatry, 129*, 669–678.

Alterman, A.I., Gottheil, E. & Crawford, H.D. (1975). Mood changes in an alcoholism treatment program based on drinking decisions. *American Journal of Psychiatry, 132*, 1032–1037.

American Psychiatric Association (1980). *Diagnostic and Statistical Manual of Mental Disorders* (3rd ed.). Washington, D.C.: Author.

Brown, J.S., & Crowell, C.R.(1974). Alcohol and conflict resolution: A theoretical analysis. *Quarterly Journal of Studies on Alcohol, 35*, 66–85.

Caddy, G.R. (1978). Toward a multivariate analysis of alcohol abuse. In P.E. Nathan, G.A. Marlatt, & T. Loberg (Eds.), *Alcoholism: New Directions in Behavioral Research and Treatment.* New York: Plenum Press, pp. 71–117.

Cappell, H., & Herman, C.P. (1972). Alcohol and tension reduction: A review. *Quarterly Journal of Studies on Alcohol. 33*, 33–64.

Chafetz, M.E (1966). Alcohol excess. *Annals of the New York Academy of Sciences, 133*, 808–813.

Conger, J.J. (1951). The effects of alcohol on conflict and avoidance behavior. *Quarterly Journal of Studies on Alcohol 12,* 1–29.
Conger, J.J. (1956). *Manual of instructions: SAQS.* Chicago: Psychometric Affiliates.
Cox, W.M. (1979). The alcoholic personality: A review of the evidence. *Progress in Experimental Personality Research, 9,* 89–148.
Cox, W.M. (Ed.) (1983). *Identifying and measuring alcoholic personality characteristics.* San Francisco: Jossey-Bass.
Davis, D. (1971). Mood changes in alcoholic subjects with programmed and free-choice experimental drinking. In N.K. Mello & J.H. Mendelson (Eds.), *Recent Advances in Studies of Alcoholism: An Interdisciplinary Approach.* Washington, D.C.: U.S. Government Printing Office, pp. 596–618.
Dollard, J., & Miller, N.E. (1950). *Personality and Psychotherapy.* New York: McGraw-Hill.
Freed, E.X. (1978). Alcohol and mood: An updated review. *International Journal of the Addictions, 13,* 173–200.
Glatt, M.M. (1967). The question of moderate drinking despite "loss of control." *British Journal of Addiction, 62,* 267–274.
Glatt, M.M. (1974). *A Guide to Addiction and its Treatment.* New York: Wiley.
Goldman, M.S., Taylor, H.A., Carruth, M.L., & Nathan, P.E. (1973). Effects of group decision-making on group drinking by alcoholics. *Quarterly Journal of Studies on Alcohol, 34,* 807–822.
Gottheil, E., Murphy, B.F., Skoloda, T.E., & Corbett, L.O. (1972). Fixed interval drinking decisions, II: Drinking and discomfort in 25 alcoholics. *Quarterly Journal of Studies on Alcohol, 33,* 325–340.
Holloway, I. (1969). *Some psychological concomitants of addiction.* Unpublished doctoral dissertation, University of Adelaide.
Horn, J.L., & Wanberg, K.W. (1969). Symptom patterns related to excessive use of alcohol. *Quarterly Journal of Studies on Alcohol, 30,* 35–58.
Jellinek, E.M. (1952). Current notes: Phases of alcohol addiction. *Quarterly Journal of Studies on Alcohol, 13,* 673–684.
Jellinek, E.M. (1960). *The Disease Concept of Alcoholism.* Highland Park, N.J.: Hillhouse Press.
Keller, M. (1972). On the loss of control phenomenon in alcoholism. *British Journal of Addiction, 67,* 153–166.
Lang, P.J. (1971). The application of psychophysiological methods in the study of psychotherapy and behavior modification. In A. E. Bergin & S.L. Garfield (Eds.), *Handbook of Psychotherapy and Behavior Change.* New York: Wiley, pp. 75–125.
Luborsky, L., Singer, G., & Luborsky, L. (1975). Comparative studies of psychotherapies: Is it true that "everyone has won and all must have prizes?" *Archives of General Psychiatry, 32,* 995–1008.
Marlatt, G.A. (1976). Alcohol, stress and cognitive control. In I.G. Sarason & C.D. Spielberger (Eds.), *Stress and anxiety*: Vol. 3. Washington, D.C.: Hemisphere Publishing, pp. 271–296.
Marlatt, G.A. (1978). Craving for alcohol, loss of control, and relapse: A cognitive-behavioral analysis. In P.E. Nathan, G. A. Marlatt, & T. Loberg (Eds.), *Alcoholism: New directions in behavioral research and treatment.* New York: Plenum Press.
Masserman, J.H., & Yum, K.S. (1946). An analysis of the influence of alcohol on experimental neurosis in cats. *Psychosomatic Medicine, 8,* 36–52.

McGuire, M.T., Stein, S. & Mendelson, H.H. (1966). Comparative psychosocial studies of alcoholic and nonalcoholic subjects undergoing experimentally-induced ethanol intoxication. *Psychosomatic Medicine, 28,* 13–26.

McNamee, H.B., Mello, N.K., & Mendelson, J.H. (1968). Experimental analysis of drinking patterns of alcoholics: Concurrent psychiatric observations. *American Journal of Psychiatry, 124,* 1063–1069.

Mello, N.K. (1975). A semantic aspect of alcoholism. In H.D. Cappell & A.E. LeBlanc (Eds.), *Biological and Behavioral Approaches to Drug Dependence.* Toronto: Addiction Research Foundation.

Mello, N.K., & Mendelson, J.H. (1965). Operant analysis of drinking patterns of chronic alcoholics. *Nature, 206,* 43–46.

Mendelson, J.H., Ladou, J., & Solomon, P. (1964). Experimentally-induced chronic intoxication and withdrawal in alcoholics. *Quarterly Journal of Studies on Alcohol, 25* (suppl. 2).

Nathan, P.E., & Lisman, S.A. (1976). Behavioral and motivational patterns of chronic alcoholics. In R.E. Tarter & A.A. Sugerman (Eds.), *Alcoholism: Interdisciplinary Approaches to an Enduring Problem.* Reading, Mass: Addison-Wesley, pp. 470–522.

Nathan, P.E., & O'Brien, J.S. (1971). An experimental analysis of the behavior of alcoholics and nonalcoholics during prolonged experimental drinking: A necessary precursor of behavior therapy? *Behavior Therapy, 2,* 455–476.

Nathan, P.E., Titler, N.A., Lowenstein, L.M., Solomon, P., & Rossi, A.M. (1970). Behavioral analysis of chronic alcoholism. *Archives of General Psychiatry, 22,* 419–430.

Nathan, P.E., Zare, N.C., Ferneau, E.W., Jr., & Lowenstein, L. M. (1970). Effects of congener differences in alcoholic beverages on human behavior. *Quarterly Journal of Studies on Alcohol, 31* (suppl. 5), 87–100.

Pattison, E.M. (1976). Non-abstinent drinking goals in the treatment of alcoholism. In R.J. Gibbons, Y. Israel, H. Kalant, R.E. Popham, W. Schmidt, & R.G. Smart (Eds.), *Research advances in alcohol and drug problems.* vol. 3. New York: Wiley, pp. 590–611.

Pattison, E.M., Sobell, M.B., & Sobell, L.C. (Eds.) (1977). *Emerging concepts of alcohol dependence.* New York: Springer.

Pihl, R.O., & Smith, S. (1983). Of affect and alcohol. In L. A. Pohorecky & J.Brick (Eds.), *Stress and alcohol use.* New York: Elsevier, pp. 203–228.

Pohorecky, L.A. (1981). The interaction of alcohol and stress: A review. *Neuroscience and Biobehavioral Reviews, 6,* 209–229.

Steffen, J.J., Nathan, P.E., & Taylor, H.A. (1974). Tension-reducing effects of alcohol: Further evidence and some methodological considerations. *Journal of Abnormal Psychology, 83,* 542–547.

Tamerin, J.S., & Mendelson, J.H. (1969). The psychodynamics of chronic inebriation: Observation of alcoholics during the process of drinking in an experimental group setting. *American Journal of Psychiatry, 125,* 886–889.

Tamerin, J.S., Weiner, S.T., & Mendelson, J.H. (1970). Alcoholics' expectancies and recall of experiences during drinking. *American Journal of Psychiatry, 126,* 1697–1704.

Tracey, D.A., & Nathan, P.E. (1976). Behavioral analysis of chronic alcoholism in four women. *Journal of Consulting and Clinical Psychology 44,* 832–842.

Vaillant, G.E. (1983). *The natural history of alcoholism: Causes, patterns, and paths to recovery.* Cambridge, Mass: Harvard University Press.

Wanberg, K.W (1969). Prevalence of symptoms found among excessive drinkers. *International Journal of the Addictions 4,* 169–185

West, J. A., & Sutker, P. B. (in press). Alcohol consumption, tension-reduction and mood enhancement. In W. M. Cox (Ed.), *Why people drink: Parameters of alcohol as a reinforcer*. New York: Gardner Press.

SEVEN

LEARNING AND MOTIVATIONAL FACTORS IN ALCOHOL CONSUMPTION

JOHN BRICK, Ph.D.

There are several approaches that one can take in an attempt to understand the reasons why people drink and the factors that contribute to the inability to stop drinking. Traditionally, the goals of the psychologist are to understand, predict, and, in some cases, modify behavior. Although some behaviors are innate, the overwhelming majority of behavioral responses in the human repertoire are learned. In other words, we learn to modify our own behavior on the basis of previous experience. For example, thirst, a primary drive, is reduced by drinking. Consuming water reduces this drive and acts as a negative reinforcer via a process of instrumental conditioning. We quickly learn that we stop feeling thirsty and feel better after drinking.

One theory of alcohol use is that alcohol also acts as a reinforcer; its consumption is rewarding and increases the probability that drinking will be repeated. Understanding learning and motivational factors that lead to and sustain the consumption of alcohol is an important goal for clinicians and alcohol researchers. Obviously, if one can define the learned variables that contribute to alcoholism, or to drinking patterns associated with alcohol abuse, then perhaps such information may be applied to modify drinking behaviors or to target potential alcohol abusers. The range of research areas that address such factors is quite broad. A cursory examination of the table of contents of this book, for example, shows a number of research areas whose focus, in whole or in part, is to define learning-related variables associated with alcohol use.

On the surface, the answer to the question "What makes people drink?" might seem to be simply that alcohol is reinforcing. Yet not all doses of alcohol are reinforcing, and what is reinforcing for one person may be punishing for another. Many people, for example, if they drink to the point of illness, will stop drinking. Drinkers learn to recognize certain indicia of intoxication, and if those pharmacological effects are reinforcing or punishing, the drinker will alter his or her consumption accordingly. With further consumption, either during a single drinking episode or over many such episodes, tolerance to the pharmacological effects of the drug develops and consumption is increased even more.

The Alcohol Behavior Research Laboratory (ABRL) has conducted a number of studies aimed at elucidating those learning variables that may lead an individual to drink, contribute to the development of tolerance, or alter in some way the control of drinking, once it has begun. This chapter will focus primarily on the studies conducted at our laboratory that address learning and motivational factors in alcohol use in both alcoholics and nonalcoholic populations. It will specifically discuss work from our laboratory on blood alcohol discrimination, nonpharmacological (learning) factors in the development of alcohol tolerance, the interaction between alcohol and stress, vicarious learning, and learning strategies that decrease alcohol consumption in alcoholics.

LEARNING TO DISCRIMINATE BAL

One approach to alter alcohol consumption may be through a program of controlled drinking. Although the consumption of alcohol by alcoholics runs contrary to the philosophy of many health-care centers and clinicians, the concept of controlled drinking has been systematically explored by many investigators (Lovibond & Caddy, 1970; Caddy & Lovibond, 1976; Bois & Vogel-Sprott, 1974). Several studies examining the utility of controlled drinking treatment have used blood alcohol level (BAL) discrimination training as part of their training program. The underlying logic is that if alcoholics could be trained to "recognize" a particular BAL, they could learn to stop drinking before they become intoxicated and lose control. A number of ABRL studies have addressed this important issue.

Silverstein, Nathan, and Taylor (1974) used four male volunteers who were inpatients in New Jersey public hospitals to determine if alcoholics could learn to identify cues associated with alcohol intoxication. All subjects were diagnosed as gamma alcoholics, had a five-year history of excessive drinking, but exhibited no evidence of organic brain impairment or psychoses. Subjects also had a strong desire to learn to control their drinking. In this study, subjects were asked to estimate their BALs on the basis of internal feelings and sensations, internal cues with and without accurate feedback as to their actual BAL (external feedback). The intent was to determine whether subjects could learn to associate different feelings and sensations with different BALs. Initially the ability of alcoholic subjects to discriminate BALs improved with external feedback training. However, subsequent training, in which the feedback was removed during the final posttraining phase of the study, resulted in a substantial decrease in the accuracy of estimation.

Results from the above-cited study suggested that alcoholics were not able to learn to discriminate levels of intoxication. Nathan and colleagues then broadened their question, and in a subsequent study, Huber, Karlin, and Nathan (1976) examined whether nonalcoholic subjects could learn to make accurate blood alcohol estimates. This study addressed two questions: (1) could nonalcoholics discriminate BALs on the basis of internal cues, and (2) were there any differences in blood alcohol estimation accuracy after discrimination training that focused on internal cues, external cues, or both. The results showed that there were significant differences between alcoholics and nonalcoholics. In contrast to the results found with alcoholics, nonalcoholics were able to learn to use internal, subjective cues (feelings and sensations) as well as external cues (BAL-dose relationships) to estimate BALs. The results suggested that one of the qualitative differences between alcoholics and nonalcoholics lay in the strategy they used to estimate BALs.

Lansky, Nathan, and Lawson (1978) extended the study by Huber et al. (1976) by comparing the efficacy of external and internal cue training with alcoholic drinkers. These investigators reasoned that, unlike nonalcoholic subjects, alcoholics would be less able to acquire accurate blood alcohol discrimination ability using internal cues. All eight alcoholic subjects in this study showed similar pretraining inability to estimate BALs accurately. During training, when accurate blood alcohol feedback was provided, estimate accuracy increased significantly regardless of whether subjects received internal-oriented or external-oriented feedback. When feedback of actual BALs was removed, however, only externally trained subjects managed to maintain the ability to estimate BALs accurately. Unlike the nonalcoholic subjects studied by Huber and colleagues, alcoholics did not learn to discriminate BALs using internal cues.

These studies could be interpreted to suggest that alcoholics were unable to learn and retain the association between internal cues and external feedback. Quite possibly, alcoholics were receiving such weak or poorly defined internal cues that they needed continual external feedback in order to maintain whatever discrimination ability they had learned. The next study, by Lansky, Nathan, Ersner-Hershfield, and Lipscomb (1978), shed additional light on this issue.

Lansky and co-workers (1978) asked both alcoholics and nonalcoholics to estimate BALs after various doses of alcohol. Subjects were given scales with the low end representing "sober" and the high end "very high, about as high as you've ever been," but no training of any sort. This method may have been less restrictive in pinpointing internal cues than in previous studies since it was more open to whatever cues the alcoholics utilized in drinking to attain this high. These investigators found that alcoholics were less effective than nonalcoholics in discriminating alcohol intoxication. Unlike in the previously described studies, the inability of alcoholics to make discriminations seemed to be independent of learning ability, since no specific discrimination training was used in this study.

One explanation for the inability of alcoholics and the ability of nonalcoholics to utilize internal cues may be related to different levels of tolerance between the two subject populations. In other words, with repeated alcohol use, alcoholics experienced less and less of an effect from the drug. Using the results obtained from these studies, Lipscomb and Nathan (1980) hypothesized quite logically that because alcoholics were tolerant to the effects of alcohol, they attributed the same set of intoxication cues to different BALs or they experienced very few or no internal cues. In both cases, tolerance would interfere with the association of a consistent set of internal cues with specific BALs and therefore disrupt an accurate blood alcohol estimate. To test this hypothesis, Lipscomb and Nathan tested 24 male undergraduates who were assigned to one of four experimental groups on the basis of previous drinking patterns (heavy versus light) and familial alcoholism (present in close biological relative versus absent from any relative). Subjects were also tested for their ability to stand steadily (bodysway) while under the influence of alcohol. Subjects participated in a three-session BAL discrimination training program that utilized only internal cue training. During session 1, the baseline session, subjects consumed alcohol in six programmed doses and made eight estimates of intoxication without training or feedback on actual BALs. In session 2, accurate BAL feedback following each estimate and internal cue training was provided through relaxation training and adjective checklists to help subjects identify bodily sensations and feelings. In the test session (session 3), subjects were asked to make estimates of BALs without training or feedback.

The results revealed that groups differing in drinking pattern or familial alcoholism did not differ in ultimate blood alcohol estimation accuracy after internal training. In contrast, the subject's degree of tolerance played a significant role in predicting accurate blood alcohol estimates. In this study, low tolerant subjects were defined as those whose body sway differed markedly between sober and intoxicated states, whereas high tolerant subjects differed little on this measure whether they were drunk or sober. Low tolerant subjects were found to be significantly more accurate in their session 3 estimates than high tolerant subjects. This effect could not be accounted for by pretraining differences, suggesting that low tolerant subjects were better able to use internal training. These results also suggest that previously observed differences between alcoholics and nonalcoholics in their ability to monitor internal cues of intoxication may be related to the development of tolerance by alcoholics. This finding further reinforces the view that internal cues training is not an effective means of teaching BAL discrimination to alcoholics.

How might these results be explained? Nathan and colleagues have postulated that differences in the sensitivity to internal cues to intoxication may serve to modulate drinking by nonalcoholics, but that in alcoholics, cellular tolerance, or other physiological factors that contribute to tolerance, may decrease the ability of the alcoholic to recognize these cues. This would explain the inability of alcoholics to learn to estimate BALs based on sensations and feelings (they are tolerant) and describes one motivational factor in continued drinking (the desire to achieve pharmacological effects of the drug that were previously obtained with lower doses). To test the hypothesis that higher tolerance may interfere more with the alcoholic's accurate estimation of BALs at low rather than high BALs, Shapiro, Nathan, Hay, and Lipscomb (in press) trained alcoholics to discriminate BALs under both high and low blood alcohol levels. Somewhat surprisingly, these investigators found that higher alcohol doses appeared to disrupt rather than enhance discrimination accuracy, suggesting that factors besides tolerance affect the ability of alcoholics to discriminate BALs.

Overall, these studies suggest that alcoholics are less able than nonalcoholics to estimate their BALs on the basis of internal cues. The precise mechanism responsible for this inability to recognize internal cues is not known. Nathan and colleagues have postulated that alcoholics may have a deficit or dysfunction of internal "receptors." Although alcohol does not exert its pharmacological effects through a receptor per se, the term receptor is useful since it may be interpreted broadly to mean changes in sensory receptors relaying information from the peripheral nervous system or membrane-induced changes in the functional activity of central nervous system neurons. The subsequent direct or indirect effect on various pre—and postsynaptic receptors undoubtedly contributes to alcohol's behavioral and physiological effects. Nathan and colleagues have postulated that whatever the receptor mechanisms are, such internal receptors were damaged in the alcoholic as a result of (1) high circulating levels of ethanol (ethanol toxicity), (2) some genetic dysfunction that has resulted in altered sensitivity or functional activity of some receptor system, or (3) an alteration in receptor sensitivity due to tolerance. Changes in the functional activity of those neuronal systems mediating ethanol's action may be responsible for within- and between-group differences in response to acute actions of ethanol. Such changes may also mediate the development and maintenance of tolerance and the ability to learn to discriminate BALs.

HORMONAL FACTORS INFLUENCING BAL DISCRIMINATION

Just what are the physiological factors involved in learning alcohol discrimination to which Nathan alluded? One possibility, but by no means the only avenue of inquiry (see Chapter 3), is that hormonal variations play some role in this phenomenon. Alcohol, as a drug, is capable of producing a wide range of physiological changes in an organism, including changes within the endocrine system. Alterations in the concentration of hormones and resultant hormone-receptor interactions, for example, may affect sympathetic nervous system arousal or cellular respiration, or alter the behavioral responsiveness of the organism to any number of internal or external stimuli, including pharmacological agents. One such change may be in the development and expression of tolerance or individual differences in availability or detection of cues used in estimating BAL. The effect of hormonal variation on the behavioral and physiological responses to alcohol may be tested via a study of women during various phases of their menstrual cycle.

THE MENSTRUAL-CYCLE PHASE AND ITS EFFECT ON ALCOHOL ESTIMATION, MEMORY, AND BEHAVIOR

A number of studies have suggested a relationship between the response to alcohol and menstrual-cycle phase. For example, women tested during the premenstrual phase of their cycle have been reported to absorb alcohol faster and to have significantly higher peak BALS than at other phases of their menstrual cycle (Jones & Jones, 1976a, b; Zeiner & Kegg, 1980; Podolsky, 1963). Since the rate at which alcohol concentration rises is related to subjective and objective measures of intoxication, hormonal variations may alter learning and sensitivity to cues associated with alcohol consumption.

To test further the effect of menstrual-cycle phase on alcohol-level discrimination ability, Hay, Nathan, Heermans, and Frankenstein (1984) tested 20 female social drinkers who consumed moderate doses (0.5–1.5 ounces/subject) of alcohol on three occasions during one complete menstrual cycle (premenstrual, menstrual flow, and midcycle). No differences in total time of intoxication or other indices of alcohol metabolism were found between women as a function of menstrual-cycle phase or the use of birth control pills. More important, menstrual-cycle phase did not affect the accuracy of BAL estimation. There was, however, a significant interaction between menstrual-cycle phase and tolerance to body sway; women who were very tolerant were significantly less accurate than women with low alcohol tolerance in estimating BALS during the midcycle phase of their menstrual cycle (Hay et al., 1984). These results again point to a negative correlation between tolerance BAL estimation accuracy and extend those findings to women.

In a related study, Brick, Nathan, Westrick, and Frankenstein (1986) determined whether the behavioral effects of alcohol were altered by menstrual-cycle phase in ten women between 21 and 24 years of age. Subjects were brought into the laboratory for three different experimental sessions, to coincide with the flow, midcycle, and premenstrual phases of their cycles. During each session, the effects of a 0.65g/kg alcohol dose were measured on memory for words, standing steadiness, coding vigilance, and BAL. Measures were obtained during a prealcohol baseline and on the ascending and descending limb of the blood-alcohol curve. Alcohol impaired standing steadiness and memory, but not coding-vigilance performance. On the coding-vigilance task, subjects performed better during the flow phase of their cycle than they did in either the midcycle or premenstrual phase. There were no significant differences in BAL peak or area under the curve as a function of menstrual-cycle phase. Further examination of the behavioral responsiveness of these subjects revealed no significant alcohol times menstrual-cycle phase interaction, suggesting that neither the pharmacokinetics nor the behavioral effects of alcohol were affected by menstrual-cycle phase.

ROLE OF LEARNING IN THE DEVELOPMENT OF TOLERANCE

We learned earlier that cellular tolerance may be an important factor in the development of tolerance and in the ability of alcoholics to learn blood-alcohol discrimination. Nonbiological factors may also influence tolerance to alcohol. Although there has been considerable recent interest in the role of nonpharmacological factors in the development of tolerance, this notion is not new. One of the earliest learning theories of tolerance was the demonstration of state-dependent learning (Overton, 1966). "State dependency" refers to the phenomenon that a task learned and practiced in a drug state is better performed in the same drug state. The demonstration of state-dependent learning with alcohol suggested the possibility that tolerance and dependence can be explained in terms of state-dependent effects. Performance steadily improves in the drug state until tolerance is learned. Abrupt withdrawal of the drug shifts the organism to the nondrug state and performance deficits, such as withdrawal occur.

The role of learning in alcohol tolerance was further suggested by Chen (1968), who tested the performance of rats in a circular maze before and after alcohol. Chen found that if rats were injected with alcohol before a daily test session, initial performance was markedly impaired. Predictably, with repeated injections performance improved until there was little effect of alcohol and tolerance developed. However, if rats were injected with alcohol after each test session rather than before and were then tested later, they did not show tolerance after a single dose of alcohol. In other words, they lost their tolerance. Since both groups of subjects received identical amounts of alcohol, their degree of "cellular" tolerance should have been identical. The fact that the first group did better than the second strongly suggested that tolerance was a learned phenomenon.

LeBlanc, Gibbons and Relant (1973) employed a similar design, but instead of a complex maze, used a moving belt test. Rats were trained to walk on a moving belt until they reached a specified criterion of performance; if they fell or strayed off, they received an aversive electric shock. It was also found that tolerance to the disruptive effects of alcohol on performance developed in the animals who were injected after testing, but it took longer. Perhaps part of this discrepancy is attributable to task complexity. Using human subjects, Gregson, Smith, Strelow, and Brabyn (1978) found that heavy drinkers displayed more tolerance than light drinkers when tested on a simple walking task; when task complexity was increased, however, the difference between the groups disappeared. In a related study, Henry, Davis, Enselkeen, Triebwasser, and Lancaster (1974) drew similar conclusions from the study of air force pilot trainees on a flight simulator.

For the most part, tolerance in humans has been most easily measured using cognitive tasks rather than sensory-perceptual tasks. This may be due, in part, to motivational differences. For example, Mann and Vogel-Sprott (1981) demonstrated greater development of tolerance to performance on a pursuit-rotor task when subjects were paid more if they performed well.

PAVLOVIAN CONDITIONED TOLERANCE

The work of Siegel and his associates has provided additional evidence that learning plays a significant role in the development of tolerance. Siegel's model (1978) of drug tolerance is by far the most influential and best supported model of its kind. Siegel suggests that environmental stimuli preceding drug intake elicit a conditioned compensatory response that attenuates the drug effect. Within what Siegel conceives of as a classical Pavlovian conditioning paradigm, the conditioned stimuli (CS) consist of the various experimental procedures and environmental stimuli associated with the administration of the drug. The unconditioned stimuli (UCS) are the actual direct pharmacological effects of the drug. The conditioned response (CR), once formed by repeated administrations of the drug, may then be demonstrated with a placebo by presenting the usual drug administration cues (CS) in the absence of the pharmacological effects of the drug (UCS). According to Pavlovian conditioning theory, the conditioned responses should then mimic the unconditioned response.

Seward (1970) reported that the conditioned response to certain drugs of abuse appears in many instances as preparation for, rather than as a replica of, the unconditioned response. After examining a number of such studies, Siegel concluded that the conditioned responses to drug-associated stimuli are often in the direction opposite to the pharmacological effects of the drug. The responses are presumably physiological changes made by the organism to negate the disruption in homeostasis produced by the pharmacological agent. For example, after tolerance to alcohol-induced hypothermia developed, the administration of a placebo would produce a hyperthermic response. According to Siegel's current theory, the repeated pairing of stimuli associated with drug intake with the pharmacological effects of the drug leads to an increase in the magnitude of the conditioned compensatory response. Accordingly, when the drug is administered in conjunction with the usual predrug cues, the drug effect is reduced by these anticipatory conditioned compensatory responses. As these compensatory conditioned responses increase in magnitude with continued drug intake, the effect of the drug continues to decrease. The decreasing effect of a drug as a function of repeated intake defines chronic tolerance.

Up until recently, most studies of conditioned tolerance utilized animal subjects but a preliminary exploration of the role of classical conditioning processes in human tolerance to ethanol was reported by Lightfoot and Vogel-Sprott (1981). These researchers assigned 24 male social drinkers to four groups. After an initial pretest session to familiarize subjects with coding-vigilance and bead-stringing measures of tolerance, subjects underwent a four-session tolerance-development sequence. During each session, subjects in group one were tested on both tolerance measures before and after receiving 0.79g/kg of ethanol in the presence of a distinct set of environmental cues. Subjects in a second group were treated identically, except that they were not tested. Subjects in a third group received alcohol under a different set of environmental cues (and were tested before, rather than after, receiving alcohol). Subjects in a fourth group received a placebo during the phase of the study when tolerance developed. This phase was followed by a tolerance test session in which all subjects received alcohol in the distinct environment and were then tested on the perceptual motor tasks. Subjects in the first and second groups were significantly less impaired,—that is, more tolerant—on the coding-vigilance task than those in group 3, just as the classical conditioning model of tolerance would predict.

A more extensive study of Pavlovian conditioning and tolerance was performed by Shapiro and Nathan (1986). In that study, 16 male subjects classified as light to moderate drinkers were randomly assigned to one of two groups and then participated in the four experimental phases.

Following a pretest session (phase I) to familiarize subjects with the experimental tasks, both groups received five administrations of alcohol (0.75 g/kg) and during the ten-session tolerance-development phase (phase II), five administrations of an equal volume of tonic on an alternating schedule. Subjects in group 1 received alcohol in a "distinctive environment" (barlike setting) and received tonic in the "home environment" (featureless experimental room). Subjects in group 2 were treated exactly the same, except that the environmental cues with which the substance consumed was paired were reversed. In the subsequent session to test for tolerance (phase III), both groups received alcohol in the distinctive environment. Tolerance was assessed cognitively (coding-vigilance task) motorically (body sway), physiologically (skin and core temperature, blood volume amplitude, sensation questionnaire), and affectively (Nowlis Mood Adjective Checklist).

The results of this study were consistent with a classical conditioning model of tolerance. Subjects who received alcohol in the presence of cues previously associated with alcohol consumption (group 1) were significantly less impaired (more tolerant) during phase III on the coding-vigilance task than subjects who received alcohol in the presence of cues never before associated with alcohol (group 2). Furthermore, in the last session (phase IV), when subjects in group 1 received tonic under conditions previously associated with alcohol, they evidenced compensatory responses opposite to the unconditioned response to the drug. That is, subjects in group 1 performed significantly better on the coding-vigilance task than subjects in group 2. Although all other measures appeared sensitive to the effects of alcohol, cues paired with alcohol consumption did not have a significant effect on these responses.

The results of the Shapiro and Nathan (1986) study support Siegel's (1978) classical conditioning model of tolerance. There are, however, alternative explanations. For example, members of group 1 may have exhibited more tolerance during phase 3 because of their having practiced while under the influence of the drug during the previous phase of testing. Similarly, during phase IV, when all subjects received tonic in the distinct environment, the presence of cues predicting alcohol consumption may have served as discriminative stimuli to elicit the "compensatory" responses learned as a function of practice during intoxication to compensate for the disruptive effects of alcohol.

EFFECT OF DRUGGED PRACTICE ON TOLERANCE

The results of the above-mentioned study suggested that one way in which tolerance to alcohol may develop is by practice in the presence of the drug (drugged practice) received during the tolerance-development phase. To extend these results and provide an initial test of this alternative state-dependent learning hypothesis, Nathan and colleagues recently completed a study in which they varied the number of drugged practice trials and compared the subsequent effects of the varied practice on the development of acute tolerance. In that study, male social drinkers were tested on a battery of cognitive, psychomotor, self-report, and psychophysiological indices before and after consuming a moderate dose of alcohol. To test whether acute tolerance is due to drugged practice, half the subjects in each cell were tested at the same ascending and descending levels of the blood-alcohol curve and the other half were tested on the descending limb only and during a double prealcohol baseline, so that each group had the same number of practice trials. An initial analysis of those data revealed a significant drug (alcohol, tonic) x times practice (one or two drugged practice trials) interaction for the coding vigilance task (a divided-attention, psychomotor test). Subjects tested only once after consuming alcohol (one drugged practice measured on the descending limb of the blood-alcohol curve) performed *better* than subjects tested on both the ascending and descending limbs of the blood-alcohol curve.

These results suggest that practice in a drugged state does not contribute to tolerance since subjects who practiced twice under alcohol were more impaired only once after the drug. Further analyses of these data are under way, but a similar pattern of results has already been seen using a different dependent variable, memory recall.

MODELING

Social learning theory seeks to identify the psychological determinants of behavior by drawing heavily on the tenets of classical and instrumental conditioning. For example, Bandura (1977) describes a two-step process by which formerly neutral stimuli become anxiety producing via conditioning. Initially, the person learns that, based upon experience, there is a predictive relationship between two stimuli (instrumental conditioning). A second process (classical conditioning) then develops that involves self-arousal of anticipatory feelings of anxiety in response to the antecedent event. Unlike a strict operant conditioning approach, social learning theorists emphasize the importance of cognitive processes in weighing the salience of various environmental events and modifying behavior based upon an ongoing cognitive evaluation of the environment and its consequences for behavior (Bandura, 1977).

Modeling is a process proposed by social learning theorists whereby an individual learns by watching others (Bandura, 1977; Biddle, Bank & Marlin, 1980). Bandura believes that from a social learning perspective, "alcoholics are people who have acquired, through differential reinforcement and modeling experiences, alcohol consumption as a widely generalized dominant response to aversive stimulation" (Bandura, 1969, p. 536). It has been suggested for some time that some drinking practices are learned through modeling we observe and are influenced by the behaviors of others. One of the first experiments designed to assess the role of modeling was performed by Caudill and Marlatt, (1975). A subsequent study at the ABRL (Rosenbluth, Nathan, & Lawson, 1978) has also addressed this issue by examining the effect of gender on alcohol consumption in a dyadic setting.

A direct test of the theory that drinking behavior may be influenced by the drinking of others was carried out by Rosenbluth and colleagues (1978.) These investigators examined beer drinking behavior in randomly selected patrons at a college pub during the evening hours, over a three-month period. Drinking patterns of male and female subjects were recorded unobtrusively, along with the number and sex of drinking companions. It was found that males who drank with other males consumed the most beer per hour and had the highest consumption rates, whereas females who drank with other females drank the least amount and had the slowest consumption rate. In this study, drinking in a group facilitated the consumption of alcohol as compared with drinking in a dyadic setting. The sex × times setting relationship was greater in women than in men, but the authors point out that "one reason for this apparent sex difference may be that many men were already consuming alcohol at high rates, regardless of the interpersonal context of their drinking... [and as a result may have] approached a ceiling unaffected by drinking context" (p. 120).

In earlier studies, we found that alcoholics and nonalcoholics differed in their ability to learn cues associated with the effects of alcohol intoxication. Could alcoholics also differ in the degree to which they modeled the behavior of others? Hay, Frankenstein, Nathan, and Heermans (1983) extended these findings to female alcoholics to determine if the gender of the model would influence consumption patterns. Three female alcoholics were recruited to participate in four one-hour experimental sessions. In each session, subjects were paired with either a male or female confederate. In the first two sessions, alcoholic confederate pairs rated wines in a "taste-testing" task. The other two sessions programmed one hour *ad lib* access to wine in a naturalistic bar setting. In all sessions, confederates alternated between 15-minute periods of heavy and light drinking.

Alcohol consumption was recorded unobtrusively. Results indicated that subjects did not model confederates' drinking patterns in the taste-testing task. However, there was a dramatic modeling effect during *ad lib* drinking irrespective of the gender model. When interacting with male confederates, subjects averaged a 57 percent drop in consumption from "high" to "low" consumption periods and a 38 percent rise from "low" to "high" periods. Corresponding values with female confederates were 37 percent and 59 percent respectively. The results demonstrated that alcohol consumption by female alcoholics was increased or decreased dramatically by modeling influences in the social/bar setting only. These results were in contrast to previous findings that male alcoholics modeled confederate drinking in both settings (Caudill & Lipscomb, 1980). Modeling occurred for both male and female confederates equivalently in the bar setting. In general, these results strongly suggest that social-setting variables have a major effect on alcohol consumption.

ALCOHOL-STRESS INTERACTION

In the past decade, a number of studies in the social and biological sciences have demonstrated an interaction between alcohol and stress. Two excellent reviews of this topic are available (Cappell & Greeley, 1987; Pohorecky, 1980) as well as a recent international symposium on stress and alcohol use (Pohorecky & Brick, 1983; also see Chapters five and six, this volume). This interaction between alcohol and stress has been formalized as the "tension-reduction hypothesis" (TRH). Basically, the TRH states that alcohol reduces tension and that individual organisms drink in order to reduce tension. In the context of a reinforcement theory of alcohol use, the drinking response becomes associated with a reduction in the strength of the tension. The first laboratory study that led to the suggestion of a TRH of alcohol use came from the work of Masserman and Yum (1946). In that initial study, they demonstrated that alcohol reduced phobic reactions in cats that had previously learned to open a door led to an aversive stimulus. Conger (1951) reasoned that alcohol produced a reduction in the fear motivating the animal's avoidance of aversive stimuli.

Conger hypothesized that alcohol acted as a reinforcer because it reduced either primary or learned drives. In other words, if alcohol reduced psychological or physiological tension, it became a reinforcer and its use was continued.

One of the earliest ABRL studies on tension reduction was performed by Steffen, Nathan, and Taylor (1974), who found a negative correlation between BAL and an objective measure of tension, EMG, but a positive correlation between BALS alcohol levels and subjective reports of distress. Although the authors interpreted these results as support for the TRH, they also were self-critical, noting that the data were correlational and that a casual relationship between alcohol and tension could not be identified. They additionally noted that peripheral muscle tension may not be a good index of autonatic nervous system arousal.

Wilson and Abrams (1977) examined the interaction between alcohol and social anxiety using heart rate and self-reports as measures of anxiety. Male undergraduates were brought into the laboratory and told that they would drink either an alcoholic or a non alcoholic beverage (either alcohol was actually administered or a placebo beverage substituted). Thus the pharmacological effects of alcohol could be partitioned from the expectancy effects of the drug (see Marlatt & Rohsenow, 1980; Bradlyn & Young, 1983). The stressor in this study was social interaction with a female confederate. During the interaction, the male subjects had three minutes in which to make as favorable an impression as possible on the female confederate. The confederate was instructed to listen attentively but not to provide any verbal or non verbal feedback to the subject during the interaction. Subjects who believed they had consumed alcohol showed significantly less increase in heart rate during the social interaction than subjects who believed that they drank the nonalcoholic beverage. There was no main effect of alcohol alone.

In a related study, Abrams and Wilson (1979) used the same design and experimental procedure described above (Wilson & Abrams, 1977), except that female social drinkers were used as subjects. In contrast to males, females who believed they had consumed alcohol showed greater physiological arousal and were rated as being more anxious than subjects who believed that they had consumed tonic.

These studies show that cognitive expectations can be more important than actual pharmacological effects of alcohol in altering tension. Interestingly, expectations about the effects of alcohol on tension were very different in males than in females. Thus the importance of cognitive variables acquired through individual learning histories must be carefully considered before generalizing about the effects of alcohol on behavior. The interested reader is referred to several excellent discussions on the effects of alcohol expectancy and stress reduction (Wilson, in press; Abrams, 1983; Marlatt, 1983; (Chapter 8, this volume).

Whether or not it is the pharmacological effects or the nonpharmacological expectancy effects of alcohol that alter tension, the question remains as to whether or not tension reduction plays a significant role in continued alcohol consumption by alcoholics. Nathan and O'Brien (1971) examined alcohol consumption in four chronic alcoholics and four control nonalcoholic subjects and found that "most alcoholic subjects showed heightened depression, anxiety, and hostility and more symptoms of psychopathology during drinking. Nonalcoholics, by comparison, demonstrated essentially no change in affect with alcohol and only a mild increase in psychopathology" (p. 492). These results offer very little support for the TRH as an explanation for alcohol consumption by either alcoholics or nonalcoholics. However, as Wilson (in press) has suggested people may drink because alcohol initially reduces tension (i.e., is negatively reinforcing) despite the fact that chronic alcohol use increases anxiety (i.e., is punishing).

Not only has alcohol or the expectation that one has drunk alcohol led to decreased anxiety, but the perception of anxiety in others is altered in a similar manner. Wilson, Perold, and Abrams, (1981) examined the effects of beliefs about drinking alcohol in a dyadic setting. In this study, half of the male subjects were led to believe they had received alcohol and the other half tonic (actually no alcohol was served to either group). Half of the subjects in each beverage condition were told they would be interacting with another subject, a female, and the other half were told that they would be interacting with another subject, a female who had consumed a moderate dose of alcohol (confederates did not receive alcohol). Subjects who were led to believe that the female had consumed alcohol showed significantly less anxiety than subjects who were told only that the female was another subject. This study has some very broad implications regarding the preceived effect of alcohol in our society. Not only does alcohol, or the expectation of alcohol, alter stress in individual subjects, but the belief that someone else has consumed alcohol significantly alters one's own anxiety. In considering these results along with those of Wilson and Abrams (1977), it is tempting to speculate that males believe that females are more accepting and less critical when they are intoxicated.

ALCOHOL AND SELF-AWARENESS

Another explanation of the TRH has been proposed by Hull (1981). Hull's self-awareness model of why people drink is based upon the notion that alcohol interferes with encoding processes fundamental to self-awareness and self-evaluation. Hull suggests that alcohol inhibits self-awareness processing and provides a source of psychological relief. The psychological relief from self-awareness acts as a negative reinforcer and increases alcohol consumption.

In support of this model, studies by Hull, Levenson, Young, and Sher (1983) demonstrated that alcohol reduced self-awareness as operationalized by the use of self-focused statements and first-person pronouns during a short speech. Several additional studies by Hull and colleagues (1983) supported the notion that "alcohol reduces self-awareness by inhibiting self-relevant encoding processes."

Wilson (1983) has criticized Hull's theory on several grounds. At the heart of Wilson's critique is the observation that other investigators have failed to find evidence of decreased self-awareness using either Hull's measure (self-focused statements and first-person pronouns) or other measures of self-awareness. For example, Frankenstein, Nathan, Hay Sullivan, and Cocco (1985) studied the effects of alcohol on alcoholics marital interactions. Alcoholics talked significantly more during social interactions when they were intoxicated than when they were sober; moreover, the ratio of first-person pronouns to total number of words did not differ with intoxication.

ROLE OF LEARNING AND MOTIVATION IN TREATMENT

The application of the principles of classical and instrumental conditioning to the treatment of alcoholism stemmed from early work in experimental psychology. The pioneering work of Garcia, Kimeldorf, and Koelling (1955) demonstrated that conditioned taste aversion could be produced in rats by pairing saccharin-flavored water with illness produced by whole-body exposure to gamma rays. Subsequent studies have demonstrated conditioned taste aversions by pairing saccharin with a number of drugs, including lithium chloride (Nachman, 1963), apomorphine (Garcia & Koelling, 1967), and cyclophosphamide (Garcia, Ervin, & Koelling, 1967).

In the early 1960s, investigators explored the efficacy of aversive conditioning using electric shock as the UCS as a possible treatment for alcoholism (McGuire & Vallance, 1964; Blake, 1965, 1967; MacCulloch, Feldman, & Oxford, 1966; Sandler, 1969). Although initial reports on the effectiveness of this treatment indicated varying degrees of success, Nathan and Niaura (1985) have criticized the majority of these studies on methodological grounds, pointing out that none had appropriate control groups with which to compare treatment results. For the most part, conditioning procedures involving electric shock as the aversive stimulus to alter alcohol consumption were ineffective (Wilson, 1978). Part of the reason for the failure of this approach may be related to the salience of the stimuli used or the lack of response-contingent consequences of alcohol use. Cohen, Liebson, Faillace, and Allen (1971) found that alcoholics restricted their drinking if their sobriety was rewarded with access to an enriched social and physical environment rather than being left in an impoverished laboratory setting. Wilson, Leaf, and Nathan (1975) reported that if alcoholics received mildly aversive electric shock after every drink, they decreased their alcohol consumption substantially. In the same study, alcoholics also self-administered shock as a way of controlling their alcohol consumption. Wilson emphasizes that an important factor in the successful use of shock to decrease drinking is that the contingency between drinking and shock must be constant. Subjects must learn that each and every time they take a drink, they will be shocked. Without such a contingency, the use of electrical aversion to treat alcoholism has generally been unsuccessful (Nathan, 1976; Nathan & Briddell, 1977; Wilson, 1978, in press).

Wilson and Davidson (1969) theorized that one explanation for the lack of effectiveness of aversion therapy was that the unconditioned stimulus itself was not biologically appropriate since shock was associated more readily with audiovisual and tactile cues than with the gustatory cues associated with drinking. In animals such as rats (the most popular subject in the earlier taste-aversion studies), gustatory cues may be more relevant and so are attended to more. Wilson and Davison suggested that a more appropriate aversive stimulus for treating alcoholism may be nausea-producing drugs such as emetine. Disulfiram (Antabuse), an aldehyde dehydrogenase inhibitor, also has aversive properties, as it allows for the accumulation of toxic alcohol-derived acetaldehyde. Although the disulfiram reaction includes flushing, headache, palpitations, weakness, nausea, and vomiting, the delay in onset of these symptoms (up to 30 minutes after drinking alcohol) may make it undesirable as an aversive treatment even with patients who are motivated to take the drug.

The last issue to be discussed is that of relapse. Although a variety of techniques have been utilized to prevent relapse, more than half of alcoholics who are treated relapse within the first few months. What causes relapse? An earlier section of this chapter, discussed the interaction between alcohol and stress and emphasized that alcohol acts as a negative reinforcer via a process of instrumental conditioning. Although there is equivocal evidence from laboratory studies that alcohol is a negative reinforcer for alcoholics, it is interesting to note that almost half of the relapse episodes are associated with aversive such social events as rejection, criticism, arguments, or loss of a spouse, friend, or child (Walker, Sanchez-Craig, & MacDonald 1974). Relapse not associated with a preceding aversive event may be associated with thoughts and feelings about past or future aversive events (Walker et al., 1974). One way in which this association may be explained is through a process of classical conditioning. Solomon (1977) has suggested an opponent-process theory of alcohol use and relapse. He suggests that the nervous system opposes and suppresses any affective change (reinforcing or punishing) experienced by the organism. He calls these primary affective changes "a-processes" and the opposing changes, "b-processes." The b-processes have an affective or hedonic quality that is opposite to that of the a-processes. The a-process produces an affective A state, and the b-process produces an affective B state. Alcohol initially causes an increase in the a-process, which is characterized by relaxation and tension reduction, as discussed earlier. Solomon believes that with prolonged alcohol use, the b-process becomes more intense as do the aversive stimuli associated with the B state. Such processes may explain the observation that among alcoholics the reinforcing properties of alcohol is replaced by anxiety, depression, and irritation (Nathan & O'Brien, 1971). The alcoholic also learns that the unpleasant B state can be reduced by increased alcohol consumption. Drinking is further reinforced because it increases the A state and decreases the B state. Through a process of classical conditioning, both the A and B states can be associated with previously neutral stimuli. For example, just the sight and smell of a drink and the act of holding it may elicit a number of conditioned responses associated with the A state (Dolinsky, 1987). Similarly, negative emotional states produced by stressors may be confused with the B state that is normally experienced when one's BAL decreases. Under such circumstances, alcoholics may seek to reduce the B state by consuming alcohol (Donovan & Chaney, 1985).

SUMMARY

Learning and motivational factors appear to play a significant role in the maintenance of alcohol use and the development of alcoholism. Whereas most people might stop drinking after several drinks, alcoholics continue, possibly because they are tolerant to the pharmacological effects of alcohol and fail to recognize cues associated with increasing levels of intoxication. We have seen that alcoholics are less able than nonalcoholics to learn to discriminate cues associated with intoxication. Although traditionally, studies have focused on biochemical and hormonal factors in the development of tolerance, our laboratory has demonstrated that environmental factors predicting the effects of alcohol can be learned through a process of classical conditioning. Environmental cues paired with alcohol can and do alter subsequent responsiveness to alcohol's effects on behavioral measures of tolerance. Hormonal changes (at least those associated with the female menstrual cycle) do not appear to play a significant role in mediating the effect of alcohol on behavior.

Alcohol may, under certain circumstances, act as a negative reinforcer, decreasing anxiety through a number of possible mechanisms. Data from our laboratory suggest that through a process of instrumental learning, alcohol use may come to be reinforcing at least initially. Among alcoholics, however, continued alcohol use is associated with increased anxiety and depression. Alcoholics may be motivated to continue drinking because of their earlier experiences when alcohol served as a negative reinforcer. In other words, the learned association between alcohol use and the reduction of negative emotional states does not extinguish among alcoholics even though their continued alcohol use is actually punishing (i.e., it increases anxiety, depression, and irritability). Whether or not the ability to recognize that alcohol is no longer reinforcing is due to some underlying characteristic of individuals who become alcoholics or to an effect of alcohol use per se might be an interesting topic of future research.

Finally, it is quite reasonable to use the principles of learning to treat alcoholics. It seems plausible that alcoholics would reduce or discontinue their alcohol consumption if they can be taught that their drinking leads to punishment. In shaping the appropriate behavior, however, clinicians must carefully select appropriate reinforcement and punishment, as well as appropriate schedules to deliver them if a learning strategy is to be successful.

REFERENCES

Abrams, D.B. (1983). Psycho-social assessment of alcohol and stress interactions: Bridging the gap between laboratory and treatment outcome research. In L.A. Pohorecky & J. Brick (Eds.), *Stress and Alcohol Use.* New York: Elsevier, p. 61–86.

Abrams, D.B. & Wilson, G.T. (1979). Effect of alcohol on social anxiety in women: Cognitive vs. physiological processes. *Journal of Abnormal Psychology, 68* 68, 168–173.

Bandura, A. (1969). *Principles of behavior modification,* New York, Holt, Rinehart & Winston

Bandura, A. (1976). *Social learning theory.* Englewood Cliffs, N.J., Prentice Hall

Blake, B.C. (1965). The application of behavior therapy to the treatment of alcoholism. *Behavior Research and Therapy, 3* 241–252.

Blake, B.C. (1967). A follow-up of alcoholics treated by behaviour therapy. *Behaviour Research and Therapy, 5* 89–94.

Bois, C. & Vogel-Sprot, M. (1974). Discrimination of low blood alcohol levels and self-titration skills in social drinking. *Quarterly Journal of Studies on Alcohol 35,* 87–97.

Brick, J.B. Nathan, P.E., Westrick, E., & Frankenstein, W. (1986). Effect of menstrual cycle phase on behavioral and physiological responses to alcohol. *Journal of Studies on Alcohol, 47,* 472–477.

Cappell, H., & Greeley J. (1987). Alcohol and tension reduction: An update on research and theory. In H.T. Blane & K. E. Leonard (Eds.), *Psychological theories of drinking and alcoholism.* New York: Guilford.

Caudill, D.B. & Marlatt, G.A. (1975). Modeling influences in social drinking: an experimental analogue. *Journal of Consulting and Clinical Psychology, 43,* 405–415

Cicero, T.J. (1981). Neuroendocrinological effects of alcohol. *Annual Review of Medicine,* 32, 123–142.

Cohen, M., Liebson, I.A., Faillace, L.A., & Allen, R.P. (1971). Moderate drinking by chronic alcoholics, *Journal of Nervous and Mental Disease 53:* 434–444.

Collins, R.L., & Marlatt, G.A. (1981). Social modeling as a determinant of drinking behavior: Implications for prevention and treatment. *Addictive Behaviors, 6* 233–240.

Conger, J.J. (1956). Reinforcement theory and the dynamics of alcoholism. *Quarterly Journal of Studies on Alcohol, 17,* 296–305.

Dolinsky, Z.S., Morse, D.E., Kaplan, R.F., Meyer, R.E., Corry, D., & Pomerleau, O.F. (1987), Neuroendocrine, psychophysiological and subjective reactivity to an alcohol placebo in male alcoholic patients. *Alcoholism: Clinical and Experimental Research 11,* 296–300.

Donovon, D.M., & Chaney, E.F. (1985). Alcoholic relapse prevention and intervention: Models and method In G.A. Marlatt & Gordon, J.R. (Eds.), *Relapse prevention.* New York: Guilford Press, pp 363–415.

Frankenstein, W., Nathan, P.E., Hay, W.M., Sullivan, R.F., & Cocco, K.M. (1985). Asymmetry of influence in alcoholics' maritial communication: Alcoholics' effects on interaction dominance. *Journal of Marital and Family Therapy,* 11, 399–410.

Garcia, J., Ervin, R., & Koelling, R.A. (1967). Bait-shyness: A test for toxicity with N = 2. *Psychonomic Science,* 7, 245.

Garcia J., Kimeldorf, D.J. & Koelling, R.A. (1955). Conditioned aversion to saccharin resulting from exposure to gamma radiation. *Science,* 122, 157.

Gregson, R.A., Smith, D.A., Strelow, E.R., & Brabyn, J. (1978). Acute effects of alcohol on measures of walking performance. *Applied Psychological Measurement,* 2, 203–219.

Hay, W.M. Frankenstein, W., Nathan, P.E. & Heermans, H.M. (1983). Modeling influences on female alcoholics rate of alcohol consumption. Paper presented at the American Psychological Association meeting. Anaheim, California Henry, P.H., Davis, T.Q., Enselkeen, E.J., Triebwasser, J.M., & Lancaster, M.C. (1974). Alcohol induced performance decrements assessed by two link trainer tasks using experienced pilots. *Aerospace Medicine,* 45, 1180–1189.

Huber, H., Karlin, R., & Nathan, P.E. (1976). Blood alcohol level discrimination by non-alcoholics: The role of internal and external cues. *Journal of Studies on Alcohol,* 37, 27–39.

Hull, J.A. (1981). A self-awareness model of the causes of and effects of alcohol consumption. *Journal of Abnormal Psychology,* 90, 586–600.

Hull, J.A., Levenson, R., Young, R., & Sher, K. (1983). The self awareness reducing affects of alcohol consumption. *Journal of Personality and Social Psychology,* 44, 461–473.

Jones, B.M., & Jones, M.K. (1976a). Alcohol effects in women during the menstrual cycle. *Annals of New York Academy of Sciences,* 273, 567–587.

Jones, B.M., & Jones, M.K. (1976b). Women and alcohol: Intoxication metabolism and menstrual cycle. In M. Greenblatt & M.A. Schuckit (Eds.), *Alcoholism problems in women and children.* New York: Grune & Stratton.

Lansky, D., Nathan, P.E., Ersner-Hershfield, S.M., & Lipscomb, T.L. (1978). Blood alcohol level discrimination: Pretraining monitoring accuracy of alcoholics and nonalcoholics. *Addictive Behaviors,* 3, 209–214.

Lansky, D., Nathan, P.E., & Lawson, D.M. (1978). Blood alcohol level discrimination by alcoholics. Internal and external cue training. *Journal of Consulting and Clinical Psychology,* 46, 953–960.

LeBlanc, A.E., Gibbons, R.J., & Kalant, H. (1973). Behavioral augmentation of tolerance to ethanol in rats. *Psychopharmacology,* 30, 117–122.

Lightfoot, & Vogel-Sprott, M. (1981). Behavior tolerance to low doses of alcohol in social drinkers. Paper presented at Canadian Psychological Association.

Lipscomb, T.R., & Nathan, P.E. (1980). Blood alcohol level discrimination: The effects of family history of alcoholism, drinking pattern and tolerance. *Archives of General Psychiatry,* 37, 577–582.

Lovibond, S.H. & Caddy, G. (1970) Discriminated aversive control in the moderation of alcoholic's drinking behavior. *Behavior Therapy,* 1, 437–444.

MacCulloch, M.J., Feldman, M.P., & Oxford, J.F. (1966). Anticipatory avoidance learning in the treatment of alcoholism: A record of therapeutic failure. *Behavior Research and Therapy,* 4, 187–196.

Mann, R.E., & Vogel-Sprott, M. (1981). Control of alcohol tolerance by reinforcement in nonalcoholics. *Psychopharmacology,* 85, 315–320.

Marlatt, G.A. (1983). The controlled drinking controversy: A commentary. *American Psychologist,* 38, 1097–1110.

Marlatt, G.A., & Rohsenow, D. (1980). Cognitive processes in alcohol use: Expectancy and the balanced placebo design. In N. Mello (Ed.), *Advances in substance abuse; Behavioral and biological research.* Greenwich, Conn. JAI Press.

Masserman, J.H. & Yum, K.S. (1946). An analysis of the influence of alcohol on experimental neuroses in cats. *Psychosomatic Medicine,* 8, 36–52.

McGuire, R.J., & Vallance, M. (1964). Aversion therapy by electric shock, a simple technique. *British Medical Journal.* 1, 151–152.

McNamee, H.B., Mello, N.K., & Mendelson, J.M. (1968). Experimental analysis of drinking patterns of alcoholism, current psychiatric observations. *American Journal of Psychiatry,* 124, 1063–1069.

Mendelson, J.H., LaDou, J., & Solomon, P. (1964). Experimentally induced chronic intoxication and withdrawal in alcoholics. *Quarterly Journal of Studies on Alcohol,* 2, 40–52.

Nachman, M. (1963). Learned aversion to the taste of lithium chloride and generalization to other salts. *Journal of Comparative Physiology and Psychology,* 56, 342.

Nathan, P.E. (1976). Alcoholism. In H. Leithenberg (Ed.), *Handbook of behavior modification.* New York: Appleton-Century Crofts.

Nathan, P.E., & Briddell, D.W. (1977). Behavioral assessment and treatment of alcoholism. In B. Kissin & H. Begleiter (Eds.). *The biology of alcoholism.*

Vol. 5. *Treatment and Rehabilitation of the chronic alcoholic.* New York: Plenum Press.

Nathan, P.E., & Niaura, R. (1985). Behavioral assessment and treatment of alcoholism. In J.H. Mendelson & N.K. Mello (Eds.). *The diagnosis and treatment of alcoholism.* New York: McGraw-Hill.

Nathan, P.E., & O'Brien, J.S. (1971). An experimental analysis of the behavior of alcoholics and nonalcoholics during prolonged experimental drinking. *Behavior Therapy, 2,* 455–476.

Overton, D.A. (1966). State dependant learning produced by depressant and atropine-like drugs. *Psychopharmacologia,* 10, 6–31.

Podolsky, E. (1963). The woman alcoholic and premenstrual tension. *Journal of American Medical Womens Association,* 18, 816–818.

Pohorecky, E. (1980). Ethanol-stress interaction: A review. *Neuroscience Biobehavioral Review,* 5, 209–229.

Pohorecky, E., & Brick, J.B. (1983). *Stress and alcohol use.* New York: Elsevier.

Rosenbluth, J., Nathan, P.E., & Lawson, D.M. (1978). Environmental influences on drinking by college students in a college pub: Behavioral observation in the natural environment. *Addictive Behaviors,* 3, 117–121.

Sandler, J. (1969). Three aversive control procedures with alcoholics: A preliminary report. Paper read at Southeastern Psychological Association.

Seward, J.P. (1970). Condition theory. In M. Marx (Ed.). *Learning theories.* New York: Macmillan.

Shapiro, A., & Nathan P.E. (1986). Human tolerance to alcohol: The role of Pavlovian conditioning processes. *Psychopharmacology* 88: 90–95.

Shapiro, A., Nathan, P.E., Hay, W., & Lipscomb, T.L. (in press). Influence of dosage level on blood alcohol level discrimination by alcoholics. *Journal of Consulting and Clinical Psychology..*

Siegel, S. (1978). A Pavlovian analysis of morphine tolerance. In N.A. Krasnor (Ed.)., *Behavioral tolerance: Research treatment implications.* NIDA Monograph, USDHEW Publication no. 78–551, p.27–53.

Silverstein, S.J., Nathan, P.E., & Taylor, H.A. (1974). Blood alcohol level estimation and controlled drinking by chronic alcoholics. *Behavior Therapy,* 5, 1–15.

Solomon, R.L. (1977). An opponent-process theory of acquired motivation: The affective dynamics of addiction. In J.D. Maser & M.E. Seligman (Eds.), *Psychopathology: Experimental models.* San Francisco Freeman, pp. 66–103.

Steffen, J., Nathan, P.E., & Taylor, H.A. (1974). Tension reducing effects of alcohol; Further evidence and some methodological considerations. *Journal of Abnormal Psychology,* 83, 442–547.

Walker, K., Sanchez-Craig, M. & MacDonald, K. (1974). *Teaching coping strategies for interpersonal problems.* Paper presented at the North American Congress on Alcohol and Drug Problems, San Francisco.

Wilson, G.T. (in press). Alcohol use and abuse: A social learning analysis. In C.D. Chaudron and D.A. Wilkinson (Eds.). *Theories of alcoholism.* Toronto: Addiction Research Foundation.

Wilson, G.T., & Abrams, D.B. (1977). Effects of alcohol on social anxiety and physiological arousal: Cognitive versus pharmacological processes. *Cognitive Therapy and Research,* 1, 195–210.

Wilson, G.T. & Davison, G.C. (1969). Aversion techniques in behavior therpay: Some theoretical and metatheoretical considerations, *Journal of Consulting and Clinical Psychology,* 33, 327–329.

Wilson, G.T., Leaf, R.C., & Nathan, P.E. (1975). The aversive control of excessive alcohol consumption by chronic alcoholics in the laboratory setting. *Journal of Applied Behavioral Analysis*, 8, 13–26.

Wilson, G.T, Perold, E.T., & Abrams, D.B. (1981). Effects of expectations on self-intoxication and partners drinking on anxiety in dyadic social interaction. *Cognitive Therapy and Research*, 5, 251–264.

Zeiner, A.R., & Kegg, P.S. (1980). Menstrual cycle and oral contraceptive effects on alcohol pharmacokinetics in caucasian females. *Alcoholism: Clinical and Experimental Research*, 4, 233–237.

EIGHT

EXPECTANCY EFFECTS IN REINFORCEMENT FROM ALCOHOL

ALAN R. LANG, Ph.D. and
ELIZABETH M. MICHALEC, M.

Argument over the preeminence of biological as opposed to psychosocial variables pervades nearly every avenue of exploration of alcohol use and its many concomitants and consequences. This is unquestionably the case when the focus is on why people drink. Yet, despite all the controversy, relevant research often proceeds unidimensionally, almost as if the superiority of its particular position in the debate were a foregone conclusion. Biochemists, for instance, may perform blood assays and examine tissue slides with little systematic consideration of the learning or environmental backgrounds of the organisms whose reactions to intoxication they are so carefully evaluating. Meanwhile, cultural anthropologists observe and chronicle drunken behavior, describing in detail the related rites and traditional alcohol-usage patterns, but may neglect to analyze precisely the ethanol and cogener contents of the beverages consumed or their possible interactions with the diet, physical condition, or unique tolerance of those partaking. Although there are probably many technical and practical reasons for such oversights, understanding of the reinforcing aspects of alcohol use could benefit

Preparation of this chapter was supported, in part, by National Institute of Alcohol Abuse and Alcoholism grant R01 AA06267 to Alan R. Lang from efforts to study the relative contributions of biological and psychosocial factors to drinking more intensively and, where possible, simultaneously. We believe that an expectancy analysis of why people drink encompasses more of the extraordinarily diverse parameters of alcohol as a reinforcer than is typical of many perspectives, and in doing so it offers added insight into the separate and potentially interactive determinants of drinking behavior.

At the outset, two specific meanings that the general term "expectancy" can assume should be identified. First, there are *alcohol-response* expectancies, which make up the domain of beliefs people hold about how drinking will affect them directly. These beliefs are often presumed to reflect the intrinsic powers of alcohol as a pharmacological agent with specific biobehavioral actions. Hypothetically, drinking should occur to the extent that these allegedly unconditioned responses are regarded as predominantly reinforcing. The second category of expectations can be described as *response-outcome* alcohol expectancies. These are beliefs about the indirect effects of drinking, that is, about the way that being intoxicated alters psychosocial evaluations and the other consequences one experiences. Such beliefs are typically presumed to reflect intrapersonal standards, prevailing sociocultural norms, and specific situational constraints. Where response-outcome alcohol expectancies are involved, drinking should occur to the extent that operative contingencies produce more favorable reinforcement opportunities for the drinker than for the same person when sober. The role of response-outcome expectancies in alcohol-related behavior has often been obscured, perhaps because it is more subtle and complex than that of the sometimes overlapping alcohol-response expectancies. Expectancy theory and research make an effort to disentangle these two classes of variables.

As a complex biopsychosocial construct, expectancy addresses drinking in terms of an alcohol × person × environment interaction. This permits consideration of the biological actions of alcohol, but anticipates the potential importance of the psychosocial and even physical context in which they occur. Moreover, the expectancy approach makes room for genetic, personality, conditioning and learning, and other influences, without exclusive or exaggerated emphasis on any one factor. In short, although alcohol expectancies are widely regarded as primarily cognitive mediators of the relationship between drinking and behavior, one objective here is to show that they represent more.

This broader perspective is reflected in the diverse methods of expectancy research. On the one hand, surveys of popular opinions about alcohol-response and response-outcome alcohol expectancies, as well as solicitation of self-reported motives for using alcohol, are among the tactics that have been employed to obtain clues about what people think or expect drinking might offer them. Yet the most remarkable feature of expectancy research is its experimental investigation of the separate and possibly interactive effects of the largely distinct classes of biological and psychosocial variables thought to influence alcohol-related behavior. The best empirical analyses of the relative contributions of these variables employ a balanced-placebo design in which actual beverage content (alcoholic or nonalcoholic) and subjects' expectations about beverage content (alcoholic or nonalcoholic) are manipulated independently in all possible combinations. Thus the thrust of this chapter is on studies that use this approach.

It should be made clear at the outset that the methods, but more important the results and interpretations, of alcohol expectancy research constitute a significant departure from many traditional analyses of and conventional wisdoms about the reinforcing aspects of drinking. Consequently this exposition may sound like a polemic—and this is intentional. We selected studies to underscore our position that the notion of direct and specific intrinsic actions of alcohol on behavior, and particularly on psychosocial behavior, has been overrated. This is not to deny that ethanol is a potent drug which, in large doses, is capable of producing dramatic, physiologically mediated impairment of cognitive, sensory, and psychomotor functioning that can lead to stupor, convulsions, and even death. Nor do we wish to propose a preemptive role for expectancy and psychosocial variables in the explanation of alcohol use, abuse, and dependence. Nevertheless, we maintain that the nature and direction of many alcohol-related behaviors, especially those involving psychosocial reinforcement or punishment as an important dimension, are dictated largely by the environmental contingencies operating when people drink and by the expectancies people develop from repeated exposure to such associations.

At an intuitive level, we take as evidence for our position the fact that many of the behavioral correlates of drinking are highly unreliable or variable both across *and* within individual drinkers. Moreover, these differences do not seem to be explicable in terms of the blood-alcohol level (BAL), the general physical condition, or the specific, acquired tolerance of the subject under observation. It appears instead that internal/experiential changes (e.g., altered mood) and external/interpersonal changes (e.g., altered sociability) occasioned by drinking may be less a product of specific biobehavioral actions of ethanol than they are a consequence of environmental stimuli and contingencies and of the expectancies they engender. The point is illustrated nicely by Pliner and Cappell's (1974) study of social versus solitary drinking, in which they found that subjects receiving comparable doses of alcohol reported different affective and physical reactions as a function of drinking either alone or in a group. Inasmuch as group drinking produced markedly greater feelings of euphoria than drinking alone, despite comparable levels of intoxication, it would appear that psychosocial changes, precipitated by situation factors and cognitions merely associated with alcohol use, can constitute potentially significant sources of reinforcement for drinking. Unfortunately, few studies in the human literature have varied drinking situations in the manner of Pliner and Cappell. Furthermore, the practical problems involved in any effort to sustain systematic manipulations of the way the environment responds to drinkers have proved insurmountable. Thus the focus of this review will be on analyzing the expectations that drinkers have acquired through everyday experience, with the understanding that environmental contingencies probably played a prominent role in their development. The tenability of this assumption is bolstered by extensive cross-cultural studies (MacAndrew & Edgerton, 1969) suggesting that the behavioral concomitants of drinking vary dramatically as a function of the nature and degree of tolerance societies and subcultures show for the behavior of intoxicated individuals. Drinking cues thus may be regarded as discriminative stimuli signaling that a new—and in many societies, more permissive—set of environmental contingencies is in operation (cf. Falk, 1983). With the reinforcing potential of such changes in mind, we argue further that individual differences in expectations about and reactions to drinking may be as much a result of varied environmental responses to different classes of drinkers (e.g., males versus females) as they are a product of unique genetic or personality characteristics of the individual often thought to be directly relevant to alcohol reactions per se.

EXPECTANCY SURVEYS

Knowledge of people's alcohol-response and response-outcome expectancies could prove valuable in efforts to understand both the reinforcing properties of alcohol and, ultimately, why people drink. Moreover, exploration of exactly why, when, and for whom certain alcohol expectations arise and operate could serve to clarify the multiplicity of factors probably involved in drinking motives. Survey research conducted in recent years has begun to offer some insight into these areas. Let us begin by summarizing the expectations of adult drinkers, and later compare these with the beliefs about alcohol effects held by adolescents and younger children to secure a developmental perspective. An examination of how alcohol expectancies vary as a function of presumed level of intoxication, beverage type, social context, and drinking patterns and gender of the respondent is then undertaken. The issue of how drinking is expected to affect oneself differentially, as opposed to others, is addressed as well. Most of this discussion focuses on alcohol-response expectancies because few surveys to date have considered response-outcome expectancies, except where violent crime is concerned [see Critchlow (1983), for a review]. Nevertheless, the potential importance of response-outcome expectations is noted as appropriate.

Probably because of easy access to research subjects, the alcohol expectations of university students are the best-documented examples of adult beliefs about alcohol. Although students cannot be regarded as totally representative of the adult population, the results from numerous surveys of this group are remarkably consistent despite differences in methods and diversity of samples. Among the leaders in the field, Goldman and his colleagues (Brown, Goldman, Inn & Anderson, 1980) have developed the Alcohol Expectancy Questionnaire (AEQ), a checklist emphasizing positive outcomes expected from drinking. Factor analyses of AEQ data obtained from large samples of university students revealed that this group expects alcohol (1) to transform experiences in a positive way, (2) to enhance social and physical pleasure, (3) to enhance sexual performance and experience, (4) to increase power and aggression, (5) to increase social assertiveness, and (6) to reduce tension. Besides the first two more global expectations, these subjects obviously anticipated that drinking would produce some specific affective and social-behavioral changes having components of both positive and negative reinforcement.

Similarly, Southwick, Steele, Marlatt, and Lindell (1981) found that university students, when asked to indicate the effects of alcohol on bipolar adjective scales, reported that drinking increased their sense of stimulation/dominance and produced pleasurable disinhibition, although they acknowledged that some psychomotor-behavioral impairment could result. Meanwhile, across the sea, Crawford (1984a) used open-ended questions to poll Scottish university students about alcohol expectations. Results showed that these undergraduates also anticipated disinhibition of important social behaviors along with a mixture of positive and negative changes in affect. Minor departures from the expectations of American students might as easily have been a product of diverging methodology as of cultural contrast.

In sum, the studies of these young adults showed that, despite some reports of adverse physical and emotional reactions, their expectations about drinking were predominantly positive. Additionally, it is noteworthy that many of the more reinforcing features of alcohol's alleged effects take place in the social arena and involve rather specific changes in sexual, aggressive, and other interpersonal behaviors. This suggests that any pharmacological actions of alcohol might be augmented by social learning and environmental contexts and contingencies. Perhaps some clues about the interplay of these factors can be gleaned from an examination of the alcohol expectancies of adolescents as they make the transition from nondrinkers to drinkers.

Christiansen, Goldman, and Inn (1982) surveyed 12-to 19-year-olds using a modified version of the AEQ. Results showed subjects across this age range reported expecting physical-tension reduction, diversion from worry, increased interpersonal power, magical transformation of experiences, enhanced pleasure, and modification of social-emotional behavior from alcohol. The striking correspondence of the adolescents' expectations to those of adults and the minimal variations in them as a function of personal experience with alcohol consumption are remarkable. It appears that the main effect of direct experience with alcohol's pharmacological action, an effect to some extent confounded with age in this sample, was to crystalize and homogenize existing expectancies evidently developed through observation.

Cross-cultural comparisons of alcohol-response expectations, employing the same instrument with both American and Irish adolescents (Christiansen & Teahan, 1985), offered a better opportunity to evaluate social learning effects on beliefs about drinking. The two groups showed overall agreement regarding alcohol as a change agent capable of global positive impact. However, American youths believed more strongly that drinking enhances social, sexual, and certain cognitive and motor performances, while Irish teenagers felt its action was greater in increasing aggression and arousal. Perhaps the folklore regarding the Irish tradition of drunken brawls as a form of recreation is reflected here. In any case, the presence of cross-cultural differences in the specific effects expected from alcohol supports the reinforcing potential of alcohol acquired through its operation as a discriminative stimulus. In other words, drinking may signal greater access to whatever otherwise inhibited behaviors the society will tolerate when its people are intoxicated. Thus alcohol-response expectancies may reflect underlying response-outcome expectancies endemic to a particular culture.

Turning to younger children's expectations, there is some evidence of cross-cultural agreement about alcohol's effects, but these beliefs differ markedly from those held by adults or even adolescents. Jahoda and Cramond (1972) were among the first investigators to evaluate the knowledge and attitudes about alcohol of primary-school aged children. Unlike many adolescents and most adults, the vast majority of their young Scottish subjects had never had more than a small amount of alcohol to drink, and many not even that. Therefore, their expectations were based almost exclusively on observations of drinking and other indirect sources of information. Nevertheless, these children were quite knowledgeable about alcohol use and expressed firm opinions about its effects and correlates. In contrast to older populations, however, their attitudes and expectations were predominantly negative. The majority regarded being drunk as an unpleasant state and failed to comment on the potential of alcohol either to improve emotional experience or to disinhibit social behavior. Spiegler (1983) reported similar findings in a study of American six- to ten-year olds, while Isaacs (1977) showed even U.S. seventh-graders held stereotypes of social drinkers as slightly meaner, more aggressive, louder, sloppier, and less fun to be with than persons who were not drinking. Back in Scotland, Aitken's (1978) study of ten- to 14-year olds suggested that early puberty is the critical period for a dramatic transition from negative alcohol attitudes to the more positive expectations that Christiansen et al. (1982) found among American adolescents.

The question then becomes, what accounts for this shift? Christiansen et al.(1982) have already indicated that level of direct experience with being intoxicated was not central to adolescents' positive expectations about drinking, although Christiansen and Goldman (1983) did find more anticipated enhancement of social behavior among teenagers who drank more. Other investigators have suggested that younger children might simply be repeating what parents and authority figures have told them in efforts to discourage youthful drinking. Adolescents, on the other hand, might be more inclined to rebel against what grownups say about alcohol, choosing instead to report their observations of intoxicated behavior by adults.

Another plausible explanation for the shift in expectancies as children grow older can be generated from survey data gathered by members of our own research team (Lang, Murray, & Pelham, 1984). Rather than asking children for global stereotypes of drinkers, these investigators focused on primary-schoolers' reports of how the behavior of adults *toward them* changed as a function of drinking by the adult. Results showed overwhelmingly that interactions with drinking adults were expected to be aversive, lacking in general support and attention, and fraught with inconsistency and erratic behavior. In short, for dependent young children, alcohol's effects are rather frightening and serve to undermine the security of a pleasant and predictable environment. Moreover, as nondrinkers with little genuine desire to be independent and with little real need for an excuse to be socially disinhibited, these children possess no positive expectations about alcohol. Only later, when they are more sophisticated, more concerned and self-conscious about interpersonal expression, and more capable of tolerating unpredictability, do they come to find drinking and the alleged effects of alcohol on psychosocial behavior more appealing.

Besides developmental influences on alcohol expectations, survey research has uncovered a number of other variables that affect the nature and distribution of beliefs about alcohol in the population. Not surprisingly, among these factors were the presumed level of intoxication and other characteristics of the drinkers about which respondents were queried. Isaacs (1979) asked subjects to estimate the effects of "a few drinks" on "social drinkers" and of "being drunk" on "alcoholics." He found that moderate amounts of alcohol were expected to make the first group kinder, more fun, feel better, more energetic, and more active, while large doses of alcohol were thought to leave the latter group meaner, less fun to be with, and more lethargic than when sober. Clearly, heavier drinking was thought to yield more negative results, but in this study differences in drinking amount were confounded with descriptions of the target drinker (social drinker versus alcoholic). The Southwick et al. (1981) study described earlier did not suffer from this problem, asking instead how having a "moderate amount" of alcohol or "too much" alcohol would affect the respondents themselves. Results showed that lower doses were expected to produce increased pleasure and stimulation with less of the behavioral impairment that dominated anticipated effects at high doses. Although the method of this study lacked objectivity and precision in operational definitions of dosage, it clearly illustrated that expectations about drinking are not uniformly linear in relation to dosage. Furthermore, it appears that the maximal reinforcement, and especially the psychosocial benefits expected from drinking, occur at lower levels of intoxication.

Expectations have also been shown to vary with beverage type (Lang, Kaas, & Barnes, 1983). Undergraduates were asked to indicate which type of beverage, equated for ethanol content, was most likely to produce each outcome in an extensive and varied set of possibilities. Wine was primarily related to positive expectations, beer and mixed drinks to a balance of desirable and undesirable outcomes, and straight drinks to mostly negative effects. These results suggest that it may be not so much the ethanol one consumes that determines the specific cognitive, affective, and behavioral consequences of drinking but, the "social meaning" and environmental context typically associated with drinking certain types of alcoholic beverages.

In another study offering support for the hypothesis that the environment surrounding drinking affects alcohol expectations, Brown (1985a) found marked differences in the expectancies of alcoholics depending on the social context in which they reported that they typically drank. Those who usually drank with family members expected less reinforcement from alcohol than did those who drank alone or in other social contexts. This difference was significant not only for global positive effects, but also for sexual enhancement, social assertiveness, and tension reduction. Arguably, reinforcement contingencies operating in the social environment influenced both general and specific effects of drinking.

To this point we have provided evidence suggesting that alcohol expectancies may vary with level of intoxication, beverage type, and social context. But, when considering the potency of alcohol as a reinforcer and how it influences why people drink, it might be most important to evaluate the relation between expectations and the drinking habits of those holding them. Both Brown et al. (1980) and Southwick et al. (1981) performed such analyses using data they collected on the drinking patterns of university students. Results showed that heavier drinkers had stronger expectations of specific, positive effects than light drinkers, whose beliefs were more global and less intense. These findings were later replicated by Rohsenow (1983), who noted that heavy and moderate alcohol users expected alcohol to enhance their social and sexual pleasure, to increase aggression, and to promote tension reduction more than did light drinkers, although both groups anticipated an equal degree of psychomotor impairment and other aversive consequences. On balance, then, heavier drinkers expected more positive reinforcement from alcohol than did light drinkers.

Also using university students, categorized as nonproblematic social drinkers, frequent drinkers with alcohol-related problems, and contextually influenced drinkers, Brown (1985b) attempted to predict category membership using distinctive alcohol expectancies. She found that frequent, nonproblem drinkers emphasized social and physical pleasure as the primary expected reinforcement. For problem drinkers, on the other hand, anticipation of tension reduction (both physical and psychological) was the best predictor of category membership. These results suggest that in addition to the stronger overall positive expectancies of heavier drinkers, persons having alcohol problems may assign different relative importance to specific effects than lighter drinkers do.

Broadening their sample to include medical patients and alcoholics as well as university students, Brown, Goldman, and Christiansen (1985) also showed that heavier drinking was associated with stronger, more positive alcohol expectancies both across and within subject subgroups. Brown (1985c) expanded on these findings in a one-year follow-up study of 42 alcoholics and discovered that those abstaining or drinking at a nonproblem level when contacted were less inclined to hold strong expectations that alcohol produced relaxation. Again, individuals with the most severe drinking problems seemed to expect greater tension reduction from alcohol.

The results of studies relating adolescents' alcohol expectations to their levels of drinking and drinking problems closely parallel those reported for adults. Using data from the 1982 Christiansen et al. survey, Christiansen and Goldman (1983) expanded on the finding that low-frequency drinkers in the 12-to-19 age range held moderate expectations of generally enhanced pleasure and social functioning, whereas high-frequency drinkers believed in stronger increases, including increases in sex, power, and tension reduction. Across subgroups of frequent drinkers, those without problems stressed alcohol's enhancement of their social behavior, while adolescents with similar drinking frequencies that resulted in problems most expected alcohol to improve their cognitive and motor functioning. Christiansen and Brown (1985) went on to show that within a clinical sample of adolescent alcohol abusers, the belief that drinking improves cognitive/motor performance was associated with a positive family history of alcohol problems. Perhaps there is something unique about the alcohol-response expectations of those most vulnerable to problem drinking.

What conclusions can be drawn from the connection between one's alcohol expectations and the level of drinking and drinking problems? Generally, those who use and abuse alcohol more have positive beliefs about its effects, perhaps including some specific expectations that might be "critical markers" of vulnerability to drinking problems (see Christiansen, Goldman, & Brown, 1985). But what does this tell us about why people drink? Speculation about a genetic diathesis seems too simplistic, yet something must maintain the association. Clearly, the more excessively one drinks, the more liable or she is to experience negative outcomes, so that clinging to positive alcohol expectations seems paradoxical. Perhaps problem drinkers are people whose lives are fraught with other problems which makes the initial, if only short-term, pleasure or relief obtain from drinking appear more positive by contrast. Or maybe these individuals hold positive expectations in order to rationalize their addiction. Or could it be that heavier drinkers are accustomed to drinking in social contexts that offer at least indirect encouragement and support for their excessive use of alcohol? In all probability, it is some combination of these factors, but effects due to any of them would argue that direct, pharmacological actions of ethanol on the individual constitute substantially less than the whole explanation for variations in drinking behavior and problems.

As a final dimension of alcohol expectancies, let us consider the role that the gender of the drinker plays. This attribute was selected because it has been the most widely investigated and is among the most obvious individual characteristics that could influence the environmental reactions to a drinker that we hypothesize to be critical to the development of alcohol expectancies. Thus, if the alcohol expectations of males and females were found to be significantly different, despite comparable biological actions of ethanol in most people regardless of gender, this would lend support to our argument that many specific psychosocial effects associated with drinking are more learned than they are innate or unconditioned responses to alcohol per se.

The literature on children's stereotypes of male and female drinkers reveals no strong differences in expectations as a functions of gender of the target. Jahoda and Cramond (1972) found Scottish children had slightly more negative views of drinking women than of drinking men, but Spiegler (1983) failed to replicate this result using a U.S. sample. Similarly, Isaacs (1977) noted only negligible differences in 12-year-olds' stereotypes of both male and female social drinkers and male and female alcoholics. Overall, it appears that children do not distinguish between the expected effects of alcohol according to the drinker's gender. Perhaps this reflects children's lack of discriminative ability, their generally negative view of the results of any drinking by adults, a narrowing of sex-role stereotypes, or some combination of all of these explanations. Among older subjects, however, there is evidence of gender-based differences in alcohol expectations. Furthermore, these differences appear both in observers' beliefs about the distinctive effects of alcohol on men and women, and in the contrasting expectations that men and women hold about how alcohol will affect them personally.

Crawford (1984a, b) found that both male and female respondents expected men, but not women, to become more aggressive and generally more unpleasant while drinking. Drinking women, in contrast, were significantly more likely to be thought of as giggly and laughing when intoxicated. Moreover, alcohol was regarded as a major cause of male, but not female aggression. This contrast in expected effects as a function of drinker gender repeated an earlier finding by Brown et al. (1980) that male subjects anticipated more aggressive arousal from alcohol than did females, who instead focused on socially acceptable, pleasurable changes. Such results, however, could have been an artifact of gender differences in rates of alcohol consumption, since, on the average, men drink more than women and so might experience different effects due to higher BALs. Rohsenow (1983) attempted to control for this factor and still noted expectancy contracts between the sexes, although she found they were of a different nature. Women reported expecting less pleasure and relaxation and more cognitive/motor impairment after a few drinks than did men, but no gender difference in expected sexual enhancement, aggression, expressiveness, or irresponsibility was evidenced. There appears to be little question about the existence of some gender differences in alcohol expectancies, although their exact nature is not altogether clear.

Using clinical populations of adult alcoholics and adolescent alcohol abusers, Creamer and Brown (1985) have uncovered both gender differences and cross-generation discrepancies in alcohol expectancies. Adult male alcoholics anticipated more global positive reinforcement from drinking, along with greater specific enhancement of sex, social/physical pleasure, and relaxation/tension reduction, than did female alcoholics, perhaps reflecting greater societal disdain for women alcoholics. However, parallel differences were not present among younger alcohol abusers, again raising the possibility that socialization was incomplete or that the culture is moving toward a reduction in gender discrimination. The younger problem drinkers may also be more homogeneous in their expectations because their alcohol abuse itself may be symbolic of a common rebellion against adult society.

Whatever the dynamics, there appears to be ample evidence that, at least for some groups, the expectations about reactions and behaviors apt to be elicited by drinking differ as a function of gender. Moreover, the nature of these differences suggests that they cannot be fully explained in terms of gender-specific intrinsic effects of alcohol. The inescapable conclusion would appear to be that environmental reactions to male versus female drinking and to the behavioral changes that accompany it should receive some consideration in attempts to explain differences in the appeal of alcohol.

Summary. Overall, the results of survey research show that the majority of adults and adolescents hold alcohol-response expectancies consistent with the notion that the direct effects of alcohol can be reinforcing. This, in turn, suggests that people may drink in order to obtain such expected effects, although self-reported expectations are not necessarily synonymous with or exhaustive of motives behind alcohol use. Additional evidence linking variations in expectancies to culture, typical drinking setting, and beverage type, as well as to the age, gender, and drinking experience of the respondent, indicates that alcohol-response expectancies may be heavily influenced by factors other than the specific pharmacological actions of ethanol. In particular, it appears that the environmental contingencies impinging upon drinkers may create reinforcement opportunities more favorable than those available to the same persons when sober. Thus alcohol response-outcome expectancies at best tapped only indirectly by most surveys of expectations about drinking, could play a crucial role in explaining why people drink. Moreover, because they are the product of environmentally determined operant conditioning rather than reflective of the intrinsic properties of alcohol, response-outcome expectancies should naturally vary according to the particular environments in which drinkers find themselves and as a function of any personal characteristics of the drinkers that might affect environmental responses to them. This sort of variation in expectations about drinking is consistent with available survey data and therefore supports arguments for a reduction in the emphasis on strictly pharmacological explanations of reinforcement from alcohol.

EXPECTANCY EXPERIMENTS

Let us assume that the domain of alcohol-related expectations endorsed by the vast majority of drinkers (and nondrinkers) has been fairly thoroughly identified by surveys. It seems clear that realization of just a few of the generally positive alcohol-response effects people anticipate could provide the impetus to drink and the motivation to continue drinking via direct reinforcement. Furthermore, if there in is validity to the response-outcome expectancy that alcohol intoxication produces more favorable environmental contingencies by altering evaluations of otherwise inhibited and/or highly scrutinized responses, then a potent source of indirect reinforcement in evident. Certainly such expectations could help explain why people drink. The critical questions to be addressed are how such expectancies operate, what their basis is, and what factors influence them. To provide a partial answer to these questions, we present a selective review of well-controlled experiments on expectancy effects. We emphasize those studies designed to examine the relative contributions of the pharmacology/biology of ethanol's action and the psychosocial/contextual aspects of drinking. We also analyze the role of individual differences in expectancy effects.

Investigations into the separate and interactive effects of pharmacological and psychosocial variables, and of related expectancies, as antecedents and consequences of drinking have been improved considerably by an increasing utilization of the "balanced-placebo design" (Marlatt & Rohsenow, 1980). This design, originally developed by Ross and his colleagues (Ross, Krugman, Lyerly, & Clyde, 1962) and later popularized by Marlatt and his associates (e.g. Marlatt, Demming & Reid, 1973), systematically manipulates the alcoholic content of beverages consumed *and* the beliefs subjects hold regarding the contents of those beverages. The result is four distinct, belief/beverage, combinations: (1) expect alcoholic beverage/receive alcoholic beverage, (2) expect alcoholic beverage/receive placebo, (3) expect nonalcoholic beverage/receive nonalcoholic beverage, and (4) expect nonalcoholic beverage/receive alcoholic beverage. The design thereby permits investigators to test hypotheses about the extent to which physiological factors, expectancy factors, or some combination of the two account for responses typically associated with drinking. Balanced-placebo experiments have helped shed new light on the processes underlying the cognitive-behavioral concomitants of drinking, highlighting expectancy influences both on how much drinking one will do under what circumstances and on consequences associated with drinking.

Antecedents of Drinking: Alcohol Consumption as the Dependent Variable

In a landmark study of expectancy factors in alcohol use, Marlatt et al. (1973) applied a variate of the balanced-placebo design to investigate the alleged "loss of control" drinking phenomenon in alcoholics. They presented separate groups of male alcoholics and social drinkers with a bogus taste-rating task, telling them that the beverages being sampled were either vodka and tonic or tonic only. The actual beverage contents were systematically varied to be either congruent or discrepant with the instructional set. The main finding was that both alcoholic and nonalcoholic subjects drank significantly more when they thought their beverages contained alcohol—regardless of the actual contents. These results seriously challenged traditional conceptualizations of alcoholism, which hold that alcoholics' difficulties in controlling their drinking stem from a physiologically mediated loss of control triggered by the introduction of alcohol into the body. Instead, it appeared that subjects' beliefs about beverage content, and presumably some expectancies about alcohol's effect, were the crucial determinants of drinking. The alcoholics' belief that they were drinking alcohol and that doing so would automatically lead them to further drinking, might have resulted in a self-fulfilling prophecy. Alternatively, subjects who believed that they were drinking alcohol may have consumed more of the beverage simply because they sought the effects they thought alcohol would provide them.

Whatever the specific reasons for the results obtained in this experiment, and at least partially replicated in other analogous studies (e.g. Berg, Laberg, Skutle, & Ohman, 1981), the potential significance of "expectancy effects" was established. Accordingly, investigators have attempted to elaborate on the role of expectations in drinking behavior. One approach borrows heavily from the tension-reduction model of alcohol consumption (Conger, 1956; also see Chapter 5 in this volume). This model proposes that alcohol reduces tension and that organisms drink it in order to obtain this effect. Although reviews of the empirical literature on the tension-reduction model (e.g. Cappell & Greeley, 1987) reveal inconsistent support and sometimes contradictory results, research guided by it have produced some important insights into motives and expectations for drinking.

Higgins and Marlatt (1973) studied the effects of threatened, impersonal stressors (painful and nonpainful electric shock) on ad lib drinking. Despite evidence that differing levels of anxiety were prompted by the high and low stress manipulations, alcohol consumption did not vary as a consequence. Apparently the type of tension occasioned by the threat of electric shock is unrelated to drinking or the expectations that might influence it. Interpersonal stress in the form of threatened social evaluation, on the other hand, has been shown to affect alcohol consumption.

Using heavy drinking males in a design very similar to that employed in their earlier work, Higgins and Marlatt (1975) manipulated social anxiety prior to drinking. Participants in the high-threat condition were told that immediately after drinking they would interact with a group of women students who would be asked to rate them on personal attractiveness. Subjects exposed to low threat were simply told that a small group interaction would follow the drinking. Results indicated that subjects anticipating the threatening social evaluation consumed nearly twice as much alcohol as those in the low-threat condition. Thus, unlike the impersonal shock stressor, apprehension over interpersonal evaluation did promote more drinking. Perhaps subjects facing social evaluation expected alcohol to enhance their social responding directly; or maybe drinking increased following threat of psychosocial evaluation so that any negative outcomes could be attributed to alcohol. Unfortunately, subjects were not specifically queried about such expectancies. In any event, several other experiments on interpersonal stress and drinking underscore the connection between alcohol expectancies and psychosocial evaluation.

Holroyd (1978) created an experimental "party" situation and measured the BALs of high and low socially anxious subjects after they had received either a positive or a negative social evaluation. The only significant difference in drinking across groups and treatments was that high social anxiety individuals drank less after negative evaluations, and so the temporal relation between alcohol consumption and interpersonal stress seems critical. If drinking takes place after a negative evaluation is already complete, it may be too late for attempts to use alcohol to enhance social performance or to insulate oneself against potentially ego-threatening evaluations by creating the opportunity to attribute any poor performance to intoxication.

In addition to suggesting the importance of temporal factors involved in the operation of expectancies as they related to psychosocial stress and alcohol use, Hylroyd (1978) also noted some individual difference effects. Miller, Hersen, Eisler, and Hilsman (1974) had earlier called attention to such factors in an even more dramatic fashion. They showed that alcoholics, but not social drinkers, significantly increased their alcohol consumption when confronted with stressful social situations requiring assertive responses. Apparently, the different alcohol expectations of problem drinkers and/or the relative inadequacy of their assertive behavior repertoires mad drinking a more attractive response for them than for normal drinkers in this context. The possible use of drinking as a psychosocial coping response is evident, and this is a theme that pervades a number of other relevant studies.

Marlatt, Kosturn, and Lang (1975) examined the possible use of drinking as a coping response in an experiment involving an anger-provoking, insulting confederate for two groups of subjects and a neutral confederate for a third. All groups engaged in ad lib drinking ("wine tasting") after the interaction. The two provoked groups differed in that only one had an opportunity to retaliate (administer electric shocks in a bogus feedback task) against the insulting confederate prior to drinking. Results showed that the provoked-no retaliation group consumed significantly more wine than the provoked-retaliation subjects, with those in the neutral condition drinking an intermediate amount. The authors concluded that when an alternative and satisfactory interpersonal coping response (e.g. retaliation in this case) is available, subjects will not react to psychosocial stress by drinking more. Similarly, Strickler, Tomaszewski, Maxwell, and Suib (1979) found that subjects threatened with exposure to a stressful public speaking situation drank less if a relaxation rather than a sensitization treatment preceded access to the alcohol. Thus the role of expectancies and the probability of reliance on drinking as a means of tension reduction appear to depend on the availability of other options within the immediate environment and on the behavioral repertoire of the individual. This point has been further illustrated in a number of experiments involving intellectual performances. For instance, Noel and Lisman (1980) and Tucker, Vuchinich, Sobell, and Maisto (1980) found drinking increased in connection with the psychosocial stress of intellectual performance and evaluation, but Tucker, Vuchinich, and Sobell (1981) later showed that if a reasonable performance-enhancing option (e.g. access to relevant study materials) is made available, social drinker subjects will generally minimize their use of alcohol.

Summary. Investigations of antecedents of drinking indicate that levels of beverage consumption may be determined more by psychosocial/

contextual factors in the situation than by the biological state of the organism. In particular, interpersonal and perhaps some overlapping intrapersonal psychosocial stressors appear to exert more influence on drinking than do more impersonal physical stressors—despite comparable levels of discomfort in the individual. Additionally, the fact that individual differences and situational constraints affect the likelihood that response alternatives other than drinking will be enacted in the face of stress make plausible the conceptualization of alcohol use as a coping mechanism. Exactly how expectations about alcohol are involved in the function of drinking as a coping response has not been made clear as yet. However, an examination of the ways in which alcohol expectancies and ethanol's pharmacological actions influence the responses and outcomes associated with drinking is revealing.

Consequences of Drinking: Alcohol Consumption as the Independent Variable

The literature on how drinking affects human behavior is, of course, far too large for a complete review here. We merely sample balanced-placebo experiments in each of three major areas to which we have already alluded: (1) impersonal effects—ethanol and cognitive/motor performance; (2) intrapersonal—alcohol and internal reactions ordinarily associated with mood or affect, including both physiological and subjective components; and (3) interpersonal effects—drinking and socially important responses, such as general social behavior, sexually relevant reactions, and overt aggression. Although the review could be structured differently and there is obvious potential for overlap among the three broad areas, our organization should facilitate illustration of how the reinforcing potential of alcohol expectancies varies as a function of the particular behavior with which drinking is associated. Special emphasis is placed on distinguishing between direct pharmacological actions of alcohol and cognitive expectancy factors in reactions to drinking, and on how each might contribute to why people use alcohol. Since expectancies have already been shown to play a relatively larger role in drinking situations where psychosocial variables are salient, our focus is on how drinking affects behavior involving psychosocial consequences.

Impersonal Effects: Cognitive/Motor Performance For years most authorities have agreed that, from very modest BALs of about 0.04 upward, drinking adversely affects cognitive and motor performance in a direct and linear fashion, moderated mainly by individual tolerance (cf. Birnbaum & Parker, 1977; Moskowitz, Daily, & Henderson, 1974). Still, until 1975 no balanced-placebo study of this kind of performance had been carried out. At that time, Lang, Goeckner, Adesso, and Marlatt (1975) showed that, in fact, only actual alcohol and not expectancy, caused a decrement in the reaction time of their heavy social drinker subjects. Two more balanced-placebo studies using lower ethanol' doses, but more difficult perceptual-motor tasks involving divided attention in pursuit rotor and choice reaction-time responses, yielded a similar main effect for alcohol (Connors & Maisto, 1980; Vuchinich & Sobell, 1978). Of some interest was the additional finding by Vuchinich and Sobell (1978) that subjects deceived about beverage content performed more poorly than their correctly informed counterparts, leaving open the possibility that some effects of expectancy might operate even in impersonal, psychomotor performances. Finally, on a simulated driving task, Rimm, Sininger, Faherty, Whitley, and Perl (1982) noted that alcohol ingestion had a debilitating effect on driving, whereas the belief that one had consumed alcohol had no discernible consequence.

In the more cognitive realm, Miller, Adesso, Fleming, Gino, and Lauerman (1978) showed that the storage and retrieval of verbal material were also impaired by alcohol, but were unaffected by any other treatment in the balanced-placebo design. Several other studies that included information-processing measures as part of efforts to discover a cognitive basis for the effect of drinking on sexual response (Lansky & Wilson, 1981; Wilson, Niaura, & Adler, 1985) and perception of emotion (Tucker & Vuchinich, 1983) also demonstrated the detrimental impact of alcohol on memory, but little or no expectancy effect.

More equivocal results were obtained by Williams, Goldman, and Williams (1981), who included both cognitive and motor tasks in their study and failed to find main effects for either alcohol or expectancy. On some cognitive tasks, however, they reported better performance by subjects who knew they were receiving alcohol than by those who were misinformed, a finding similar to that of Vuchinich and Sobell (1987). One last balanced-placebo study (Lang, Verret, & Watt, 1984) examined the effects of drinking on both cognitive/motor performances and on subjects' own assessments of how well they had done. Standardized tests of creativity were given to participants after the beverage manipulations. Results showed neither low doses of alcohol nor expectancies about beverage contents influenced creative performance, but that those subjects who thought they had received alcohol gave significantly more positive evaluations of their creativity than did those who believed they had drunk no alcohol.

On balance, these well-controlled investigations of drinking and cognitive-motor responses attest to the potent and apparently direct effect alcohol can have in impairing performance on a variety of laboratory tasks, though none of these effects could be regarded as particularly reinforcing. Two additional points about these results are noteworthy. First, most of the tasks themselves had little or no psychosocial meaning, that is, they could not be readily extrapolated to some real-life performance of significant intrapersonal or interpersonal consequence. However, when potential for psychosocial relevance was increased (e.g., in the case of creativity), results were different in that they suggested a role for expectancy. Second, in two of the studies it appeared that subjects who knew they had received alcohol acted to "compensate" for alcohol-induced impairment. Other investigators have shown similar effects in individuals with BALs as high as 0.10 by instructing them to "try to stay sober" (Young & Pihl, 1980) or by offering monetary inducements for maintaining good performance (Myrsten, Lamble, Frankenhauser, & Lundberg, 1979) despite intoxication. Under these conditions, subjects exhibited relatively better memory and psychomotor behavior, and even better mood, than drinkers not receiving such instruction or incentive. A certain cognitive or volitional control, capable of modifying some of the least controversial impersonal consequences of drinking thus has been demonstrated. It should not be too surprising if more complex and multiply determined intrapersonal and interpersonal behaviors show substantially greater susceptibility to cognitive and expectancy effects—especially since they also offer greater opportunity for reinforcement.

Intrapersonal Effects: Physiology and Affect We have already noted that Pliner and Cappell (1974) were among the first to demonstrate that perceived effects of alcohol on physical sensations and affect can be influenced by the circumstances under which drinking occurs (social versus solitary). Other investigators have replicated and expanded upon these results. For instance, differing reactions to group versus individual drinking were reported by Sher (1985). O'Malley and Maisto (1984) also found that when subjects were asked to perform a distracting task in connection with their beverage consumption, they appeared to be less attuned to changes in internal sensations and affect ordinarily associated with intoxication, were less able to detect variations in alcohol dose, and were more easily deceived by placebos. Moreover, individual differences in internal reactions and affective changes experienced while drinking have been shown to occur as a function of acquired tolerance (O'Malley & Maisto, 1984), family history of alcoholism (O'Malley & Maisto, 1985), and alcohol-response expectancies (Sher, 1985). The results of these studies suggest that changes in physical sensations and mood can be precipitated by drinking and that such changes can be influenced by multiple, and potentially interactive, contextual and individual difference variables. However, determination of any direct and specific actions of alcohol on physiological responses and perceived sensations and on affect might best be achieved by applying balanced-placebo manipulations to a relatively homogeneous group of individuals in a neutral setting. Only a few such studies have been carried out.

McCollam, Burish, Maisto, and Sobell (1980) varied both beverage content and instructional set, and then monitored indices of physiological arousal as well as self-reports of bodily sensations and affect in male social drinkers. Only subjects who received alcohol showed a significant change in subjective reactions, reporting increased sensations, more positive, affect, and less depression. Physiological responses (pulse rate and skin conductance) were influenced by both instructions and alcohol in a complicated there-way interaction with measurement trials, leading the authors to conclude that the objective arousal measures taken were too broad and ambiguous to interpret confidently. Connors and Maisto (1979) also found that it was mainly alcohol that produced changes in physical sensations and improved affect in men, but they noted that expectancy and rate of drinking selectively influenced some self-reported responses (e.g. "expect alcohol" subjects scored higher on "nonchalance").

Bolon and Barling (1980) took a different tack in their balanced-placebo investigation of the effects that drinking has on intrapersonal responding in a neutral setting. They included both male and female subjects, varied drinking context (alone versus in small group), and then compared pretest and posttest responses on the Zung Depression Scale. Their results showed a main effect for actual alcohol, but in this case intoxicated subjects reported *increased* depression, especially depressive ideation. Female subjects also noted more physical symptoms of depression after receiving alcohol. The simple belief that alcohol had been consumed again exerted little influence on reactions experienced, but otherwise the interpretations of alcohol-induced changes seemed remarkably inconsistent with those detected by McCollam et al. (1980) and Connors and Maisto (1979). They also contradicted Levenson, Sher, Grossman, Newman, and Newlin (1980) who found that high doses of alcohol produced a mixed pattern of stimulant (e.g. increased skin conductance) and relaxant (e.g., decreased finger pulse rate) physiological effects, but did yield self-reports of greater cheerfulness and reduced anxiety.

Taken together, these heterogeneous findings indicate that, although ethanol ingestion obviously can cause physiological changes and influence reports of certain bodily sensations apparently correlated with them, the specific impact of drinking on mood in neutral situations is unclear. To be reinforcing, such changes require interpretation, which, in turn, is subject to specific task, general environmental, and individual difference factors. Yet, despite the fact that alcohol does not appear to have reliable, direct effects on mood under "normal" circumstances, the possibility that drinking can somehow counteract or compensate for elevations in unpleasant affect cannot be ruled out. Indeed, since amelioration of distress (i.e., tension reduction) is among the most common alcohol-response expectancies, such negative reinforcement could be an important determinant of why people drink. A detailed analysis of alcohol and tension reduction appears elsewhere in this volume, so only a brief review of the balanced-placebo studies relevant to the topic will be undertaken here.

Physical Threats. Most studies attempting to examine the hypothesis that drinking reduces tension or anxiety elicited by threats of exposure to physical stimuli have involved anticipation of electric shock. Polivy, Schueneman, and Carlson (1976), for instance, told male subjects they would receive shocks for any errors made on a reaction-time task that was to be performed after drinking. Mood measures collected at several points surrounding balanced-placebo beverage administration revealed that subjects reported lower anxiety if they actually received alcohol than if they consumed nonalcoholic drinks, thus suggesting a direct, tension-reducing effect of ethanol ingestion. It was also found, however, that subjective anxiety was significantly *higher* among men who thought they had drunk alcohol than among those who thought they had not, regardless of the actual contents of their drinks. Perhaps the subjects' fear that alcohol would impair their reaction-time task performance and thereby increase exposure to punishment produced this remarkable finding for expectancy.

The complexities of the impact of drinking on fear arising from anticipation of faradic stimulation are further underscored by results obtained by Sutker, Allain, Brantley, and Randall (1982). Using a design similar to that of Polivy et al. (1976), except with the threat of shock tied to errors on a paired associates learning task, these investigators obtained alcohol, expectancy, and gender difference effects. Overall, actual alcohol increased heart rate, while an alcohol expectancy elevated the level of skin conductance. Subjective measures of distress, however, showed no changes as a function of either alcohol or expectancy, at least where male subjects were concerned. On the other hand, women reported the greatest anxiety when they thought they had consumed alcohol, but actual receipt of alcohol produced a mixed pattern of increases and decreases in anxiety depending upon when in the sequence of trials anxiety was measured.

Another balanced-placebo study, apparently more successful in ruling out any expectancy effects and demonstrating that alcohol directly reduces stress responses in physically threatened subjects, was men-

Figure 8–1. The balanced-placebo design

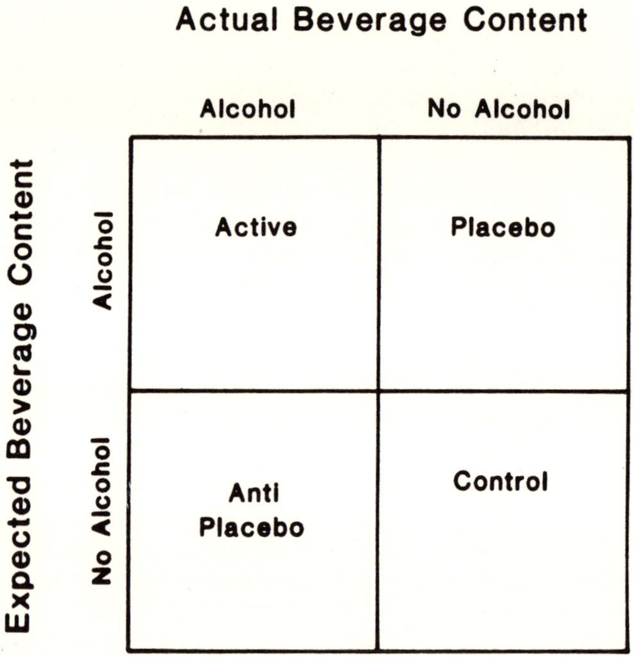

tioned earlier in connection with physiological responses to drinking (Levenson et al., 1980). These researchers used the threat of an uncontrollable shock as their fear manipulation, thereby avoiding the potential problem of confounding fear of shock with fear of alcohol-induced performance decrements when shocks are made contingent upon errors on psychomotor or learning tasks. They found that regardless of instructional set, subjects who actually received alcohol in this experiment exhibited a "stress-response dampening effect." In other words, actual alcohol consumption reduced the magnitude of subjective (and also physiological) anxiety responses in subjects exposed to a threat of shock. Unfortunately, these experimenters were unable to maintain reasonably effective beverage treatment deceptions as required by the balanced-placebo design, so that a true test of expectancy effects was impossible.

One final study of drinking and physical threats used snakes rather than shocks to induce fear (Rimm, Briddell, Zimmerman, & Caddy, 1981). These investigators selected subjects who were afraid of snakes, gave them drinks according to a balanced-placebo design, and measured their subjective anxiety as well as their approach behavior in the presence of a snake. There were no effects due to expectancy, but subjects who drank alcohol reported less anxiety than those who had only tonic. Despite its apparent tension-reducing effect, however, the alcohol treatment did not affect the likelihood that subjects would approach the snake. This prompted the authors to suggest that some additional motive is required if alcohol-induced changes in anxiety are to result in overt behavioral changes.

In summary, the action of alcohol in reducing anxiety arising from physical threat appears to be scarcely more reliable than its ability to improve affect in neutral situations. Again, task demands and individual differences must qualify any strictly pharmacological theory that drinking ameliorates the mood of individuals in distress. On the other hand, the belief that one has consumed alcohol either increases or has no effect on anxiety, although at least one experiment failed to provide an adequate test of expectancy effects. Therefore, if drinking produces consistent reinforcement through its intrapersonal consequences, this effect apparently must occur mainly under circumstances other than those we have examined so far.

Psychosocial Threats. Early work (Higgins & Marlatt, 1973; 1975) on stress-induced drinking suggested that the nature of the stressor is critical in determining whether alcohol consumption will rise following exposure to it. In particular, it was shown that fear of social evaluation precipitated increased drinking, whereas physical threats typically did not. Cognizant of these results, several investigators have conducted balanced-placebo studies of how drinking influences affective responses to psychosocial threats.

Tucker, Maisto, Vuchinich, and Blumenthal (1979) had subjects drink and then told them that they were to be evaluated on either a test of motor coordination or a task involving conversational skills. Since participants indicated that they expected drinking to impair coordination, but to facilitate conversation, the experiment seemed to provide an opportunity to test the relative strengths of pharmacological and expectancy effects. However, the results were difficult to interpret both because of a failure to implement the balanced-placebo design successfully and because significant beverage effects interacted with gender as well as type of task. Male subjects given alcohol were more aroused (increased pulse) and more anxious (subjective measures) in the motor task condition, but less aroused and less anxious in the conversational task condition. Conversely, women were more anxious about the motor task when they received nonalcoholic beverages, and neither alcohol nor expectancy affected anxiety about the evaluation of conversational skills. One can only speculate about the basis for this complex pattern of findings, but certainly the overall results again call into question the universality of any direct and specific effects of alcohol on affect as a reliable source of reinforcement.

Levenson et al. (1980) provided an additional assessment of drinking and psychosocial threat. They tested the effects of a relatively high alcohol dose and of expectancy on the anxiety responses of subjects who anticipated either an uncontrollable shock or the task of recording a speech about their physical appearance. Results for the latter, intrapersonally threatening, task were virtually identical to those discussed earlier for the physical, shock threat. Specifically, actual alcohol consumption produced a stress-response dampening, that is, a suppression of physiological and subjective responses indicative of distress. No expectancy effects were observed, but beverage expectancy manipulations were largely unsuccessful in this experiment and so a role of expectations could not be ruled out.

These two representative studies of how drinking affects subjects anticipating psychosocial threats provide only modest support for the notion that alcohol alone acts as a reinforcer by reducing or suppressing negative affect in such situations. Available data suggest that, just as in the case of evaluations of alcohol's impact on mood in physically threatening situations, whatever effects do occur are probably influenced by environmental contexts, task demands, and individual differences. Moreover, the case for cognitive expectancy as a determinant of the consequences of drinking, though still not compelling, appears stronger were intrapersonal effects of any kind are concerned than it did for effects of an impersonal nature. We take this to suggest that the more closely alcohol use is associated with important psychosocial responses, the greater the role of expectancy factors in reinforcement from drinking is likely to be. In the following section, we seek to illustrate how expectancies about the effects of alcohol on interpersonal behavior can play a critical role in why people drink.

Interpersonal Effects: Social Behaviors One of the most strongly held expectancies about alcohol is that it reduces personal inhibitions and/or eases social restraints ordinarily governing certain potentially reinforcing interpersonal behaviors. Hypothetically, if drinkers express themselves more freely while under the influence of alcohol, then therein lies part of the attractiveness of drinking. Among the specific interpersonal behaviors sometimes expected to increase following drinking are general sociability, sexual response, and aggression. Balanced-placebo research, emphasizing study of these particular behaviors, has sought to determine whether any observed alcohol-related changes in them are due to the direct physiological action of ethanol or involve cognitive expectancies and changes in environmental contingencies merely associated with the presence of drinking cues.

Sociability. Some research on how alcohol affects anxiety produced by psychosocial threats has already been discussed, but those studies did not evaluate the influence of drinking on responses manifested in actual, face-to-face interactions. Given the popular reputation of alcohol as a presumably reinforcing "social lubricant," exploring its effects in interpersonal contexts could be critical to determining why people drink. Several well-controlled investigations have taken this approach.

Wilson and Abrams (1977) were the first to employ a balanced-placebo design to study alcohol effects in social interactions. After consuming assigned beverages, male subjects had to "try to make a good impression" in an interaction with a female confederate who had been trained to respond neutrally. Both physiological (heart rate) and subjective (self-report) measures of anxiety indicated that the men who thought they had received alcoholic drinks were less socially anxious than those who believed they had consumed nonalcoholic beverages—regardless of actual beverage content. Also of interest in this context is independent work by Keane and Lisman (1980) indicating that ethanol impaired the type of social performance called for in the task used by Wilson and Abrams (1977). Thus, while the direct effect of ethanol may be a potentially punishing interference with social facility, relaxation constituting a potential reinforcement resulted only from the *belief* that one had consumed alcoholic beverages.

Abrams and Wilson (1979) followed up their 1977 study, this time with female subjects receiving balanced-placebo beverage treatments before interacting with a male confederate. Again, significant expectancy effects, but no actual beverage effects, were obtained, but the pattern for women was generally the reverse of that for men. In other words, females who thought they had drunk alcohol evidenced *more* physiological arousal as indicated by increases in heart rate and skin conductance and were rated as *more* anxious by observers. Actual alcohol had no effects on these measures and, in fact, self-reports of anxiety were not influenced by any of the beverage manipulations.

Perhaps the gender differences in expectancy effects found in social interactions can be accounted for by positing a disparity in the potential consequences risked by drinking men and women in our culture. For instance, it may be that the woman who is presumed to be intoxicated is viewed (and may regard herself) as more sexually vulnerable when drinking, particularly in the company of strangers. Hence she may have good reason to exhibit increased anxiety, although she may be reluctant to acknowledge it. Such an explanation is consistent with the experimental finding (Wilson, Perold, & Abrams, 1981) that men felt more at ease and appeared more confident in heterosexual interactions when they believed their female partner was intoxicated. Wilsnack, Klassen, and Wilsnack (1983) also reported that the majority of female respondents they surveyed had experienced unwanted sexual advances by inebriated men.

In summary, the two best-controlled investigations of how drinking affects responses in face-to-face interpersonal situations have indicated that expectancy, and not the physiological action of alcohol, contributed most to the changes observed. Clearly apparent gender differences in the specific nature of these expectancies further suggest that men may find the effects reinforcing, whereas empirical results offer little insight into why women would drink in the sorts of contexts examined in the studies. Additional research using varied interpersonal tasks and measures as well as different dyad or group compositions is obviously needed to clarify the reinforcing parameters that lead drinking to be so closely associated with sociability. Nevertheless, it appears that, at least for men in heterosexual situations, drinking cues and expectancies promote a sense of social ease and may motivate increases drinking.

Sexuality. As indicated earlier, many people hold the belief that alcohol can enhance sexual response/performance and overall enjoyment of sexual activity. Moreover, in our discussion of alcohol and sociability we alluded to the possibility that drinking might somehow facilitate sexual advances by men. Given the intrinsically reinforcing nature of sexual expression, it is obvious that such expected effects of alcohol could constitute important motives for drinking. Balanced-placebo research on drinking and sexuality, aimed at determining the basis for common beliefs about their connection, has been especially active in recent years and has generated evidence with implications for why people drink (also see Lang, 1985). A sample of this important work is reviewed here.

Wilson and Lawson (1976) randomly assigned male social drinkers to alcoholic or nonalcoholic beverage conditions after independently manipulating expectations about beverage contents. Subjects then viewed erotic films depicting heterosexual and homosexual scenes while measures of penile tumescence were recorded. Results showed that actual alcohol failed to influence erections significantly, but that beverage expectancy did affect arousal during both films. Subjects who believed they had drunk alcohol exhibited greater sexual response, as indicated by direct physiological measures, than those who believed they had received nonalcoholic drinks. In addition, subjective ratings of sexual arousal correlated positively with the physiological reactions. These findings clearly illustrate the power of expectancies to influence sexual behavior associated with drinking. They also suggest that men may experience reinforcement from drinking through its enhancement of their sexual arousal, although this effect appears to be psychosocially rather than pharmacologically determined.

In 1978, Wilson and Lawson replicated their balanced-placebo study of drinking and sexual arousal using female social drinkers as subjects. The results were quite different. This time expectancy did not affect physiological indicies of sexual arousal. Instead, actual alcohol produced a decrease in sexual response. Paradoxically, however, the more intoxicated the women said they felt, the more intense the sexual arousal they reported, suggesting confusion in their interpretation of internal sensations. In any case, the authors attempted to reconcile the gender differences observed across the two studies by noting that women tend to hold weaker expectancies of alcohol's facilitative effect on sexual response, that they are less aware of the specific sensations and signs of initial stages of sexual arousal, and that females might experience more anxiety and other possibly disruptive feelings of vulnerability while drinking in an unfamiliar laboratory situation. Whatever the actual reasons for the gender differences, there is little reason to believe that the pharmacological effects of alcohol on sexual response in women would be so different from that in men. Instead, cognitive expectancies and the social learning that spawns them must play a role in determining whether or not drinking is reinforced by its effects on sexual response.

In the first balanced-placebo study to include subjects of both sexes in the same design (McCarty, Diamond, & Kaye, 1982), the investigators posited that expectancy effects are most influential in situations involving personal and/or social conflicts over the acceptability of sexual responsiveness, so they attempted to maximize the ease with which subjects could register sexual reactions. Accordingly, they utilized very tasteful, conventional sexual stimuli pretested to evoke moderate sexual arousal and minimal inhibitions. It was hypothesized that under these conditions response-outcome expectancies of the sort that excuse increased sexual self-indulgence by attributing its cause to alcohol, would not be salient. Thus differences in responses as a function of beverage treatment could reflect confusion of alcohol-induced arousal with sexual arousal due to the presence of sexual cues in the environment. Indeed, the strongest perception of sexual arousal and the highest-level sexual fantasy were found in the antiplacebo condition where external alcohol cues were absent, allowing internal sensations actually precipitated by alcohol to be attributed to sexual cues in the environment. Significantly, McCarty et al. (1982) did not find gender differences in sexual arousal related to drinking, perhaps because they chose less explicit sexual stimuli and used subjects' initial ratings of the arousing value of those stimuli as covariates in their analyses. In any case, the authors argued convincingly that drinkers in the natural environment are often insensitive to their level of intoxication and may be inclined to confuse alcohol-induced physical sensations with sexual arousal if proximal cues are erotic. Repetition of such associations could give rise to functionally autonomous alcohol-response expectancies regarding sexuality and so could provide a potent source of reinforcement from drinking.

Focusing more on the expectancy that drinking will reduce culpability for deviant, but nevertheless potentially reinforcing sexual responses, Briddell, Rimm, Caddy, Krawitz, Sholis, and Wunderlin (1978) studied male college students' reactions to audiotaped portrayals of heterosexual intercourse, rape, and sadism. Like Wilson and Lawson (1976), their results showed that alcohol expectancy, but not actual alcohol led to greater physiological and subjective sexual arousal. In addition, one especially noteworthy finding was that expectancy effects increased as the sexual stimuli became increasingly deviant. More recently, George and Marlatt (1986) also showed that alcohol expectancy alone was sufficient to produce increases in male subjects' attention to violent-erotic slides and increases in their subjective sexual arousal when presented with such stimuli. These effects were greater the more deviant the slide content and were not influenced by actual alcohol. Thus in both studies inhibitions about expressions of sexual arousal seem to have been lifted when the belief that one had been drinking was available as an explanation or excuse for greater latitude in the types of sexual stimuli to which one responded.

If alcohol expectancies can facilitate potentially reinforcing sexual arousal in response to stimuli widely acknowledged to be deviant (e.g., forcible rape), then they may help to explain why some people drink. Lang, Searles, Lauerman, and Adesso (1980) have further proposed that disinhibiting expectancy effects not only take place in connection with external, societal standards of deviance, but also can be seen in variations of sexual response as a function of personal standards and self-regulatory processes. Lang et al. (1980) hypothesized that the probability that an alcohol expectancy will disinhibit sexual responses varies according to the utility or reinforcing value that attributing one's behavior to drinking has for that particular person. To test this prediction, male social drinkers classified as high, medium, or low in "sex guilt" were first administered beverages according to the balanced-placebo design, and then asked to evaluate photographic slides of varying erotic content and report on the degree of their sexual arousal. The time spent looking at each slide was unobtrusively recorded and was considered to reflect interest in that stimulus. Men who thought they had received alcoholic beverages evinced greater sexual arousal, regardless of actual intoxication, thus replicating the results of Wilson and Lawson (1976). However, the novel finding of the Lang et al. (1980) study was that level of sex guilt mediated the effect of alcohol expectancy on time spent in viewing the slides. Most subjects viewed the more sexually explicit slides longer regardless of beverage treatment, but the men high in sex guilt did so only if they thought they had drunk alcohol. Unlike the other men, the sexually inhibited subjects apparently needed drinking as an excuse to indulge their prurient interests. Here, expectancies again seemed more important than the pharmacological effect of alcohol in determining reinforcement derived from drinking. In addition, it was shown that the extent to which sexual disinhibition occurs in connection with alcohol use may depend upon the values or other personal characteristics of the individual drinker (also see Lansky & Wilson, 1981).

Another approach to the topic of drinking and sexuality has focused on how alcohol affects subjects' restraint or control of arousing experiences. Abrams and Wilson (1983) theorized that if subjects can attribute arousal to intoxication, they should be less inclined to try to control their sexual responses or to deny themselves access to erotic stimuli. These investigators used a delay-of-gratification paradigm to explore this hypothesis. Once male subjects in a modified balanced-placebo design with two dose levels had consumed their beverages, they were shown a brief segment of an erotic film. Then they were told that the longer they chose to wait before going on to the final viewing and measurement phase of the experiment, the more of the film they would get to see. While waiting, subjects were told to attend to their thoughts, feelings, and arousal so that they could report on them later. Despite no group differences in physiological measures of sexual arousal during the waiting period, men who thought they had drunk alcohol chose longer delays in order to see more film and reported having more sexual thoughts while waiting. In addition, subjects who believed they had consumed alcohol reported less embarrassment, less boredom, and greater pleasure while waiting. These results were interpreted to mean that subjects' belief that they were intoxicated reduced their self-consciousness, thereby enabling them to pursue greater sexual gratification (i.e., more extensive viewing of the erotic film) because this self-indulgence could be attributed to alcohol.

In summary, the relation between drinking and sexual expression is by no means simple. At high doses, alcohol acts as a pharmacological depressant for virtually all aspects of physiological functioning, and hence seems unlikely to provide any reinforcement via enhancement of sexual responding. On the other hand, the low to moderate BALs reached in most balanced-placebo studies have been shown to have little or no impact on sexual functioning. In these studies, however, the belief that one had drunk alcohol exerted a significant influence on sexually-relevant behavior, and did so in such a way that it would tend to reinforce drinking. For men in particular, an alcohol expectancy was found to cause increased physiological and subjective sexual arousal in response to erotic stimuli, to reduce reluctance to seek and attend to sexual materials, and to broaden the range of sexual stimuli that evoked arousal. Moreover, these disinhibiting effects appeared to be greater in people who had a high level of guilt about sexual expression. Although additional research is needed to clarify the basis of expectancy effects and why they operate differently for different subject populations (e.g., women and men), clearly these effects constitute a potentially important motive for drinking.

Aggression. With the possible exception of psychoanalysts, people generally do not consider aggression to be as inherently reinforcing as sexual expression. Still there are times when exercising power and dominance can be personally rewarding, when aggression can be instrumental in the attainment of goals, and even when impulsive retaliation or revenge can be satisfying. If drinking in some way facilitates expression of aggression, this effect could motivate alcohol use.

A large body of evidence (Collins, 1981) indicates that, alcohol use is associated with an inordinate proportion of aggressive, violent, and criminal behaviors. Traditionally, this correlation has been explained in terms of the presumed pharmacological effect of ethanol either to stimulate aggression directly or to release it from inhibition through an anesthetic action on certain higher brain centers (Pernanen, 1976). It is also possible that a tension-reducing effect of alcohol could facilitate aggression by diminishing fears about aversive consequences. Or perhaps ethanol interferes with cognitive processes and produces greater aggression because drinkers have difficulty making decisions about instigators' intentions or about the appropriate behavioral contingencies in ambiguous situations with potential for aggression. Whatever the particular pharmacological theory, a number of published laboratory experiments appear to support the claim of a causal link and a positive linear relation between alcohol dose and level of expressed aggression (see Taylor & Leonard, 1983). However, these studies typically have failed to rule out expectancy as a potential contributor to the increased aggression observed in drinkers. In particular, there is a need to consider the possibility that merely because of the beliefs surrounding it, alcohol provides the drinker with greater freedom to engage in aggressive behavior. Thus expectancy analyses of drinking and aggression appear warranted.

Using a balanced-placebo design, Lang et al. (1975) studied effects of alcohol on aggression in male college students who reported high levels of alcohol use. After drinking, subjects experienced a brief interaction with either an anger-provoking or a neutral confederate. Subsequently, aggression was assessed by measuring the intensity and duration of electric shocks subjects were willing to administer to their confederate partners during a bogus teaching task. Results revealed that subjects who thought they had drunk alcohol were significantly more aggressive than those who thought they had consumed nonalcoholic beverages, regardless of the actual beverages consumed. There were no differences due to alcohol itself and, although provocation had a main effect in increasing aggression, it did not interact with any of the beverage treatments. In this situation alcohol expectancies clearly facilitated aggressive responding.

Pihl, Zeichner, Niaura, Nagy, and Zacchia (1981) employed a variate of the balanced-placebo design to examine further the role that subjects' beliefs about beverage content play in alcohol-mediated aggression. Prior to participation in an aggressive interchange, male subjects were given either alcoholic or nonalcoholic drinks, which were described as containing either a high or low alcohol dose, despite the fact that the beverages of all subjects who received alcohol contained the same moderately high dose. Measures of aggression included intensity and duration of shock given to a bogus partner and scores on a posttask attitude questionnaire. Results showed that the effects of drinking on aggression varied according to which dependent measure was being considered. Consistent with the findings of Lang et al. (1975), men who thought they had received a high dose of alcohol chose to deliver more punishing shocks to their partners than did men who believed they had drunk only a low alcohol dose, regardless of actual beverage content. The only effect for alcohol itself was that, compared with subjects receiving nonalcoholic drinks, those who actually had consumed alcohol evinced more negative attitudes toward their partners on the posttask questionnaire. Thus the stronger the alcohol expectancy, the greater was the physical aggression, although verbal aggression seemed to be more responsive to actual consumption of alcohol. Perhaps because it is more widely accepted than physical aggression, the written negative evaluation form of verbal aggression used in this experiment did not require an alcohol attribution to excuse or justify it and so it was influenced by other features of the situation.

Also using a high-dose and low-dose expectancy manipulation, this time including drinks with two levels of actual alcohol content as well as the usual nonalcoholic beverages, Kreutzer, Schneider, and Myatt (1984) found that self-reported hostility and oral verbal aggression were differentially affected by drinking. Self-reported hostility was higher at moderate levels of actual intoxication than when subjects had either a high dose of alcohol or none at all, and it also increased with increases in expected dosage. Verbal aggression, on the other hand, was affected only by actual alcohol, reaching its highest level in subjects who consumed the most alcohol. In this experiment it was again shown that nonphysical forms of aggressive expression were influenced by pharmacological actions of alcohol, while expectancy played a more minor role.

Finally, in the only balanced-placebo investigation of drinking and aggression that included female subjects, Rohsenow and Bachorowski (1984) examined the verbal responses of participants following an anger-provocation manipulation. Three separate experiments using varied doses of alcohol yielded a complicated pattern of results. Actual alcohol consumption led to a modest increase in aggression only when women who had received a low dose were compared with those who had consumed a nonalcoholic beverage. The main finding, however, was that among all subjects who consumed high alcohol doses, and also among males receiving the lower dose, subjects who thought they had received alcohol were *less* aggressive than those who thought they had not. The authors attempted to reconcile these surprising results with those of other balanced-placebo studies of aggression by noting that subjects in the alcohol expectancy conditions reported feeling "happier" after drinking than did those who thought they had received nonalcoholic beverages. This competing expectation may have overwhelmed any belief that drinking increases aggression, particularly since other research (Rohsenow, 1983) has indicated that the vast majority of woman, as well as a substantial proportion of men, think alcohol leads to greater aggressiveness in *others,* but not in themselves. In any case, alcohol expectancy was still the major determinant of behavior change in this experiment.

In general then, multiple factors appear to influence the relation between drinking and aggression. At least for men, the belief that one has consumed alcohol clearly can facilitate the expression of more physical aggression than would be seen in individuals without an alcohol expectancy, irrespective of actual alcohol consumption. Results from studies using self-report and verbal measures of aggression, however, were more equivocal, and also highlighted the role of situational and task demands as well as individual difference variables in alcohol's link to aggression. Still, to the extent that aggressive expression is reinforcing, the belief that it is facilitated by alcohol consumption can provide a reason for drinking. This expectancy, however, may be a reflection of social learning rather than an illustration of specific, biobehavioral actions of ethanol.

Summary Overall, balanced-placebo investigations of the consequences of drinking indicate that the simple belief that one has consumed alcoholic beverages, relatively independent of the actual contents of those beverages, can contribute to potentially reinforcing outcomes that sometimes accompany drinking. In our analysis of such cognitive expectancy effects, we argue further that their impact increases as the class of consequences under consideration involves a greater element of psychosocial evaluation. This argument has been bolstered by a recent meta-analysis of balanced-placebo studies (Hull & Bond, 1986) that used a somewhat different scheme to classify behavioral consequences of drinking, but arrived at similar conclusions. In general, we noted that impersonal behaviors, such as cognitive and motor performances, are ordinarily impaired by drinking, and that this effect is due almost exclusively to deleterious pharmacological actions of ethanol. Conversely, alcohol expectancy operates as a critical determinant of the facilitating effect that drinking can have on certain reinforcing interpersonal behaviors, particularly those that are subject to conflict-inducing inhibitions or restraints (cf. Steele & Southwick, 1985). Finally, both alcohol and expectancy appear to be potential contributors to the intrapersonal consequences of drinking, but have their effect in a rather inconsistent manner that varies greatly across situations and individuals. Overall, we feel justified in the assertion that alcohol expectancy exerts its greatest influence on social behaviors having considerable psychological importance for the individual. Recognition of this connection has the potential to improve our understanding of why people drink.

CONCLUSIONS

At a time when we seem to be on the verge of discovering physiological, family/genetic, and other relatively stable individual difference variables affecting the reinforcing actions of ethanol and consequent vulnerability to drinking problems, abandonment of a biological perspective on alcohol use and abuse seems ill-advised. It would be equally foolhardy to disregard the useful insights into drunken behavior provided by careful analyses of the ways alcohol might affect information processing. Certainly alcohol's enhancement of feelings of power (McClelland, Davis, Kalin, & Wanner, 1972), reduction of self-awareness (Hull, 1981), and distortion of attention/perception (Pihl, 1983) could have rewarding consequences. Unfortunately, all these approaches depend directly or indirectly on certain specific pharmacological effects of alcohol and, as such, fail to account fully for alcohol expectancies manifested in the balanced-placebo studies reviewed in this chapter. Moreover, they often appear to shortchange the contributions that non-pharmacological processes, involving psychological and social-environmental contingencies, can make to why people drink. Without attempting to integrate expectancy effects into a broader biopsychosocial perspective on drinking, let us highlight their possible role.

Alfred Adler (1956) was among the first to suggest that addictive behavior often begins as a way of dealing with acute feelings of anxiety, insecurity, and inferiority about personal and social functioning. He argued that indulging in substance use can protect one's self-esteem and permit avoidance of threatening interpersonal responsibility by providing an excuse or externalization of blame for any incompetent performance or socially inappropriate behavior. Meanwhile, the individual can maintain high aspirations and lofty morals since a true test of ability and intentions is not possible except under conditions of sobriety. Other more contemporary theorists appear to share Adler's ideas. For instance, Jones and Berglas (1978) coined the term "self-handicapping" in a description of how people sometimes drink to obscure the meaning of performance feedback, especially when the behaviors in question involve precarious (though not entirely negative) aspects of self-concept. Finally, a related and potentially reinforcing aspect of drinking in this culture is the way that it alters reactions to or evaluations of one's behavior. Falk's (1983) treatise on psychoactive substances as discriminative stimuli outlined this argument. In particular, the inebriate's behavior is often taken less seriously, be it criminal, distasteful, or simply inappropriate (cf. Critchlow, 1983; Suls, 1978).

If drunken behavior is not regarded as a true reflection of oneself and the drinker is treated with greater tolerance than when sober, then the reinforcing potential of drinking is indeed considerable. In essence, alcohol use enhances one's latitude for expression by diminishing responsibility for behavior. In MacAndrew and Edgerton's (1969) words, it provides "time out" from rules normally governing conduct. There are naturally some limits to this alcohol-induced freedom. However, the ambiguity of the "social contract" that establishes them is evident, and may itself contribute to the problems associated with drinking.

In summary, our position is that many of the specific alcohol-response expectancies generally regarded as reinforcing were not born of intrinsic biobehavioral actions of ethanol. Instead, the appeal of drinking appears to arise largely from observation and experience of environmentally supported response-outcome expectancies that enable one to cope with psychosocial conflicts in rewarding ways (cf. Steele & Southwick, 1985). Evidence from studies using the balanced-placebo design provides striking support for this argument. Where personal and social inhibitions restrain desired expression of psychosocially meaningful behavior (e.g., sexual response), expectancy effects often play a key role in facilitating enactment. On the other hand, if there is little motivation or significance to enactment of a behavior (e.g., trivial cognitive/motor performance), expectancy effects do not influence it, though actual alcohol may if its more general pharmacological actions are relevant. Furthermore, observed gender differences and situational effects on alcohol-behavior relations would appear to support social learning and environmental determination of these phenomena. Finally, the virtually total lack of interactions between actual alcohol effects and expectancy effects in balanced-placebo studies indicates that expectancy ought to be regarded as an independent source of reinforcement from drinking.

From the point of view of prevention and resolution of alcohol problems, the demonstrated importance of expectancies may provide reason for optimism. After all, it is probably easier to change what people believe and will tolerate about drinking than it is to change their physiological reactions to it.

REFERENCES

Abrams, D., & Wilson, G. (1979). Effects of alcohol on social anxiety in women: Cognitive vs. physiological processes. *Journal of Abnormal Psychology*, 88, 161–173.

Abrams, D., & Wilson, G. (1983). Alcohol, sexual arousal, and self-control. *Journal of Personality and Social Psychology,* 45, 188–198.

Adler, A. (1956). *The individual psychology of Alfred Adler.* New York: Basic Books.

Aitken, P. (1978). *Ten-to-fourteen-year-olds and alcohol: A developmental study in the Central Region of Scotland* (vol.3). Edinburgh: HMSO.

Berg, G., Laberg, J., Skutle, A., & Ohman, A. (1981). Instructed versus pharmacological effects of alcohol in alcoholics and social drinkers. *Behavior Research and Therapy,* 19, 55–66.

Birnbaum, I., & Parker, E. (Eds.). (1977). *Alcohol and human memory.* New York; Erlbaum.

Bolon, K., & Barling, J. (1980). Alcohol, expectancies, sex, and social effects on depression. *South African Journal of Psychology,* 10, 46–49.

Briddell, D., Rimm, D., Caddy, G., Krawitz, G., Sholis, D., & Wunderlin, R. (1978). Effects of alcohol and cognitive set on sexual arousal to deviant stimuli. *Journal of Abnormal Psychology,* 87, 418–430.

Brown, S. (1985a). Context of drinking and reinforcement from alcohol: Alcoholic patterns. *Addictive Behaviors,* 10, 191–195.

Brown, S. (1985b). Expectancies versus background in the prediction of college drinking patterns. *Journal of Consulting and Clinical Psychology, 53,* 123–130.

Brown, S. (1985c). Reinforcement expectancies and alcohol treatment outcome after one year. *Journal of Studies on Alcohol,* 46, 304–308.

Brown, S., Goldman, M., & Christiansen, B. (1985). Do alcohol expectancies mediate drinking of adults? *Journal of Consulting and Clinical Psychology, 53,* 512–519.

Brown, S., Goldman, M., Inn, A., & Anderson, L. (1980). Expectations of reinforcement from alcohol: Their domain and relation to drinking patterns. *Journal of Consulting and Clinical Psychology,* 48, 419–426.

Cappell, H., & Greeley, J. (1987). Alcohol and tension reduction; An update on Research and theory. In H. Blane & K. Leonard (Eds.), *Psychological theories of drinking and alcoholism.* New York: Guilford Press.

Christiansen, B., & Brown, S. (1985). *Adolescent alcohol expectancies: Further evidence of their robust nature.* Paper presented to the American Psychological Association. Los Angeles, Calif.

Christiansen, B., & Goldman, M. (1983). Alcohol-related expectancies versus demographic/background variables in the prediction of adolescent drinking. *Journal of Consulting and Clinical Psychology,* 51, 249–257.

Christiansen, B., Goldman, M., & Brown, S. (1985). The differential development of adolescent alcohol expectancies may predict adult alcoholism. *Addictive Behaviors,* 10, 299–306.

Christiansen, B., Goldman, M., & Inn, A. (1982). Development of alcohol-related expectancies in adolescents: Separating pharmacological from social learning influences. *Journal of Consulting and Clinical Psychology,* 50, 336–344.

Christiansen, B., & Teahan, J. (1985). *Cross culture comparisons of Irish and American adolescent drinking practices and beliefs.* Unpublished manuscript. University of Wisconsin Medical School.

Collins, J.J. (Ed.) (1981) *Drinking and crime.* New York: Guilford Press.

Conger, J. (1956). Reinforcement theory and the dynamics of alcoholism. *Quarterly Journal of Studies on Alcohol,* 17, 296–305.

Connors, G., & Maisto, S. (1979). Effects of alcohol, instructions, and consumption rate on affect and physiological sensations. *Psychopharmacology,* 62, 261–266.

Connors, G., & Maisto, S. (1980). Effects of alcohol, instructions and consumption rate on motor performance. *Journal of Studies on Alcohol,* 41, 509–517.

Crawford, A. (1984a). Alcohol and expectancy: I Perceived sex differences in the effects of drinking. *Alcohol and Alcoholism,* 19, 63–69.

Crawford, A. (1984b). Alcohol and expectancy: II. Perceived sex differences in the role of alcohol as a source of aggression. *Alcohol and Alcoholism,* 19, 71–75.

Creamer, V., & Brown, S. (1985). *Alcohol expectancies of reinforcement: A gender or generational gap?* Paper presented to the American Psychological Association, Los Angeles, Calif.

Critchlow, B. (1983). Blaming the booze: The attribution of responsibility for drunken behavior. *Personality and Social Psychology Bulletin,* 9, 451–473.

Falk, J. (1983). Drug dependence: Myth or motive? *Pharmacology Biochemistry and Behavior,* 19, 385–391.

George, W., & Marlatt, G. (1986). The effects of alcohol and anger on interest in violence, erotica, and deviance. *Journal of Abnormal Psychology,* 95, 150–158.

Higgins, R., & Marlatt, G. (1973). Effects of anxiety arousal on the consumption of alcohol by alcoholics and social drinkers. *Journal of Consulting and Clinical Psychology,* 41, 426–433.

Higgins, R., & Marlatt, G. (1975). Fear of interpersonal evaluation as a determinant of alcohol consumption in male social drinkers. *Journal of Abnormal Psychology,* 84, 644–651.

Holroyd, K. (1978). Effects of social anxiety and social evaluation on beer consumption and social interaction. *Journal of Studies on Alcohol,* 39, 737–744.

Hull, J. (1981). A self awareness model of the causes and effects of alcohol consumption. *Journal of Abnormal Psychology,* 90, 586–600.

Hull, J., & Bond, R. (1986). Social and behavioral consequences of alcohol consumption and expectancy: A meta-alalysis. *Psychological Bulletin,* 99, 347–360.

Isaacs, M. (1977). Stereotyping by children of the effects of drinking on adults. *Journal of Studies on Alcohol,* 38, 913–921.

Isaacs, M. (1979). College students' expectations of the results of drinking. *Journal of Studies on Alcohol,* 40, 476–479.

Jahoda, G., & Cramond, J. (1972). *Children and alcohol: A developmental study in Glasgow.* London: HMSO.

Jones, E., & Berglas, S. (1978). Control of attributions about the self through self-handicapping strategies: The appeal of alcohol and the role of underachievement. *Personality and Social Psychology Bulletin,* 4, 200–206.

Keane, T., & Lisman, S. (1980). Alcohol and social anxiety in males: Behavioral, cognitive, and physiological effects. *Journal of Abnormal Psychology,* 89, 213–223.

Kreutzer, J., Schneider, H., & Myatt, C. (1984). Alcohol, aggression and assertiveness in men: Dosage and expectancy effects. *Journal of Studies on Alcohol,* 45, 275–278.

Lang, A. (1985). The Social psychology of drinking and human sexuality. *Journal of Drug Issues,* 15, 273–290.

Lang, A., Goeckner, D., Adesso, V., & Marlatt, G. (1975). Effects of alcohol on aggression in male social drinkers. *Journal of Abnormal Psychology,* 84, 508–518.

Lang, A., Kaas, L., & Barnes, P. (1983). The beverage type stereotype: An unexplored determinant of the effects of alcohol consumption. *Bulletin of the Society of Psychologists in Addictive Behaviors,* 2, 46–49.

Lang, A., Murray, A., & Pelham, W. (1984). *Children's perceptions of the effects of alcohol on adult-child interactions.* Paper presented to the Southeastern Psychological Association, New Orleans, La.

Lang, A., Searles, J., Lauerman, R., & Adesso, V. (1980). Expectancy, alcohol, and sex guilt as determinants of interest in and reaction to sexual stimuli. *Journal of Abnormal Psychology,* 89, 644–653.

Lang, A., Verret, L., & Watt, C. (1984). Drinking and creativity: Objective and subjective effects. *Addictive Behaviors,* 9, 395–399.

Lansky, D., & Wilson, G. (1981). Alcohol, expectations, and sexual arousal in males: An information processing analysis. *Journal of Abnormal Psychology,* 90, 35–45.

Levenson, R., Sher, K., Grossman, L., Newman, J., & Newlin, D., (1980). Alcohol and stress response dampening: Pharmacological effects, expectancy, and tension reduction. *Journal of Abnormal Psychology,* 89, 528–538.

MacAndrew, C., & Edgerton, R. (1969). *Drunken comportment: A social explanation.* Chicago: Aldine.

Marlatt, G., Demming, B., & Reid, J. (1973). Loss of control drinking in alcoholics: An experimental analogue. *Journal of Abnormal Psychology,* 81, 233–241.

Marlatt, G., Kosturn, C., & Lang, A. (1975). Provocation to anger and opportunity for retaliation as determinants of alcohol consumption in social drinkers. *Journal of Abnormal Psychology,* 84, 652–659.

Marlatt, G., & Rohsenow, D. (1980). Cognitive processes in alcohol use: Expectancy and the balanced placebo design. In N. Mello (Ed.), *Advances in substance abuse: Behavioral and biological research.* Greenwich, Conn.: JAI Press.

McCarty, D., Diamond, W., & Kaye, M. (1982). Alcohol, sexual arousal, and the transfer of excitation. *Journal of Personality and Social Psychology,* 42, 977–988.

McClelland, D., Davis, W., Kalin, R., & Wanner, E. (1972). *The Drinking man.* New York: Free Press.

McCollam, J., Burish, T., Maisto, S., & Sobell, M. (1980). Alcohol's effects on physiological arousal and self-reported affect and sensations. *Journal of Abnormal Psychology,* 89, 224–233.

Miller, M., Adesso, V., Fleming, J., Gino, A., & Lauerman, R. (1978). The effects of alcohol on the storage and retrieval processes of heavy social drinkers. *Journal of Experimental Psychology: Human Learning and Memory,* 4, 246–255.

Miller, P., Hersen, M., Eisler, R., & Hilsman, G. (1974). Effects of social stress on operant drinking of alcoholics and social drinkers. *Behavior Research and Therapy,* 12, 67–72.

Moskowitz, H., Daily, J., & Henderson, R. (1974). Acute tolerance to behavioral impairment by alcohol in moderate and heavy drinkers. System Development Corp. Santa Monica, Calif., Tech Report. HS-009–2–332.

Myrsten, A., Lamble, R., Frankenhauser, M., & Lundberg, U. (1979). Interaction of alcohol and reward in an achievement situation. *Psychopharmacology*, 62, 211–215.

Noel, N., & Lisman, S. (1980). Alcohol consumption by college women following exposure to unsolvable problems: Learned helplessness or stress-induced drinking? *Behavioral Research and Therapy*, 18, 429–440.

O'Malley, S., & Maisto, S. (1984). Factors affecting the perception of intoxication: Dose, tolerance, and setting. *Addictive Behaviors*, 9, 111–120.

O'Malley, S., & Maisto, S. (1985). Effects of family drinking history and expectancies on responses to alcohol in men. *Journal of Studies on Alcohol*,46, 289–297.

Pernanen, K. (1976). Alcohol and crimes of violence. In B. Kissin & H. Begleiter (Eds.), *The biology of alcoholism* (vol.4). New York and London: Plenum Press.

Pihl, R. (1983). Alcohol and aggression: A psychological perspective. In E. Gottheil et al. (Eds.), *Alcohol, drug abuse, and aggression*. Springfield, IL: Charles, C. Thomas.

Pihl, R., Zeichner, A., Niaura, R., Nagy, K., & Zacchia, C. (1981). Attribution and alcohol mediated aggression. *Journal of Abnormal Psychology*, 90, 468–475.

Pliner, P., & Cappell, H. (1974). Modification of affective consequences of alcohol. A comparison of social and solitary drinking. *Journal of Abnormal Psychology*, 83, 418–425.

Polivy, J., Schueneman, A., & Carlson, K. (1976). Alcohol and tension reduction: Cognitive and physiological effects. *Journal of Abnormal Psychology*, 85, 595–600.

Rimm, D., Sininger, J., Faherty, M., Whitley, M., & Perl, M. (1982). A balanced placebo investigation of the effects of alcohol vs. alcohol expectancy on simulated driving behavior. *Addictive Behaviors*, 7, 27–32.

Rimm, D., Briddell, D., Zimmerman, M., & Caddy, G. (1981). The effects of alcohol and the expectancy of alcohol on snake fear. *Addictive Behaviors*, 6, 47–51.

Rohsenow, D. (1983). Drinking habits and expectancies about alcohol's effects for self versus others. *Journal of Consulting and Clinical Psychology*, 51, 752–756.

Rohsenow, D., & Bachorowski, J. (1984). Effects of alcohol and expectancies on verbal aggression in men and women. *Journal of Abnormal Psychology*, 93, 418–432.

Ross, S., Krugman, A., Lyerly, S., & Clyde, D. (1962). Drugs and placebos: A model design. *Psychological Reports*, 10, 383–392.

Sher, K. (1985). Subjective effects of alcohol: The influence of setting and individual differences in alcohol expectancies. *Journal of Studies on Alcohol*, 46, 137–146.

Southwick, L., Steel, C., Marlatt, A., & Lindell, M. (1981). Alcohol-related expectancies: Defined by phase of intoxication and drinking experience. *Journal of Consulting and Clinical Psychology*, 49, 713–721.

Spiegler, D. (1983). Children's attitudes toward alcohol *Journal of Studies on Alcohol*, 44, 545–552.

Steele, C., & Southwick, L. (1985). Alcohol and social behavior I: The psychology of drunken excess. *Journal of Personality and Social Psychology*, 48, 18–34.

Strickler, D., Tomaszewski, R., Maxwell, W., & Suib, M. (1979). The effects of relaxation instructions on drinking behavior in the presence of stress. *Behavior Research and Therapy,* 17, 45–51.

Suls, J. (1978). Estimating behavior-belief congruence in intoxicated persons. *Journal of Studies on Alcohol,* 39, 1299–1301.

Sutker, P., Allain, A., Brantley, P., & Randall, C. (1982). Acute alcohol intoxication, negative affect, and autonomic arousal in women and men. *Addictive Behaviors,* 7, 17–26.

Taylor, S., & Leonard, K. (1983). Alcohol and human physical aggression. In R. Green & E. Donnerstein (Eds.), *Aggression: Theoretical and empirical reviews* (vol.2), New York: Academic Press, pp. 77–101.

Tucker, J., Maisto, S., Vuchinich, R,. & Blumenthal, L. (1979). Alcohol and anxiety: The role of drinking context, expectancy, and sex of subject. *Behavioral Psychotherapy,* 7, 75–84.

Tucker, J., & Vuchinich, R. (1983). An information processing analysis of the effects of alcohol on perceptions of facial emotions. *Psychopharmacology,* 79, 215–219.

Tucker, J., Vuchinich, R., & Sobell, M. (1981). Alcohol consumption as a self-handicapping strategy. *Journal of Abnormal Psychology,* 90, 220–230.

Tucker, J., Vuchinich, R., Sobell, M., & Maisto, S. (1980). Normal drinkers' alcohol consumption as a function of conflicting motives induced by intellectual performance stress. *Addicitve Behaviors,* 5, 171–178.

Vuchinich, R., & Sobell, M. (1978). Empirical separation of physiologic and expected effects of alcohol on complex perceptual motor performance. *Psychopharmacology,* 60, 81–85.

Williams, R., Goldman, M., & Williams, D. (1981). Expectancy and pharmacological effects of alcohol on human cognitive and motor performance: The compensation for alcohol effect. *Journal of Abnormal Psychology,* 90, 267–270.

Wilsnack, S., Klassen, A., & Wilsnack, R. (1983). *Drinking, sexual experience, and reproductive dysfunction among women in a 1981 national survey.* Paper presented at the 14th Annual Medical-Scientific Conference of the National Alcoholism Forum, Houston, Texas.

Wilson, G., & Abrams D. (1977). Effects of alcohol on social anxiety and physiological arousal: Cognitive versus pharmacological processes. *Cognitive Therapy and Research,* 1, 195–210.

Wilson, G., & Lawson, D. (1976). Expectancies, alcohol, and sexual arousal in male social drinkers. *Journal of Abnormal Psychology,* 85, 587–594.

Wilson, G., & Lawson, D. (1978). Expectancies, alcohol and sexual arousal in women. *Journal of Abnormal Psychology,* 87, 358–367.

Wilson, G., Niaura, R., & Adler, J. (1985). Alcohol, selective attention and sexual arousal in men. *Journal of Studies on Alcohol,* 46, 107–115.

Wilson, G., Perold, E., & Abrams, D. (1981). The effects of expectations of self-intoxication and partner's drinking on anxiety in dyadic social interaction. *Cognitive Therapy and Research,* 5, 251–264.

Young, J., & Pihl, R. (1980). Self-control of the effects of alcohol intoxication. *Journal of Studies on Alcohol,* 41, 567–571.

NINE

SOCIAL REINFORCEMENT AND ALCOHOL CONSUMPTION

HELENE RASKIN WHITE, Ph.D., MARSHA E. BATES, Ph.D., and VALERIE JOHNSON, Ph.D.

Drinking alcohol, like other acquired human behaviors, is learned and usually performed in a social context. There are many socially acceptable reasons and occasions for alcohol use, social rewards for drinking, and role models of drinking behaviors resulting in a wide variety of drinking practices being integrated into our day-to-day life. Strictly speaking, of course, the act of drinking is an individual behavior, but usually drinking also has a social function. That is, it often involves two or more persons interacting with one another and/or reacting to some social stimulus. The focus of this chapter is on social rewards and incentives for drinking that are dependent upon peoples' experiences within the context of specific social environments. We discuss the most proximal social determinants of drinking, including family, friends, and members of other meaningful peer groups who are powerful agents of social influence at various stages of development. In addition, we con-

The authors thank Drs. Ronald L. Akers and Erich W. Labouvie for their valuable comments on an earlier draft of this chapter. The writing of this manuscript was supported, in part, by grants from the National Institute of Alcohol Abuse and Alcoholism (#AA-05823) and the National Institute of Drug Abuse (#DA-03395).

sider the potentially influential yet noninteractional models of drinking that are widely observed in the electronic and printed media, both in an advertising context and during the recreational viewing of television and movies. Before discussing social influences on the initiation and development of drinking behaviors, we provide a brief orientation to the major features of a social learning approach to the question of why people drink. We also present a general model within which to consider significant influences in the social environment.

SOCIAL LEARNING PERSPECTIVE

Social reinforcers—that is, those provided by other people—are important determinants of many human behaviors. If others' reactions are perceived as approving (positive reinforcement) or consisting of the withdrawal of disapproval (negative reinforcement), they will increase the likelihood that the behavior will be performed again. If the reactions of others are perceived as disapproving (punishment), they will decrease the probability that the behavior will be engaged in again. The idea that consequences of behavior determine whether new behaviors will be acquired and existing ones will be modified is central to most learning theories. In addition, social learning theories emphasize that symbolic mental events (e.g., thought processes) and the observation of others also influence learning. Hence theories of social learning integrate learning principles derived from observable behavior with constructs based on cognitive processes that are not directly observable (see Bandura, 1969; Rotter, 1982; Skinner, 1971).

Observational Learning

Much social learning occurs in the absence of direct experience. That is, human thought and behavior may be markedly influenced by observing other people engage in behavior that is reinforced (vicarious or anticipated reinforcement) (Bandura, 1977). The behavior of others is modeled because observers expect that their own behavior will produce the same positive consequences that they observed the model experience (Bandura, 1977). The terms modeling, imitation, and observational learning have been used to refer to the same phenomenon, but we prefer the distinction made by Bandura (1977), Rimm and Masters (1979), and others, who clearly differentiate between the temporary copying of a model's behavior (imitation) and the acquiring of more enduring behaviors (observational learning).

It has been demonstrated that observational learning can occur without actual performance (e.g., Flanders, 1968), presumably because of humans' ability to symbolically represent, store, and covertly rehearse behaviors. Thus, in the case of drinking, we suspect that observational learning of ones' parents' drinking behaviors can take place long before those behaviors are actually performed. The child or adolescent may not actually engage in these learned drinking behaviors until some later age or in an appropriate social, very likely peer, setting.

During the past ten years, a number of experimental studies have confirmed that, under certain conditions, individuals imitate the specific characteristics of drinking behavior (e.g., rate of consumption) that they observe among confederates in laboratory settings (e.g., Collins, Parks, & Marlatt, 1985), "real world" bar settings (e.g., Reid, 1978), and seminaturalistic bar settings (e.g., Caudill & Lipscomb, 1980). Experimental manipulations have included varying the social status of the confederate model, as well as the degree of the social interaction between model and subject. For example, in a recent study by Collins et al. (1985), moderate to heavy drinking male subjects drank in a laboratory bar setting while paired with a light- or heavy-consumption model. The model either behaved in a warm, sociable manner while drinking with the subject or was cold and uncommunicative. A significant interaction on subjects' drinking behavior was found between the model's consumption rate and level of sociability. In the sociable condition, subjects modeled the confederate in terms of amount of alcohol consumed, while in the unsociable condition, all subjects tended to drink heavily. Thus the negative social stimulus created by the nonsociable model seemed to precipitate heavy drinking by all subjects. A comparison of these laboratory results with those of Reid (1978), whose study manipulated sociability of the model in a natural bar, however, indicates that the number of behavioral alternatives to drinking available to the subjects may be a significant consideration in determining their response to unpleasant social conditions. In this study, subjects exposed to an unsociable model exhibited a "flight" response; they had one drink and then left the bar. Thus the number of actual or perceived alternatives to alcohol consumption for the relief of social stress may be one determinant of whether alcohol consumption will be used to regulate socially induced negative internal states.

Complementing the experimental modeling research, there have been several observational studies of drinking behaviors in natural settings. These studies have found that the duration of the drinking occasion, the rate of consumption, and the amount consumed depend on the size and gender of the drinking group. For example, Rosenbluth, Nathan, and Lawson (1978) found that individuals drink more rapidly in groups of three or more persons than in dyads. Cutler and Storm (1975) also found that consumption is greater in larger than in smaller groups. They attribute this difference to the fact that larger groups as compared with smaller groups drink for longer periods of time.

Cognitions and Social Expectations

Throughout the socialization process, symbolic representations of experience, including internalized values, beliefs, and expectancies, are formed and modified first through exposure to parents (or other primary caretakers) and later through the influence of other meaningful social agents (e.g., peers, teachers). Basic experimental research has demonstrated that differing beliefs about how often a behavior is likely to be reinforced (Kaufman, Baron, & Kopp, 1966) and why a particular behavioral consequence has occurred (Dulany, 1968) significantly modify how different individuals will behave in response to identical stimuli in the environment. It thus seems likely that (1) the reinforcing properties of alcohol will be perceived differently by various individuals depending upon their previous exposure to specific others and social contexts for drinking and (2) resultant expectations about the effects of alcohol will actually modify how people experience and react to alcohol. Reasons for drinking and drinking behaviors themselves may thus be influenced by meaningful others even when others are not present (see Jones & Gerard, 1967).

Survey research has demonstrated that expectations regarding alcohol's function as a facilitator of other social behavior is a powerful determinant of drinking behaviors. In general, the reasons for drinking most frequently endorsed by nonproblem drinkers involve the enhancement of already pleasurable internal states and social occasions. In contrast, alcoholics and problem drinkers expect more global positive changes, social assertiveness, social and physical pleasure, relaxation, and tension reduction from alcohol use than do other drinkers. (See chapter 8, this volume, for an in-depth discussion of alcohol expectancies.) The expectancy research suggests that people at risk for or currently experiencing alcohol problems may have more social and nonsocial reinforcers connected with drinking and/or more generalized stimulus conditions that trigger drinking behavior than do those who are not experiencing problems. (Stimulus generalization is seen when an individual gives a conditioned response to stimuli that are similar to the one to which he or she was originally conditioned.)

Generalization of stimulus conditions for drinking or generalized expectations of reinforcement from drinking may evoke (1) more intensive drinking behaviors and (2) nonadaptive drinking responses to stressful social stimuli. The latter may be at least as important for the development of problem drinking as the former because drinking in response to stressful life events presents a temporary respite at best. At worst, the state of induced intoxication is counterproductive to adaptive problem solving and may create additional stress, exacerbate existing problems, and preempt the development of adaptive coping skills.

SOCIAL LEARNING MODEL

According to Bandura (1977), "Social learning theory approaches the explanation of human behavior in terms of a continuous reciprocal interaction between cognitive, behavioral and environmental determinants" (p. vii). Hence a social learning approach seems well suited to examining why people drink because drinking seems to be determined by complex interactions among alcohol, the person who drinks it, and the environment (see, for example, Akers, 1985; Sher, 1985). A schematic representation of personal, behavioral, and environmental determinants of drinking behavior is presented in Figure 9–1. The personal and environmental variables shown represent, but do not exhaust, the list of potentially significant influences on drinking behaviors. The double-headed arrows signify that each domain contains influences that affect, and are affected by, influences in the other domains. Note that this model is quite different from those that view behavior solely as a unidirectional function of personal and environmental determinants (see Bandura, 1977).

The Person

The social learning model depicts the individual as bringing to the environment a unique endowment that (1) imposes certain limits on what can be learned and how it is learned and (2) influences his or her selection of various environments. Learning experiences transform one's genetic potentialities into behavioral repertoires (Doby, 1966). Because the foci of this chapter are important environmental influences on drinking behaviors, we will make little mention of relevant intrapersonal characteristics, including "self-efficacy," a construct that occupies

Figure 1. Interactive schema of person, environment, and drug variables affecting and affected by drinking behaviors.

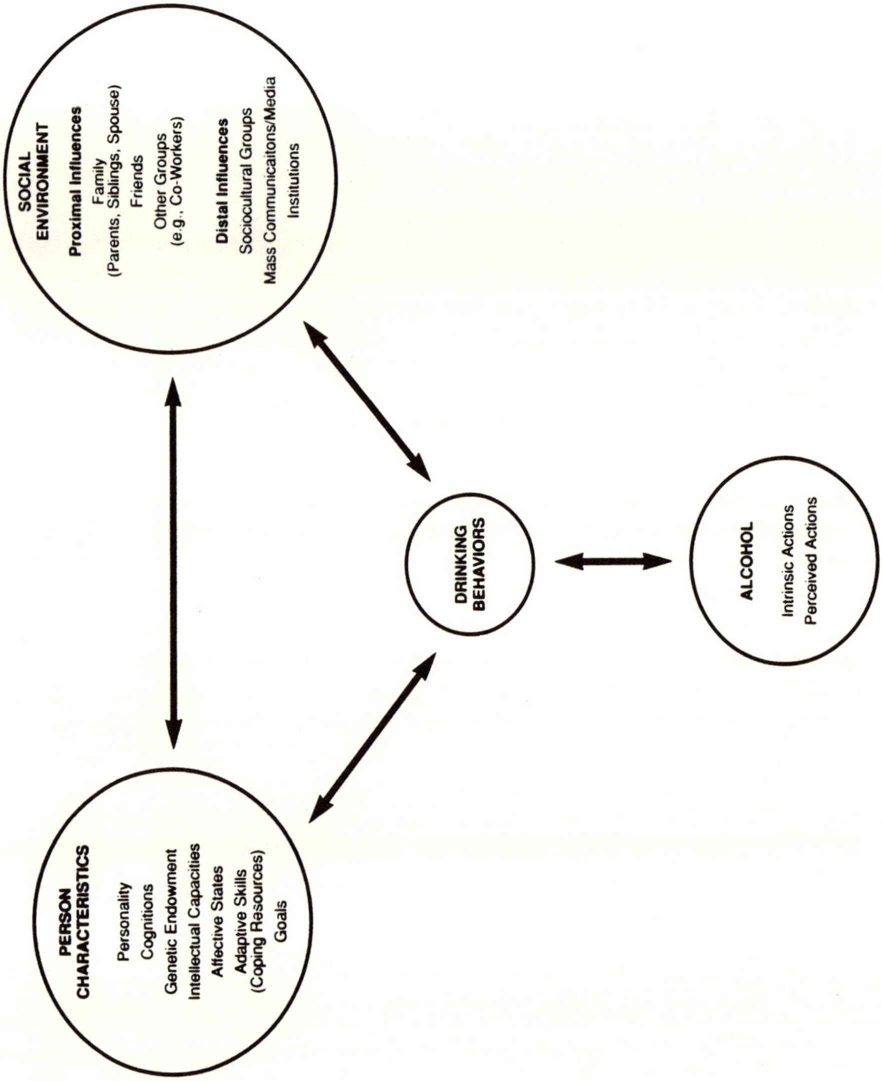

a central position in Bandura's (1982) formulation of social learning. Individual differences in self-efficacy (e.g., Love, Ollendick, Johnson, & Schlesinger, 1985) and other intrapersonal characteristics seem to mediate the impact of social stresses and pressures on a person's subsequent behavior.

Understanding the scope and limits of environmental influences on drinking, however, requires an appreciation that personality characteristics will modify (e.g., Bates, Labouvie & White, 1986) and be modified by (e.g., Pandina & Bates, 1985) drinking behaviors themselves as well as by models and reinforcers in the relevant social environments. For example, in a three-year prospective longitudinal study, Pandina and Bates (1985) found that initial level and patterns of change in adolescents' drinking behaviors accounted for a reliable proportion of change found in certain personality characteristics. Personality characteristics may also partly determine the effect of environmental influences. For instance, an adolescent who has strong needs for affiliation and approval is likely to be more vulnerable to peer pressure to drink than one who does not. Reciprocally, adolescents' heavy use of alcohol to cope during their development may prevent their acquiring adaptive social skills needed later in life (Falk, Schuster, Bigelow, & Woods, 1982).

Alcohol

One also needs to consider the pharmacological effects of alcohol when examining why people drink within a social learning framework. Because alcohol is a psychoactive drug that produces powerful and relatively immediate effects, it can serve as a potent primary reinforcer. Primary reinforcing effects are the result of "intrinsic" pharmacological actions of alcohol and the strength of these effects may be genetically determined in part (see Goodwin, 1985; Chapter 2, this volume). "Perceived" actions of alcohol would be most correctly located within the person rather than the alcohol domain of Figure 9-1 because they are attributed to alcohol by the individual. We have included them in the alcohol domain, however, because increasing evidence suggests that socially mediated expectancies and cognitions strongly influence effects of alcohol that have been traditionally attributed to its pharmacological actions (see Chapter 8 in this volume; Falk, 1983; MacAndrew & Edgerton, 1969; Marlatt & Rohsenow, 1981).

The Environment

The environment imposes limitations on the nature and content of learning experiences. The distal environment consists of the larger cultural, religious, and other groups that help determine to what extent drinking behaviors will be reinforcing for the individual. Humans' capacity to symbolically represent and transmit information to one another, and thus to succeeding generations, provides avenues for the transference of integrated patterns of behavior whereby actions can be regulated through thought and language (Bandura, 1977). The learning of behavior patterns through experiencing common social reinforcers contributes to certain commonalities observed within large social groups (such as ethnic and religious groups, societies, and cultures) with respect to their attitudes, expectations, and patterns of alcohol use. These large groups typically have at their disposal legal, ethical, and/or educational institutions that function to promote those patterns of drinking that are consistent with the interests, beliefs, and goals of the group. (These broad-based channels of social influence are the focus of the next chapter).

In addition to social motivations for drinking that are rather common in our society, family members and peers also prescribe why, when, and how much to drink. These smaller social groups reinforce or punish certain drinking behaviors both by their example and by their expressed or implied attitudes toward drinking. Such groups also teach members the appropriate manner in which to comport themselves while intoxicated (Falk et al., 1982). Behaviors that are perceived as acceptable to engage in during intoxication may be highly idiosyncratic, depending upon the social group considered and the individual's unique experiential history. In this chapter we focus on these proximal environmental, as well as media, influences on drinking.

It is important to note that a social learning framework for studying the interindividual processes that influence drinking behaviors is not advanced here as an alternative to pharmacological, genetic, or other more molecular explanations of drinking phenomena and effects. Rather it should be considered as providing a complementary descriptive and predictive level of analysis for what is clearly a complex, multidimensional causal process.

In summary, a social learning approach that emphasizes the reciprocal interaction among the person, the environment, and behavior has been offered as a framework for examining why people drink. Environmental influences are examined in detail in the remainder of this chapter.

PROXIMAL ENVIRONMENTAL INFLUENCES

This section examines some of the empirical findings relating to influences of the proximal environment on drinking behavior. While the majority of these studies do not test a social learning model per se, variables that represent various components of the model have been investigated.

There are three ways in which interpersonal influences have been postulated to operate: (1) directly (i.e., setting an example, providing reinforcement, or as a result of the quality of the relationship); (2) indirectly (i.e., influencing the development of values, attitudes, and behaviors and the formation of ties); and (3) conditionally (i.e., influencing the susceptibility to be influenced by another individual). Observational learning and reinforcement are the two primary social learning processes by which these influences are transmitted. The ways in which these processes operate depend upon many conditions, including the quality and nature of the relationship between individuals as well as situations (Kandel, Kessler, & Margulies, 1978). The following sections examine ways in which interpersonal influences directly affect the development of drinking behaviors.

The Family

Parents During infancy and early childhood, the family is the primary facilitator of the socialization process. Hence parents (guardians) have the primary responsibility for providing status, nurturance, training, and other elements of socialization. Basic research in modeling efficacy has found that models with higher status or power over the life events of an individual are more effective behavioral models than are others (e.g., Bandura, 1977). These findings suggest that, at least during childhood, parents are potentially powerful models of drinking behavior due to their initially exclusive control over the daily life of their children.

Kandel et al. (1978) have suggested that initiation to alcohol use results from direct modeling in which adolescents imitate the behavior of significant others. Similarly, Barnes (1977) makes a case for the "model building" theory of alcohol use; various patterns of alcohol use are learned by imitation of the example set by parents. (We have defined this more enduring learning resulting from modeling as observational learning.) Barnes claims that the best predictors of youthful drinking are the attitudes and behaviors of parents in regard to alcohol use. She presents evidence that abstainers tend to come from homes in which parents abstain; moderate drinkers come from homes in which parents drink moderately; and a disproportionate number of heavy drinkers come from homes in which parents drink heavily.

Much of the empirical research on alcohol use supports Barnes' conclusions. That is, parental drinking has been found to be strongly related to adolescent initiation (e.g., see Rachal, Williams, Breham, Cavanaugh, Moore & Eckerman, 1975; Bacon & Jones, 1968; Fontane & Layne, 1979; Gorsuch & Butler, 1976; Jessor & Jessor, 1975; Maddox, 1970). The majority of these studies, however, have been atheoretical and not designed to investigate the processes of social learning.

Newcomb, Huba, and Bentler (1983) compared "direct (classical) modeling" and "cognitive mediational" explanations of maternal influence on adolescent alcohol and drug use. The former implies that direct observation and modeling are the essential processes for the acquisition of a behavior. The latter stresses that modeling effects are important but only to the extent that they influence the child's cognitive mediation, assimilation, and perceptions, which, in turn, motivate drinking. The cognitive mediational approach emphasizes that it is more the behavior that children perceive their parents to display that is acquired than the parents' actual behavior. In the study by Newcomb and colleagues, cognitive mediations best explained both sons' and daughters' acquiring the drinking behavior of their mother.

Most research suggests that parents who drink teach their children to drink, but whether the social learning that results is primarily through direct or vicarious social reinforcement has not been adequately addressed. There are several plausible ways in which parents may differentially influence, either intentionally or unintentionally, their childrens' use of alcohol. One way is to forbid or punish use. Studies have found that when parents forbid use of alcohol, their adolescent offspring are less likely to use alcohol than are the offspring of parents who permit use (Mandell, Cooper, Silberstein, Novich, & Koloski, 1963). Alternatively, individuals may drink because they perceive that their parents expect them to drink. In fact, parents are generally the first ones to introduce alcohol to their children (Mandell et al., 1963). Fontane and Layne (1979) found that the second most frequently identified situation in which college students felt that drinking was expected was in the family context. (The first was at parties). Rachal et al. (1975) also reported that a majority of adolescents consume alcohol with some regularity in the home on special occasions or with dinner. Thus youth may learn to drink because drinking on special occasions with their family is associated with positive consequences.

Another way adolescents may be socially reinforced for drinking is when they do so in order to deceive their parents. That is, an adolescent who is forbidden to drink but drinks anyway and does not get caught may be reinforced for his or her behavior. Even explicit punishment by parents for drinking could paradoxically serve to increase drinking behaviors by bringing the adolescent some secondary gain, such as attention. On the other hand, feeling guilty about drinking when one is not permitted to do so may serve to inhibit the behavior. Such diverse parental influences on child drinking behaviors illustrate the enormous complexity of this influence and the need for research to identify the particular circumstances under which one or the other of these influences is likely to arise.

Smart, Gray, and Bennett (1978) found that factors that predict whether or not a student will initiate drinking are different from those that predict the frequency and degree of drinking after it has started. For example, parental modeling appeared to be an important predictor of initiation, whereas contextual variables (e.g., drinking in cars) were the most important predictors of heavy drinking. Lack of parental knowledge of the child's drinking was the best predictor of drunkenness.

Although a full discussion of the quality of the parent-child relationship as it relates to drinking behavior is beyond the scope of this chapter, note that this variable influences social learning processes (see Zucker, 1976). Because family members are the primary agents of socialization, they set up initial reinforcement contingencies and thus influence all stages of development. The quality of the interaction between the adolescent and his or her parents and the quality of the home environment have been shown to influence adolescents' drinking regardless of what their parents' habitual use might be. For example, positive family relationships and the adolescent's attachment to family appear to inhibit the acquisition and extent of drinking behavior among adolescents (e.g., Prendergast & Schaefer, 1974). For a detailed discussion of the way in which family variables affect alcohol and other drug use, see Kandel et al. (1978) and Glynn (1981).

Likewise, family background variables have consistently been shown to affect the likelihood of subsequent alcoholism. Parent-child attachments, as well as personality and child-rearing practices of the parent, are strongly related to later problem drinking and alcoholism in the offspring (McCord, McCord, & Gudeman, 1960; Zucker, 1976). Barnes (1977) suggests that problem drinking behavior results from incomplete and inadequate socialization of children within the family.

Being reared in a home with an alcoholic parent can also contribute to children's subsequent development of alcoholism. Attitudes about alcohol and motivations to use it have been shown to be important determinants of alcohol problems (see White, 1982). For example, those individuals who believe in using alcohol for utilitarian or escape reasons are more likely to experience alcohol problems than those who use it for ritualistic or social purposes (Bales, 1946; Cahalan, 1970). Hence through observational learning within the home, children of alcoholics may learn inappropriate reasons for, and patterns of, alcohol use. The alcoholic parent conveys the attitude that heavy drinking is positively reinforcing. Parents are also models for the development of coping strategies (Knight, 1980). Therefore, a child may learn to use alcohol to escape from problems rather than developing more positive coping mechanisms if he or she is exposed to alcohol use as a predominant coping mechanism and views the strategy as effective. There are additional characteristics of a home with an alcoholic parent that could contribute indirectly to the later development of alcoholism in the children (see Knight, 1980; Orford, 1979).

Parents are not the exclusive adult agent of influence over children and adolescents; other adults play influential roles as well. Likewise, a young person's perceptions of adults in general and the transitions into adulthood can affect how his or her drinking develops. According to Jessor and Jessor (1975), the initiation to drinking alcohol marks a transition in the life cycle that for many adolescents represents a symbolic means of dissolving their adolescent status and identifying with adults. Adolescents may drink because they feel that it is the "adult thing to do." Maddox and McCall (1964), for example, found a relationship between the number of teenagers who report themselves to be drinkers and their perception of an adult as a drinker. Barnes (1981) also presented evidence that adolescent alcohol use reflects the norms and behaviors in the larger adult society. Some research suggests that adolescents drink to conform to or reject traditional sex-role standards. According to Wilsnack and Wilsnack (1979), adolescent males drink to signal their manliness by being able to consume large amounts of alcohol and by showing generosity to and comradeship with other males by sharing drinks. In contrast, adolescent females drink in defiance of traditional feminine roles.

Unlike most researchers who have addressed parental influences on adolescent use, Cahalan, Cisin, and Crossley (1969) examined parental influence on adult offspring. These investigators found a strong association between an adult's drinking pattern and that of his or her parents. Frequent drinking on the part of parents was found to be highly correlated with later heavy drinking among their adult offspring. Cahalan et al. also found that parental attitudes about the use of alcohol were strongly related to their adult children's attitudes and patterns of use. The researchers suggested that this strong association could result from the fact that both generations are subjected to the same environmental and cultural influences on their drinking rather than as a result of childrens' observational learning of parental drinking behavior. They add, however, that regardless of the reason for the relationship, it is clear that when parents' drinking patterns and attitudes regarding drinking are known, the ability to predict their offsprings' drinking pattern is enhanced.

Other Family Members. Another potential agent of interpersonal influence on patterns of alcohol use is the sibling. Although the literature on this topic is scant, a few studies have identified an association between siblings' use of psychoactive drugs (Pedraza, 1985; Spevack & Pihl, 1976; Clayton & Lacy, 1982). However, when alcohol alone has been analyzed, this relationship has not held (Clayton & Lacy, 1982).

Cahalan and his colleagues (1969) found a strong association between husband's and wife's drinking habits. Female and male heavy drinkers were much more likely to have spouses who were also heavy drinkers. Likewise, when husbands were light drinkers or abstainers, nine out of ten of the wives were also. Researchers have consistently found high rates of problem drinking and alcoholism among husbands of female alcoholics (Jacob, Favorini, Meisel, & Anderson, 1978), although the explanation for this association is unclear. It may be due either to observational learning, to direct reinforcement, or to the fact that an individual selects his or her spouse on the basis of shared attitudes and behaviors.

The research presented thus far provides a strong case for the association among family members' alcohol use, and especially between parental drinking and use by offspring. However, the specific learning processes involved remain unclear.

Peer Groups

Adolescent Peer Groups. In addition to parental models of alcohol use, some research indicates that both the actual or perceived number of peers using alcohol and peer attitudes regarding use of alcohol substantially influence adolescent use. (For a review, see Kandel, 1978; Radosevich, Lanza-Kaduce, Akers, & Krohn, 1980.) Kandel and her colleagues (1978) found that, in addition to friends' use and attitudes regarding alcohol, the degree to which adolescents were involved in peer activities (e.g., driving around in cars, attending parties) was an important factor predicting initiation. Although research has established that peers influence one another's use, it has not been determined to what extent the behavior is learned from the peer group and to what extent adolescents select friends whose drinking behaviors seem attractive.

Bacon and Jones (1968) hypothesized that adolescents drink for social approval, that is, they need to belong. But these researchers also found that the teenage group as a whole was unlikely to reject a person just because he or she abstained from drinking. Drinkers and non-drinkers were just as likely to be included in school and social organizational activities. Nevertheless, a study that examined situations where adolescents felt most tempted to drink alcohol found that they almost always involved two or more people, usually in the context of a party or some other unstructured social occasion (Stetson, Brown & Beatty, 1985). Either direct or indirect social pressures to drink were reported in 91 percent of these situations.

A few recent studies have operationalized and tested Akers' (1977, 1985) social learning model using parental and peer behavior and attitudes as predictors of adolescent drinking. Akers' social learning theory combines aspects of Sutherland's (1947) differential association perspective (i.e., the importance of significant others in learning "deviant" behavior) with Bandura's (1977) principles of social learning. According to Akers' (1977), social learning theory proposes a process whereby differential associations (significant others) provide the environment in which exposure to definitions (beliefs and attitudes), imitation of models, and reinforcement take place. The definitions, in interaction with models and anticipated reinforcers, produce initial use. After initial use, imitation becomes less important while definitions and consequences become more important.

Akers, Krohn, Lanza-Kaduce, and Radosevich (1979) investigated the relative importance of imitation, alcohol use by significant others, beliefs about alcohol, and reinforcers of alcohol use for explaining adolescent alcohol use. Their data demonstrated that friends' use of alcohol was the best predictor of alcohol use. Beliefs were the second best predictor. The concept of imitation, defined as the number of admired models the respondent had observed engaging in the behavior, was less related to drinking behavior than the other social learning variables. Overall, the model explained 55 percent of the variance in alcohol use. In a second analysis, the same independent variables explained 32 percent of the variance in alcohol abuse; differential association variables again explained the greatest amount of variance. In the analyses of abusive drinking, beliefs ranked fourth in accounting for abuse while reinforcement ranked higher. These researchers interpreted these results as suggesting that, over time, alcohol abusers begin to respond to direct reinforcement (from the effects of the drug itself) and definitions come to play a less significant role.

Lanza-Kaduce and Radosevich (1980) also tested Akers' model and found strong evidence of one general learning process that operates across all stages and substances. Definitions appeared to be the most powerful set of predictor variables, followed by reinforcement and differential association variables. Again, the effect of imitation was weakest. In addition, stages of use were less differentiated by consequences of use than by normative definitions of use. Thus the authors concluded that definitions may be more than mere stimuli to which reinforcement or punishment is conditioned.

Applying casual modeling techniques to data from the Rutgers Health and Human Development Project (a longitudinal study of adolescents), Johnson (1988) tested a social learning model of continued alcohol use. Like Akers et al. (1979), she found that the proportion of friends who use and friends' opinions about use were the best predictors of continued use of alcohol. Contrary to the two studies described above, however, attitudes had a negligible effect. She found that punishments were positively related to continued use. That is, as the number of reported punishments experienced increased, the amount and frequency of use also increased. There are several possible explanations for this unexpected result: (1) punishments may only temporarily decrease substance use; (2) adolescents may not view intended punishments as such; and (3) the need for immediate gratification from alcohol may outweigh the delayed punishment. It is also possible that survey research may not be able to capture the concept of punishment that has been measured in laboratory research.

Parents Versus Peers. Researchers with different theoretical orientations disagree about the relative influence of parents and peers during adolescence. Our own research (White, Johnson, & Horwitz, 1986) indicates that peers exert a significantly stronger influence on adolescent alcohol and drug use than do parents. Yet parental permission to drink and parental drinking are related to various stages of initiation and extent of alcohol use. Similarly, Huba and Bentler (1980) found that, by the ninth grade, an adolescent's use of alcohol was more strongly associated with use by peers than with use by adult models (i.e., parents and other significant adults). On the other hand, in the study by Akers and his associates, when adolescents at all grade levels were asked from whom they had learned the most about alcohol and who had the greatest influence on their decisions to drink or not to drink, parents and other significant adults were ranked ahead of peers (Akers, 1985).

Fontane and Layne (1979) indicate that the peer culture reinforces drunkenness if parents display it and co-opts the parental influence of those parents who do not drink to drunkenness. They found that respondents were more likely to have gotten drunk if both their parents did than if neither did. However, three-fourths of students from homes where parents did not get drunk had been drunk themselves. Maddox (1966) argues that while peer groups are important for learning how to drink and in providing occasions and support for drinking, teenagers first learn to drink from adult models. The peer group may provide support for drinking that has already been learned in the home (Barnes, 1977). In addition, parents can influence their children's values as well as their choice of friends and so can make their children susceptible to the influence either of friends who use drugs or those who do not. Zucker (1976) suggests that, at the very least, the family indirectly influences drinking by defining the child's socioeconomic status, ethnic/cultural background, and environmental milieu.

In his review of the literature on parental and peer influences on alcohol and other drug use, Glynn (1981) concludes: "There does not appear to be any point at which the drug [use] behavior of most adolescents is wholly influenced by either family or peers . . . parent and peer influences on adolescent alcohol use appear to be relatively equal . . . the most effective family influences appear to be those that are developed in advance of adolescence" (pp. 68–69).

Adult Peer Groups. For adolescents, the peer group is usually defined as either close friends or the larger circle of persons similar in age with whom one interacts. For adults, however, the notion of peer group is more ambiguous. In experimental research on modeling of drinking behavior, the definition of peer group has ranged from those with similar drinking patterns (e.g., Caudill & Lipscomb, 1980) to those with similar socioeconomic or other demographic characteristics (e.g., Collins et al. 1985). In survey research on alcohol, adult peer groups have been defined to include friends, neighbors, co-workers, and drinking companions. This section examines the influence of these various adult peer groups on drinking patterns and the related social environments in which they occur.

The importance of social learning processes for adult drinking was shown in a recent study by Akers, LaGreca, Sellers, and Cochran (1985) using an elderly population. In that study, 67 percent of the variance in elderly drinking was accounted for by a social learning model similar to the one that Akers and his colleagues (1979) tested with the adolescent sample (excluding imitation). The balance of reinforcement variables (the sum of reinforcers minus punishers) perceived as coming from the effects of alcohol itself was more important for this age group than for the teenagers. Nevertheless, the behaviors and reactions of spouses, other family members, and friends were also highly related to elderly drinking.

In a national survey, Cahalan and his colleagues (1969) identified various patterns of drinking and related social activities among heavy and nonheavy drinkers. In general, they found that men, regardless of the extent of their drinking, and heavy drinking women drank most often with their friends (regardless of the type of beverage consumed), while nonheavy drinking women tended to drink beer and wine most often with their family but spirits most often with friends. They also found that heavy drinkers more than other drinkers were likely to drink alone, but that only a minority of drinkers from all categories drank alone (25 percent of heavy drinkers and 13 percent of nonheavy drinkers). Most drinking by all types of drinkers was in homes rather than in bars and restaurants, yet more heavy than light drinkers drank in bars and restaurants.

Furthermore, Cahalan et al. (1969) found that, in general, alcoholic beverages were served relatively more often when meeting socially with people from work than with close friends. In addition, heavy drinkers were more likely than others to get together socially with people from work rather than from church or neighborhood. Cahalan and colleagues suggest that heavy drinkers are less subject to certain social controls; however, they do not argue that the lack of controls causes heavy drinking. It is just as likely that heavy drinkers choose the company of other heavy drinkers who tend not to be friends from neighborhood and church.

The above findings suggest that friends from work may provide the social reinforcement for drinking that may be important in the adult stages of the life cycle. The link between various occupations and alcohol use and abuse has been well documented in the literature (Plant, 1979). Peer pressure on the job, as well as off, can strongly influence drinking patterns. In addition to the familiar "three-martini lunch," many occupational groups stop at local taverns on the way home from work to have a drink. Members of occupations with high rates of excessive drinking include seamen, lawyers, domestic servants, military personnel, physicians, and persons working in the alcohol production and distribution field.

Plant (1979) identified job-related risk factors that contribute to the development of heavy drinking patterns. Among these are jobs in which (1) alcohol is available or there is social pressure to drink (e.g. entertainment); (2) workers are separated from normal social/sexual relationships (e.g., the military); (3) there is freedom from supervision (e.g., traveling salespeople); and (4) there are job pressures and stress (e.g., policeofficers) (see also Roman & Trice, 1977). In his longitudinal study, Plant found that high-risk jobs (e.g., in the alcohol industry) attract high-risk individuals (heavy drinkers with poor work histories). However, high-risk jobs independently provide the impetus for changing a person's drinking pattern because they provide an opportunity and positive reinforcement for drinking.

Trice (1966, 1984) also considers the interaction of high-risk individuals and drinking groups in his theory of the development of alcoholism. He asserts that drinking persists because it enhances sociability in groups (e.g., in tavern cliques, recreation groups) which he labels "drinking groups." People with vulnerable personalities (i.e., those with a conflict over dependency needs) obtain needed emotional support in these groups. If repeatedly reinforced, drinking by vulnerable people becomes their predominant coping strategy to deal with life stresses, while other coping techniques are not developed or disappear. Trice believes that some form of group tutelage is crucial in the progression toward alcoholism and that heavy drinking groups with norms that define alcohol as having extraordinary personal effects for the individual sharply contribute to it. By merely complying with the norms of heavy drinking, a group member may become an excessive drinker. Eventually, as excessive drinking extends beyond the norms of the group, the heavy drinker is ostracized. He or she voluntarily withdraws from the original drinking group and seeks another. With movement from one group to the next, more tolerant group, the alcoholic continues to be reinforced by the sense of belonging he or she experiences with other stigmatized, excessive drinkers. Eventually a process of progressive isolation sets in ("reward–rejection–relocation experience") and exclusion from society becomes permanent.

From the principles of social learning, one would expect that rejection by one's peers would extinguish heavy drinking. However, the permissive reinforcement of the excessive drinking occurs earlier in the incorporation into the group and shapes the deviant drinking; by the time the ostracism takes place, it is too little (because other groups that are tolerant and reinforcing of a higher level of drinking are available) and too late (see Akers, 1985). Prolonged excessive drinking may produce physical dependence and the alcoholic continues to drink heavily in order to forestall withdrawal symptoms. Moreover, immediate reinforcement from drinking outweighs later negative consequences, such as social ostracism.

In the previous sections, we examined proximal environmental influences of family and peers on drinking behaviors. There are other potentially influential models of drinking behaviors in the environment with whom one does not interact directly. These models are often observed in the printed and electronic media and are the focus of the next section.

MASS COMMUNICATION/MEDIA INFLUENCES

The media furnish an array of additional social reinforcements for alcohol use. According to Bandura (1977), the abundant and varied symbolic models provided by television and films strongly influence social learning. Research has demonstrated that media play an influential role in shaping social attitudes and behaviors for both children and adults (Bandura, 1973; Liebert, Neale, & Davidson, 1973). Bandura (1977) claims that symbolic modeling, provided especially by television, influences the development of moral judgments by portraying conduct as acceptable or reprehensible and by applying sanctions to such behavior. He suggests that with the increasing use of symbolic modeling, proximal role models may occupy less prominent roles in social learning.

The role that the media play in socially reinforcing alcohol use has been a topic of increasing controversy over the past decade. Learning theorists suggest that the media may (1) affect viewers' expectations concerning the use of alcohol, (2) affect viewers attitudes about the acceptability or appropriateness of use, and (3) motivate people to model drinking behaviors (Greenberg, Fernandez-Collado, Graef, Korzenny, & Atkin, 1979). The media provide the means for the learning of drinking behavior through observational learning, including vicarious reinforcement. Models for observational learning are available through the advertisements on television and radio, in newspapers and magazines, or on billboards, and the demonstration of alcohol consumption by characters in television shows and movies. While it is generally accepted that the media provide information to people about the goals of drinking (i.e., to have fun, to socialize, and to feel better) and about brand choices, the role played in influencing attitudes and motivations regarding alcohol use is less clear. The causal connection between exposure to mass media and individual drinking behavior has yet to be systematically explored. Although more than 2,000 studies have examined the effects of television violence on children (Wallack, 1983), little attention has been paid to the effects on viewers of alcohol use as portrayed in the media.

Advertising and Entertainment

There have been many content analyses both of alcohol use as portrayed in television dramas and of the relative amount of advertising time devoted to alcoholic beverages (e.g., Garlington, 1977; Atkin & Block, 1981; De-Foe, Breed, & Breed, 1983; De-Foe & Breed, 1979; 1983; Breed & De-Foe, 1979; 1981; 1984). These analyses provide basic descriptions concerning the amount of time that viewers are exposed to alcohol use, but do not measure the degree of causal influence on behaviors. Content analyses suggest that television portrayals of alcohol use lead to favorable attitudes toward drinking, tend to normalize drinking, or emphasize only desirable concomitants such as wealth, success, and social approval (Atkin & Block, 1981; De-Foe & Breed, 1983; Breed & De-Foe, 1984). In a study by Smart and Krakowski (1973), the use of alcohol by television characters was found to be more frequent than televised alcohol advertisements; however, the former were shorter in duration. In addition, while television characters at times exhibited signs of problem drinking, such problems were typically portrayed as short-lived and in response to a crisis, and the characters often made speedy and unrealistic recoveries. Movies appear to have done a better job of realistically presenting the negative aspects of alcohol use (see Herd & Room, 1982). Viewers have been exposed to the punishing consequences of heavy drinking in such classics as *The Lost Weekend* and *Days of Wine and Roses.* However, other movies have depicted drunkenness as a means of promoting euphoria and humor (e.g., *Arthur*) and the seduction of women (e.g., *That Touch of Mink).*

Content analyses indicate that advertisements of alcoholic beverages portray users as healthy, attractive, and happy, and accentuate such themes as wealth, success, hedonism, and sex (Breed & De-Foe, 1979). People may be vicariously reinforced from watching characters in advertisements who consume alcohol and are also depicted as attractive, healthy, and having a good time. For example, viewers may come to expect that beer drinking will make them more masculine or athletic (see Royce, 1981). Similarly, viewers may expect that wine drinking will make them more cultured and romantic while drinking hard liquor will enhance success and sexiness. To combat these criticisms, in 1978 the Wine Institute adopted a new code of advertising standards that includes eliminating (1) the use of athletes, (2) the implication of health benefits of use, (3) sexual exploitation, and (4) appealing explicitly to youth. However, our casual viewing of advertisements prompts us to question the extent to which the advertisers actually adhere to all of these standards.

The alcohol industry contends that its advertisements are not aimed at initiating new drinkers, but at changing drinkers' preferences from one type of beverage to another. The brewers, for example, claim that they merely want to relay the message that beer is an attractive alternative to wine. Alcohol advertisers, in general, have long maintained that their advertisements only affect brand choice, and that advertising influences only the market shares of the commodity (Mosher & Wallack, 1981). To date, some econometric studies have concluded that advertising only modestly increases hard liquor sales and that restrictions on alcohol advertising do not decrease consumption (e.g., Ogborne & Smart, 1980). Two recent reviews on the content of alcohol advertising in magazines and television concluded that there is a lack of evidence supporting a causal relationship between advertising and consumption rates. (Strickland, Finn, & Lambert, 1982; Finn & Strickland, 1982).

There are also conflicting results as to the influence of the media on the development of heavier use patterns. Atkin, Neuendorf, and McDermott (1983) conducted a survey of adolescents and young adults and concluded that advertising stimulates consumption, which, in turn, may lead to heavy drinking. When Breed and De-Foe (1981) analyzed prime-time television shows, they found that almost 60 percent of the drinking scenes involved drinking five or more drinks. Compared with the societal norms, this would be considered atypical (heavy) drinking. These researchers also report that they observed little or only mild disapproval of alcohol abuse among TV characters. In addition, 25 percent of the drinking took place before or during work, and a primary reason for drinking was to cope with stress and anxiety.

Other authorities assert that different factors underlie the motivation for social drinking versus problem drinking (Pittman & Lambert, 1978; Rossiter & Robertson, 1980). Although advertisements may cause drinking to be acceptable for more people in more places, it is less likely that they promote drunkenness since they rarely display models suggesting that drunkenness is appropriate. On the other hand, such beer slogans as "when you're having more than one" may encourage people to have more than one drink. The research suggests that the media exert influence on particular people, such as social isolates, or those who otherwise are predisposed to heavy drinking or are already at risk for problem use.

It appears that several factors mediate the influence of the media on alcohol consumption, including communication with significant others and one's expectations of alcohol. Strickland & Wilson (1982) reported that high levels of communication within families moderated the influence of media on consumption by adolescents. In addition, we would expect such variables as repetitiveness of exposure, attention to the message, acceptance of the message, and motivation to act on the message influence use (see, for example, Strickland, 1982).

Prevention and Attitude Change

Mass media campaigns to prevent alcohol problems have solicited air time to publicize the negative aspects of alcohol use. Typically, these media campaigns have concentrated on preventing problems associated with use (e.g., drunk driving, child abuse/neglect, fetal alcohol syndrome) or on promoting responsible use and increasing awareness of the potential problems and warning signs of alcoholism. Hewitt and

Blane (1984) reviewed evaluations of 15 media campaigns conducted from 1971 to 1982. In examining outcome measures, they found that the majority of campaigns promoted desired change in the degree of knowledge about alcohol problems but that attitudes and behaviors did not significantly change as a result of the exposure to these media prevention programs. (See also Nathan & Niaura, 1987.)

Additional empirical work suggests that the media are a source of knowledge about alcohol, but that they may not directly influence attitudes (see Smart & Fejer, 1972). Blane and Hewitt (1980) found that the effects of media prevention campaigns are largely limited to reinforcing established attitudes or behaviors. Still others (Dembo, Miran, Babst, & Schmeidler, 1977) found that friends, experts, or former users were considered much more credible in relaying information about drugs than were the media. Strickland (1983) also found that media influences are less salient than the influence of parents and peers.

In sum, while it seems clear that the media provide viewers with vicarious, positive social reinforcers for drinking, there is, as yet, no strong empirical evidence that exposure to alcohol use in the media increases the number of new drinkers, the overall consumption level, or the number of alcoholics. However, the role of media influences has not been thoroughly studied. Research needs to focus on children and adolescents because they are in their formative years when influences of models are most salient and social reinforcements and consequences of alcohol use appear to be more powerful than nonsocial reinforcers (Strickland & Pittman, 1984; Christiansen, Goldman, & Inn, 1982). The need for more research on this age group is underscored by the fact that, from childhood through high school years, television viewing consumes more time than any other leisure or work activity (Rubenstein, 1978).

DISCUSSION

We have explored the social mechanisms that underlie why people drink by examining the influences of direct social reinforcements provided by family and peers, as well as the symbolic processes involved in observational learning and noninteractional media models. Although behavior is often regarded solely as a dependent variable, in the social learning perspective we present, patterns of alcohol use are seen as arising from a continual interplay of personal, environmental, and behavioral influences. As Bandura (1977) explains, "Although the reciprocal sources of influence are separable for experimental purposes, in everyday life two-way control operates concurrently. In ongoing interchanges, one and the same event can be a stimulus, a response, or an environmental reinforcer depending upon the place in the sequence at which analysis arbitrarily begins" (p. 204). The complexity of any model embracing the concept of reciprocal determinism presents an enormous challenge for survey research. This challenge is especially evident when studying behaviors such as drinking for which the potential for harmful consequences makes temporal ordering of influences a paramount concern.

In conclusion, we briefly discuss some limitations of using social learning models to address the question of why people drink and make suggestions for future research. Critics suggest that social learning approaches overemphasize social influences on behavior (e.g., Wrong, 1981) and do not give sufficient attention to individual motivations and actions. This criticism may be warranted in some cases, but several social learning theorists have, in fact, incorporated motivations, attitudes, and other internal influences in their formulations of social learning theory (see Bandura, 1977). Jessor and Jessor (1977), for example, have included personality and motivational variables in their empirical research on the development of problem behaviors, including alcohol abuse. Most researchers, however, have included only cognitions, (i.e, beliefs and attitudes) and have ignored other person variables.

Another common criticism of the social learning perspective is that the concepts are difficult to operationalize, and thus the deductions are difficult to test. Processes of observational learning involving vicarious reinforcement versus directly experienced reinforcement are difficult to distinguish. That is, while we can identify a positive relationship between an adolescent's drinking pattern and that of his or her parents, we cannot assess whether the youth models his or her parents because the parents are perceived to be enjoying themselves (vicarious reinforcement) or because he or she wants social approval (direct positive reinforcement) from the parents.

In using social learning models to study why people drink, additional definitional and measurement problems are often encountered. For instance, researchers have not specified the number of times a behavior needs to occur for it to be considered learned or the number of times a punishment needs to take place in order to extinguish behavior. Individual differences in speed of learning and in assigning importance to specific behavioral consequences have not been addressed or measured. Also, important potential social reinforcers, (e.g., teachers, characters in books) have often been missed during data collection, which has concentrated solely on obviously significant models (e.g., parents and peers).

Given the presumed multiple causes of drinking, the current fragmentation in research efforts between different disciplines is unfortunate. There is a clear need for research to study characteristics of the individual as well as proximal and distal aspects of the environment, including family, peer, media, and ethnic/cultural group influences in varying contexts. A few integrative conceptual frameworks seem to be emerging. Strickland and Pittman (1984), for example, examined conceptual parallels between social learning approaches and the consumer socialization paradigm and suggested how research on alcohol use may benefit from combining concepts from both of these approaches. We, at the Rutgers Health and Human Development Project, are studying the development of drinking behaviors in the broader context of individuals' physical, psychological, and social development. Our approach considers changes in drinking in relation to other developmental transitions rather than relating static differences at one time only (Pandina, Labouvie, & White, 1984). To answer the question of why people drink, longitudinal studies are often preferable to cross-sectional ones. The former can provide more information regarding the temporal sequencing of events and changes in behaviors and influences over time. More multidisciplinary longitudinal studies are needed to further our understanding of drinking behaviors.

REFERENCES

Akers, R.L. (1977). *Deviant behavior: A social learning approach.* Belmont, Calif.: Wadsworth.

Akers, R.L. (1985). *Deviant behavior: A social learning approach.* Belmont, Calif.: Wadsworth.

Akers, R.L., Krohn, M.D., Lanza-Kaduce, L., & Radosevich, M. (1979). Social learning and deviant behavior: A specific test of a general theory. *American Sociological Review,* 44, 636–655.

Akers, R.L., La Greca, A.J., Sellers, C., & Cochran, J. (1985, Nov.). *Alcohol behavior among the elderly: Preliminary findings on social learning and experience with the legal system.* Paper presented at the 37th Annual Meeting of the American Society of Criminology. San Diego, Calif.

Atkin, C., & Block, M. (1981). *Content and effects of alcohol advertising.* Springfield, Va. Bureau of Alcohol, Tobacco, and Firearms (NTIS No. PB82–123142).

Atkin, C. K., Neuendorf, K., & McDermott, S. (1983). The role of alcohol advertising in excessive and hazardous drinking. *Journal of Drug Education,* 13, 313–325.

Bacon, M., & Jones, M.B. (1968). *Teen-age drinking.* New York: Crowell.

Bales, R.F. (1946). Cultural differences in rates of alcoholism. *Quarterly Journal of Studies on Alcohol,* 6, 480–499.

Bandura, A. (1969). *Principles of behavior modification.* New York: Holt, Rinehart & Winston.

Bandura, A. (1973). *Aggression: A social learning analysis.* Englewood Cliffs, N.J.: Prentice-Hall.

Bandura, A. (1977). *Social learning theory.* Englewood Cliffs, N.J.: Prentice-Hall.

Bandura, A. (1982). Self-efficacy mechanism in human agency. *American Psychologist,* 37, 122–147.

Barnes, G.M. (1977). The development of adolescent drinking behavior: An evaluative review of the impact of the socialization process within the family. *Adolescence,* 12, 571–591.

Barnes, G.M. (1981). Drinking among adolescents: A subcultural phenomenon or a model of adult behaviors. *Adolescence,* 16, 211–229.

Bates, M.E., Labouvie, E.W., & White, H.R. (1986). The effect of sensation seeking on alcohol and marijuana use in adolescence. *Bulletin of the Society of Psychologists in Addictive Behaviors,* 5, 29–36.

Blane, H.T., & Hewitt, L.E. (1980). Alcohol, public education, and mass media: An overview. *Alcohol Health and Research World,* 5, 2–16.

Breed, W., & De-Foe, J.R. (1979). Themes in magazine alcohol advertisement: A critique. *Journal of Drug Issues,* 9, 511–522.

Breed, W., & De-Foe, J.R. (1981). The portrayal of the drinking process on prime-time television. *Journal of Communications,* 31, 58–67.

Breed, W., & De-Foe, J.R. (1981). Drinking and smoking on television, 1950–1982. *Journal of Public Health Policy,* 5, 257–270.

Cahalan, D. (1970). *Problem drinkers.* San Francisco: Jossey-Bass.

Cahalan, D., Cisin, I.H., & Crossley, H.M. (1969). *American drinking practices.* New Brunswick, N.J. : Rutgers Center of Alcohol Studies.

Caudill, B.D., & Lipscomb, T.R. (1980). Modeling influences on alcoholics' rates of alcohol consumption. *Journal of Applied Behavior Analysis,* 13, 355–365.

Christiansen, A., Goldman, S., & Inn, A. (1982). Development of alcohol-related expectancies in adolescents: Separating pharmacological, from social learning influences. *Journal of Consulting and Clinical Psychology,* 50, 336–344.

Clayton, R.R., & Lacy, W.B. (1982). Interpersonal influences on male drug use and drug use intentions. *International Journal of the Addictions,* 17, 655–666.

Collins, R.L., Parks, G.A., & Marlatt, G.A. (1985). Social determinants of alcohol consumption: The effects of social interaction and model status on the self-administration of alcohol. *Journal of Consulting and Clinical Psychology,* 53, 189–200.

Cutler, R.E., & Storm, T. (1975). Observational study of alcohol consumption in natural settings: The Vancouver beer parlor. *Journal of Studies on Alcohol,* 36, 1173–1183.

De-Foe, J.R., & Breed, W. (1979). The problem of alcohol advertisements in college newspapers. *Journal of American College Health Association,* 27, 195–199.

De-Foe, J.R., & Breed, W. (1983). Television's heavy drinking problem. *Alcoholism/National Magazine,* 3(7), 62 63.

De-Foe, J.R., Breed, W., & Breed, L.A. (1983). Drinking on television: A five-year study. *Journal of Drug Education,* 13, 25–38.

Dembo, R., Miran, M., Babst, D.V., & Schmeidler, J. (1977). The believability of the media as sources of information on drugs. *International Journal of the Addictions,* 12, 959–969.

Doby, J.T. (1966). *Introduction to social psychology.* New York: Appleton.

Dulany, D.E. (1968). Awareness, rules and propositional control: A confrontation with S-R behavior theory. In T.R. Dixon & D.L. Horton (Eds.), *Verbal behavior and general behavior theory.* Englewood Cliffs, N.J.: Prentice-Hall.

Falk, J.L., (1983). Drug dependence: Myth or motive? *Pharmacology, Biochemistry and Behavior,* 19, 385–391.

Falk, J.L., Schuster, C.R., Bigelow, G.E., & Woods, J.H. (1982). Progress and needs in the experimental analysis of drug and alcohol dependence. *American Psychologist,* 37, 1124–1127.

Finn, T.A., & Strickland, D.E. (1982). A content analysis of beverage alcohol advertising. II. Television advertising. *Journal of Studies on Alcohol,* 43, 964–989.

Flanders, J.P. (1968). A review of research on imitative behavior. *Psychological Bulletin,* 69, 316–337.

Fontane, P.E., & Layne, N.R., Jr. (1979). The family as a context for developing youthful drinking patterns. *Journal of Alcohol and Drug Education,* 24(3), 19–29.

Garlington, W.K. (1977). Drinking on television: A preliminary study with emphasis on method. *Journal of Studies on Alcohol,* 38, 2199–2205.

Glynn, T.J. (1981). From family to peer: Transitions of influence among drug-using youth. In D.J. Lettieri, & J.P. Ludford (Eds.,) *Drug abuse and the American adolescent.* (NIDA Res. Monogr. Ser. No. 38). Washington, D.C; U.S. Government Printing Office.

Goodwin, D.W. (1985). Genetic determinants of alcoholism. In J.H. Mendelson & N.K. Mello (Eds.); *The diagnosis and treatment of alcoholism* (2nd ed.). New York: McGraw-Hill.

Gorsuch, R.L., & Butler, M.C. (1976). Initial drug abuse: A review of predisposing social psychological factors. *Psychological bulletin,* 83, 120–137.

Greenberg, B.S., Fernandez-Collado, C., Graef, D., Korzenny, F., & Atkin, C.K. (1979). Trends in use of alcohol and other substances on television. *Journal of Drug Education,* 9, 243–253.

Herd, D., & Room, R. (1982). Alcohol images in American film 1909–1960. *Drinking and Drug Practices Surveyor,* 18, 24–35.

Hewitt, L.E., & Blane H.T. (1984). Prevention through mass media communication. In P.M. Miller & T.D. Nirenberg (Eds.). *prevention of alcohol abuse,* New York: Plenum.

Huba, G.H., & Bentler, P.M. (1980). The role of peer and adult models for drug-taking at different stages in adolescence. *Journal of Youth and Adolescence,* 9, 449–465.

Jacob, T., Favorini, A., Meisel, S.S., & Anderson, C.M. (1978). The alcoholic's spouse, children and family interactions. *Journal of Studies on Alcohol,* 39, 1231–1251.

Jessor, R., & Jessor, S.L. (1975). Adolescent development vs. the onset of drinking: A longitudinal study. *Quarterly Journal of Studies on Alcohol,* 36, 27–51.

Jessor, R., & Jessor, S.L. (1977). *Problem behavior and psychological development: A longitudinal study of youth.* New York: Academic Press.

Johnson, V. (1988). Adolescent alcohol and marijuana use. A longitudinal assessment of a social learning perspective. *American Journal of Drug and Alcohol Abuse,* 14, 419–439.

Jones, E.E., & Gerard, H.B. (1967). *Foundations of social psychology.* New York: Wiley.

Kandel, D. (1978). Convergences in prospective longitudinal surveys of drug use in normal populations. In D. Kandel (Eds.), *Longitudinal research in drug use: Empirical findings and methodological issues.* Washington, D.C.: Hemisphere J. Wiley.

Kandel, D., Kessler, R.C., & Margulies, R.S. (1978). Antecedents of adolescent initiation into stages of drug use: A developmental analysis. In D. Kandel (Ed.), *Longitudinal research in drug use: Empirical findings and methodological issues. Washington, D.C.: Hemisphere J. Wiley.*

Kaufman, A., Baron, A., & Kopp, R.E. (1966). Some effects of instructions on human operant behavior. *Psychonomic Monograph Supplements,* 1, 243–250.

Knight, J.A. (1980). The family in the crisis of alcoholism. In S.E. Gitlow & H.S. Peyser (Eds.), *Alcoholism a practical treatment guide.* New York: Grune & Stratton.

Lanza-Kaduce, L., & Radosevich, M. (1980). *Can a processual theory discriminate among stages of substance use? A test of social learning theory.* Unpublished manuscript, University of Florida, Gainesville.

Liebert, R.M., Neale, J.M., & Davidson, E.S. (1973). *The early window effects of television on children and youth.* New York: Pergamon Press.

Love, S.Q., Ollendick, T.H., Johnson, C., & Schlesinger, S.E. (1985). A preliminary report of the prediction of bulemic behaviors: A social learning analysis. *Bulletin of the Society of Psychologists in Addictive Behaviors,* 4, 93–101.

MacAndrew, C.R., & Edgerton, B. (1969). *Drunken comportment: A social exploration.* Chicago: Aldine.

Maddox, G.L. (1966). Teeangers and alcohol: Recent research. *Annals of the N.Y. Academy of Sciences,* 133, 856–865.

Maddox, G.L. (Ed.) (1970). *The domesticated drug: Drinking among collegians.* New Haven, Conn.: College and University Press.

Maddox, G.L., & McCall B.C. (1964). *Drinking among teenagers.* New Haven, Conn.: College and University Press.

Mandell, W., Cooper, A., Silberstein, R.M., Novick, J., & Koloski, E. (1963). *Youthful drinking: New York State 1962.* Staten Island, N.Y.: Wakoff Research Center.

Marlatt, G.A., & Rohsenow, D.J. (1981). The think-drink effect. *Psychology Today,* 15(12), 60–62, 64, 66, 68–69, 93.

McCord, W., McCord, J., & Gudeman, J. (1960). *Origins of alcoholism.* Palo Alto Calif. Stanford University Press.

Mosher, J.R., & Wallack, L.M. (1981). Government regulation of alcohol advertising: Protecting industry profits versus promoting public health. *Public Health Policy,* 2, 333–353.

Nathan, P.E., & Niaura, R.S. (1987). Primary and secondary prevention of alcohol problems. In W.M. Cox (Ed.), *Treatment and prevention of alcohol problems: A resource manual.* New York: Academic Press.

Newcomb, M.D., Huba, G.J., & Bentler, P.M. (1983). Mothers' influence on the drug use of their children: Confirmatory tests of direct modeling and mediational theories. *Developmental Psychology,* 19, 714–726.

Ogborne, A.C., & Smart, R.G. (1980). Will Restrictions on alcohol advertising reduce alcohol consumption? *British Journal of Addictions,* 75, 293–296.

Orford, J. (1979). Alcohol and the family. In M. Grant & P. Gwinner (Eds.), *Alcoholism perspectives.* Baltimore: University Park Press.

Pandina, R.J., & Bates, M.E. (1985, Feb.). *The relationship between stability and change in personality formation and drug use patterns.* Paper presented at the

Colombia University Seminar on Drugs and Society 1984–1985: Longitudinal Research, New York, NY.

Pandina, R.J., Labouvie, E.W., & White, H.R. (1984). Potential contributions of the life span developmental approach to the study of adolescent alcohol and drug use: The Rutgers Health and Human Development Project, a working model. *Journal of Drug Issues,* 14, 253–268.

Pedraza, M. (1985). *The role of siblings in adolescent substance use and delinquency.* Unpublished masters thesis, Rutgers University, New Brunswick, N.J.

Pittman, D.J., & Lambert, M.D. (1978). Alcohol, alcoholism and advertising: A preliminary investigation of asserted associations. St. Louis: Social Science Institute, Washington University.

Plant, M. (1979). *Drinking careers.* London: Tavistock.

Prendergast T.J., & Schaefer E.S. (1974). Correlates of drinking and drunkenness among high school students. *Quarterly Journal of Studies on Alcohol,* 35, 232–242.

Rachal, J.V., Williams, J.R., Breham, M.L., Cavanaugh, B., Moore, R.P., & Eckerman, W.C. (1975). *A national study of adolescent drinking behavior, attitudes and correlates.* Springfield, V.A. National Institute of Alcohol Abuse and Alcoholism, (NTIS No. PB-246–002).

Radosevich, M., Lanza-Kaduce, L., Akers, R.L., & Krohn, M.D. (1980). The sociology of adolescent drug and drinking behavior: A review of the state of the field, Part 2. *Deviant Behavior,* 1, 145–169.

Reid, J.B. (1978). Study of drinking in natural settings. In G.A. Marlatt & P.E. Nathan (Eds.), *Behavioral approaches to alcoholism.* New Brunswick, N.J.: Rutgers Center of Alcohol Studies.

Rimm, D.C., & Masters, J.C. (1979). *Behavior therapy.* New York: Academic Press.

Roman, P.M., & Trice, H.M. (1977). Alcohol abuse and work organizations. In B. Kissin & H. Begleiter (Eds.), *The biology of alcoholism, Vol. 4, Social aspects of alcoholism.* New York: Plenum Press.

Rosenbluth, J., Nathan, P.E., & Lawson, D.M. (1978). Environmental influences on drinking behavior by college students in a college pub: Behavioral observation in the natural environment, *Addictive Behaviors,* 3, 117–121.

Rossiter, J.R., & Robertson, T.S. (1980). Childrens' dispositions toward proprietary drugs and the role of television drug advertising. *Public Opinion Quarterly,* 44, 316–329.

Rotter, J.B. (1982). *The development and application of social learning therory.* New York: Praeger.

Royce, J.E. (1981) *Alcohol problems and alcoholism.* New York: Free Press.

Rubenstein, E. (1978). Television and the young viewer. *American Scientist,* 66, 685–693.

Sher, K.J. (1985). Subjective effects of alcohol: The influence of setting and individual differences in alcohol expectancies. *Journal of Studies on Alcohol,* 46, 137–146.

Skinner, B.F. (1971). Social behavior. In E. McGinnies & C.B. Ferster (Eds.), *The reinforcement of social behavior.* Boston: Houghton Mifflin.

Smart, R.G., & Fejer, D. (1972). Credibility of sources of drug information for high school students. *Journal of Drug Issues,* 2(2), 8–18.

Smart, R.G., Gray, G., & Bennett, C. (1978). Predictors of drinking and signs of heavy drinking among high school students. *International Journal of the Addictions,* 13, 1079-1094.

Smart, R.G., & Krakowski, M. (1973). The nature and frequency of drugs content in magazines and on television. *Journal of Alcohol Education,* 18(3), 16–23.

Spevack, M., & Pihl, R.O. (1976). Nonmedical drug use by high school students. Three year survey study. *International Journal of the Addictions,* 11, 755–792.

Stetson, B.A., Brown, S.A., & Beatty, P.A. (1985, Aug.). *Coping with high-risk drinking situations: Abusing versus nonabusing adolescents.* Paper presented at the 93rd Annual Meeting of the American Psychological Association, Los Angeles, Calf.

Strickland, D.E. (1982). *Parents, peers, and problem drinking: An analysis of interpersonal influences on teenage alcohol abuse in the U.S.* Paper presented at the 28th Internationl Institute on the Prevention and Treatment of Alcoholism, Munich, Germany.

Strickland, D.E. (1983). Advertising exposure, alcohol consumption and misuse of alcohol. In M. Grant, M. Plant, & A. Williams (Eds.), *Economics and alcohol: Consumption and controls,* New York: Gardner Press.

Strickland, D.E., Finn, T.A. & Lambert, M.D. (1982). A content analysis of beverage alcohol advertising. I. Magazine advertising. *Journal of Studies on Alcohol,* 43, 655–682.

Strickland, D.E., & Pittman, D.J. (1984). Social learning and teenage alcohol use: Interpersonal and observational influences within the sociocultural environment. *Journal of Drug Issues,* 14, 137–150.

Strickland, D.E., & Wilson, J.B. (1982). *Social learning, family communication, and teenage drinking patterns.* St. Louis: Washington University Social Science Institute Working Paper Series.

Sutherland, E.H. (1947). *Principles of criminology.* Philadelphia: Lippincott.

Trice, H.M. (1966). *Alcoholism in America.* New York: McGraw-Hill.

Trice, H.M. (1984). 'Alcoholism in America' revisited. *Journal of Drug Issues,* 14, 109–123.

Wallack, L. (1983). *Television programming, advertising and the prevention of alcohol-related problems.* San Francisco: Medical Research Institute of San Francisco, Prevention Research Group.

White, H.R. (1982). Sociological theories of the etiology of alcoholism. In E.L. Gomberg, H.R. White, & J.A. Carpenter (Eds.), *Alcohol, science and society revisited.* Ann Arbor, Mich.: University of Michigan Press and Rutgers Center of Alcohol Studies.

White, H.R., Johnson, V., & Horwitz, A. (1986). An application of three deviance theories to adolescent substance use. *International Journal of the Addictions,* 21, 347-366.

Wilsnack, S.C., & Wilsnack, R.W. (1979). Sex roles and adolescent drinking. In H.T. Blane & M.E. Chafetz (Eds.), *Youth, alcohol, and social policy.* New York: Plenum Press.

Wrong, D. (1981) The Oversocialized concept of man in modern sociology. *American Sociological Review,* 26, 183–193.

Zucker, R.A. (1976). Parental influences upon drinking patterns of their children. In M. Greenblatt & M.A. Schuckit (Eds.), *Alcoholism problems in women and children.* New York: Grune & Stratton.

TEN

ANTHROPOLOGICAL AND SOCIOCULTURAL PERSPECTIVES ON ALCOHOL AS A REINFORCER

DWIGHT B. HEATH, Ph.D.

Drinking is an ancient custom, one of the most common customs that have survived over the centuries. And this has happened despite almost universal recognition that there are potential hazards connected with excessive or careless drinking. In many cultures, there is—and has long been—some opposition to it, at least with respect to certain segments of the population. Large categories of people (e.g., children, women) are often forbidden to drink, and even those for whom drinking is allowed are usually restricted in terms of time, place, and various other factors. Nevertheless, in many societies a majority of the population drink regularly and suffer no ill effects. Obviously, the rewards that most people derive from drinking alcoholic beverages far outweigh the costs, most of the time. Each of the contributors to this volume has taken some effort to spell out, in both theoretical and substantive terms, different ways in which alcohol is a reinforcer. The emphasis in this chapter is more on public and social reinforcements as they relate to groups and categories of people, and even cultural reinforcements that impact favorably on institutions.

Ethanol, the most widely used psychoactive drug in the world today, has probably been in use longer than any other throughout human history. The fact that it can be dangerous if misused has been widely described for as long as we have written records, and elaborate sets of legal, religious, and other norms have been developed to regulate who drinks how much of what, where and when, in the company of whom, and with what outcomes.

Ethanol is peculiar inasmuch as it can be used as a food, a medicine, or a poison, and also as a symbol. It qualifies as a food both in terms of the calories it provides (7 per gram, or over 200 per ounce), and in terms of the ways many people use it. Although the calories in ethanol are "empty" (in the sense that they lack vitamins, minerals, and other nutritional values), there is often substantial food value in the beer or wine of which ethanol is only a small part. Medicinal uses of beverage alcohol have varied throughout history and throughout the world; one need not refer to remote and exotic cultures to find examples, such as the counterproductive use of whiskey for snake bite, or the increasing prescription of drinks as mild tranquilizers in nursing homes.

Ethanol is a poison in the same sense that common table salt is a poison—a little can add zest, but too much can be toxic. The toxic quality of alcohol is recognized in lay language—(most people know that "intoxication" means being poisoned)—but few people realize how easy it is to overdose. The fact that alcohol can also be a symbol will be further developed in this chapter, but, for present purposes, it should be sufficient to point out the very different meanings that are conjured up by wine at religious communion, beer at a student beach-party, brandy after a lavish dinner, champagne at a wedding, or cocktails with a business lunch.

These facts demonstrate that ethanol is an unusual substance. And yet it is also a very common substance. It is a product that appears naturally throughout temperate and tropical climates. It has long been observed that birds, insects, and other small animals become intoxicated on overripe fruits and berries that have fermented because free-floating yeasts convert their sugars into alcohol.

But ethanol is also an artifact to the degree that human societies have learned how to use and control the process of fermentation, and some have added distillation. There is a natural limit to the concentration of alcohol that can occur in fermentation—most of the microorganisms that convert the carbohydrates themselves become ineffective when the concentration of ethanol approaches 15 percent. Distillation takes advantage of the different boiling points of water and alcohol to extract water, thereby achieving a much higher concentration of alcohol than is possible by fermentation alone. Although fermented beverages (such as beer, wine, ale, mead, chicha, pulque, and various home brews) are most commonly used, distillation (which yields whiskeys, rum, gin, vodka, and similar "strong" or "hard" liquors) is a simpler process than many people realize.

Regardless of the ingredients—which can be virtually any fruit, grain, or vegetable in which carbohydrates convert to sugars—and regardless of the techniques that are brought to bear in fermentation or distillation, alcoholic beverages normally have special meanings and uses in every culture where they are known. It is these special socially shared meanings and uses that are crucial when we address the issue of alcohol as a reinforcer in sociological and anthropological terms.

Throughout history, different populations have evinced different patterns of belief and behavior with respect to alcoholic beverages. Furthermore, they derive different kinds of satisfactions and dissatisfactions from drinking. Cross-cultural analysis of alcohol use focuses more on attitudes, values, and other normative aspects of alcohol use than on sheer quantity of alcohol ingested (Heath 1982; Marshall, 1979a; Frankel & Whitehead, 1981). The same tends to hold true when we compare various groups and categories of people within a given population (e.g., by sex, age, occupation, socioeconomic class, religious affiliation, etc.).

For all of the apparent damage that is attributed to beverage ethanol, there are evident benefits as well. Repeated surveys of representative samples of the overall population of the United States have demonstrated that close to two-thirds of the people over 15 years of age drink more than once a year, and that only about 10 percent of them suffer appreciable deleterious consequences (U.S. DHEW/DHHS, 1971–83). That figure does not relate merely to physical dependence, severe liver damage, serious traffic injuries, and similar problems that are often thought to result from long-term drinking, but it also includes many other kinds of alcohol-related problems, such as disabling feelings of guilt, trouble on the job, depression, strains in relationships with friends and family, and minor accidents. Another way of looking at the same well-established and persistent statistic is that fully 90 percent of those who drink alcoholic beverages in this country do so without suffering any negative outcomes, according to the governmental agency that is primarily concerned with monitoring drinking problems.

In short, although some drinking results in problems, much more does not. In attempting to understand the interaction of alcohol and the human animal, scientists are increasingly recognizing that no single disciplinary perspective is adequate. In fact, the study of alcohol inherently demands a multidisciplinary approach, combining biological, psychological, and sociocultural or behavioral methods and concepts. Whereas other chapters in this volume have focused on reinforcements in biological and psychological terms, from the point of view of individual users, this one focuses more on sociocultural or behavioral reinforcements, from the point of view of groups, societies, and cultural systems.

THE ENHANCEMENT OF SOCIABILITY

The enhancement of sociability by using alcohol has been eulogized in song and story for centuries. In most societies, drinking is a social act, an adjunct to hospitality, the accompaniment of eating. It intensifies social bonds and acts as a social lubricant. There are a wide variety of beliefs and behaviors associated with alcohol but its invariant biochemical effects seem to be important with respect to some of its values as a social reinforcer. Ethanol is unusual among drugs in having a biphasic effect on the nervous system. In small doses, it is a stimulant, but as it accumulates in the body, it quickly acts as a depressant on the central nervous system. The stimulation of an initial drink is often subjectively interpreted as bolstering one's confidence, putting one at ease, overcoming shyness, or otherwise adding some special verve or vivacity to one's general demeanor. The depressive action of the next few drinks may paradoxically be felt to be continuing stimulation. As certain learned and customary inhibitions of muscle tone, reserve vis-à-vis other people, and so forth, are progressively depressed, one may feel more relaxed, more at ease, increasingly "natural," and otherwise relatively uninhibited. Many people talk more in such a state, are more outgoing, and are less self-conscious or concerned about failure. These changes occur in most individuals long before there is any slurring of speech, failure in motor coordination, or other gross outward evidence of inebriation, so that people not only feel as if they are being stimulated (rather than depressed), but they also tend to act that way, which has prompted some scientists to speak of this as a phase of "pseudostimulation."

Apart from the physiological effects of alcohol, there is a significant psychological component to the effect of alcohol on conviviality. Many of the effects of drinking are determined less by the quantity of alcohol in one's system than by one's expectations. As explained in Chapter 8, experiments using the balanced-placebo design have demonstrated that the expectancy effects of alcohol are often stronger than the pharmacological effects (cf., Marlatt & Rohsenow, 1980). The culturally learned expectation that alcohol enhances sociability might, therefore, also be viewed as a self-fulfilling prophecy. In the contemporary United States, this expected effect of alcohol is learned early. As discussed in chapter 8, a recurrent theme in the reports of 17–19-year-old students asked about the effects of alcohol is that "alcohol enhances social and physical pleasure (... makes it easier to talk with people... makes people feel more interesting)" (Christiansen Goldman, & Inn, 1982; p. 341). When Brown, Goldman, Inn, & Anderson (1980) studied college students' expectations of reinforcement from alcohol, the primary factor that emerged was "alcohol enhances social and physical pleasure."

A neuropharmacological view of what is going on when people have a few drinks may be very different from the drinkers' own subjective view of it. And a social scientist might stress other factors. But there is no question that for many people, alcohol in small quantities serves as a relaxant and tends to lighten their mood, which makes it useful as a social lubricant. In most of the societies that derive from Western European cultures, alcoholic beverages are considered a normal and appropriate adjunct to sociability. Many people expect to have the opportunity to drink at both formal and informal social gatherings. Since the 1930s, "the cocktail hour," "a cocktail party," or simply "cocktails" served as a general label for many kinds of sociable and conversational meetings (de Voto, 1951). In recent years, "wine and cheese" often carries the same meaning. Although guests are not necessarily expected to drink, the mention of drink implies an opportunity to meet and talk with people in a setting that is less formally structured than most work contexts, and the availability of light refreshments (but without the expectation of a complete meal).

The custom of greeting visitors with a hearty exhortation to "have a drink" or the invitation that someone "come over for a drink" has evolved to a specifically alcohol-related implication, although, in a strict linguistic sense, it might well refer generically to any kind of beverage (Heath, 1986). A Finnish visitor to England was surprised to find that alcohol was intended when he expected coffee (Salo, 1962), and many Muslims must conceal their dismay when such an offer does not include tea.

Although ethanol is neither an indispensable adjunct to conviviality nor a guarantor that amicable relations will ensue, it is often used to help people who do not know each other well to feel at ease, and its effectiveness is often demonstrated. It may be imagined that this kind of "crutch" is needed only in large and complex societies, where extreme concern with individualism and privacy make for alienation, whereas smaller and simpler societies allow for greater openness and spontaneity in social relationships, especially where everyone in a group already knows everyone else. However, that is not always the case. The atomistic quality of social relations in many nonindustrialized societies is such that drinking parties tend to be important as rare occasions or which people who normally are unaccustomed to close or sustained interaction can feel at ease with others and enjoy conviviality that is lacking in other realms of their lives (e.g., Bunzel, 1940; Heath, 1958; Mandelbaum, 1965). The idea of alcohol as facilitating sociability among otherwise isolated individuals seems also to be relevant to some of the stereotypes that have to do with drinking among various occupational categories: sailors in port, cowboys at the end of a cattle drive, loggers out of the woods, fur trappers at the trading posts, crews ashore from oil rigs, and others for whom socializing is a sporadic and uncertain enterprise.

A recent review of cultural conceptions about alcohol held by urban blacks in the United States emphasizes that: "Certainly alcohol in black culture is seen as enhancing the sociability of gatherings, including talking or 'rapping' [Brown, 1972], and projecting a particular image of self [Sterne & Pittman, 1972; Borker, Herd, and Hambry, 1980] and thus has a very important and positive role in black culture" (Gaines, 1985, p. 191). Drinking in bars is similarly an important social activity for blacks in Bermuda (Manning, 1979) and throughout the Caribbean, and for immigrants to U.S. cities from Cape Verde (Cabral, 1980) and various Latin American countries (Gordon, 1981, 1985).

One formulation about alcohol as a reinforcer that many academic and professional people find difficult to comprehend is the frequent assertion by Indians, Eskimos, and members of other economically and culturally disadvantaged populations that drinking is valued as a pastime "because there's nothing else to do" (e.g., Hurt, 1961; Nagler, 1970; Norick, 1970). Although such a statement may seen absurd, it is obviously meaningful to those who say it, and investigators should not dismiss it without determining what might be viewed as worthwhile "things to do." For example, the boisterous drunken comportment that some may find offensive is often valued by others as exhilirating and appropriate (e.g., Hill, 1974, 1980; Marshall, 1979b). "Getting rowdy with the boys" is seen as a brief but important phase in the life of Irish-American males (Burns, 1980), just as being a "hell raiser" is for urban Indian youths (Hill, 1974), with both the expectation and the normal pattern in both cultures being that they "grow out of it," "settle down," and drink less in later years. Contemporary middle-class North American culture does not explicitly approve such behavior, but much adolescent drinking and drunken behavior appear to be ambivalently accepted on grounds that "boys will be boys," or "at least it's better than other drugs." Among many populations, drinking is important as a recreational activity among groups of men. Although many readers may find it incomprehensible that becoming intoxicated in a public place could be anything but shameful, there are populations who view it as one of the few ways of having a "good time" (e.g., Hamer, 1965; Lithman, 1979; Little, 1979).

GROUP IDENTIFICATION & ETHNIC BOUNDARIES

In an earlier comprehensive review of the anthropological literature on alcohol, the writer made the point that, "with respect to non-Western and peasant cultures, the drinking of alcoholic beverages is probably most often cited as an act which has important value in promoting social cohesion or conviviality... Somewhat more strongly phased interpretations occasionally speak of group drinking as 'symbolizing social unity' and the unity theme is even more dramatic when a few authors refer to the importance of group solidarity vis-à-vis another reference group" (Heath, 1975). Quite apart from its widespread role in the general enhancement of sociability, alcohol often serves more specifically as a social and cultural reinforcer with respect to the conceptions that people hold of themselves and the images that they want or expect others to have of them. In many different ways, drinking often is an important aspect of group identification, and patterns or styles of alcohol use serve as clear markers of the boundaries among ethnic groups.

One extreme version of drinking as a social boundary marker is the self-righteous pride that some teetotalers take in considering abstinence a proof of their moral superiority to anyone who ever drinks. This attitude is found among both individuals and groups. One of many guesses about the reason why Mohammed proscribed wine for his followers is that such behavior would be a clear distinguishing feature between adherents to Islam and all others in the region, among whom wine was commonly used and highly esteemed (Badri, 1976). In a 20th century example, several "cults" in the United States stress abstinence as a crucial feature that distinguishes their members from others (Galanter, 1981). Black Hebrews do the same (Singer, 1980), as do evangelical Protestant coverts in some predominantly Catholic communities in Latin America (Kearney, 1970; Muratorio, 1980).

Another extreme of drinking as a social boundary marker is represented by those who exalt heavy drinking and frequent drunkenness as important and appropriate behavior. Even while Westermeyer (1974) was pointing out some fallacies that prevail in connection with the widespread "myth of 'the drunken Indian,'" he also took pains to demonstrate that some Indians embrace the stereotype and use it as a way of asserting their ethnicity, differentiating themselves from others, and offending sensibilities of those whites who decry such behavior. It was this kind of behavior that led Lurie (1971) to the insightful characterization of American Indian drinking as "the world's oldest on-going protest movement." A Finnish researcher recently demonstrated that, on the basis of a survey, Finns' description of their own customary behavior is markedly more moderate than the popular stereotype, which emphasizes physical violence—and yet, those same people take pride in the "myth" that emphasizes episodic binges and knife fights as typifying alcohol use in Finland (Simpura, 1984).

Between these extremes of abstinence and drunken brawling lies a broad range of beliefs and behaviors that emphasize particular beverages, drinking patterns, or other aspects of culture as distinctive and important in differentiating one population from others. A well-known example is traditional Jewish emphasis on moderation. The phase *Schikker ist ein Goy* is widely used, even among English speakers, meaning that drunkenness is a vice of Gentiles (Snyder, 1958; Glassner & Berg, 1980). By contrast, the image of the hard-drinking Irishman, caricatured on both sides of the Atlantic, has evolved into an object of ethnic identity during the past 100 years (Stivers, 1976, 1985).

It is not yet axiomatic that "you are what you drink" (as it long has been that "you are what your eat"), but experienced bartenders often pride themselves on their skill at predicting how many of what kind of drink people will order (Spradley & Mann, 1975). Sex, age, and "class" (often inferred from dress) play a role in such estimates, but so does "ethnicity" (which often refers to "race" or presumed ancestral national derivation). Such interpretations are not simply projections from outsiders; they are also articulated by members of the reference groups themselves.

The Camba of the Bolivian jungle poke fun at the relatively mild drinks of other populations, while downing large draughts of 186-proof rum (Heath, 1958), and many a Balkan octagenarian attributes his or her longevity to the special local plum brandy with which he or she starts every day. Villagers in the Andes pride themselves on the taste, texture, bouquet, and other qualities of their chicha, just as villagers in Western Europe discuss and compare their wines. The *aguardiente* or vodka that outsiders consider raw and unpleasant may be "the only beverage worth drinking" in the judgment of a local peasant. Styles of toasting not only serve as public pledges of social commitment within a group, but they also dramatically distinguish a given population from others who do not participate. Many an anthropologist has, rightly or wrongly, felt that an important hurdle in terms of rapport had been passed when native drinking companions expressed approval that the anthropologist "drinks like us." Inclusion within a group where drinking is a focal activity is often a mark of social acceptance, just as exclusion from such a group may well signal rejection. In all of these ways, drinking can be viewed as a kind of social boundary marker, useful in determining who "we" are and who "they" are.

The mid-century misconception that homeless persons were asocial and that Skid Rows were peopled by derelicts who cherished isolation was effectively laid to rest as a few anthropologists and sociologists spent enough time to get to know the people and their way of life. Our new understandings tend to emphasize social relationships that had not previously been recognized. "The bottle gang" (Rubington, 1968) has clear and important etiquette, procedures, and understandings about division of labor, long-term reciprocity, and other relational niceties. Many types of "bums" are differentiated (Spradley, 1970), and an elaborate code of conduct is understood and manipulated among judges and the police so that knowledgeable Skid Rowers can "beat the drunk charge" (Spradley, 1974). Although drinking is by no means all they do, it plays an important role much of the time (except for a few abstainers); learning how to get drinks and how to share them are of fundamental importance to those who want to adapt to the dominant pattern of life on any Skid Row. In a major Canadian city, Brody (1970) found that the moral imperative of buying drinks serves as an economic leveler and the conviviality of drinking is not only viewed as reassuring and supportive, but as "basic to the community" inasmuch as it "unites Indians as Indians."

A very different perspective is offered in some societies where the very act of drinking has taken on the symbolism of the dominant (usually white) culture. Where this does occur, it almost always follows a period of legal restrictions in which members of a colonialized population were forbidden access to alcohol. Some of the many contexts in which native drinking has been explicity characterized as a kind of symbolic passing or "identification" with non natives are Coast Salish of southwestern Canada (Jilek-Aall, 1974), Bougainville in the southwestern Pacific (Ogan, 1966), Australian aborigines (Eastwell, 1979), and Trukese (Marshall, 1979b).

Although a tenuous physiological basis was cited for the generalized value of alcohol in initially facilitating sociability among individuals who might otherwise be ill at ease, these examples of drinking as a feature that helps to distinguish an "in-group" from an "out-group" clearly have their roots in custom, the habitual patterns that are passed from generation to generation by means of socialization and enculturation. Other important cultural meanings and uses of alcohol relate to stratification and exchange, or ranking in social and economic terms.

STRATIFICATION AND EXCHANGE

Whatever else they may be, alcoholic beverages are not free goods. They incorporate raw materials that might otherwise have served as food, labor that might have been invested in other ventures, and often considerable energy used as fuel for distillation, and so forth. As economic commodities, they tend to represent relatively high value in small volume and play a variety of roles in the economics and prestige systems of societies that use them. Even simple alcoholic beverages are sumptuous in the sense that they are not requisite to survival in the way that food, shelter, and many other goods are. As a luxury, drinking can be used as a symbolic marker, not only of ethnicity and other reference-group membership, but also of social and economic status. Illustrative customs include occasional use of a few exceptionally valuable beverages by only a select few, drinking as conspicuous consumption, and drinks as gifts in systems of prestation that signal one's affluence, power, prestige, philanthropy, sophistication, or other special qualities.

Drinking and providing opportunities for others to drink are highly visible and esteemed activities in many populations, serving as bases for prestige and social credit. Instead of viewing liquor as a "social problem," an Australian anthropologist focussed on "the recognition that Aborigines construct their relationships with each other through the sharing of liquor. Indeed, sharing liquor is a fundamental way by which some Aborigines order their contemporary communities" (Collmann, 1979, p. 202), with long-term reciprocity focused on the exchange of alcohol and social obligations. Binge drinking or "sprees," far from reflecting a breakdown of traditional society as is often presumed by outsiders, can fruitfully be viewed as "especially appropriate ways of establishing potential credit among a generalized collectivity" (p. 212), or "trying to develop funds of credit against long-term uncertainties, by spending current surpluses on liquor" (p. 221).

Similarly, in a longitudinal study, Waddell (1973, 1975) discerned, among Papagos who had migrated to the city an elaborate pattern of "treating" and implicit "accounting" by drinking partners. This pattern provides opportunities for the accrual of individual power and social credit, thereby enhancing the social standing of a few in a culture that generally stresses egalitarianism. There is a pervasive moral imperative to share, so it is expected that someone who can afford it will buy drinks for others, and that one who receives a little extra money will not hoard it or spend it selfishly but will share with drinking buddies at the bar. This is a pattern in which all can participate, even when there is no expectation that the investments will "even out in the long run." On the contrary, those who invest most heavily—as long as they do so in a culturally appropriate manner, without boasting or complaining—gain prestige from doing so. Occasional reciprocity by even the poorest beneficiary of such largesse maintains the imagery of communal sharing, without subverting the recognition that some have been more generous than others. Over the long run, Waddell points out, the "individual power" of a few is enhanced, but that occurs within a milieu of widespread "social credit," as among Australian aborigines.

Alcoholic beverages also help us to understand the bases for authority of native leadership in some communities where authority derives from neither election nor hereditary succession. The pidgin English term "big man" is often applied in Melanesia, *caudillo* in Hispanic America, or "patron" in generic analysis by social scientists, with reference to those few individuals who are especially adept at brokering. They can build networks among individuals, and sometimes even alliances among communities, on the basis of amassing certain goods and strategically redistributing them on special occasions. Pigs and yams were traditionally used in Pacific island cultures, but beer is increasingly serving the purpose. Liquor has traditionally been important among the spoils doled out to reward supporters in shifting alliances throughout Latin American history (Wolf & Hansen, 1967). Recent archaeological evidence suggests that the ruler of the Incas in pre-Columbian Peru and other Andean countries, even though he inherited a sort of divine kingship as a supposed direct patrilineal descendent of the Sun God, may not been above using a monopoly of chicha (maize beer), or at least of a special grade of it prepared by an elite class of brewers (Morris, 1979). Documents from the Colonial period support the interpretation that the Inca leader maintained order among regional leaders throughout his extensive empire at least in part by allocating chicha from his special stores (Rostworowski de Diez Canseco, 1977).

The use of alcoholic beverages as a gift for the establishment and manipulation of social credit is also well known among the Giriama of Africa (Parkin, 1972), Finnish farmers and townspeople (Suuronen, 1973), and businesspeople in Catalonia (Hansen, 1976). A measure of the importance of this pattern is Hagaman's (1980, p. 205) assertion that maize beer "is the most important thread in the loose fabric of LoBir life." In a similar way, the *tesguinado* (communal work bee, with maize beer provided by the host) is the basis of reciprocal labor exchange that is crucial in the Tarahumara culture of northern Mexico (Kennedy, 1978). Landowners' providing home brew to neighbors who visit in order to share the work is commonplace among the Quechua of Andean South America (e.g., Doughty, 1971), Bantu (Hutchinson, 1961), and Basuto (Brownlee, 1933) of South Africa, as it was at barn raisings and husking bees in many earlier frontier areas in the United States (Rorabaugh, 1979).

The social credit aspect of drinking and treating can be manipulated not only by individuals but by families, such as those among the Ecuadorean Quechua (Barlett, 1980), highland Maya of southern Mexico

(Nash, 1972), and Kwakiutl of Canada (Rohner & Rohner, 1970). The sharing of alcohol need not necessarily be the subject of long-term accounting that redounds to the advantage of the relatively wealthy or prestigious; it can be an important part of sharing among those who have little, as on Skid Row. A vivid example is a Canadian Ojibway community marked by extreme social and psychological stress, where it was found that "alcohol is perhaps the only commodity that is shared widely" (Shkilnyk, 1985, p. 21).

As a commodity, beverage alcohol can be bought, sold, and bartered, as well as shared. Some of the most vivid accounts in the social history of drinking have to do with just such economic transactions, especially as they occurred in transcultural contexts. The victims of imperialism and exploitation have suffered in many ways, and one can often point to both ecological and cultural disasters that ensued. Such negative consequences, however, should not obscure the fact that, rightly or wrongly, those who used liquor for conquest were amply reinforced.

The popular image of "the triangle trade" in the 18th century Atlantic basin (with molasses from the West Indies going to New England in exchange for rum, which was in turn sent to Africa and exchanged for slaves, who went to the West Indies to produce molasses) has been challenged by historians, but there is no question that liquor was a useful tool in the expansion of European empires in other contexts. The value of liquor as a medium of exchange was enhanced by the fact that it was readily consumed by natives, who did not usually learn how to make it. It is a convenient commodity for frontier traders also because it combines high value in small volume, with infinite divisibility, and with no spoilage. Such use of "firewater" (as liquor was often called) as a way of cheating American Indians is not merely a convention of Hollywood movies but a well-documented historical fact (e.g., MacLeod, 1928; Deloria, 1969); it was similarly used in Australia (e.g., Sargent, 1979), South Africa (e.g., Onselen, 1976), Micronesia (e.g., Marshall & Marshall, 1975), and elsewhere.

Even people who do not themselves drink often view alcohol as a reinforcer in social terms. Heavy excise taxes are common in many jurisdictions, so that drinking underwrites a variety of public services. More obvious is the employment that is provided by the production and distribution of alcoholic beverages, especially significant when alcohol provides work for people who have few other opportunities. For example, women rarely can become independent entrepreneurs in many male-dominated peasant societies such as South Africa (Hellman, 1934), highland Peru (Doughty, 1971; Vazquez, 1967), or colonial Mexico (Taylor, 1979), and yet they often dominate the commercially important production and sale of home brew in those areas.

CEREMONIAL AND RITUAL ASPECTS

One of the pioneers in the scientific study of alcohol was also one of the most venturesome in offering broadly based impressionistic hypotheses. Although E. M. Jellinek is probably best known for a book on *The Disease Concept of Alcoholism*, his mythic phrasing of universal symbolism deserves mention in any discussion about the significance of alcohol as a social reinforcer. Citing diverse literary and classical historical allusions, he asserted that those who drink together "become brethren," that toasting or pledging with drink "was an act of identification, a symbolic covenant. Through drinking together, people are able to identify with each other, to form symbolic blood covenants" (Jellinek, 1977, p. 864).

Although Jellinek's sources are of questionable validity and his rhetoric overblown, ceremonial toasting remains vitally in force in many African and Latin American peasant or tribal communities, where a truce is still pledged with drink, or drinking together is required as a public gesture of mutual acceptance when a dispute settlement is negotiated between two parties. Vestiges of a similar custom can be seen among cosmopolitan industrialists or entrepreneurs who insist, to seal a bargain, "Let's drink on it." The exchanging of toasts, often with an elaborate intertwining of arms, harks back at least to "pledging in the cup" that was integral to diplomacy in the highly fragmented and faction-ridden Europe of the 16th and 17th centuries.

We have already mentioned the importance of drinking patterns as inclusive and exclusive social boundary markers. There are some societies in which such distinguishing behavior is so formalized as to constitute a secular ritual. For example, "alcohol plays a predominantly integrative role in [Bolivian] Camba society, where drinking is an elaborately ritualized activity and alcoholism is unknown. The anxieties which are often cited as bases for common group drinking are not present, but fiestas constitute virtually the only corporate form of social expression. Drinking parties predominate among rare social activities, and alcohol serves to facilitate rapport between individuals who are normally isolated and introverted" (Heath, 1958). Much the same could be said of the Mexican Tarahumara (Kennedy, 1978), Andean Aymara (Carter, 1977), and some other atomistic populations around the world.

Those who are unaccustomed to thinking, as social scientists do, of ritual as a secular phenomenon, will certainly recognize some of the important roles that alcoholic beverages play in various religious rituals. Most Christians seem not to think of taking Communion as "drinking alcohol," but sacramental wine was so crucial to some churches that it was exempted from the prohibition that was intended to keep the United States "dry" from 1919 through 1933. A few pedants set out early in this century to prove that Biblical allusions to "wine" referred to unfermented grape juice, but their work has not fared well under linguistic and other scholarly criticism. Without belaboring the complex theological theory of transubstantiation, one cannot help but be impressed by the supposed potency of a substance that is said to incorporate an essence of the divine, and is then ingested by the congregants. The fact that Jews learn to drink early in life, in the warm and supportive context of religious rituals at home with the family, is often thought to provide a special view of the act that serves as a kind of "immunization" against alcoholism. Although it obviously does not always serve that function, Jews have, for centuries, tended to drink in moderation, and to emphasize the contrast between themselves and their neighbors in this respect (Snyder, 1958; Glassner & Berg, 1980). The sacred symbolism of abstinence on the part of some fundamentalist Muslims has already been cited as an important marker of a crucial social boundary. The same holds true for many ascetic Protestant sects, certain castes of Hindus, and members of some other religious groups.

The association of alcoholic beverages with religion and the supernatural has taken many other forms throughout human history. Bacchus was the Roman god of wine, and the ancient bacchanalian revels included drunkenness as a profoundly religious aspect of worship. The terminology persists in English to this day although most bacchic behavior is now viewed as eminently secular; the same holds true for the Greek Dionysus and dionysian rites. On the basis of largely ancient Near Eastern sources, Klausner (1964) suggested that the ritual use of wine probably grew out of its early substitution for blood, with both standing equally for "the stream of life" in sacrifices made to demanding deities. In ancient Egypt, the goddess Isis was appreciated in part for having invented beer and other intoxicants. The Aztec pantheon in pre-Columbian Mexico included a deity credited with introducing pulque to humankind, and that beverage is still often referred to as "the milk of the Virgin," reflecting the syncretic incorporation of Christian symbolism in the folk Catholicism of contemporary Mexican Indians (Madsen & Madsen, 1969).

In many parts of the world, both drinking and drunkenness have a sacred quality. Widespread examples are the Ainu of Japan (Kubodera, 1965), Tiriki of Kenya (Sangree, 1962), early religions of India (Ravi Varma, 1950), Zapotecs of Mexico (Kearney, 1970), and Quechuas of Peru (Mangin, 1957). The case of the Seneca is especially striking for indicating how drinking patterns and norms can change through time (Wallace, 1970). North America is unusual in that few of the native populations had alcoholic beverages before the arrival of Europeans. In the early years of sporadic contact, most of the several Iroquoian-speaking tribes around the Great Lakes adopted brandy but used it in an unusual way. It became a tool in the vision quest, by which a young man set out to communicate with the guardian spirit that would become helpful and religiously important throughout the rest of his life (Carpenter, 1959). Only after some decades did drinking lose that mystical religious role and become a secular activity, associated with frequent violence, economic exploitation, and other problems. By the end of the 18th century, alcohol had caused so much disruption in Seneca society that a recovering alcoholic with a messianic vision found strong popular response when he preached a return to traditional Indian values, imaginatively combined with selected tenets and symbols of Christianity. This became the Handsome Lake Religion, which, including abstinence from alcohol, remains a vital force among Seneca Indians today.

Even in cultures where alcohol has no specifically religious use or meaning, drinking has been observed sometimes to have almost a mystical quality. Even Jellinek (1977), a long-term friend of Alcoholics Anonymous and proponent of the disease concept of alcoholism, waxed eloquent about how "drunkenness can be a kind of shortcut to the higher life, the achievement of a higher state without an emotional and intellectual effort" (p. 858). A more sinister, but equally supernatural, association was posited on the basis of the supposed equivalence of blood and wine: "Under strain, people turn to alcohol as the modern representative of the sacrificial cults for the riddance of evil" (Klausner, 1964, p. 141).

One need not look to ancient history or exotic primitive cultures in order to see that ceremonial and ritual values are important among the various social and cultural reinforcements offered by alcohol. Witness, for example, the breaking of a bottle of champagne over the bow of a ship to be launched, the long and intricate toasting that is a highlight of many political and social occasions, the spilling of alcohol over winners in an athletic contest, and so forth.

OTHER THEORETICAL AND EMPIRICAL CONSIDERATIONS

There are a number of ways in which alcohol use serves as a reinforcer socially and culturally that do not fit conveniently into the categories described. Among such functions are those served by bars, taverns, and other public drinking establishments. The sociability of drinking in a bar has already been noted, but without mention of the fact that, for many regular patrons, certain kinds of bars can be important sources of information and services as well as companionship. Just as was the case for international immigrants early in this century, urban bars frequented by American Indians are key centers for a wide range of socially important interactions. Quite apart from the recreation, socializing, and other relations that are commonly appreciated in bars anywhere, these also serve as valuable settings for education, employment, and social welfare. Education is used here in the broad sense of learning specific skills and adaptive strategies that are helpful—newcomers can often find housing, learn how to look for work, "get the lowdown" on the availability of various public services, and so forth. For people whose earlier lives have been spent on isolated and sparsely populated reservations or in other rural areas, such a bar can be an important and useful center for acculturation to a complex and vastly different ambience (Waddell, 1973). In those respects, the "Indian bars" of Tucson are similar to those of Los Angeles (Fiske, 1979) or other major cities (Price, 1975).

Another unusual societal benefit of drinking came to light in a recent account of modern Navajo patterns: "As they shared the wine, the men would talk about their work, their herds, and the ceremony. Often, as a treat to younger men and as a means of showing their competence and position in life, the older men would share some of their ceremonial knowledge. These discussions could become quite competitive if two medicine men were present and if they had a little too much to drink. At such times a considerable amount of knowledge about ceremonies and their myths of origin might be disclosed. In this way drinking served as a vehicle for cultural transmission" (Topper, 1985, p. 234). Incidentally, among the Navajo, it is those who are less acculturated and wealthier who have the most alcohol-related problems, the opposite of what many expect who view poverty and/or the stresses concomitant to acculturation as major causes for Indians' become alcoholic (Levy & Kunitz, 1974).

It is not all clear what meaning or importance should be attributed to the widespread social pattern of "matched sipping" and the "modeling" between people who drink together. This is an unusual pattern of drinking, and one of which most people are not even aware. Even those scientists who discovered it on the basis of meticulous sustained observation do not know what to make of the fact that nearby persons who do not know each other tend, rapidly but unconsciously, to synchronize their sipping of alcoholic drinks, adjusting toward the more rapid rate. This finding has been noted consistently, both under controlled laboratory conditions and in field observations (Collins & Marlatt, 1981; Schaefer,

Sobell, & Mills, 1971; Billings, Gomberg, Nash, Kessler, & Weiner, 1978). Another interesting observation that is not readily explainable is that, in small groups of U.S. whites, the rate of drinking varies in direct proportion to the rate of talking at high rates of talking, but the relationship is inverse at low rates (Burley, MacLeod, & Genmil, 1978).

Drinking has always and everywhere been essentially a social act, usually viewed as enhancing sociability, except in those few societies in which it is strictly forbidden on specifically religious grounds. Nevertheless, a less reinforcing link between drinking and social relations is also widely recognized and deplored. What are we to make of the fact that aggression (defined broadly here to include fighting, assaults with weapons, verbal abuse, inappropriate sexual overtures, or other acts by which an individual can offensively encroach on others) is often thought to be a normal concomitant or result of drinking?

One important point in this connection is the simple fact that no such association exists or is posited in many of the world's cultures. Further evidence that the supposed linkage between alcohol and aggression is more cultural than biological—that is, a learned rather than a chemically determined response—is the fact that, wherever drunken aggression does occur, the aggression is not random but follows patterns predicted from social organization and cultural norms. The game imagery proposed by MacAndrew and Edgerton (1969) is helpful in this connection: although some people act as if being drunk gives them "time out" (temporary suspension of the normal rules of conduct), such freedom is always subject to limitations. For example, even in ceremonies that include drunkenness combined with communal license and sexual promiscuity, certain people remain "off limits" because of the incest taboo. Similarly, drunken fighting is rarely directed against those persons who happen to be in closest proximity; even an apparently "out-of-control" drunk will usually seek out an individual against whom he or she has a long-term grievance. Every society's widespread allowance of time out for inebriates is limited. Even drunks continue to conform to broadly expanded, but still culturally limited, norms. The classic formulation, amply illustrated with historical and ethnographic evidence, is that of MacAndrew and Edgerton (1969, p. 67): "Although there can be no doubt that the limits governing drunken comportment are often far less confining than those obtained under conditions of sobriety, it is our contention that the continued existence of limits of *any* kind gives the lie to the conventionally accepted notion that when one is drunk, his now 'uninhibited impulses' take over and his resulting comportment is no longer under control." It is for this reason that the writer has elsewhere referred to the supposed connection between alcoholic and aggression as a "missing link" (Heath, 1983).

Another important theoretical consideration with respect to drinking in sociocultural perspective has to do with the supposed linkages between alcohol use and other aspects of a given culture. In cross-cultural research an effort is made to discover which of various customs and traits occur in association with each other in a statistically significant number of cultures. Correlations do not prove cause-and-effect relationships, but they often suggest hypotheses that can, in turn, be tested by other means. For example, undoubtedly one of the best-known "explanations" of why people drink is "to reduce tension." One of the most commonly cited sources of evidence to support this is a systematic review of the anthropological literature conducted by a sociologist: "*The primary function of alcoholic beverages in all societies is the reduction of anxiety*" (Horton, 1943, p. 223; italicized in the original). A subsequent restudy of the same data by another sociologist has been virtually ignored, although it clearly contradicted Horton's principal finding and replaced it with another that focuses on relations within groups rather than on emotions within the individual. Using the same worldwide sample of 62 cultures, but with more reliable methods of rating and more sophisticated statistical techniques, Field's (1962) "most important single conclusion was that the degree of drunkenness at periodic communal drinking bouts is related to variables indicating a personal (or informal) rather than a corporate (or formal) organization, but is substantially unrelated to the level of anxiety in the society" (p. 72). A number of other hypotheses about alcohol as a reinforcer have been generated and tested with such elaborate cross-cultural methods, emphasizing such varied traits as child rearing, patterns of marriage and residence, feelings of power, and themes in folklore, (Heath, 1984). But such theorizing is often viewed as less socially significant than are practical recommendations for how to increase positive and decrease negative reinforcements that are associated with alcohol.

IMPLICATIONS FOR ACTION

The enduring popularity of alcohol, despite the problematic consequences than can result from drinking it, is not a recent phenomenon. Neither is it a product of advertising, rock music, urbanization, industrialization, or any of the forces that tend to be simplistically blamed by those who would like to do away with alcohol, or drastically to limit popular access to it. There is a perverse sense in which drinking is often no less important to those who oppose it than it is to those who favor it.

An insightful sociological analysis of the movement that culminated in Prohibition in the United States aptly characterized that as a "symbolic crusade," important as a gesture demonstrating that the nation still held to some of the values of a group whose traditional dominance was rapidly becoming eclipsed (Gusfield, 1963). According to that view, enactment of the Constitutional amendment was symbolically important, even when the enabling legislation was unenforceable.

Something similar is happening today, as groups vociferously attack the advertising of alcoholic beverages, oblivious to the fact that some of the nations that have the highest rates of alcohol-related problems have had no advertising of any kind for decades. It is true that drunk driving causes much pain and death in the United States, but one must wonder why there appears to be so much public clamor at this moment in history, when the rate of alcohol-related traffic fatalities has been decreasing steadily for as long as relevant statistics have been kept. Those who call for heavier taxation, indexed price regulation, and a variety of other controls to limit per-capita consumption of alcohol appear not to realize that Americans are drinking only about one-third as much today as they did 150 years ago (Rorabaugh, 1974; USDHHS, 1983). In some senses, media advertisers and the alcohol industry seem to have become scapegoats for parents who are frustrated by not having control of their children, and by others trying to fix blame for a variety of problems over which they have no control. Their very opposition to alcohol appears to be strongly reinforcing for them, quite apart from whatever other kinds of reinforcement it may bring.

There has been an unfortunate tendency, through the few decades in which scientific alcohol studies have been conducted, for most researchers also to focus on negative outcomes of drinking and the problems that result from excessive use of alcohol, a tendency long deplored by Bacon (1943), 1979) and Kilty (1982). In such a context, it is striking to have Brissett's (1978) explicit rejection of the presumption that heavy drinking is problematic: "Heavy drinking is, in many ways, functional for the drinker." Similarly, although it is not presented in a challenging way, many would find Littman (1970) heretical in his assertion that abstention may not be an appropriate goal for American Indian alcoholism treatment, inasmuch as alcohol "promotes psychological and social integration in an alien culture."

It is a striking aspect of most of the anthropological literature on alcohol that it has, over the years, included frequent mention of the benefits of drinking. In some instances, interpretations of alcohol as a social and cultural reinforcer have been those of the social scientist, observing patterns and interpreting them in terms of how they relate to the ongoing system of individual human beings and their interactions.

In other cases, the positive judgments about alcohol are those of the people under study, who are themselves often the best judges of the reinforcing quality of any behavior. Attempts to reflect this social reality have brought serious charges about the competence of ethnographers. An internationally recognized sociologist who specializes in epidemiological studies that stress the negative outcomes of alcohol use suggested that we may be perpetrating "problem deflation" on a systematic basis (Room, 1984), but most respondents disagree forcefully.

In attempting to identify some of the fruitful implications for action that derive from this analysis of alcohol as a reinforcer, probably the cardinal one is the need for broader and deeper recognition that social and cultural factors play an important role, in combination with physiological and psychological factors, in shaping not only how people drink, but also the outcomes of drinking. It is widely recognized that different attitudes and values concerning alcohol are linked with different kinds of reactions to drinking. Similarly, alcohol-related problems—if they occur at all—occur in different ways and at variable rates that closely correlate with the basic norms that a population hold about drinking. Any attempt at better understanding alcohol use and its outcomes must necessarily be multidisciplinary, and afford more than lip service to the proposition that we are dealing with a biopsychosocial phenomenon.

One of the most dramatic ways in which awareness of cultural differences has already proved its practical utility is in the use of culture-specific modalities for the treatment of alcohol-related problems of many kinds. It has become widely accepted that treatment for "minorities" in this country should be "culture sensitive." A number of successful efforts have been made along these lines (see, e.g., Heath, Waddell, & Topper, 1981; Heath, 1987, Weibel-Orlando, 1984), and the Indian Health Service is systematically evaluating the many experiments that have been made under its auspices (Mail & Menter, 1985; Mason, Mail, Palmer, & Zephier, 1985).

A number of interesting "natural experiments" in this respect also deserve attention, in which native practices result in healing of a kind that could not be replicated by Western medicine or by the self-help approach that is most popular among the overall population. A well-documented example is participation in ceremonial dances by young Salish men in southwestern Canada, many of whom turn to this activity deliberately as a way of discontinuing the pattern of heavy drinking that was getting them into various kinds of trouble (Jilek, 1981).

In the northeastern United States, participation in various traditional Medicine Lodge ceremonies serves the same purpose for many Iroquoian youths. These activities not only engage the attention and energies of the participants, but they do so in a uncompetitive setting, jointly with others (including respected elders), before large and appreciative audiences. Presumably also important is the fact that they include strong reaffirmation of traditional values, which include periodic austerity in terms of food, drink, and sex, as well as pride in one's heritage and way of life. This last factor assumes special importance in relation to the widespread theory that much of the problem drinking on the part of minority populations is a reaction to anomic depression, "a chronic dysphoric state characterized by feelings of existential frustration, defeat, lowered self-esteem, sometimes with discharges of randomly aggressive behavior against self or others" (Jilek, 1981, p. 161). That psychoreactive syndrome often develops in reaction to alienation from aboriginal culture under Westernizing influences; it is the psychiatric counterpart of what Dozier (1966) referred to, in ethnographic terms, as "sociocultural deprivation." Jilek (1981) gives details about how the Guardian Spirit Ceremony can be viewed as a "culture-congenial therapy" for anomic depression and alcohol-related problems that are linked with it.

Similarly therapeutic for many problem drinkers is participation in the Native American Church, often called "the Peyote Cult" (Jilek, 1974; LaBarre, 1969; Pascarosa & Futterman, 1976), which combines Christian principles with a drug-assisted vision guest that has strong traditional roots. The syncretic peyote religion is not distinctive of a particular tribe, as are the others that have been mentioned; it has swept across the United States as part of a pan-Indian movement that embraces several intertribal commonalities while retaining distinctive local cultural characteristics. Another pan-Indian activity that has been gaining popularity in recent years, especially among men who have had problems they associate with excessive drinking, is participation in the sweat lodge (Hall, 1985), a sort of sacred sauna that combines ideas of purification with reaffirmations of some basic values that are brought to be traditionally Indian. Although psychological interpretations of such activities may seem to go deeper, there is an important social and cultural component that cannot be ignored.

The key role that attitudes, values, and expectations play with respect to drinking and its effects also highlights the potential value of education as a means of preventing and diminishing drinking problems in the first place. Legislative controls of many kinds have been tried in many jurisdictions, and it is striking that they seem almost always to have been ineffective, except when combined with religious proscriptions. A comprehensive approach to education, involving the entire community rather than only schoolchildren, and geared to the knowledge, beliefs, and interests of the population, has not yet been given an adequate long-term trial. In view of the many ways in which alcohol serves as a reinforcer, it seems only sensible that this promising approach be given a fair chance, including diverse techniques and content relevant to the varied cultural systems that are to be addressed. It does seem ironic that so many people in the United States today, generally thought to be an exceptionally permissive society, should hold a view far to the right of Increase Mather, a Puritan minister in the Massachusetts Bay Colony, who declared, "Drink is in itself a Creature of God, and to be received with thankfulness" (1673, pp. 3–4).

REFERENCES

Bacon, S. (1943). Sociology and the problems of alcohol: Foundations for a sociological study of drinking behavior. *Quarterly Journal of Studies on Alcohol,* 4, 399–445.

Bacon, S. (1979). Alcohol research policy: The need for an independent, phenomenologically oriented field of study. In M. Keller (Ed.), *Research priorities on alcohol.* New Brunswick, N.J.: *Journal of Studies on Alcohol Supplement* 8, pp. 2–26.

Badr, M. (1976). *Islam and alcoholism.* Indianapolis: American Trust Publications.

Barlett, P. (1980). Reciprocity and the San Juan fiesta. *Journal of Anthropological Research,* 36, 116–130.

Billings, A., Gomberg, C., Nash, B., Kessler, M., & Weiner, S. (1978). Synchronized sipping in alcoholics and social drinkers: A preliminary investigation. *Journal of Studies on Alcohol,* 39, 554–559.

Borker, R., Herd, D., & Hembry, K. (1980). *Ethnographic report for the Black Drinking Practices Study* (3 vols.). Berkeley, Calif.: Source.

Brissett, D. (1978). Toward an interactionist understanding of heavy drinking. *Pacific Sociological Review,* 21, 3–20.

Brody, H. (1970). *Indians on Skid Row.* Ottawa: Northern Science Research Group, Department of Indian Affairs and Northern Development *Publication* 70–2.

Brown, A., Goldman, M., Inn, A., & Anderson, L. (1980). Expectations of reinforcement from alcohol: Their domain and relation to drinking patterns. *Journal of Consulting and Clinical Psychology,* 48, 419–426.

Brown, H. (1972). Street talk. In T. Kochman (Ed.), *Rappin' and stylin' out: Communication in urban black America,* Urbana, Ill.: University of Illinois Press, pp. 205–208.

Brownlee, F. (1933). Native beer in South Africa. *Man,* 33,75–76.

Bunzel, R. (1940). The role of alcoholism in two Central American cultures. *Psychiatry,* 3, 361–387.

Burley, P., MacLeod, C., & Gemmil, J. (1978). Effects of social interaction on rate of alcohol consumption. *Psychological Reports,* 42, 49–50.

Burns, T. (1980). Getting rowdy with the boys. *Journal of Drug Issues,* 10, 273–286.

Cabral, S. (1980). "Time out": The recreational use of drugs by Portuguese-American immigrants in southeastern New England. *Journal of Drug Issues,* 10, 287–299.

Carpenter, E. (1959). Alcohol in the Iroquois dream quest. *American Journal of Psychiatry,* 116, 148–151.

Carter, W. (1977). Ritual, the Aymara, and the role of alcohol in human society. In B. du Toit (Ed.), *Drugs, rituals, and altered states of consciousness.* Rotterdam: A.A. Halkema, pp. 101–170.

Christiansen, B., Goldman, M., & Inn, A. (1982). Development of alcohol-related expectancies in adolescents: Separating pharmacology from social-learning influences. *Journal of Consulting and Clinical Psychology,* 50, 336– 344.

Collins, R,. and Marlatt, G. (1981). Social modeling as a determinant of drinking behavior: Implications for prevention and treatment. *Addictive Behaviors,* 6, 233–239.

Collmann, J. (1979). Social order and the exchange of liquor: A theory of drinking among Australian Aborigines. *Journal of Anthropological Research,* 35, 208–224.

Deloria, V., Jr. (1969). *Custer died for your sins: An Indian manifesto.* New York: Macmillan.

de Voto, B. (1951). *The hour.* Cambridge, Mass.: Riverside Press.

Doughty, P. (1971). The social uses of alcoholic beverages in a Peruvian community. *Human Organization,* 30, 187–197.

Dozier, E. (1966). Problem drinking among American Indians: The role of sociocultural deprivation. *Quarterly Journal of Studies on Alcohol,* 27, 172–187.

Eastwell, H. (1979). A pica epidemic: A price for sedentarism among Australian ex-hunter-gathers. *Psychiatry,* 42, 264–273.

Field, P. (1962). A new cross-cultural study of drunkenness. In D. Pittman & C. Snyder (Eds.), *Society, culture, and drinking patterns.* New York: J. Wiley, pp. 48–74.

Fiske, S. (1979). Urban Indian institutions: A reappraisal from Los Angeles. *Urban Anthropology,* 8, 149–172.

Frankel, B., & Whitehead, P. (1981). *Drinking and damage: Theoretical advances and implications for prevention.* New Brunswick, N.J.: Rutgers Center of Alcohol Studies.

Gaines, A. (1985). Alcohol: Culture conceptions and social behavior among urban blacks. In L. Bennett & G. Ames (Eds.), *The American experience with alcohol: Contrasting cultural perspectives.* New York: Plenum Press, pp. 171–197.

Galanter, M. (1983). Sociobiology and informal controls of drinking: Findings from two charismatic sects. *Journal of Studies on Alcohol,* 42, 64–79.

Glassner, B., & Berg, B., (1980). How Jews avoid alcohol problems. *American Sociological Review,* 45, 647–664.

Gordon, A., (1981). The cultural context of drinking and indigenous therapy for alcohol problems in three migrant Hispanic cultures: An ethnographic report. In D. Heath, J. Waddell, & M. Topper (Eds.), *Cultural factors in alcohol research and treatment of drinking problems.* New Brunswick, N.J.: *Journal of Studies on Alcohol Supplement* 9, pp. 217–240.

Gordon, A., (1985). Alcohol and Hispanics in the Northeast: A study of cultural variability and adaptation in alcohol use. In L. Bennett & G. Ames (Eds.), *The American experience with alcohol: Contrasting cultural perspectives.* New York: Plenum Press, pp. 287–313.

Gusfield, J. (1963). *Symbolic crusade: Status politics and the American temperance movement.* Urbana, Ill.: University of Illinois Press.

Hagaman, B. (1980). Food for thought: Beer in a social and ritual context in a West Africa society. *Journal of Drug Issues,* 10, 203–214.

Hall, R. (1985). Distribution of the sweat lodge in alcohol treatment programs. *Current Anthropology,* 26, 134–135.

Hamer, J. (1965). Acculturation stress and the functions of alcohol among the Forest Potawatomi. *Quarterly Journal of Studies on Alcohol,* 26, 285–302.

Hansen, E. (1976). Drinking to prosperity: The role of bar culture and coalition formation in the modernization of the *Alto Panades.* In J. Aceves, G. Levitas, & E. Hansen (Eds.). *Economic transformation and steady-state values: Essays in the ethnography of Spain.* New York: Queens College *Papers in Anthropology* 2, pp. 42–51.

Heath, D. (1958). Drinking patterns of the Bolivian Camba. *Quarterly Journal of Studies on Alcohol,* 19, 491–508.

Heath, D. (1964). Prohibition and post-repeal drinking patterns among the Navaho. *Quarterly Journal of Studies on Alcohol,* 25, 119–135.

Heath, D. (1975). A critical review of ethnographic studies of alcohol use. In R. Gibbins, Y. Israel, H. Kalant, R. Popham, W. Schmidt, & R. Smart (Eds.), *Research advances in alcohol and drug problems* (Vol. 2). New York: J. Wiley, pp. 1–92.

Heath, D. (1982). Sociocultural variants in alcoholism. In E. Pattison & E. Kaufman (Eds.), *Encyclopedic handbook of alcoholism* New York: Gardner Press, pp. 426–440.

Heath, D. (1983). Alcohol and aggression: A "missing link" in worldwide perspective. In E. Gottheil, K. Druley, T. Skoloda, & H. Waxman (Eds.), *Alcohol, drug abuse, and aggression.* Springfield, Ill.: Charles C. Thomas, pp. 89–93.

Heath, D. (1984). Cross-cultural studies of alcohol use. In M. Galanter (Ed.), *Recent developments in alcoholism* (Vol. 2). New York: Plenum Press, pp. 405–416.

Heath, D. (1986). Cultural definitions of drinking: Notes toward a semantic approach. *Drinking and Drug Practices Surveyor,* 21, 17–22.

Heath, D. (1987). "Addictive behaviors" and "minority populations" in the United States: American Indian drug use as a cultural case study. In T. Nirenberg & S. Maisto (Eds.), *Developments in the assessment and treatment of addictive behaviors.* Norwood, N.J.: Ablex, pp. 339–351.

Heath, D. (in press). American Indians and alcohol: Epidemiological and sociocultural relevance. In *Epidemiology of alcohol use and abuse among U.S. minorities.* Rockville Md.: National Institute on Alcohol Abuse and Alcoholism Research Monograph 18.

Heath, D., Waddell, J., & Topper, M. (Eds.), (1981). *Cultural factors in alcohol research and treatment of drinking problems.* New Brunswick, N.J.: *Journal of Studies on Alcohol Supplement* 9.

Hellmann, E. (1934). The importance of beer-brewing in an urban Native yard. *Bantu Studies,* 8, 38–60.

Hill, T. (1974). From hell raiser to family man. In J. Spradley & D. McCurdy (Eds.), *Conformity and conflict: Readings in cultural anthropology* (2nd ed.). Boston: Little, Brown, pp. 186–200.

Hill, T. (1980). Life styles and drinking patterns of urban Indians. *Journal of Drug Issues,* 10, 257–272.

Holmberg, A. (1971). The rhythms of drinking in a Peruvian coastal mestizo community. *Human Organization,* 30, 198–202.

Honigmann, J. (1963). Dynamics of drinking in an Austrian village. *Ethnology,* 2, 157–169.

Honigmann, J., & Honigmann, I. (1945). Drinking in an Indian-white community. *Quarterly Journal of Studies on Alcohol,* 5, 575–619.

Horton, D. (1943). The functions of alcohol in primitive societies: A cross-cultural study. *Quarterly Journal of Studies on Alcohol,* 4, 199–320.

Hurt, W. (1961). The urbanization of the Yankton Indians. *Human Organization,* 20, 226–231.

Hutchinson, B. (1961). Alcohol as a contributing factor in disorganization: The South African Bantu in the nineteenth century. *Revista de Antropologia* (Sao Paulo), 9, 1–13.

Jellinek, E. (1977). The symbolism of drinking: A culture-historical approach. *Journal of Studies on Alcohol,* 38, 849–866 [originally published 1966].

Jilek, W. (1974). Indian healing power: Indigenous therapeutic practices in the Pacific Northwest. *Psychiatric Annals,* 4, 13–21.

Jilek, W. (1981), Anomic depression, alcoholism, and a culture-congenial Indian response. In D. Heath, J. Waddell, & M. Topper (Eds.), *Cultural factors in alcohol research and treatment of drinking problems.* New Brunswick, N.J.: *Journal of Studies on Alcohol Supplement* 9, pp. 159–170.

Jilek-Aall, L. (1974). Psychosocial aspects of drinking among Coast Salish Indians. *Canadian Psychiatric Association Journal,* 19, 357–361.

Kearney, M. (1970). Drunkenness and religious conversion in a Mexican village. *Quarterly Journal of Studies on Alcohol,* 31, 132–152.

Kennedy, J. (1978). *Tarahumara of the Sierra Madre: Beer, ecology, and social organization.* Arlington Heights, Ill.: AMH Publishers.

Kilty, K. (1982). Scientific ideologies and conceptions of drinking behavior and alcoholism. *Journal of Sociology and Social Welfare,* 9, 755–765.

Klausner, S. (1964), Sacred and profane meanings of blood and alcohol. *Journal of Social Psychology,* 64, 27–43.

Kubodera, I. (1965), *On the practice and ritual of brewing among the Ainu.* Toronto: Addiction Research Foundation Substudy 1–2 and Y-65 [originally published in Japanese, 1935].

LaBarre, W. (1969). *The Peyote Cult.* New York: Schocken.

Lemert, E. (1964). Forms and pathology of drinking in three Polynesian societies. *American Anthropologist,* 66, 361–374.

Levy, J., & Kunitz, S. (1974). *Indian drinking: Navajo practices and Anglo-American theories.* New York: Wiley-Interscience.

Lithman, Y. (1979). Feeling good and getting smashed: On the symbolism of alcohol and drunkenness among Canadian Indians. *Ethnos.* 44, 119–133.

Little, K. (1979). Nobody knows the good times: Drinking in Athapaskan communities. *Journal of Anthropology at McMaster,* 5, 126–179.

Littman, G. (1970), Alcoholism, illness, and social pathology among American Indians in transition. *American Journal of Public Health,* 60, 1769–1787.

Lurie, N. (1971). The world's oldest on-going protest demonstration: North American Indian drinking patterns. *Pacific Historical Review,* 40, 311–332.

MacAndrew, C., & Edgerton, R. (1969). *Drunken comportment: A social explanation.* Chicago: Aldine.

MacLeod, W. (1928). *The American Indian frontier.* New York: Knopf.

Madsen, W., & Madsen, C. (1969). The cultural structure of Mexican drinking behavior. *Quarterly Journal of Studies on Alcohol,* 30, 701–718.

Mail, P., & Menter, G. (1985). Evaluation of Indian alcoholism programs: Lessons learned over three years. Paper read at U.S. Public Health Service Professional Association.

Mandelbaum, D. [et al.] (1965). Alcohol and culture [with comments]. *Current Anthropology*, 6, 281–294.

Mangin, W. (1957). Drinking among Andean Indians. *Quarterly Journal of Studies on Alcohol*, 18, 55–66.

Manning, F. (1979). *Black clubs in Bermuda: Ethnography of a play world*. Ithaca, N.Y.: Cornell University Press.

Marlatt, G., & Rohsenow, D. (1980). Cognitive processes in alcohol use: Expectancy and the balanced placebo design. In N. Mello (Ed.), *Advances in substance abuse: Behavioral and biological research* (vol. 1), Greenwich, Conn.: JAI Press, pp. 159–199.

Marshall, M. (Ed.) (1979a). *Beliefs, behaviors, and alcoholic beverages: A cross-cultural survey*. Ann Arbor, Mich.: University of Michigan Press.

Marshall, M. (1979b). *Weekend warriors: Alcohol in a Micronesian culture*. Palo Alto, Calif.: Mayfield.

Marshall, M., & Marshall, L. (1975). Opening Pandora's bottle: Reconstructing Micronesians' early contacts with alcoholic beverages. *Journal of the Polynesian Society*, 84, 441–465.

Mason, R., Mail, P., Palmer, I., & Zephier, R. (1985). *Briefing book for the alcoholism program review*. Albuquerque, N.M.: Program Branch, Indian Health Service.

Mather, I. (1673). *Wo to drunkards: Two sermons testifying against the sin of drunkenness*... Cambridge, Mass.: Marmaduke Johnson.

Morris, C. (1979). Maize beer in the economics, politics, and religion of the Inca Empire. In C. Gastineau, W. Darby, & T. Turner (Eds.), *Fermented food beverages in nutrition*. New York: Academic Press, pp. 21–34.

Muratorio, B. (1980). Protestantism and capitalism revisited, in the rural highlands of Ecuador. *Journal of Peasant Studies*, 8, 37–60.

Nagler, M. (1970). *Indians in the city*. Ottawa: Canadian Research Centre for Anthropology, Saint Paul University.

Nash, J. (1972). The betrothal: A study of ideology and behavior in a Maya community. In H. Siverts (Ed.), *Drinking patterns in highland Chiapas*. Bergen, Norway: Universitetforlaget, pp. 89–120.

Norick, F. (1970). Acculturation and drinking in Alaska. *Rehabilitation Record*, 11, 13–17.

Ogan, E. (1966). Drinking behavior and race relations. *American Anthropologist*, 68, 181–187.

Onselen, C. (1976). Randlords and rotgut, 1886–1903: An essay on the role of alcohol in the development of European imperialism and South African capitalism. *History Workshop*, 1, 33–89.

Parkin, D. (1972). *Palms, wine, and witnesses: Public spirit and private gain in an African farming community*. San Francisco: Chandler.

Pascarosa, P., & Futterman, S. (1976). Ethnopsychedelic therapy for alcoholics: Observations on the peyote ritual of the Native American Church. *Journal of Psychedelic Drugs*, 8, 215–221.

Price, J. (1975). U.S. and Canadian Indian urban ethnic institutions. *Urban Anthropology*, 4, 35–52.

Ravi Varma, L. (1950). Alcoholism in Ayurveda. *Quarterly Journal of Studies on Alcohol*, 11, 484–491.

Rohner, R., & Rohner, E. (1970). *The Kwakiutl Indians of British Columbia.* New York: Holt, Rinehart & Winston.
Room, R. [et al.] (1984). Alcohol and ethnography: A case of "problem deflation"? [with comments]. *Current Anthropology,* 25, 169–191.
Rorabaugh, W. (1979). *The alcoholic republic: An American tradition.* New York: Oxford University Press.
Rostworowski de Diez Canseco, M. (1977). *Etnia y sociedad.* Lima, Peru: Instituto de Estudios Peruanos.
Rubington, E. (1968). The bottle gang. *Quarterly Journal of Studies on Alcohol,* 29, 943–955.
Salo, K. (1962). "Have a drink..." —engelska alkoholvanor. *Alkoholpolitik,* 25, 167–169.
Sangree, W. (1962). The social functions of beer drinking in Bantu Tiriki. In D. Pittman & C. Snyder (Eds.), *Society, culture and drinking patterns.* New York: Wiley, pp. 6–21.
Sargent, M. (1979). *Drinking and alcoholism in Australia: A power relations theory.* Melbourne: Longmans Cheshire.
Schaefer, H., Sobell, M., & Mills, K. (1971). Baseline drinking in alcoholics and social drinkers: Kinds of drink and sip magnitude. *Behavior Research and Therapy,* 9, 23–27.
Shkilnyk, A. (1985). *A poison stronger than love: The destruction of an Ojibway community.* New Haven, Conn.: Yale University Press.
Simpura, J. (1984). Det finska ölsinnet till vardags och till fest: Dryckessituationerna och drickandets sociala betydelser. *Alkoholpolitik,* 73–83.
Singer, M. (1980). The function of sobriety among black Hebrews. *Journal of Operational Psychiatry,* 11, 162–168.
Snyder, C. (1958). *Alcohol and the Jews: A cultural study of drinking and sobriety.* Glencoe, Ill.: Free Press.
Spradley, J. (1970). *You owe yourself a drunk: An ethnography of urban nomads.* Boston: Little, Brown.
Spradley, J. (1974). Beating the drunk charge. In J. Spradley & D. McCurdy (Eds.), *Conformity and conflict: Readings in cultural anthropology.* Boston: Little Brown & Co., pp. 377–384.
Spradley, J., & Mann, B. (1975). *The cocktail waitress: Woman's work in a man's world.* New York: Wiley.
Sterne, M., & Pittman, D. (Eds.) (1972). *Drinking patterns in the ghetto* (Vol. 1). St. Louis: Washington University Social Science Institute.
Stivers, R. (1976). *A hair of the dog: Irish drinking and American stereotype,* University Park, Pa.: Pennsylvania State University Press.
Stivers, R. (1985). Historical meanings of Irish-American drinking. In L. Bennett & G. Ames (Eds.), *The American experience with alcohol: Contrasting cultural perspectives.* New York: Plenum Press, pp. 109–129.
Suuoronen, K. (1973). *Traditional festive drinking in Finland according to responses to an ethnological questionnaire.* Helsinki: Social Science Research Institute of Alcohol Studies *Report* 76.
Taylor, W. (1979). *Drinking, homicide, and rebellion in colonial Mexican villages.* Stanford, Calif.: Stanford University Press.
Topper, M. (1985). Navajo "alcoholism": Drinking, alcohol abuse, and treatment in a changing cultural environment. In L. Bennett & G. Ames (Eds.), *The American experience with alcohol: Contrasting cultural perspectives,* New York: Plenum Press, pp. 227–251.

United States, Department of Health, Education and Welfare/Health and Human Services, 1971–1984. *Alcohol and health: Special report to the U.S. Congress* (Eds. 1–5). Rockville, Md.: National Institute on Alcohol Abuse and Alcoholism.

Vázquez, M. (1967). La chicha en los paises andinos. *América Indígena,* 27, 265–282.

Waddell, J. (1973). "Drink, friend!" Social contexts of convivial drinking and drunkenness among Papago Indians in an urban setting. In M. Chaftez (Ed.), *Proceedings of the 1st Annual Alcoholism Conference of the National Institute on Alcohol Abuse and Alcoholism.* Washington: U.S. Government Printing Office, pp. 237–251.

Waddell, J. (1975). For individual power and social credit: The use of alcohol among Tucson Papagos. *Human Organization*, 34, 9–15.

Wallace, A. (1970). *The death and rebirth of the Seneca*. New York: Knopf.

Weibel-Orlando, J. (1984). Indian alcoholism treatment programs as flawed rites of passage. *Medical Anthropology Quarterly,* 15, 62–67.

Westermeyer, J. (1974). "The drunken Indian": Myths and realities. *Psychiatric Annals,* 4, 29 ff.

Wilson, G., & Abrams, D. (1977). Effects of alcohol on social anxiety and physiological arousal: Cognitive versus pharmacological processes. *Cognitive Therapy and Research,* 1, 195–210.

Wolf, E., & Hansen, E. (1967). *Caudillo* politics: A structural analysis. *Comparative Studies in Society and History,* 9, 168–179.

ELEVEN

INCENTIVE MOTIVATION, AFFECTIVE CHANGE, AND ALCOHOL USE: A MODEL

W. MILES COX, Ph.D., and
ERIC KLINGER, Ph.D.

The preceding chapters in this volume illustrate a variety of categories of variables have been investigated as causes for why people drink. The chapters have shown, for example, that the degree of reinforcement that people derive from drinking is determined by their biochemical reactivity to alcohol (Chapters 3 and 4), their conditioned responses to stimulus cues associated with alcohol (Chapter 7), their expectations about imbibing alcohol (Chapter 8), various social pressures to drink or not to drink (Chapter 9), and the attitudes about drinking that are fostered by the society in which they live (Chapter 10). A major question that remains to be answered, however, is the manner in which the various parameters of alcohol as a reinforcer interact with one another. Thus our motivational model of alcohol use seems especially appropriate to present as the culminating chapter in this volume because it takes into account all of the variables that are known to affect drinking and shows how these variables are interrelated.

Despite the fact that multiple factors influence drinking, the final, common pathway to alcohol use is, in our view, motivational. The motivation to drink, moreover, is closely tied to people's incentive motivation

This chapter is reprinted with the kind permission of the APA and the affective changes that they derive from their incentives. We begin, therefore, by defining incentive motivation and affective change and showing how these two concepts are related to people's use of alcohol.

INTRODUCTORY DEFINITIONS

Incentive Motivation

The term *incentive motivation* was introduced by Clark L. Hull (1951, 1952) as a theoretical construct to account for the vigor and intensity of behavior. Previously, Hull (1943) had assumed that organisms can perform a learned response to the extent that they have acquired habit strength (the learned association between a stimulus and the response), and that the response is energized solely by the organism's current level of drive (which was assumed to be proportional to its physiological need). Subsequent experiments, however, prompted Hull to modify this view.

These landmark experiments were conducted by Crespi (1942) and Zeaman (1949), who trained albino rats to traverse a straight runway for one magnitude of food reward and then shifted them to either a larger or smaller magnitude of reward. The shifts in reward were accompanied by precipitous changes in the speeds with which the rats traversed the apparatus. With an increase in reward, the rats abruptly increased their running speeds and ran more rapidly than a control group that received only the large reward (a positive incentive contrast effect). With a decrease in reward, the rats abruptly decreased their running speeds and ran more slowly than a control group that received only the small reward (a negative incentive contrast effect). Since the rats' performance of the learned response was a function of the current attractiveness of their incentive (relative to what it had been previously), and since their current performance could not be explained entirely by drive and habit strength, Hull (1951, 1952) introduced the new motivational construct, incentive motivation, to account for their behavior. Other learning theorists (Black, 1965, 1968, 1969, 1976; Spence, 1956) have modified and extended Hull's (1951, 1952) view of incentive motivation and have elaborated on the manner in which it combines with other learning and motivational constructs.

In the present chapter, the term "incentive motivation" is used simply to refer to an organism's motivation to pursue incentives: positive incentives to which it is attracted and negative incentives by which it is repelled. In our view, incentive motivation forms an integral part of organisms' psychological functioning. In fact, in the case of the human organism, people's lives are organized around the pursuit and enjoyment of incentives (Klinger, 1975, 1977). A person who is committed to pursue an incentive is characterized by a distinctive motivational state, or current concern, that lasts from the initial commitment until the incentive is either consummated or relinquished. According to our model of alcohol use, a person's motivation to use alcohol is intertwined with his or her incentive motivation and the effective changes that result from that motivation.

Affective Change

Affect refers to the psychological, or experimental, component of an emotional response. By affective change we mean a change in affect from its current state—a change that may be either quantitative or qualitative in nature. Even though affective changes may occur for reasons other than through organisms' commerce with their incentives, the incentives in their life—and their relationships to them—are a major source of organisms' affective changes.

What are incentives, and why are organisms motivated to pursue them? In current motivational theory (see Klinger, 1975, 1977; Pervin, 1983), there is an emerging consensus that an incentive is any object or event that has the capacity to produce an affective change. An incentive is contrasted with a goal, which is any particular incentive that an organism has become committed to pursue. An organism may strive to achieve a positive incentive in order to enhance its positive affect, and it may seek or rid itself of a negative incentive in order to reduce its negative affect.

Among both animals (Black, 1976) and humans (Klinger, 1975, 1977), it is organisms' expectations about incentives that appear to govern their goal striving. The empirical evidence indicates that expectations about incentives (instead of drive reduction or operant reinforcement) are both necessary and sufficient for goal-directed behavior to take place. For instance, the animal research has demonstrated that vigorous goal directed behavior can occur in the virtual absence of drive (e.g., Black & Cox, 1973; Cox, 1976). Analyses of human motivation indicate that goal striving is the organizing force behind behavior and that people strive for goals because they expect that reaching them will produce affective changes (Klinger 1975, 1977; Pervin, 1983).

In the case of humans' motivation to use alcohol in particular, it has been demonstrated that clear expectations about the effects of alcohol are formed prior to the time that a person consumes any alcohol (Christiansen, Goldman, & Inn, 1982), and that people's expectations about imbibing alcohol dramatically influence their motivation to drink and the actual effects that drinking has on their behavior (Marlatt & Rohsenow, 1980). Our model of alcohol use suggests that the many variables demonstrated to have an impact on people's motivation to drink do so by virtue of the fact that they help to form expectations about the affective changes that will be experienced if a person drinks.

Alcohol Use

There are two ways in which drinking alcohol can bring about affective changes, and there are two corresponding types of effects that people expect to achieve by drinking. The first way is through the direct, chemical effects of alcohol. As we saw in Chapters 5 and 6, alcohol clearly has mood-altering effects that are often described as either "tension reducing" or "mood enhancing." As we saw in Chapter 8, however, people's expectations about the mood-altering effects of alcohol are often a more potent source of actual changes in mood than is the pharmacological action of alcohol itself. The second way in which drinking brings about affective changes is indirect and occurs by virtue of the fact that drinking alcohol can be instrumental in regulating the other incentives in one's life. Imbibing alcohol, that is, might either facilitate or interfere with a person's reaching nonchemical positive or negative goals, thereby indirectly bringing about affective changes. We saw in Chapter 9, for instance, that many of the social variables that influence drinking do so indirectly because drinking alcohol is instrumental in achieving peer approval. Later in the chapter, we provide other specific examples of how the indirect, instrumental effects of drinking alcohol can bring about affective changes.

Regardless of whether an affective change that is produced by drinking alcohol is direct or indirect, alcohol use is interwined with people's incentive motivation and the affective changes that they experience as a result of the incentives in their lives. Thus, for example, the affect that people experience before imbibing alcohol, and which they expect to change by drinking, is likely to have arisen from their goal striving, and their success or lack of success in reaching their goals. In turn, drinking alcohol, especially in excessive quantities, changes people's affect, their incentive motivation, and their subsequent motivation to use or not to use additional alcohol. Thus either directly or indirectly drinking alcohol influences, and is influenced by, the other incentives in people's lives.

Modifying Incentive Motivation with Alcohol

The first author's initial investigation of incentive motivation, affective change, and alcohol use was with albino rats in an instrumental conditioning situation similar to the one used by Crespi (1942) and Zeaman (1949). Specifically, the aim of this study was to determine whether incentive contrast effects resulting from shifts in the magnitude of food reward could be modified by alcohol.

In one view (Amsel, 1958, 1962; Crespi, 1942; Hull, 1952; Zeaman, 1949), the sudden changes in behavior that accompany incentive shifts are mediated by emotional reactions to the shift. According to this explanation, incentive contrast effects that are ordinarily observed should be modified among animals that experience the mood-altering effects of alcohol at the time that the incentive shift takes place. That is, alcohol, through its attenuation of the negative emotional reaction to a downshift in reward, might reduce or eliminate the negative incentive contrast effect. Through its enhancement of a positive emotional reaction to an upshift in reward, alcohol might contribute to a positive incentive contrast effect.

To explore these possibilities, Cox and colleagues (Cox, 1981, 1988; Cox, Klinger, & Kemble, 1987) compared reactions to incentive shifts of rats that had consumed an alcoholic solution before their conditioning trials with those that had consumed a nonalcoholic solution. Results obtained with the sober rats were consistent with those of the many incentive contrast studies that have followed those of Crespi (1942) and Zeaman (1949). That is, negative contrast effects have been consistently obtained with incentive downshifts, but positive contrast effects with incentive upshifts have usually not been seen in discrete-trial instrumental conditioning situations involving immediate reward (Cox, 1975; Flaherty, 1982). Different results, however, were obtained when the animals were under the influence of alcohol.

In one experiment (Cox, 1981), the inebriated rats (unlike the sober rats) showed a pronounced positive contrast effect. In another experiment (Cox, 1987b), the negative contrast effect differed among inebriated and sober rats in that the inebriated rats initially showed less abrupt reductions in running speeds than the sober ones, but the inebriated animals were slower to recover from the reduction in reward. The latter result suggests that coping with an incentive loss by drinking alcohol might be maladaptive. Finally, Cox, Klinger, and Kemble (1987) found that alcohol altered the orderly sequence of changes in rats' level of activity that follows an incentive loss.

In these experiments with rats, it is impossible to know, of course, whether the modifications in reactions to the incentive shifts that were produced by alcohol occurred because alcohol altered the rats' affective changes. The results, however, do appear consistent with that possibility. Moreover, the results of these experiments with animals on the apparent effects of alcohol on incentive motivation underscore the importance of understanding how humans' incentive motivation is interrelated with their motivation to use alcohol. Our motivational model of alcohol—and our research program that is based on the model—is designed to address that issue.

MOTIVATIONAL MODEL OF ALCOHOL USE

In the preceding sections, we have suggested that the nonchemical incentives in people's lives—and the affective changes that they experience as a result of their relationship to these incentives—are intertwined with their use of alcohol. We have also suggested that nonchemical incentives, as well as the other parameters of alcohol as a reinforcer that have been discussed in this volume, have their ultimate influence on people's use of alcohol because they contribute to people's motivation to drink. We believe, moreover, that each variable has an impact on a person's motivation to use alcohol insofar as that variable contributes to that person's expectations about the effect that drinking will have on his or her affect. Thus our model of alcohol use depicts people as deciding to drink or not to drink on the basis of whether the positive affective consequences that they expect to derive from drinking outweigh those that they expect to derive from not drinking.

A flow diagram of the model is shown in Figure 11–1. Cursory inspection will indicate that the variables shown there are grouped into categories and that the interrelationships among the variables are indicated by solid and broken lines that connect the variables. The solid lines lead from variables that strengthen a decision to drink, whereas the broken lines lead from variables that strengthen a decision not to drink. Thus the version of the model that is shown in Figure 11–1 depicts each variable as dichotomous. An eventual aim of our research program, however, is to determine weights to assign to each variable—weights that will differ from one individual to another and within a given individual from one point in his or her life to another.

In guiding the reader through the flow diagram, we will first discuss the end-point that is depicted at the extreme right of the figure (i.e., the final decision to drink or not to drink). We will then discuss in turn each category of variables that leads to the decision, proceeding across the flow diagram from left to right until we return to the point of the final decision.

Decision to Drink or Not to Drink

The model assumes that a person makes a decision about whether or not he or she will consume any particular drink of alcohol. However, this assumption is not intended to imply that the person is necessarily aware of either having made a decision or the factors that affected the decision. In point of fact, decisions about drinking often are unconscious and automatized. Nevertheless, the decision itself is voluntary, and a person can exercise control over it. Consider, for example, how often a person would take that next drink if he or she knew that it had been poisoned.

Experimental analyses of drinking behavior lend empirical support to our contention that people decide whether to drink or not to drink and that they decide how much alcohol to consume on the basis of the particular emotional effect that they wish to achieve rather than being driven by chemical effects or withdrawal symptoms (cf. Marlatt & Gordon, 1985; Peele, 1985b). Moreover, it has been shown that alcoholic patients placed in experimental drinking situations will decide to endure withdrawal symptoms in order to "save up" for the opportunity to go on a binge (cf. Langenbucher & Nathan, 1983). In his analysis of relapses among alcoholics, Marlatt (1985) has found that alcoholics often set the stage for a relapse to occur through a series of "mini-decisions," each of which taken individually does not appear to be related to the alcoholic's final goal of returning to drinking. In Marlatt's words:

> Each mini-decision must be justified by an "explanation" that satisfies the self and others and which does not "blow the cover" on the covert nature of the operation. The use of Apparently Irrelevant Decisions... is crucial to this process of self-deception and minimization of social surveillance. At each choice-point, the client makes a decision that leads closer to the brink of relapse and justifies the decision that leads [to a] bolstering strategy such as rationalization or denial. As such, the decision is rendered "apparently irrelevant" to the goal of relapse. Each such "move" on the

Figure 11-1 (start)

Figure 11-1. Motivational model of alcohol use

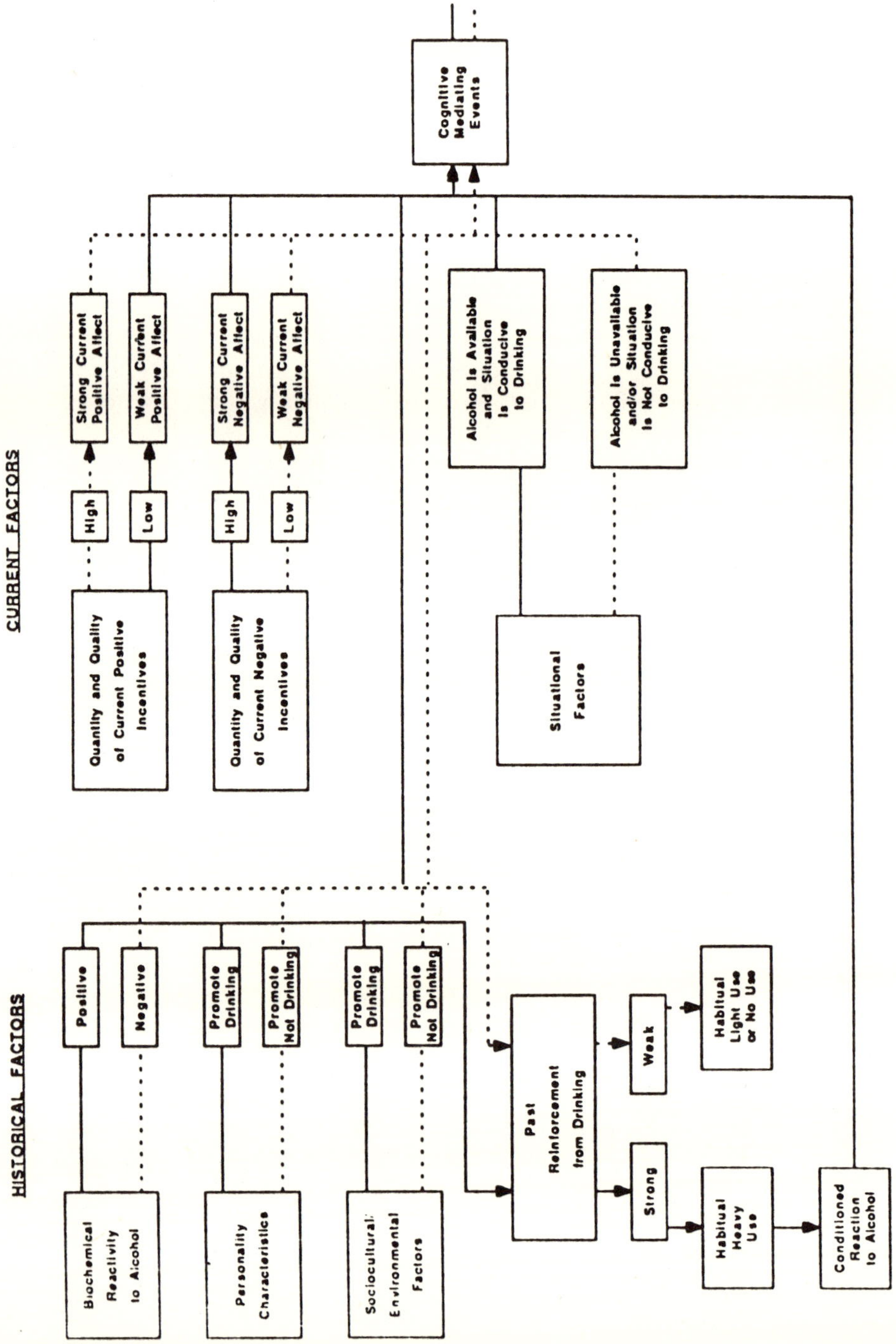

Figure 11-1 (end)

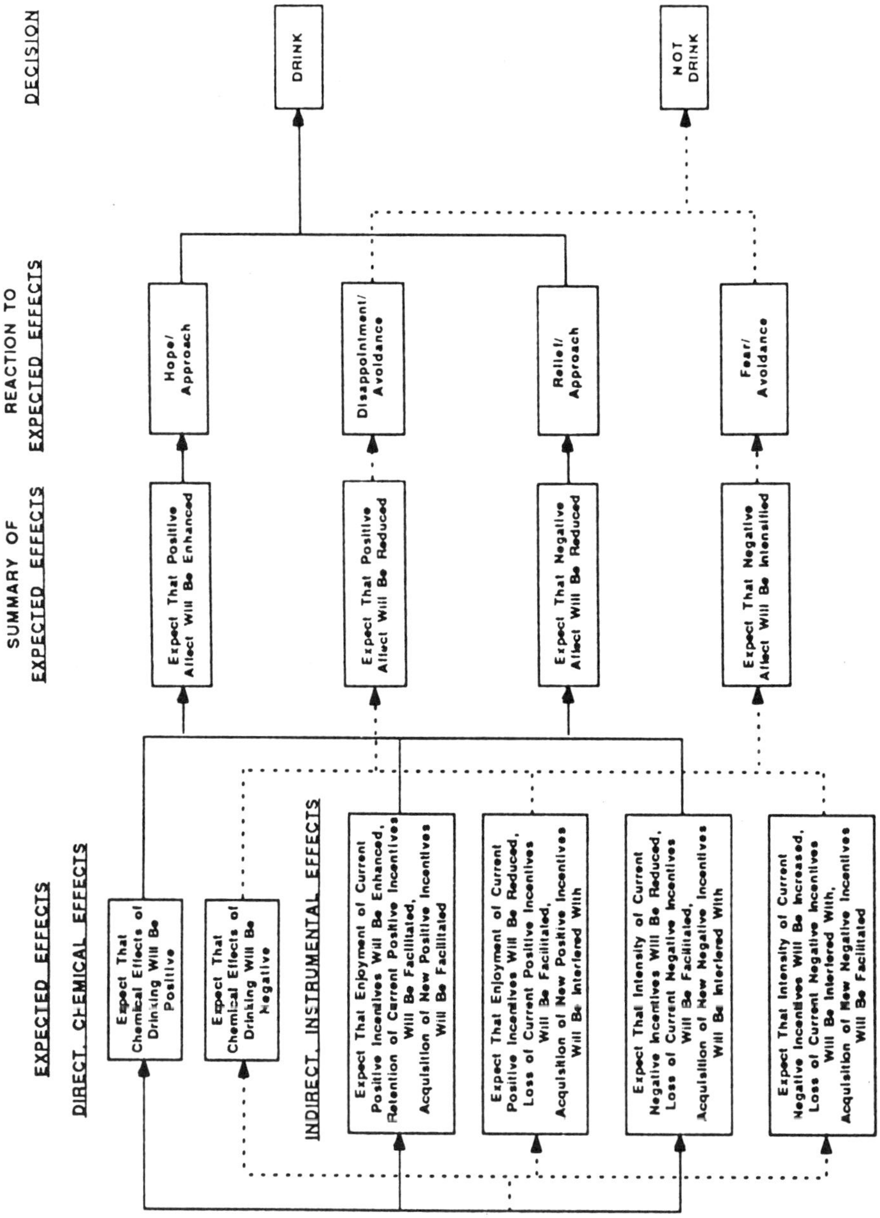

checkerboard leading to relapse can be thought of as a chain... culminating in the final set-up.... (p. 271).

Historical Factors

The category of variables that we refer to as the historical factors is shown at the extreme left of Figure 11–1. Each of the variables in this category is historical in the sense that it has helped to determine the nature of an individual's past experiences with drinking, which, in turn, influence that person's current motivation to drink. There are three kinds of historical factors: a person's biochemical reactivity to alcohol, his or her personality characteristics, and the sociocultural environment in which he or she lives.

Biochemical Reactivity To Alcohol. The research on biochemical reactivity to alcohol that was discussed by Hunt in Chapters 3 and 4 and other recent reviewers (Cloninger & Li, 1985; Schuckit, Li, Cloninger, & Deitrich, 1985; Nathan, 1986) points to the biochemical mechanisms that appear to underlie the reinforcing effects of alcohol. Moreover, as we saw in Chapter 2 by Goodwin, these mechanisms seem to be under genetic control and to predispose certain people to develop problems with alcohol.

The exact biochemical mechanisms that are responsible for the reinforcing effects of alcohol are still hypothetical. One reviewer (Peele, 1985a) believes, in fact, that the role of genetic factors in alcoholism has been overstated. What is clear, however, is that there are wide differences among people in the manner in which they metabolize alcohol and its metabolic by products—differences that are controlled by the genetically determined level of metabolic enzymes in the body. In particular, people whose enzymes are insufficient for the rapid metabolism of acetaldehyde (the first metabolic product of alcohol) experience stronger negative, physical effects of drinking than do people with adequate levels of these enzymes. As a consequence, the former are biologically predisposed not to drink large quantities of alcohol and, hence, not to develop problems with alcohol. On the other hand, the biochemical mechanisms that determine the intensity of positive effects that a person derives from alcohol (mechanisms that might also be under genetic control) seem to be related to the particular effects that alcohol and its metabolites have on neuronal membranes and neurotransmitters and their receptor sites in the brain. To the extent that a person's biochemical reaction to alcohol is such that he or she has experienced strong positive effects but weak negative effects, his or her expectations about the positive effects of drinking will have been raised and the current motivation to drink enhanced.

Personality Characteristics. None of the previous chapters has specifically discussed how people's personality characteristics help to account for why they drink. Such a discussion was not included, in part because there are a number of recent, comprehensive reviews of alcoholic personality characteristics to which the reader might refer (Barnes, 1983; Cox, 1983, 1985, 1987, 1988; Lang, 1983).

Although the notion of an "alcoholic personality" is currently passé, certain personality characteristics have been frequently observed among people who develop problems with alcohol. Characteristics such as nonconformity, impulsivity, and reward seeking are often seen both before the problems with alcohol develop and among alcoholics undergoing treatment. On the other hand, low self-esteem and negative affect seem typically to be a consequence of excessive drinking. However, although the initial pattern of reward seeking seems to characterize a large proportion of problem drinkers, a smaller proportion are initially characterized by punishment avoidance and use alcohol to cope with anxiety and depression (MacAndrew, 1983).

In our view, personality affects people's motivation to use alcohol because it modulates the impact of the other variables that influence drinking. For instance, a person whose personality characteristics are like those of the typical problem drinker and who also derives positive biochemical effects from alcohol would be more likely than another person—with different personality characteristics but a similar reaction to alcohol—to indulge impulsively in drinking while discounting the delayed negative consequences of doing so. Such an individual would also be more likely than others to adhere to social pressures to drink while discounting social strictures against using alcohol excessively.

Personality also affects the motivation to drink because of the effect that drinking has on the nonchemical incentives in a person's life. Thus the impulsive reward seeker who tends not to place importance on traditional societal values is less likely than other people to pursue incentives that are difficult to achieve but which potentially will be enduring sources of emotional satisfaction. Such a person is also less likely than others to perservere when frustrated in goal pursuits and at such times is likely to turn to alcohol as a means of coping. As a consequence of having fewer nonchemical resources with which to regulate his or her affect, this person's motivation is use alcohol would be further strengthened.

Sociocultural/Environmental Influences. White, Bates, and Johnson in Chapter 9 and Heath in Chapter 10 discussed the sociocultural and environmental factors that help to account for why people drink.

From the evidence presented in these two chapters, it is clear that these sources of influence are potent determinants of people's motivation to use alcohol.

There are striking examples of the influence that anthropological and cultural factors have on drinking behavior. For example, among cultural groups such as the Irish and French (and northern European cultures generally), there are high rates of alcohol consumption and problems associated with the use of alcohol that appear to result from the unhealthy drinking practices that these cultures foster. On the other hand, although groups such as Italians and Jews also have high rates of alcohol consumption, problems associated with its use among these groups are few, presumably because of the healthy drinking practices that these cultures reinforce. What Health's chapter has helped us to understand is the particular mechanisms by which such vastly different drinking practices are culturally transmitted. From the perspective of our model of alcohol use, it is important to understand that differences among people in their past use of alcohol and their current motivation to use or not use additional alcohol might be traceable, in part, to the drinking practices that are instilled by the culture in which they live.

Besides the pervasive cultural influences such as those that Heath discusses, there are additional social variables within particular cultural groups that help to determine why the drinking practices of one individual in that group differ from those of another. As we saw in Chapter 9, people model their drinking behavior after that of their family, friends, and peer groups, who also provide direct social rewards for drinking or not drinking. In addition, it appears that the mass media to which an individual is exposed help to instill drinking habits, especially through the drinking practices that they portray.

Past Reinforcement from Drinking. A person will have been reinforced for drinking in the past to the extent that the biochemical reactivity to alcohol has been positive, and his or her personality characteristics, as well as sociocultural and environmental influences, have promoted drinking. It is likely that a person who has been strongly reinforced for drinking in the past will become a habitual heavy user of alcohol. Such a person would expect that he or she will be reinforced for drinking in the future, and when faced with a choice between imbibing a drink or not doing so, this person would probably decide to drink. Conversely, a person will not have been reinforced for drinking in the past to the extent that the biochemical reactivity to alcohol has been negative, his or her personality characteristics have promoted not drinking, and sociocultural and environmental influences have also promoted not drinking. A person who has not been reinforced for drinking in the past will probably use alcohol lightly, if at all. Such a person would hold expectations of not being reinforced for drinking in the future. Thus when faced with a choice between drinking or not drinking, it is likely that this person would decide not to drink.

Conditioned Reaction to Alcohol. When people first taste alcohol, they often find it to be an aversive stimulus. Eventually, however, many come to highly value the opportunity to drink alcohol. That conditioning principles are involved in this transformation seems almost self-evident.

To the extent that the historical variables that we just discussed have promoted an individual's drinking in the past, he or she will have developed classically conditioned responses to alcohol and the stimuli that have been associated with drinking. However, both the evidence reviewed by Brick in Chapter 7 and other recent evidence (Newlin, 1984, 1985a, 1985c; Shipley, 1987) indicates that the classically conditioned responses to alcohol cues are often opposite to the unconditioned, pharmacological responses to alcohol itself. In terms of opponent-process theory (e.g., Solomon, 1980), the conditioned compensatory response to alcohol cues appears to reflect classical conditioning of the opponent state (or "B" state) rather than conditioning of the pharmacological response to alcohol itself (the "A" state). Conditioning of the B state, appears to underlie the tolerance to alcohol that develops after repeated exposure and the so-called craving for its effects by habitual heavy users. Finally, it has been demonstrated that the conditioned compensatory response is stronger among persons who are genetically predisposed to develop problems with alcohol than among those who are not (Newlin, 1985b).

Current Factors

Two sets of factors from one's current life situation have an impact on one's decisions about drinking: The situation in which an individual is located at any time and his or her current positive and negative incentives that are sources of the positive and negative affect that he or she experiences. These current factors are the major group of variables that are depicted second from the left in Figure 11–1.

Situational Factors. By situational factors, we mean the immediate environmental context in which a person is located when he or she decides whether or not to drink. McCarty (1985) refers to these situational factors as "microenvironmental" influences and includes among them such considerations as the physical setting, whether a person is alone or with other people, and, if with other people, the degree to which they encourage or discourage drinking. To the extent that alcohol is available and the immediate situation is conducive to drinking, weight will be added to a person's decision to drink. To the extent that alcohol is unavailable and the immediate situation is not appropriate for drinking, weight will be added to a person's decision not to drink. The microenvironmental influences are distinguished from ubiquitous, broadly based macroenvironmental influences such as governmental regulation of the price and availability of alcohol, sociocultural factors, and urbanization (Conners & Tarbox, 1985).

Current Positive and Negative Incentives. As discussed earlier in the chapter, the positive incentives that are currently available to a person to pursue and enjoy are a primary source of the positive affect that that person currently experiences. In a similar manner, the negative incentives that are noxious elements in a person's life are, to a large extent, responsible for the negative affect that that person currently experiences. In short, the intensity of a person's current positive affect and current negative affect is determined largely by the quality and quantity of that person's current positive and negative incentives. As Figure 11–1 suggests, if a person does not have satisfying positive incentives to pursue and/or is not making satisfactory progress toward reaching goals that will produce positive incentives, weight will be added to that person's expectations that he or she can better enhance positive affect by drinking. Insofar as a person's life is burdened by noxious elements and/or he or she is making unsatisfactory progress toward removing these elements, weight will be added to that person's expectations that he or she can better counteract negative affect by drinking.

Prior research indicates, in fact, that drinkers act as if they choose alcohol to obtain particular emotional effects that they are unable to obtain through nonchemical incentives. They drink, for example, to feel more powerful (McClelland, Davis, Kalin, & Wanner 1972), more womanly (Wilsnack, 1974, 1976; Benson & Wilsnack, 1983), more optimistic (Klinger, 1977), and less anxious and depressed (Langenbucher & Nathan, 1983). The choice between drinking and not drinking also has been shown to vary as a function of other activities that are available to a person to enjoy and the constraints that inhibit access to them (Vuchinich, 1982; Vuchinich & Tucker, 1983).

The evidence is particularly compelling that alcoholics' positive and negative incentives are potent determinants of their decisions about drinking. Tucker, Vuchinich, and Harris (1985), for instance, reviewed a variety of evidence indicating that alcoholics who do not return to drinking following formal treatment have more positive changes and fewer negative changes in their lives (in areas such as intimate relations, vocational functioning, financial status, and physical and emotional health) than alcoholics who return to drinking. Similarly, Vaillant (1983,

p. 190) found that developing substitute activities (e.g., work, hobbies, meditation, helping other people) was the factor to which abstinent alcoholics most frequently attributed their ability to alter their drinking habits. With regard to determinants of particular relapse episodes, both Marlatt and his colleagues (e.g., Marlatt & Gordon, 1985) and Sanchez-Craig and her colleagues (e.g., Sanchez-Craig, Wilkinson, & Walker, 1987) have reported that frustration of goal-directed activities and other negative affect are the most common reason that alcoholics give for their returning to drinking. Finally, Perri (1985) followed persons with serious drinking problems prospectively from the time that their efforts to change were initiated. Those persons who ultimately succeeded were distinguished from those who did not succeed primarily by having developed some form of alternative, satisfying behavior to take the place of drinking (e.g., a new hobby, physical exercise, consumption behaviors such as eating particular snack foods or drinking nonalcoholic beverages). Successful more than unsuccessful persons, moreover, had family and friends who supported their efforts, and they more often attended Alcoholics Anonymous meetings. Thus the empirical evidence clearly suggests that, in order for alcoholics not to return to abusive drinking once they have stopped, it is necessary for them to develop meaningful sources of satisfaction to compete with the satisfaction that they previously sought by drinking alcohol.

Cognitive Mediating Events

The historical and current factors give rise to the cognitive mediating events represented by the box at the center of Figure 11–1. The cognitive processes that this box encompasses include people's thoughts, perceptions, and memories that determine the nature of their expectations about the direct (chemical) and indirect (instrumental) effects that taking a drink will have on their affect. These expectations might concern both positive and negative effects of drinking and effects that are immediate or delayed. Also, the expected effects might not correspond to the actual effects of drinking. For example, a person might place too much emphasis on positive, immediate effects, while discounting the delayed, negative effects. The specific kinds of expectations that a person might have about the effects of drinking are shown in the next boxes in the flow diagram and are described in the following.

Expected Chemical Effects of Drinking. A person has expectations about how drinking will modify his or her affect directly through the chemical effects of the alcohol. To the extent that a person expects that the chemical effects of drinking on his or her affect will be positive, weight will be added to that person's decision to drink. To the extent that a person expects that the chemical effects of drinking on his or her affect will be negative, weight will be added to that person's decision not to drink.

Expected Instrumental Effects of Drinking. A person also has expectations about how drinking will modify his or her affect indirectly by enhancing or interfering with his or her nonchemical incentives. There are four possible expected instrumental effects of drinking that are depicted in Figure 11–1. The first two have to do with the expected, indirect effects of drinking on one's positive affect: A person may expect that drinking will be instrumental in either enhancing or reducing positive affect because it facilitates or interferes with the enjoyment of nonchemical, positive incentives. For example, a person might expect that drinking will enhance positive affect because drinking brings approval from peers. He or she might expect that drinking will reduce positive affect because it brings strife to his or her marriage. The second two expected instrumental effects of drinking have to do with its expected, indirect effects on one's negative affect: A person might expect that drinking will be instrumental in either facilitating or interfering with the nonchemical, negative incentives in his or her life. For example, a person might expect that he or she could reduce negative affect by drinking because it would relieve suffering from a physical disease. On the other hand, he or she might expect to intensify negative affect by drinking because drinking will solidify his or her identity as an alcoholic.

Summary of Expected Effects of Drinking. The direct (chemical) and indirect (instrumental) effects that a person might expect that drinking will have on his or her affect can be summarized into the four categories shown next in the flow diagram: (a) expect that positive affect will be enhanced, (b) expect that positive affect will be reduced, (c) expect that negative affect will be reduced, (d) expect that negative affect will be intensified. To the extent that a person expects that the effects of drinking on his or her affect will be positive (i.e., categories a and c), weight will be added to that person's decision to drink. To the extent that a person expects that the chemical effects of drinking on his or her affect will be negative (i.e., categories b and d.), weight will be added to that person's decision not to drink.

Reaction to Expected Effects of Drinking. People derive emotional satisfaction or dissatisfaction from their anticipation of future events that they expect to be pleasant or unpleasant. With respect to taking a drink, people react affectively to the affective changes that they expect drinking will produce. Four relevant affective reactions (hope, disappointment, relief, and fear; Mowrer [1960]) are shown in the next to the last group of boxes in Figure 11–1. We see here that a person will feel hopeful if he or she expects drinking to enhance positive affect, but will feel disappointed if he or she expects drinking to reduce positive affect. A person will feel relieved if he or she expects that drinking will reduce negative affect, but will feel fearful if he or she expects that drinking will intensify negative affect. Two of these affective reactions to the expected effects of drinking (hope and relief) will add additional weight to a person's decision to drink and his or her actual approach of alcohol. The other two affective reactions (disappointment and fear) will add additional weight to the person's decision not to drink and his or her actual avoidance of alcohol.

IMPLICATIONS FOR TREATMENT

There are many reasons why a person's goal striving and the incentives produced by that striving may not provide sufficient emotional satisfaction (Klinger, 1977; Pervin, 1983), resulting in that person's seeking to find emotional satisfaction by drinking alcohol. Accordingly, we have developed a motivational counseling technique for alcoholics that focuses on their nonchemical incentives, aiming to help them find meaningful sources of satisfaction and to rid themselves of frustration. The counseling technique consists of two major components. First, we carefully assess the patient's motivational structure (the goals that are the compelling forces in his or her life), in order to identify points for intervention. Second, we undertake a 12-step counseling procedure to modify the patient's motivational structure, helping the person to develop a meaningful life without alcohol.

Motivational Structure Questionnaire for Alcoholics

To assess alcoholics' motivational structure, we have developed the Motivational Structure Questionnaire for Alcoholics (MSQ-A). The questionnaire is based on Klinger's (1987) Interview Questionnaire Technique, which combines idiographic and nomothetic assessment. The technique is idiographic because each alcoholic completing the questionnaire lists his or her own current concerns, which may be conceptualized quite differently from the concerns of another alcoholic. The technique is also nomothetic, however, because each alcoholic also characterizes his or her current concerns on a number of variables that allow comparisons to be made across individual patients. The Interview

Questionnaire Technique has been demonstrated to be reliable, as evaluated by a modified stability measure, and valid, in the sense of predicting future behavior (Klinger, 1987).

After first listing his or her goals, concerns, activities, and involvements in the various life areas that are provided on the answer sheet, the alcoholic indicates the action that he or she wishes to take vis-à-vis each concern that was listed. The verb that the patient chooses to indicate the desired action allows us to classify each goal as appetitive (e.g., to get, obtain, accomplish), aversive (e.g., to get rid of, prevent), agonistic (e.g., to attack), or epistemic (e.g., to find out more about, resolve questions about), hence providing valuable information about the relative strength of the patient's positive motivation (i.e., feeling impelled to achieve positive, attractive goals) and negative motivation (i.e., feeling impelled to avoid negative, aversive goals). For each concern, the patient also indicates his or her role in relation to the goal (i.e., the degree to which he or she is actively participating in goal striving) and the degree to which he or she is committed to attaining the goal.

Next, the patient rates each goal along a series of dimensions. The value ratings include (1) the amount of joy that the patient imagines feeling if the goal were actually accomplished and (2) the amount of sorrow that he or she imagines feeling if the goal cannot be attained. The patient also conveys (3) ambivalence for the goal by indicating the amount of unhappiness that he or she imagines feeling upon attaining the goal. The ratings concerning expectancy and other reality factors include the patient's expected (1) probability of success in attaining each goal, (2) probability of success in attaining each goal if no action is taken, (3) time available before action must be taken on each goal, and (4) nearness to goal attainment. Finally, (5) the patient rates the impact that he or she expects continued alcohol use will have on each goal, ranging from "my old drinking pattern would virtually assure that I will reach this goal" to "my old drinking pattern would entirely prevent me from attaining this goal."

From the preceding ratings, we derive summary indices for each alcoholic regarding the value, perceived accessibility, and imminence of his or her goals, as well as patterns of commitment to these goals and the nature of the patient's desires and roles in regard to them. These indices, and other information obtained from the MSQ-A, provide the basis for beginning the motivational counseling procedure.

Motivational Counseling for Alcoholics

The counselor uses the information obtained from the MSQ-A to help the patient achieve positive goals that will bring emotional satisfaction and eliminate negative goals that are sources of frustration. We will summarize the major components of the counseling procedure here, but additional details about the individual steps are presented elsewhere (Cox & Klinger, 1987).

During the initial stages of counseling, the counselor and patient review together the information that the patient provided on the MSQ-A. The aim here is to determine whether the patient depicted his or her current concerns accurately and whether the patient's goals are appropriate and realistic. People do not always realize the value that they accord to their goals, and the discussion between the counselor and patient of the patient's assigned values allows discrepancies between the patient's actual and stated values to be identified, and gives the patient the opportunity to reevaluate goals to which he or she assigned inaccurate values on the MSQ-A. In addition, the assigned values may not reflect the degree of satisfaction that the patient will ultimately derive from his or her goals, and the counselor helps the patient to reevaluate goals to which disproportionate values were assigned. Finally, discrepancies between stated expectancies about achieving goals and the patient's apparent chances of doing so are noted, and the patient is helped to acquire more accurate and more realistic expectations.

During subsequent stages of the counseling, a goal matrix—similar to that used by Emmons (1986) and Palys and Little (1983)—is completed that depicts interrelationships among the patient's goals. For each pair of goals, a decision is made about whether having one goal facilitates, interferes with, or has no effect on the attainment of the other goal. The patient is encouraged to pursue goals that will facilitate the attainment of other goals. When conflicts among goals are identified, however, ways to resolve them are sought. If viable alternative means of pursuing two conflicting goals cannot be found, then the patient is encouraged to work toward achieving the more valuable goal, while disengaging himself or herself from the less valuable goal. Disengagement from goals is deemed appropriate not only when conflicts among goals are unresolvable, but also when goals are judged to be unachievable and when a patient overvalues a goal that does not contribute much to his or her emotional satisfaction.

Throughout the course of counseling, the counselor and patient together formulate weekly goals for the patient to work toward achieving. The patient is encouraged to pursue two kinds of goals: (1) daily or weekly activities that will be gratifying in their own right and (2) subgoals that will lead to the attainment of long-range goals that the patient named on the MSQ-A. The patient is also helped to discover new incentives. Unmet needs are explored, and goals that will help to achieve those needs and serve as new sources of satisfaction are identified.

The counselor continually helps the patient reexamine sources of self-esteem and self-condemnation. Alcoholics often have unrealistically high standards and lack the capacity to forgive themselves for not meeting these standards (Cox, 1983; Klinger, 1977). Such standards are often related to negative goals that alcoholics feel compelled to avoid in order to maintain their self-esteem, but which are not inherent sources of emotional satisfaction. The counselor attempts to reduce the self-punitiveness of such patients and their tendency to turn to alcohol to cope with frustration.

Another motivational counseling technique for alcoholics has been developed by Miller (1983, 1985). Although Miller's technique is very different from ours, the general aim of both approaches is to help the alcoholic want to change his or her drinking behavior. Our technique seeks to accomplish this end by modifying patients' motivational structure in such a way that they will have appropriate and realistic nonchemical goals to pursue and can make satisfactory progress toward reaching those goals. We believe that by achieving such a motivational structure our patients will through nonchemical means find the emotional satisfaction that they have previously sought to find by drinking alcohol. We are now evaluating the effectiveness of the procedure.

SUMMARY AND CONCLUSIONS

The chapters in this volume have discussed alcohol as a reinforcer from a variety of perspectives: biological, psychological, environmental, and sociocultural. In this concluding chapter, we present a motivational model of alcohol use that takes into account all the variables that are known to affect drinking and shows how these variables are interrelated. According to the model, people decide to drink or not to drink on the basis of whether the positive affective consequences that they expect to achieve by drinking outweigh those of not drinking. Thus, according to the model, the final, common pathway to alcohol use is motivational, in spite of the variety of factors that impinge on people's decisions about drinking.

A primary determinant of people's motivation to use alcohol is the nonchemical incentives in their lives. People are motivated to bring about affective changes through the use of alcohol to the extent that they do not have satisfying positive incentives to pursue and enjoy and to the extent that their lives are burdened by negative incentives that they are not making satisfactory progress toward removing. Accordingly, we have developed a motivational counseling technique for alcoholics that carefully assesses patients' motivational structure and then seeks to modify their motivational structure, helping them to find nonchemical sources of positive affect and eliminate nonchemical sources of negative affect.

REFERENCES

Amsel, A. (1958). The role of frustrative nonreward in noncontinuous reward situations. *Psychological Bulletin, 55,* 102–119

Amsel, A.(1962). Frustrative nonreward in partial reinforcement and discrimination learning: Some recent history and a theoretical extension. *Psychological Review, 69,* 306–328.

Barnes, G.E. (1983). Clinical and prealcoholic personality characteristics. In B. Kissin & H. Begleiter (Eds.), *The biology of alcoholism* (Vol. 6) *The pathogenesis of alcoholism: Psychosocial factors.* New York: Plenum Press.

Benson, C.S., & Wilsnack, S.C. (1983). Gender differences in alcoholic personality characteristics and life experiences. In W.M. Cox (Ed.), *Identifying and measuring alcoholic personality characteristics.* San Francisco: Jossey-Bass.

Black, R.W. (1965). On the combination of drive and incentive motivation. *Psychological Review, 72,* 310–317.

Black, R.W. (1968). Shifts in magnitude of reward and contrast effects in instrumental and selective learning: A reinterpretation. *Psychological Review, 75,* 114–126.

Black, R.W. (1969). Incentive motivation and the parameters of reward in instrumental conditioning. In W.J. Arnold & D. Levine (Eds.). *Nebraska symposium on motivation.* Lincoln, Neb. University of Nebraska Press, pp. 85–141.

Black, R.W. (1976). Reward variables in instrumental conditioning: A theory. In G.H. Bower (Ed.), *The psychology of learning and motivation.* New York: Academic Press, pp. 199–244.

Black, R.W., & Cox, W.M. (1973). Extinction of an instrumental running response in rats in the absence of frustration and nonreinforcement. *Psychological Record, 23,* 101–109.

Christiansen, B.A., Goldman, M.S., & Inn, A. (1982). Development of alcohol-related expectancies in adolescents: Separating pharmacological from social-learning influences. *Journal of Consulting and Clinical Psychology, 50,* 336–344.

Cloninger, C.R., & Li, T.-K. (1985). Alcoholism: An inherited disease [Monograph]. Rockville, M.D.: US Department of Health and Human Services.

Conners, G.J., & Tarbox, A.R. (1985). Macroenvironmental factors as determinants of substance use and abuse. In M. Galizio & S.A. Maisto (Eds.), *Determinants of substance abuse: Biological, psychological, and environmental factors.* New York: Plenum Press, pp. 283–314.

Cox, W.M. (1975). A review of recent incentive contrast studies involving discrete-trial procedures. *Psychological Record, 25,* 373–393.

Cox, W.M. (1976). Eight drive-reward combinations: A test of incentive-motivational theory. *Bulletin of the Psychonomic Society, 7,* 121–124.

Cox, W.M. (1981). Simultaneous incentive contrast effects with alcoholic and nonalcoholic beverages as the discriminanda for reward magnitude. *Physiological Psychology, 9,* 276–280.

Cox, W.M. (Ed.) (1983). *Identifying and measuring alcoholic personality characteristics.* San Francisco: Jossey-Bass.

Cox, W.M. (1985). Personality correlates of substance abuse. In M. Galizio & S.A. Maisto (Eds.), *Determinants of substance abuse: Biological, psychological, and environmental factors.* New York: Plenum Press.

Cox, W.M. (1987). Personality theory and research. In H.T. Blane & K. E. Leonard (Eds.), *Psychological theories of drinking and alcoholism.* New York: Guilford Press.

Cox, W.M. (1988). Effects of alcohol on successive incentive contrast. *Bulletin of the Psychonomic Society, 26,* 67–70.

Cox, W.M. (1988). Personality theory. In C.D. Chaudron & D.A. Wilkinson (Eds.), *Theories of alcoholism.* Toronto: Addiction Research Foundation.

Cox, W.M., & Black, R.W. (1975). Shifts in magnitude of delayed and immediate reward. *Bulletin of the Psychonomic Society, 6,* 35–38.

Cox, W.M., & Klinger, E. (1987). Research on the personality correlates of alcohol use: Its impact on personality and motivational theory. *Drugs and Society,* 61–83.

Cox, W.M., Klinger, E., & Kemble, E.D. (1987). Effects of alcohol on activity level following incentive shift. *Bulletin of the Psychonomic Society, 25,* 286–288.

Crespi, L.P. (1942). Quantitative variation of incentive and performance in the white rat. *American Journal of Psychology, 55,* 467–517.

Emmons, R.A. (1986). Personal strivings: An approach to personality and subjective well-being. *Journal of Personality and Social Psychology, 51,* 1058–1068.

Flaherty, C.F. (1982). Incentive contrast: A review of behavioral changes following shifts in reward. *Animal Learning & Behavior, 10,* 409–440.

Hull, C.L. (1943). *Principles of behavior.* New York: Appleton-Century-Crofts.

Hull, C.L. (1951). *Essentials of behavior.* New Haven, Conn.: Yale University Press.

Hull, C.L. (1952). *A behavior system.* New Haven, Conn.: Yale University Press.

Klinger, E. (1975). Consequences of commitment to and disengagement from incentives. *Psychological Review, 82,* 1–25.

Klinger, E. (1977). *Meaning and void: Inner experience and the incentives in people's lives.* Minneapolis: University of Minnesota Press.

Klinger, E. (1987). The Interview Questionnaire Technique: Reliability and validity of a mixed idiographic-nomothetic measure of motivation. In J.N. Butcher & C.D. Spielberger (Eds.), *Advances in personality assessment* (Vol. 6). Hillsdale, N.J.: Erlbaum, pp. 31–48.

Klinger, E., & Cox, W.M. (1986). Motivational predictors of alcoholics responses to inpatient treatment. *Advances in Alcohol and Substance Abuse, 6,* 35–44.

Lang, A.R. (1983). Addictive personality: A viable construct? In P.K. Levison, D.R. Gerstein, & D.R. Maloff (Eds.), *Commonalities in substance abuse and habitual behavior.* Lexington, Mass.: Lexington Books.

Langenbucher, J., & Nathan, P.E. (1983). The "wet" alcoholic: One drink ... then what? In W.M. Cox (Ed.), *Identifying and measuring alcoholic personality characteristics.* San Francisco: Jossey-Bass.

MacAndrew, C. (1983). Alcoholic personality or personalities: Scale and profile data from the MMPI. In W.M. Cox (Ed.), *Identifying and measuring alcoholic personality characteristics*. San Francisco: Jossey-Bass.

Marlatt, G.A. (1978). Craving for alcohol, loss of control, and relapse: Implications for the maintenance of behavioral change. In P.E. Nathan, G.A. Marlatt, & T. Løberg (Eds.), *Alcoholism: New directions in behavioral research and treatment*. New York: Plenum Press, 1978.

Marlatt, G.A. (1985). Cognitive assessment and intervention procedures for relapse prevention. In G.A. Marlatt & J.R. Gordon (Eds.), *Relapse prevention: Maintenance strategies in the treatment of addictive behaviors*. New York: Guilford Press.

Marlatt, G.A., Demming, B., & Reid, J.B. (1973). Loss of control drinking in alcoholics: An experimental analogue. *Journal of Abnormal Psychology, 81*, 233–241.

Marlatt, G.A., & Gordon, J.R. (1985). *Relapse prevention: Maintenance strategies in the treatment of addictive behaviors*. New York: Guilford Press.

Marlatt, G.A., & Rohsenow, D.J. (1980). Cognitive processes in alcohol use: Expectancy and the balanced placebo design. In N.K. Mello (Ed.), *Advances in substance abuse: Behavioral and biological research*. Greenwich, Conn.: JAI Press, pp. 159–199.

McCarty, D. (1985). Environmental factors in substance abuse: The microsetting. In M. Galizio & S.A. Maisto (Eds.), *Determinants of substance abuse: Biological, psychological, and environmental factors*. New York: Plenum Press.

McClelland, D.C., Davis, W.N., Kalin, R., & Wanner, E. (1972). *The drinking man: Alcohol and human motivation*. New York: Free Press.

Miller, W.R. (1983). Motivational interviewing with problem drinkers. *Behavioural Psychotherapy, 11*, 147–172.

Miller, W.R. (1985). Motivation for treatment: A review with special emphasis on alcoholism. *Psychological Bulletin, 98*, 84–107.

Mowrer, O.H. (1960). *Learning theory and behavior*. New York: Wiley.

Nathan, P.E. (1986). Some implications of recent biological findings for the behavioral treatment of alcoholism. *Behavior Therapist, 8*, 159–161.

Newlin, D.B. (1984). Conditioned compensatory response to alcohol cues. *Psychophysiology, 21*, 590.

Newlin, D.B. (1985a). Human conditioned compensatory response to alcohol cues: Initial evidence. *Alcohol, 2*, 507–509.

Newlin, D.B. (1985b). Offspring of alcoholics have enhanced antagonistic placebo response. *Journal of Studies on Alcohol, 46*, 490–494.

Newlin, D.B. (1985c). The antagonistic placebo response to alcohol cues. *Alcoholism: Clinical and Experimental Research, 9*, 411–416

Palys, T.S., & Little, B.R. (1983). Perceived life satisfaction and the organization of personal project systems. *Journal of Personality and Social Psychology, 44*, 221–230.

Peele, S. (1985a). The implications and limitations of genetic models of alcoholism and other addictions. *Journal of Studies on Alcohol, 47*, 63–73.

Peele, S. (1985b). *The meaning of addiction: Compulsive experience and its interpretation*. Lexington, Mass.: Lexington Books.

Perri, M.G. (1985). Self-change strategies for the control of smoking, obesity, and problem drinking. In S. Shiffman & T.A. Wills (Eds), *Coping and substance abuse*. Orlando, Fla.: Academic Press, pp. 295–317.

Pervin, L.A. (1983). The stasis and flow of behavior: Toward a theory of goals. In M. M. Page (Ed.), *Nebraska symposium on motivation 1982*. Lincoln, Neb.: University of Nebraska Press, pp. 1–53.

Polich, J.M., Armor, D.J., & Braiker, H.B. (1981). *The course of alcoholism: Four years after treatment.* New York: Wiley.

Sanchez-Craig, M., Wilkinson, D.A., & Walker, K. (1987). Theory and methods for secondary prevention of alcohol problems: A cognitive approach. In W.M. Cox (Ed.), *Treatment and prevention of alcohol problems: A resource manual.* Orlando, Fla.: Academic Press. pp. 287–331

Schuckit, M.A., Li, T.-K, Cloninger, C.R., & Deitrich, R.A. (1985). Genetics of alcoholism. *Alcoholism: Clinical and Experimental Research, 9,* 475–492.

Shipley, T.E., Jr. (1987). Opponent process theory. In H.T. Blane & K. E. Leonard (Eds.), *Psychological theories of drinking and alcoholism.* New York: Guilford Press.

Solomon, R.L. (1980). The opponent process theory of acquired motivation: The cost of pleasure and the benefits of pain. *American Psychologist, 35,* 691–712.

Spence, K.W. (1956). *Behavior theory and conditioning.* New Haven, Conn.: Yale University Press.

Tucker, J.A., Vuchinich, R.E., & Harris, C.V. (1985). Determinants of substance abuse relapse. In M. Galizio & S.A. Maisto (Eds), *Determinants of substance abuse: Biological, psychological, and environmental factors.* New York: Plenum Press.

Vaillant, G.E. (1983). *The natural course of alcoholism: Causes, patterns, and paths to recovery.* Cambridge, Mass.: Harvard University Press.

Vuchinich, R.E. (1982). Have behavioral theories of alcohol abuse focused too much on alcohol consumption? *Bulletin of the Society of Psychologists in Addictive Behaviors, 1,* 151–154.

Vuchinich, R.E., & Tucker, J.A. (1983). Behavioral theories of choice as a framework for studying drinking behavior. *Journal of Abnormal Psychology, 92,* 408–416.

Wilsnack, S.C. (1974). The effects of social drinking on women's fantasy. *Journal of Personality, 42,* 43–61.

Wilsnack, S.C. (1976). The impact of sex roles on women's alcohol use and abuse. In M. Greenblatt & M.A. Schuckit (Eds.), *Alcoholism problems in women and children.* New York: Grune & Stratton.

Zeaman, D. (1949). Response latency as a function of the amount of reinforcement. *Journal of Experimental Psychology, 39,* 466–483.

INDEX

ABOUT THE EDITOR

W. MILES COX, Ph.D., is currently Staff Psychologist and Associate Professor of Psychology at the North Chicago Veteran's Administration Medical Center, University of Health Sciences/The Chicago Medical School. He was formerly Director of the Drug Information Center at the University of Minnesota, Morris. Dr. Cox has published widely including over a dozen chapters to books, articles for professional journals and editor for several books. He is also Editor of the *Psychology of Addictive Behaviors Journal.*